5

SOCIOLOGY OF FILM

SOCIOLOGY OF FILM

Studies and Documents

---

by

J. P. MAYER

FABER AND FABER LIMITED
24 Russell Square
London

First published in Mcmxlvi
by Faber and Faber Limited
24 Russell Square London W.C.1
Printed in Great Britain by
R. MacLehose and Company Limited
The University Press Glasgow

To my little boy
PETER

and to all the children who helped.

May they grow up to be

good citizens . . .

What are the roots that clutch, what branches grow
Out of this stony rubbish? Son of man,
You cannot say, or guess, for you know only
A heap of broken images, where the sun beats,
And the dead tree gives no shelter, the cricket no relief
And the dry stone no sound of water . . .

T. S. ELIOT
The Waste Land

CONTENTS

CONTENTS

ILLUSTRATIONS

Preface

My studies on political parties, of which my book on *Max Weber and German Politics* was intended as a first instalment, have always kept alive in me a deep interest in films, for it seemed to me that the emotional, non-rational impact of films, particularly of feature films, shaped in the widest sense 'political' opinions.

When, therefore, in March 1944 friends introduced me to Mr. J. Arthur Rank and the latter seemed to share my interest in a closer sociological investigation of film reactions, I gladly shelved my studies on political parties for a while and proceeded to prepare the present book which follows Mrs. Thorp's *America at the Movies* to which I have written a short introduction. Another volume based on about 200 motion picture autobiographies will follow the present volume shortly.

Without Mr. Rank's technical and financial facilities which he generously gave, these studies would not have been possible. I am glad to have an opportunity of publicly acknowledging my sincere gratitude to him. Moreover, many free and fairly long conversations with Mr. Rank and with some of his chief collaborators gave me an opportunity of studying the minds of the present masters of the British film industry, a knowledge which seems indispensable for a realistic sociology of film. What I learnt from local managers would be difficult to put in one sentence. I am very grateful to all of them.

By June 1945 Mr. Rank and I agreed to part from each other. We did not quarrel; we simply terminated a vaguely defined agreement in favour of an *independent* sociological investigation. As Mr. Rank has seen vital parts of this book in the form of reports (Chapters I, V, VII, and Appendix II), he will not be surprised by my general conclusions. A writer cannot serve any individual. He should only serve truth and society as a whole. Besides, this book does not dream of attacking individuals. What Marx wrote in the preface of *Das Kapital* in 1867 is fully applicable in our case: 'To avoid possible misunderstandings one word is necessary: the personalities of capitalist and great landowner are by no means drawn in rosy colours. They are only meant to be persons in so far as they are personifications of economic categories, bearers of definite class relationships and interests. Less than any other point of view can mine, which considers the development of the economic formation of society as a process of natural history, make the individual responsible for relationships whose creature he remains socially, even if he may subjectively rise above them.'

Many others have given me enthusiastic help. I had interesting interviews with Sir Alexander Korda and Paul Rotha and a thorough discussion with Mr. Michael Balcon and Mr. Alberto Cavalcanti; Mr. Oliver Bell, the amiable Director of the British Film Institute, gave me valuable support; George Hoellering and his assistant, Miss May Harris, readily spent very many hours with me in discussing the problems of my work; Mr. A. E. Strong, Headmaster of Essendine Junior School in North Paddington, and Mrs. Phyllis Colenzo provided me with child material; Mr. Maurice Cowan, the Editor of *The Picturegoer*, kindly allowed me to use his paper for collecting adult reaction material.

To all these I am profoundly indebted and also to those many hundreds—children and adults—who either gave personal interviews, filled in questionnaires, or wrote essays. Finally, I wish to thank John Roberts, Managing Director of *The New Statesman and Nation*, and Kingsley Martin, its Editor, who kindly gave me hospitality when the Rank organisation had not a single room to spare for me to work in. My temporary home at 10, Great Turnstile had the additional advantage that I could always draw, whenever necessary, on the wide knowledge of Raymond Mortimer and Edward Sackville-West in the field of literature, and on G. W. Stonier's immense experience in films. They have tolerated my curiosity in good humour though I am sure I have too often taken advantage of a hospitality so freely given.

Yet I must emphasise that all conclusions at which this book arrives are necessarily my own. I alone must bear the responsibility for what is said and also for what is not said.

I would have preferred to call the book not *Sociology of Film*, but rather 'Matériaux pour une sociologie du film', but as I could not find an adequate English title I kept this somewhat ambitious one. I hope the reader will realise from the subtitle, 'Studies and Documents', the preliminary or introductory intention of the volume.

It opens with the exposition of some general problems of a sociology of film. This essay was written on a suggestion from H. L. Beales, my colleague at the London School of Economics and Political Science, and first published in *Agenda* (Autumn 1945). Beales followed the progress of my work closely, and his encouragement and advice have helped me greatly. The second and third chapters attempt appreciations of historic universal or popular audiences. I should have liked to give a more complete comparative sociological account of the history of audiences, but the task proved too immense for the time-table I had set myself.

Chapters IV, V, VI are studies in child and adolescent reactions. Chapter VII discusses adolescent reactions, taking Professor Blumer's pioneer work on *Movies and Conduct* as basis. Chapter VIII raises the problem of the contents of films. Chapter IX, almost a book by itself, gives documents of adult picture-goers and our comment on them. Chapter X, 'Conclusions and Postulates', was written shortly before the book went to press in order to make it as up to date as possible.

I must say I found this volume most difficult to write, not because the subject-matter is fleeting and visual and as such defying definite abstract concepts with which the sociologist must operate. No, I think the main difficulty which I had to face was that so many disciplines appear to meet when one attempts a sociological analysis of film: Psychology, Ethics, History, Political Science.

As my personal preferences in the latter three fields of human studies may easily be ascertained from my previous books, it may, perhaps, be opportune to say a word about those psychologists from whose works I had learnt before I became engaged in the present studies: Lévy-Bruhl, Malinowski and Piaget helped me to clarify the concept of *participation mystique*. By MacCurdy's *Structure of Morale*, I was confirmed in my conviction that human norms and values cannot be separated from psychological mechanisms. Trained by Scheler's and Dilthey's work, I found MacCurdy's book was to me an important confirmation of long-held views. Victor von Weizsaecker's *Studien zur Pathogenese*, together with the works by the students already mentioned, helped me to realise how far off we still are from an adequate and satisfactory contemporary doctrine of what the human being really is.

It was this difficulty which led me to write this volume in such a 'subjective' manner. It is humility, not arrogance, which explains this personal approach. From beginning to end, I tried to write the book in such a way that the reader might, as it were, take part in the actual process of writing. I always meant to apply to a sociological investigation what André Gide had asked from the novelist in his *Les Faux-Monnayeurs*:

'Et . . . le sujet de ce roman?' writes André Gide. 'Il n'en a pas. . . . Depuis plus d'un an que j'y travaille, il ne m'arrive rien que je n'y verse, et que je n'y veuille faire entrer: ce que je vois, ce que je sais, tout ce que m'apprend la vie des autres et la mienne. . . . J'y travaille d'une façon très curieuse . . . sur un carnet, je note au jour le jour l'état de ce roman dans mon esprit; oui, c'est une sorte de journal que je tiens, comme on ferait celui d'un enfant. . . . C'est-à-dire qu'au lieu de me contenter de résoudre, à mesure qu'elle se propose, chaque difficulté . . . chacune de ces difficultés, je l'expose, je l'étudie. Si vous voulez, ce carnet contient la critique continue de mon roman; ou mieux: du roman en général. Songez à l'intérêt qu'aurait pour nous un semblable carnet tenu par Dickens, ou Balzac; si nous avions le journal de *l'Education senti-mentale* ou des *Frères Karamazof*! L'histoire de l'œuvre, de sa gestation! Mais ce serait passionnant . . . plus intéressant que l'œuvre elle-même. . . .'

To a great degree sociologists construct books: they enforce a formalised unity by way of an apparent logic. I was more concerned that the reader should become familiar with the raw materials out of which, ultimately, a sociology of film (or perhaps even of society as such?) might be built. In a way this book applies to sociology what James Joyce and T. S. Eliot have achieved in *Ulysses* and *The Waste Land*, from which I was allowed to borrow the epigraph. And why should the sociologist not learn from the poet, who is so much nearer to the immediacy of human experience?

It will be obvious to the reader that this is a book which approaches film from the consumer's end, an approach which has recently been quite useful for economic theory, but I have deliberately neglected the economics of the film industry. The reader will do well to consult after, or even better before, he reads this book the admirable White Paper (Board of Trade) on *Tendencies to Monopoly in the Cinematograph Film Industry*, which is an indispensable source of information on the economic structure of the British film industry. This recommendation does not imply that I agree with all the conclusions which this important White Paper suggests. I believe the authors of this White Paper still underrate the monopolistic and restrictive effects of the cinema circuits in so far as they only advocate the restriction of 'further expansion'; nor have they studied the moral impact of films, particularly on the younger generation. It seems to me that an analysis of the economic structure of the film industry can never be separated from its moral or 'political' effect.

Furthermore, there is very little in this book about film as a

social art, almost nothing on film stars, film technique, film directors, etc. Many of those problems which I do not raise have been
discussed in other works which I list in my bibliography.

I have completed the substance of this book in the health-giving,
blessed climate of a Norfolk village, where 'the largest village store
of the world' can be found, but where there is no cinema—yet.

J.P.M.

August 1945.

CHAPTER 1

Perspectives of a Sociology of Film

It is by now a commonplace that more than 50 per cent of the inhabitants of this country—children, adolescents, and adults alike—attend cinema performances once or twice a week (or even more often). In the U.S.A. the percentage of the cinema-going public is even higher. *Why* do these millions go to the picture houses? And what is the effect of films on people's minds? While psychologists have offered us an answer to the former question—if it is an answer—that our modern *populus* seeks escape from the dreariness and mechanisation of our rationalised lives, the latter question, if asked at all by social scientists, has so far produced only negligible results.[1]

The present author is engaged in a sociological study of audience reactions, which he hopes to submit to the public in a few months' time. From the result of these investigations it will become evident that films, to be more precise, feature films, exert the most powerful influence in our lives, an influence which in all probability is stronger than that wielded by press and radio. The nature of this influence which is exerted on *all* classes of British society—though there seem to exist significant differences in class reactions—is a *moral* one. Value patterns, actual behaviour, the outlook on life generally, are manifestly shaped by film influences.

Naturally, there are still millions of us who derive their philosophies of life from other media: family, friends, church, school, university, club, book, newspaper, radio, etc.; but the majority of our contemporary society is, though not film-made, yet influenced by films.

All these problems will be documented and analysed in the above-mentioned study on audience reactions. So far, the reader of this paper must take my word for it that such a moral influence of films exists.

[1] Cf. my review of Manvell's book, *Film*, in the *Political Quarterly*, London, 1944.

What I intend to discuss here are not the qualitative features of this film influence, but rather its sociological presuppositions, which explain its possibility and potentiality.

First, of course, there is the easy availability of the cinema. But while the cheapness of a cinema seat may explain the decline of the theatre's numerical appeal, it would not explain the decline of the music hall. It seems that our modern cinema-going millions are more 'passive' than the music-hall audiences of the nineteenth century. In using the term 'passive' I refer to a profound and distinct change in our contemporary sensorium, a fact which cannot be appreciated from a purely 'psychological' approach towards cinema problems.

Graham Wallas has already in 1908 drawn our attention to 'the non-rational character' in politics, and one need only study the influence of films and 'political propaganda' which the National Socialist Party used in Germany before and after 1933 to realise the enormous potentialities of visualisation in the formation of 'political' beliefs, or of any beliefs. To give only one historical illustration: the medieval miracle play was consciously devised as a means of making the liturgical Latin intelligible. 'The growth of the medieval religious drama pursues the same course in England as in the other Catholic countries of Europe . . . Priests (we are told) had very laudably introduced this dramatic appeal "in order to fortify the unlearned in their faith". These words reveal to us the original purpose of Christian drama: it was to be a sort of living picture-book for those to whom the Latin of the liturgy was unintelligible.'[1] Yet visualisation as a legitimate means of spiritual and artistic education and the non-rational character of human conceptuality are two different problems which must be clearly distinguished.

The pre-logical structure of the human mind (even if we are able to explain this fact rationally) is present in all cultures, including our own society. I believe it to be the unchallengeable result of Lévy-Bruhl's studies on the primitive mind that he has found our modern abstractions always presuppose and suggest mythical elements. Concepts like soul, life, death, society, order, are illustrations of this thesis.[2]

---

[1] Cf. George Sampson, *The Concise Cambridge History of Literature*, Cambridge, 1941, p. 235.

[2] Perhaps I may draw the reader's attention to R. G. Collingwood's criticism of Lévy-Bruhl. Cf. Collingwood, *The Principles of Art*, p. 62. C.'s criticism is facile and unconvincing. He does not even realise that *Les fonctions mentales dans les sociétés primitives* in which Lévy-Bruhl has stated the pre-logical structure of

It would be permissible to assume that there is an element of myth which explains the contemporary longing for the cinema. Just because traditional structures of life are uprooted and are on the verge of disappearing altogether, the modern cinema-goer is seeking a *participation mystique* in the events on the screen. Here he finds a totality of an apparent life which traditional institutions like churches or communities—small or large—do not seem to be able to offer any more. 'The world would appear empty without pictures', as one of my correspondents has very aptly put it.

Malinowski's well-known interpretation of myth confirms our sociological analysis of the impact of cinema on modern man. 'Myth', writes Malinowski, 'as it exists in a savage community, that is, in its living primitive form, is not merely a story told but a reality lived . . . As our sacred story lives in our ritual, in our morality, as it governs our faith and controls our conduct, even so does his myth for the savage.'[1] In this sense we are all 'savages'. Anyone who is familiar with recent developments in child-psychology knows that the non-rational character of the child's reaction towards the world persists even then when the rationalisation of the child's mind is already fully developed. The same applies to the adult. 'In jedem echten Manne ist ein Kind verborgen—und das Kind will spielen', says Nietzsche, in one of his profoundest remarks which anticipate recent investigations in children's play. Play, *participation mystique*, behaviour patterns and conduct are certainly interlocked. This interlocked structure I have in mind, when I speak of the mythical element in our passion for the cinema.[2]

Perhaps I should strengthen this argument by another consideration. I think that the sense organs of historic audiences change during the course of ages. Take the Elizabethan audience as an example. I quote from the brilliant Shakespeare lecture to the British Academy (1944) by H. S. Bennett on *Shakespeare's*

the human mind is an entirely different book from the same author's *Mentalité Primitive*. One can only conclude from this that C. has not read the *Fonctions* and his criticism thus loses substance.

[1] Cf. B. Malinowski, *Myth in Primitive Psychology*. London, 1926, p. 21.

[2] I am fully aware of the wide implications of the term *participation*, one of the most difficult terms in the history of philosophy and sociology. I hope to deal with the theoretical implications of *participation* in another context. Meanwhile interested readers ought to consult Jean Przyluski's *Participation*, Paris, 1940. In spite of P.'s criticism I adhere to Lévy-Bruhl's exposition of *participation* as given in the *Fonctions*. Cf. also C. R. Aldrich, *The Primitive Mind and Modern Civilisation*, London, 1931, and C. F. Bartlett, *Psychology and Primitive Culture*, Cambridge, 1923.

Audience: 'The wide range of social classes from which the audience was drawn, and the various types of education and training which they had received, gave the dramatist great opportunities, but . . . it seems necessary to differentiate, so that when we are told by a modern critic that of any typical audience at the Globe the majority were likely to have received an education of the grammar-school type, we must proceed cautiously . . . Dramatists must live, and "those that live to please, must please to live", so that Shakespeare and his fellows were constantly forced to remember that "whole theatre of others". These people lacking this elaborate training in rhetoric, were as mixed in their scholarly attainments as they were in their social grades. Many were literate, but a minority were not even that. The literate ranged from those who had acquired just enough knowledge to read at their Petty or ABC schools, to those who had got into the lower forms of Grammar schools. Those who could read fluently had presumably read some of the voluminous literature which poured from the London presses, and this literature, diverse as was its nature, had a strong *rhetorical* (my italics) basis. Even the illiterate by the constant listening to sermons, proclamations, addresses of welcome, official speeches, and the like, were accustomed to certain forms of literary devices, although they were completely ignorant of the names of such things . . . *The Elizabethans were trained listeners; where we rely on the eye and the printed book, they relied on the ear.*' This is, indeed, an exemplary and masterly piece of sociological interpretation of literature.[1]

If it is correct to assume, and I think it is, that we live to-day more by way of visualisation, what are the reasons for this phenomenon, if we compare ourselves with the Elizabethans? It would seem that this is a consequence of the modern rationalised structure of our lives, as Georg Simmel has already so clearly seen in his *Soziologie* (1908, p. 650 sq.): 'Accordingly, people who see without hearing are very much more confused, perplexed, and troubled

---

[1] It is interesting to compare Mr. Bennett's lecture with another recent publication, *Shakespeare and the Popular Dramatic Tradition*, by G. L. Bethell, London, 1944. Here the author takes the Elizabethan 'audience', about whose class-structure not one word is uttered, as norm for our contemporary 'naturalism' for which Ibsen is taken as example. No modern poet—if one thinks of Ibsen's later plays—has been less naturalistic than Ibsen! Mr. Bethell attributes to the Elizabethans a 'multi-consciousness' without any attempt at a sociological concretion of the term. All the same, I believe that Mr. Bethell has a glimpse of the social purpose of drama, for he writes on p. 83: 'Only the popular mind, as revealed in the popular theatre, preserved in crude melodrama something of the ancient wonder and a sense that man is not in himself an adequate cause of his own remarkable history. On this, if on anything, the future of the drama—as of any social decency—must ultimately depend'.

than people who hear without seeing. In this matter one must make a significant allowance for the sociology of the large city. The intercourse of such a city, compared with that of a small town, shows an immeasurable preponderance of visual, over auditory, impact, and not only because a relatively high number of the street encounters in a small town are with familiar people, with whom one exchanges a word or whose appearance conjures up for us their whole and not merely their visible personalities—but above all through the medium of improved public services. Before the development of omnibuses, railways, and tramways in the nineteenth century, people were not generally in the position of being able to look at each other for hours and minutes at a time without speaking to each other. Modern communications produce something which concerns by far the greater proportion of the finer relations between man and man: this ever-increasing tendency to pure visual-mindedness must therefore provide an entirely changed basis for the general sociological attitudes to men. The above-mentioned bewilderment (*Raetselhaftigkeit*) of those people who only *see* as opposed to those who only *hear* produces the displacement which I have already discussed, and contributes to the problem of the modern attitude to life generally, isolation or loneliness and the feeling of being surrounded on all sides by locked doors.' The modern cinema and its impact on contemporary life is the most powerful confirmation of Simmel's analysis.

Simmel's sociology of the senses as indicated in these sentences is, of course, only an application of Karl Marx's theory of the estrangement of the human being (*Selbstentfremdung des Menschen*) which is the guiding theme from his early writings to *Das Kapital*. The outwardness of our contemporary life which, as I hope, is now more clearly demonstrated against the background of Elizabethan civilisation, requires vigilance and conscious re-adjustment to the powers of reason. Such a re-adjustment is not impossible in view of the fact that films are planned and made by a controllable industrial process.

Perhaps I should explain here why the economic structure of the British film industry—and that of other countries, too—is not being touched upon. Not that I regard the property or social structure of the British film industry as unimportant: on the contrary. But in recent years discussion has, in my opinion, concentrated too much on this economic aspect. The recent White Paper on *Tendencies to Monopoly in the Cinematograph Film Industry*,[1] to give

[1] London. H.M. Stationery Office, 1944.

only one instance, is utterly unconcerned with what is in this chapter called the sociological perspectives of film. A sociology of film will, and must, be built up irrespective of whether the film industry is controlled by a 'monopolist' or by a state bureaucracy.

So far, our sociological interpretation has been intentionally purely descriptive. But we must now turn to some normative reflections. Here, we take our starting point from the much discussed controversy between Plato and Aristotle about the social impact of poetry. Professor Collingwood has devoted to this controversy a few important pages in his book already mentioned, *The Principles of Art*. We agree with the facts as represented by Collingwood, but differ from him on their interpretation. 'Tragedy and comedy', Professor Collingwood writes, 'were kinds of poetry which Plato classified as representative. When he wrote Book III (of the *Republic*), it seems that he intended to admit into his republic a certain kind of drama, more or less Aeschylean . . . in character. When he wrote Book X, his view had hardened. All drama must go, and he finds himself left with that kind of poetry whose chief representative is Pindar.'[1] The reasons for Plato's attitude towards poetry are easy to understand. He regarded the 'Sophistic' character of all non-mythical poetry as disruptive to the community. A community, a state without myth is doomed. Consequently, Plato himself attempted to create a myth in his *Timaeus*.[2] Aristotle, as compared with Plato, was a realist. He interpreted what he *saw*.

We follow further Professor Collingwood's analysis:[3] '*The Poetics* (by Aristotle) . . . is a defence of poetry for pleasure's sake, or representative poetry. . . .' Aristotle agrees with Plato that Tragedy generates in the audience pity and fear. 'A mind heavily charged with these emotions is thereby unfitted for practical life. . . . Plato proceeds at once to this conclusion; therefore tragedy is detrimental to the practical life of its audience . . . Aristotle inserts one further step in the analysis. The emotions generated by tragedy . . . are not in fact allowed to remain burdening the mind of the audience. They are discharged in the experience of watching tragedy. This emotional defecation or 'purging' (katharsis) leaves the audience's mind after the tragedy is over, not loaded with pity and fear, but lightened of them. The effect is thus the opposite

[1] Cf. op. cit. p. 48.
[2] With regard to the rôle of myth in Greek civilisation see my book, *Political Thought: The European Tradition*, 1942 ed., chapter 1.
[3] Cf. op. cit. pp. 51 sq.

of what Plato had supposed.' I do not intend to discuss the difficult questions which have arisen in connection with Aristotle's *katharsis* theory.[1] Relevant here is only that Professor Collingwood regards Aristotle's *Poetics* as a contribution to a theory of amusement. 'The problem is the decadence of the Greek world: its symptoms, its causes, and its possible remedies. Among its symptoms, as Plato rightly contended, was the supersession of the old magico-religious art by a new amusement art—the art, in fact, of a Waste Land.' Now, while it is certainly true that Aristotle was not a disciple of T. S. Eliot, the problem remains whether philosophy, so far as it is concerned with a world as it *is*, can afford, *now* as then, to reject 'amusement art' as a legitimate product of human creativeness? It is certainly important to study the perennial controversy between Plato and Aristotle about poetry in order to gain norms for a possible attitude towards our contemporary amusement art as exemplified by the film. Other great transitional periods of Western civilisation are of similar importance, for example, the decline of the Roman Empire or the epoch which Huizinga has covered in his study, *The Waning of the Middle Ages*. The dangerous and disruptive character of pure amusement art is undeniable. But film is not, or need not be, a pure amusement form of art.

To be sure, a sociologically conceived aesthetics of film has still to be written, but even without such a theory there can be no doubt that there exist already in all countries a considerable number of film-classics which may indicate normative trends for future development. No country has, perhaps, contributed more— to speak only of war-time developments—than Great Britain to making film into a new popular art form.

To achieve this aim, certain prerequisites have to be fulfilled. At present the emotional attitudes of modern film audiences are

---

[1] Cf. particularly George Thomson, *Aeschylus and Athens. A Study in the Social Origins of Drama*. London, 1941. Professor Thomson's study may serve as an important and indispensable correction of Collingwood's interpretation. Aristotle's *katharsis* theory was much more in line with the mythical tradition of Greek life than Collingwood seems to admit. Cf. Thomson op. cit., pp. 372 sqq. All the same, I felt justified in using Professor Collingwood's discussion of the relation of Plato and Aristotle to poetry as an *introduction* to a theme to which so many thinkers throughout the ages of European civilisation have contributed. It must be remembered that if Aristotle's conception of katharsis was bound up with the socio-mythical background of Greek civilisation it would seem to have been a mistake of the seventeenth and eighteenth centuries to take katharsis as an *a priori* condition of any audience. I shall return to this problem in the forthcoming investigations on film audiences, and show that katharsis has to be reinterpreted according to the specific sociological conditions of *historic audiences*. *See* also: S. H. Butcher, *Aristotle's Theory of Poetry and Fine Art*, London 1895.

23

almost unknown. They have to be studied, and they *are* being studied. In this respect, the greatest attention has to be devoted to the study of the reactions to films of the younger age-groups—from five to the years of adolescence. The Soviet cinema can serve in this respect as a guiding example. It is not only that the Soviet film organisation has a considerable number of permanent special children's cinemas to which grown-ups are admitted only 'when accompanied by children'; the children all over the Union of the Soviet Republics have also a living and constructive contact with the film producers and directors. In schools and youth clubs, films are discussed and criticised, suggestions for new films come from the children themselves and are not imposed on them from above.[1]

Such studies in film reactions ought to be co-ordinated with film appreciation in *all* types of schools. Furthermore, in order to enable our teachers to provide such lessons in film appreciation the teachers themselves must be taught. Consequently, film appreciation should be taught at universities. (The present writer acknowledges with gratitude the debt he owes to the authorities of the London School of Economics and particularly to his chief, Professor H. J. Laski, who have allowed him to hold a seminar on sociology of film during one term of last year's session. The experiment has borne rich fruits.)

In addition to all kinds of youth clubs, the W.E.A. ought to be enlisted to help in educating a critical film audience. Perhaps our film critics in dailies and periodicals would then express to a lesser extent their personal likes and dislikes, but would consider films more from the point of view of the wants and needs of film audiences.

I admit that it is not easy to teach film appreciation if there is no accepted doctrine to teach. But doctrines are developed by teaching: by nothing else. In this context I should like to indicate only one set of problems on which, up to now, no serious work has been done at all. What ethical values do films teach and how are these value patterns related to the actual norms according to which modern men live? Moreover, what is the relationship of both, film norms and actual norms, to absolute value standards? To ask these questions shows, perhaps, that we know just nothing about the ultimate directives which guide, though to a large extent inexplicitly, our lives. Previous ages had a very explicit knowledge of their respective value patterns, as anyone who reads

[1] Cf. Tschernjawski, *Der Sowjetfilm*. Moscow, 1941.

Aristotle's *Nicomachean Ethics* or Thomas's *Summae* will realise. To-day value patterns are visualised on the screen, but in the absence of responsible thought and attention to challenge and criticise them, they must remain stale and vague. This is, perhaps, the reason why at present even good contemporary feature films so readily glorify the social *status quo* of the society in which we live.

Finally: once, such steps as envisaged here are taken, film directors, producers, distributors, exhibitors, will have a more articulate idea of what the public wants and it might be possible thereby to raise film standards.

It is true that many products of our contemporary film industry represent for our age what the Roman *circus* meant for the declining Roman Empire: the danger is real and imminent.

If we persist in our academic remoteness from film as mass-influence, the doom of our civilisation is certain. Film is symptom *and* cause. But this pessimistic trend is only a warning. It only illustrates the power of the film medium—as popular art and educational instrument—to serve *positive* ends if *responsibly* developed.

CHAPTER 2

On Theatre and Cinema—Universal Audiences
—Political Philosophy

Perhaps it is possible to assess the social function of our contemporary cinema correctly only when we compare it with previous historic phases of our Western cultural development. I shall choose the theatre of the Greek City State, the Roman theatre and amphitheatre as main examples to illustrate the intimate connection between state and dramatic art, including its degeneration into the Roman circuses.

In a separate chapter I shall give a comparison between the Elizabethan theatre and the modern cinema. Needless to say, I am clearly aware of the selective and almost arbitrary character of the illustrative material I have chosen in order to gain my norms for a sociological interpretation of the cinema to-day; but the subject is clearly of an encyclopaedic character and it would take a long time to investigate its full implications with regard to a theory of culture.

Drama appears in all historic societies as a late form of art. 'The stage', writes Jacob Burckhardt in his *Renaissance*,[1] 'which in its perfection is a late product of every civilisation, must wait for its own time and fortune.' When it appears in the Greek city-state —its origins and early development do not concern us here——it is intimately related to the state structure as such. Religion, art, in short culture as a whole, cannot be separated from the state. When Edmund Burke in his *Reflections on the Revolutions in France* defined the state as a 'partnership in all science, a partnership in all art, and in all perfections',[2] he obviously defined not only his own norm of the state, but also implicitly the norm of the Greek city-state. Only our modern specialisation, resulting in the separation of 'spheres' of culture—economics separated from religion,

[1] Phaidon edition, 1944.
[2] Cf. R. M. MacIver, *The Modern State*, pp. 83 sq.

religion separated from art, art separated from politics, etc.—a process which began in Europe with the decline of the Middle Ages—has made us oblivious of the normative significance of the ancient city-state.

Consequently, state and theatrical performances cannot be separated. It was the Athenian State which provided this dramatic entertainment for the whole people. 'The Athenian drama', writes Haigh,[1] 'was not only an amusement for the people: it was also part of a great religious celebration. Throughout its history it never ceases to be clearly connected with the religion of the *State* (my italics). It was developed originally out of the songs and hymns in honour of Dionysus, the god of wine. In later times its range was widened, and its tone secularised; but it continued to be performed solely at the festivals of Dionysus.' The audience attending these dramatic performances of tragedies and comedies alike, was a *universal audience*. All Athenian citizens took part, including women, children,[2] and slaves, provided their masters decided to take them with them. By 'citizens' we mean those who had the franchise.[3]

Haigh has also investigated the prices of admission to the Athenian theatres, a point which throws an interesting light on the dynamic changes which the Athenian democracy underwent. 'Until the close of the fifth century every man had to pay for his place, although the charge was a small one. But the poorer classes began to complain that the expense was too great for them, and that the rich citizens bought up all the seats. Accordingly, a measure was framed directing that every citizen who cared to apply should have the price of the entrance paid to him by the state. The sum given in this way was called 'theoric' money.[4] The state grant for this 'theoric' money was not introduced by Pericles, but presumably by the demagogue Cleophon, a successor of Cleon. It was then that the lust for theatrical amusement grew to such an intensity 'as to become a positive vice, and to sap the military energies of the people'.[5] The mental and emotional atti-

[1] Cf. Haigh, *The Attic Theatre*, Oxford, 1898, p. 4 sq.

[2] In Book VII, Chapter 17, of his *Politics*, Aristotle makes the following remark from which frequent attendance of children at the theatres may be concluded: 'It should also be illegal for young persons to be present either at *iambics* or comedies before they are arrived at that age when they are allowed to partake of the pleasures of the table'. (*Everyman* ed., p. 236).

[3] Cf. *Aeschylus and Athens. A Study in the social Origins of Drama* by George Thomson, London, 1941, p. 347 sq.

[4] Haigh, op. cit., p. 369.

[5] Haigh, op. cit., p. 380 sq.

tudes of audiences—past and present—are not easy to describe. It would appear that Grote's famous description of the Athenian audience in his *History of Greece*[1] is perhaps somewhat too rosy when one compares it with the more detailed analysis by Haigh or Professor Thomson. The latter has given a specifically striking illustration when he writes: 'How, we are led to ask, did an Athenian audience react to the performance of their tragedies? In our own London theatres, the members of the audience usually keep their emotional reactions (other than laughter) to themselves; but in the cinemas of the west of Ireland, where the spectators are peasants, the atmosphere is far more intense. At the critical moments of the plot, almost every face wears a terrified look and continuous sobbing may be heard. In this respect, an Athenian would undoubtedly have felt more at home in the west of Ireland than in the West End of London. In one of Plato's dialogues (10, 535), a professional reciter of the Homeric poems describes the effect of his performances on himself and on his audience:

'When I am describing something pitiful, my eyes fill with tears; when something terrible or strange, my hair stands on end and my heart throbs . . . And whenever I look down from the platform at the audience, I see them weeping, with a wild look in their eyes, lost in wonder at the words they hear.'

'This', Professor Thomson concludes, 'was a recital of Homer. At the dramatic festivals the excitement must have been even greater. No wonder there was a panic in the theatre at the first performance of the *Eumenides*.' Two points in this admirable interpretation are of interest to the sociologist. First, the direct contact between actor and audience and their reciprocal relationship— the latter fact is the most important difference between theatre and cinema—second, that, in spite of this difference, Professor Thomson does not hesitate to compare the contemporary cinema (in the west of Ireland) with the theatrical audiences in the Athenian city-state.

Perhaps we should add here a passage from Aristotle's *Politics*,[2] which supports this description of the Athenian audience. Aristotle deals in this chapter with an inquiry concerning harmony and rhythm: '. . . all music which has the power of purifying the soul affords a harmless pleasure to man. Such, therefore, should be the harmony and such the music which those who contend with each other in the theatre should exhibit; *but as the audience is composed of*

[1] *See* particularly vol. VIII, *Everyman* edit., p. 287.
[2] VIII, 7.

two sorts of people, the free and the well-instructed, the rude, the mean mechanics, and hired servants, and a long collection of the like, there must be some music and some spectacles to please and soothe them; for their minds are as it were perverted from their natural habits, so also is there an unnatural harmony, and overcharged music, which is accommodated to their taste; but what is according to nature gives pleasure to everyone, therefore those who are to contend upon the theatre should be allowed to use this species of music.'
Aristotle wrote when the Greek City-State was already in decline. The Alexandrinian Mass-State was just making its appearance.

Plato's austere, authoritarian Utopianism banned, as we have seen on preceding pages of this book, the non-magical poetry from his State ideal. Aristotle, the greatest analyst of the Greek civilisation, did not—in contrast to Plato—separate norm from reality. Apart from the above-quoted passage of the *Politics*, in which he incidentally refers to his *Poetics*, Aristotle's dramatic theory and his exposition of the social function of dramatic poetry take always as starting-point the things which he *saw* or, perhaps better, which show themselves. The pivotal point of Aristotle's *Catharsis* theory is the philosophical acknowledgement of an audience which has the *need* of being purified.

But there can be no doubt that even Aristotle's realism abhorred the artistic decline of the contemporary Athenian theatre into amusement-art. In the same sense in which Aristotle refused to accept the early Mass-State of the Hellenic world as State proper, so he deprecated the compromise with a cheap and easy audience. One need only read Chapter XIII of the *Poetics* to understand the *moral* purpose of his dramatic theory which—to repeat—should never have been separated from the whole and synthetic meaning of his social philosophy. 'Hence it is necessary that a plot which is well constructed should be rather single than twofold . . . and that the change should not be into prosperity from adversity, but on the contrary into adversity from prosperity, not through depravity, but through some great error . . . But the proof of this is what has taken place. For of old the poets adopted any casual fables; but *now* (my italics) the most beautiful tragedies are composed about a few families . . . and such other persons as happen either to have suffered, or done things of a dreadful nature. The tragedy, therefore, which is the most beautiful according to art, is of this construction. Hence they erroneously blame Euripides, accusing him of having done this in his tragedies, and for making many of them terminate in misfortune. For this method is . . . right. . . . And Euripides, though he does not manage other

29

things well, yet appears the most tragic of poets. The fable, however, ranks in the second place, though by some it is said to be the first composition, which has a twofold construction, such as the *Odyssey* and which terminates in a contrary fortune, both to the better and worse characters. It appears, however, to rank in the first place, through the imbecility of the spectators. For the poets, in composing their plots, accommodate themselves to the wish of the spectators.' The great tragic sense of the classic Athenian drama was already decaying when Aristotle wrote his treatise on poetry. The post-classic Greek audiences appear to have preferred, as do our modern cinema audiences, the 'happy ending', only we have no Aristotle to remind us of the true meaning of tragic art.

A modern reader of Aristotle's writings should, moreover, bear in mind that the *Poetics* was not just another book by Aristotle on an incidentally selected subject. The *Poetics* is an indispensable and organic part of a fundamental attempt to interpret the Greek world as a whole. As the origin of dramatic art leads us to the Greek state-religion, so does ethical reflection naturally turn to the example of the theatre or dramatic art. Ethical norms, analysis of social reality and art, are in Aristotle's mind a synthetic unity.[1]

The process of the decay of the Greek City-State produces the degeneration of dramatic art. This phenomenon is difficult to explain. Economic, political, religious and, generally speaking, cultural causes—all seem to speed up this process. It is not easy to say which cause was the dominant one. Nietzsche, in his *Geburt der Tragoedie aus dem Geiste der Musik*, has shown that it was mainly the Socratian rationalism which led to the decline of the Athenian world.

Burckhardt, in his *Griechische Kulturgeschichte*—writing under the impact of Napoleon III's plebiscitarian dictatorship (as I have shown elsewhere)—is inclined to explain the decline of the city-state as the result of the atomised mass (or, as he prefers to say, 'majority') democracy. I am inclined to believe that Nietzsche and Burckhardt gave only partial explanations. Professor Thomson, in his book on *Aeschylus and Athens*[2] (previously referred to), has examined the problem in a wider perspective. 'The citizens of Athens became a class of *rentiers*, living parasitically on the labour of others.' The tension within the Athenian democracy

[1] Cf. e.g., Aristotle, *Nicomachean Ethics*, Book 1, Chapter XI, or Book 4, Chapter VIII.
[2] Cf. particularly Chapter XVIII.

became thus intolerable. 'The cry of liberty, which had been raised with such fervour against the Persian invader, had taken on a hollow ring because, though Pericles might clothe it in fine words, the policy for which he stood meant that liberty was to be maintained at home by suppressing it abroad. Democracy has been transformed into the negation of democracy.' *Panem et circenses* became the watchword for the Graeco-Roman world.

Dramatic art is the self-interpretation of mature societies. It is always a late form and is intimately related to the class-structure, but, if dramatic art is great art, its artistic message is beyond class and time. Otherwise Aeschylus, Sophocles, Euripides, Shakespeare, Corneille, and Racine would be as dead to us to-day as Voltaire's *Henriade*.

The universal audiences of the great theatrical periods of western civilisation, a fact to which sociology has, if I am not mistaken, so far not paid enough attention, do not necessarily require a democratic State structure. Any generalisation from the Athenian example appears to me misleading (Professor Thomson might, I think, be blamed for being inclined to such a generalisation). Shakespeare's audience, for example, was of a universal character, and so was the audience of Molière's theatre. And yet neither the Elizabethan nor the society of Louis XIV was a democratic society. This, it seems to me, is a very important sociological fact. Great dramatists like Shakespeare and Molière do not belong to one class. Their conception is universal; and because it is universal their art speaks to *all* classes. Thus, their audiences become universal audiences. One can take, for instance, as an example of Shakespeare's universal world conception the fact that Marx, in his early study on *Political Economy and Philosophy* (1843), demonstrates his idea of money, which at this period of his life-work was more a philosophical-ethical idea than a purely economic concept, by a quotation from Shakespeare's *Timon of Athens*:

> *Gold! Yellow, glittering gold! . . .*
> *Thus much of this will make black, white; foul, fair;*
> *Wrong, right; base, noble; old, young; coward, valiant;*
> *. . . . What this, you gods? Why this*
> *Will lug your priests and servants from your sides,*
> *Pluck stout men's pillows from below their heads.*
> *This yellow slave*
> *Will knit and break religions; bless the accurs'd;*
> *Make the hoar leprosy ador'd; place thieves*

And give them title, Rule, and approbation,
With senators on the bench. This is it,
That makes the wappen'd widow wed again.

. . . .

Come damn'd earth,
Thou common whore of mankind. . . .

More than twenty years later, Marx quotes the same passage in
Das Kapital[1] as evidence for these sentences: 'Just as all the qualitative differences between commodities are effaced in money, so
money on its side, a radical leveller, effaces all distinctions. But
money is itself a commodity, an external object, capable of becoming the private property of any individual. Thus social power
becomes a private power in the hands of a private person.' Marx's
pivotal concept which he took over from Hegel, the estrangement
of the human being (*Selbstentfremdung des Menschen*) is the basis
of his often misunderstood and maligned 'materialism'. As Marx
was able to illustrate his social theory by Shakespeare's idea of
money, so perhaps the great poet's contemporary audiences may
have grasped the universal appeal of his verses.

As I shall say more presently about Shakespeare's audience, I
should perhaps illustrate the point I have made about Molière by
comparing his conception of the world and its problems by quoting
one or two *pensées* from Pascal, his great contemporary, for both
lived in the same world. 'C'est sortir de l'humanité que de sortir
du milieu. La grandeur de l'âme humaine consiste à savoir s'y
tenir; tant s'en faut que la grandeur soit à sortir, qu'elle est à n'en
point sortir.' Or: 'Gradation: Le peuple honore les personnes de
grande puissance. Les demi-habiles les méprisent, disant que la
naissance n'est pas un avantage de la personne, mais du hasard.
Les habiles les honorent, non par la pensée du peuple mais par
la pensée de derrière. Les dévots qui ont plus de zèle que de
science les méprisent, malgré cette considération qui les fait
honorer par les habiles, parce qu'ils en jugent par une nouvelle
lumière que la pitié leur donne. Mais les chrétiens parfaits les
honorent par une autre lumière supérieure. . . .' This profound
social subordination is more than political conformity.

Obviously, there are historic periods where a certain measure
of apparent social stability prevails. There are others where 'class
struggles' break up this apparent social stability and demand a
decisively new social integration. As a recent critic has put it

---

[1] Cf. *Das Kapital*, Vol. 1, Chapter III.

admirably: 'Pour Molière—et surtout pour son art, la comédie, délimitée de sa nature—il fallait, "en tout fuir les extrémités", et ne pas rompre en visière à tout le genre humain.'[1] Once this social subordination, with its Christian basis, vanishes, the theatre and its universal audience disappear also. When, later in the eighteenth century, Lessing, Goethe and Schiller attempted to found a national theatre in Germany, they were bound to fail. The history of the European drama since the late eighteenth century —from Beaumarchais to Galsworthy or to Gerhart Hauptmann, is the theatre of the *tiers état*.

If I am not mistaken, universal audiences in non-democratic societies—we confine ourselves to the historic theatre of Western civilisation—appear only within the framework of an 'organic' type of society. Shakespeare's theatre seems to illustrate this phenomenon strikingly, apart from the medieval European theatre which naturally reflects and interprets a universally held religious belief.

During the Tudor period, enough of this medieval background was still alive (and Shakespeare's image of the world was also sufficiently medieval) to ensure that a conformity between dramatic art and society as a whole was maintained. 'It,' writes R. H. Tawney, in his classic *Religion and Rise of Capitalism* (Pelican edition, p. 136 sq.), 'was (a system) of an ordered and graded society, in which each class performed its allotted function, and was secured such a livelihood, and no more than such a livelihood, as was proportioned to its status. . . . The statesmen concerned to prevent agitation saw in religion the preservation of order, and the antidote for the cupidity or ambition which threatened to destroy it, and reinforced the threat of temporal penalties with arguments that would not have been out of place in the pulpit. To both alike, religion is concerned with something more than personal salvation. It is the sanction of social duties and the spiritual manifestation of the corporate life of a complex yet united society. To both, the state is something more than an institution created for material necessities or political convenience. It is a link between the individual soul and that supernatural society of which all Christian men are held to be members. It rests not merely on practical convenience, but on the will of God.'

Yet soon capitalism cut itself loose from the body of religious traditions. Spiritual norms and economic institutions became separated, a process which lasted from the sixteenth century to the present day.

---

[1] Cf. Valdemar Videl: *Corneille et son temps—Molière*, Paris 1935, p. 507.

Our age of atomic energy faces—and this is, perhaps, its unique advantage over previous epochs of violent technical 'progress'—a fundamentally simple alternative: self-destruction or the re-discovery of a unified world in which spiritual norms and the technical stage of civilisation are once more brought together.

For dramatic art, the false autonomy of economism led to the destruction of the universal theatre of the Elizabethan epoch; what remained was a distinctive class theatre.

On the other hand, the autonomous economism set the 'working class' free, and it was Karl Marx who gave it a new mission and belief: to achieve the 'realm of the Free and Equal'.

However much in Marx genuine theory may be out-of-date now, one thing is certain. A new universal belief, integrating all classes and their aspirations, guiding 'the people', must be formulated. Such a belief, if it can establish itself, may perhaps be accompanied by the re-emergence of a new popular theatre and cinema.

After this digression let us now see to what extent the Roman theatre was influenced by its Greek predecessor. The early Roman theatres were built of wood—surely a proof that costly spectacles and gladiatorial shows appeared late in Roman life, which originally was simple and austere.

The first stone theatre was built by Pompeius in 55 B.C. It was constructed on the model of the Greek theatre at Mytilene and was able to hold 40,000 spectators. Two more stone theatres were erected later: the theatre of Marcellus and the theatre of L. Cornelius Balbus. But the influence of the Hellenistic theatre had already begun since the end of the second Punic War.

The extreme externalisation of the late Hellenistic theatre with its much stronger visual effects—so reminiscent of our contemporary cinema—was vulgar and extremely licentious. It is noteworthy, perhaps, that the female parts in the Roman theatre were acted by women. We also know from Juvenal that many Roman ladies 'of quality' fell in love with the actors in the same way as our fashionable lionesses to-day become 'movie fans' and never miss a cinema *première*.

Apart from the Roman theatre, there was the attraction of the Roman circus. The Circus Maximus which, for a long time, was the only circus, was the model for the Circus Flaminius (217 B.C.) and all other later circuses. The many imperial instructions with regard to the seating arrangements give a clear indication that all Roman citizens took a passionate interest in such performances.

The chariot races which took place in the circuses provoked heavy betting. Martial has recorded for us that popular jockeys even had statues erected in their honour.

The gladiatorial fights and the fights between men and beasts took place in the amphitheatres. The Flavian Amphitheatre, for example, was able to accommodate about 50,000 spectators. 'Sixty-four *vomitories* (for by that name they were very aptly distinguished)', writes Gibbon,[1] 'poured forth the immense multitude; and the entrances, passages and staircases were contrived with such exquisite skill, that each person, whether of the senatorial, the equestrian, or the plebeian order, arrived at his destined place without trouble and confusion. Nothing was omitted which, in any respect, could be subservient to the convenience and pleasure of the spectators. . . .'

The Roman circus and the amphitheatres were during the history of the late Roman Empire the only places where 'public opinion' could express itself. Yet even this was at times a dangerous undertaking. The Emperor might have those whose demands displeased him executed. We still can boo our Prime Ministers, though we might be mildly rebuked by the *Evening Standard*. It was the function of the rich senators to finance plays. It had become their only function.

The great Roman writers bitterly attack the decay of the austere spirit of the Romans. Thus we read in Martial's *Tenth Satire*: 'For that sovereign people that once gave away military command, consulships, legions, and everything, now bridles its desires, and limits its anxious longings to two things only—bread, and the games of the circus (*Duas tantum res anxius optat panem et circenses*).' Nor did his aristocratic contemporary, Tacitus, in this respect hold different views. In his early *Dialogue on Oratory*, he sets the facts of contemporary education against those educational norms which guided the previous age of Roman History. 'In our day we entrust the infant to a little Greek servant-girl who is attended by one or two, commonly the worst of all the slaves, creatures utterly unfit for any important work. Their stories and their prejudices from the very first fill the child's tender and uninstructed mind. No one in the whole house cares what he says or does before his infant master. Even parents themselves familiarise their little ones, not with virtue and modesty, but with jesting and glib talk, which lead on by degrees to shamelessness and to contempt for themselves as well as for others. *Really I think that the characteristic and*

---

[1] Cf. Gibbon, *Decline and Fall of the Roman Empire*.

peculiar vices of this city (Tacitus speaks of Rome), *a liking for actors and a passion for gladiators and horses, are all but conceived in the mother's womb'* (my italics). The analogy with our own historic situation is striking. Our children, as the later parts of this book will prove, are to a considerable extent 'movie-made'. Indeed, they are taken to the cinemas before they can walk.

This passage from Tacitus's dialogue is by no means an incidental remark of the great historian. In his *Germania*, which is perhaps less a factual description of early Teutonic tribal life than a Romantic Utopia for his Roman readers, Tacitus writes the significant sentence: *Ergo saepta pudicitia agunt, nullis spectaculorum illecebris, nullis conviviorum irritationibus corruptae.*[1]

We could fill many pages, if not a whole book, with similar quotations from Cicero, Livius, Plutarch, Polybius, and many other Roman classics, yet for the present purpose it may suffice to conclude with the following sentences which are taken from Augustine's *De Civitate Dei*: 'They do not trouble,' writes the Christian father, 'about the moral degradation of the Empire; all they ask is that it should be prosperous and secure. What concerns us, they say, is that every one should be able to increase his wealth so that he can afford a lavish expenditure and can keep the weaker in subjection. Let the poor serve the rich for the sake of their bellies and so that they can live in idleness under their protection, and let the rich use the poor as dependants and to enhance their prestige . . . . *Let the laws protect the rights of property and leave men's morals alone* (my italics). Let there be plenty of public prostitutes for whosoever wants them, above all for those who cannot afford to keep mistresses of their own. Let there be gorgeous palaces and sumptuous banquets, where anybody can play and drink and gorge himself and be dissipated by day or night, as much as he pleases or is able. Let the noise of dancing be everywhere, and let the theatres resound with lewd merriment and with every kind of cruel and vicious pleasure. Let the man who dislikes these pleasures be regarded as a public enemy, and if he tries to interfere with them, let the mob be free to hound him to death. But as for the rulers who devote themselves to giving the people a good time, let them be treated as gods and worshipped accordingly. Only let them take care that neither war nor plague nor any other calamity interfere with this reign of prosperity.'[2]

[1] *Germania*, Chapter XIX.
[2] Condensed from *De Civitate Dei*, II, XX; I have used Christopher Dawson's translation. Cf. his *Enquiries into Religion and Culture*, London 1934, p. 205 sq.

It is true that three hundred years lie between Tacitus, Juvenal, and Augustine. The Christian father's unforgettable sentences must be read as final verdict upon falling and fallen Rome.

It is not easy to arrive at general sociological conclusions with regard to the 'laws' which determine the decay of a civilisation. But it would appear that Professor Ehrenberg in his brilliant study on *The People of Aristophanes*[1] gives us the key to an understanding of this complex historic process when he writes: 'The people of Aristophanes had once been the people of Demosthenes. The same development which led an upper class, distinguished partly by tradition and partly by education and wealth, to the sophists, to Socrates, to philosophy and political theorising, and finally to the ethical or endaemonistic individualism of the Stoics and Epicureans, made the bulk of the citizens a people without political direction, and gradually a body of unpolitical beings. This type was nothing but 'a private person', no matter whether the individual was concerned with business or intellectual enjoyments of a general *laissez-aller*.' All the same, the people of Athens continued to exist. And it was the Greeks who never shared the delight exhibited in the Roman amphitheatre of their masters in Rome. An apparent economic freedom is compatible with moral or spiritual enslavement, but it is a dangerous state of affairs which may ultimately sap the strength of 'the people'. They may become obedient spectators, satisfied solely with *panem et circenses*—then as now.

What, then, are the lessons which the decline of Athens and Rome teaches us? Theatrical art, drama, declined when Athens and Rome became Imperial States instead of City-States. In Athens this process lasted some three hundred years; in Rome the same process began in the age of Cicero; he was, as Fowler says, 'the last-born legitimate son of the Roman City-State.'[2] A new political loyalty had to be created. Thus the principle of Empire made its appearance. Alexander the Great and Caesar became the symbols of this new loyalty which, 'from Julius Caesar onwards, deliberately extended the citizenship to destroy its association with self-government, and to empty Rome itself of the tradition of authority.'[3]

This lesson is of paramount importance for our own historic

[1] Cf. Ehrenberg, *The People of Aristophanes. A Sociology of the Old Attic Comedy*, Oxford 1943, p. 264.

[2] W. W. Fowler, *The City-State of the Greeks and Romans*, p. 315. Cf. also Fustel de Coulanges, *La Cité Antique*, p. 432 sq.

[3] MacIver, *The Modern State*, p. 99.

situation. Our contemporary State centralism may lead to the same consequences as in Athens and Rome, if we do not maintain a healthy and vigorous tradition in local government. For the time being we still live—in U.S.A. and Great Britain—on a past tradition. Politicians like Joseph Chamberlain, David Lloyd George, Herbert Morrison or Wilson and Roosevelt went through the great school of local government. I suspect they represent rather the exception than the rule. To achieve a balance between the tendency towards State centralisation and decentralisation is perhaps the most urgent task of our time.[1]

This further digression may be regarded as misplaced in the general context of this study. Yet it seems to me that in view of the centralised structure of the modern cinema with its deliberate generalised (and consequently abstract) appeal, it may ultimately prove one of the great forces in speeding up the centralising process in which we live. Our modern local universal audiences are, when compared with the old medieval pageants, mysteries, and interludes of the town guilds, merely spectators, not active participants of a communal experience. The temptation to use the cinema as a mere instrument of passive entertainment is enormous. Only when local educational authorities—from primary schools upwards to universities and adult educational institutions—recognise that a critical, and that means vigilant, attitude towards the cinema may eventually create an appreciative and selective public opinion, only then shall we be able to force the film distributor to show us films which do not drug us with sensation and political apathy.

I hope the preceding pages have reminded the modern reader that during earlier phases of our European civilisation social philosophy had a vital interest in theatrical art and in all its degenerate forms. From Plato to Augustine an uninterrupted interpretation and discussion of dramatic art continues. Theatre, plays, and shows are interpretations of society, and as such the social philosophers reflect on the moral and philosophical norms which express themselves in the art of the theatre.

This tradition was maintained in later centuries: we find reflections on the theatre in Thomas Aquinas's *Summa Theologiae*, in Luther and Melanchton, in Fénelon, Locke, Voltaire, Rousseau, and Diderot, right down to Edmund Burke, who writes in an

[1] In Great Britain, the 'organic' unity of parliamentary and municipal organisations fell 'quite apart', since the municipal reform in 1835. (Cf. Maitland, *Constitutional History of England*, p. 495.) It would now seem to be imperative to readjust by a conscious and deliberate effort what 'growth' and the society of *laissez-faire* appear in danger of destroying completely.

almost forgotten letter to Malone (Burke, we must not forget, was a close friend of Garrick) who had sent him his *History of the Stage*: 'A History of the Stage is no trivial thing to those who wish to study human nature, in all shapes and positions. It is of all things the most instructive to see not only the reflection of manners and characters, at several periods, but the modes of making this reflection, and the manner of adapting it at those periods to the taste and disposition of mankind. *The Stage may be considered as the republic of active literature, and its history as the history of that State*' (my italics).

There is another important passage in Burke's mature writings where he clearly reflects on the moral influence of the theatre.[1] Moreover Burke draws our attention to the Athenian theatre, its audience, and 'to the moral constitution of the heart'. A more convincing argument for the principal thesis of this study can hardly be found.

Burke still had a clear conception that political and social philosophy cannot be divided into watertight compartments with no relation whatsoever to each other. It is not surprising that Alexis de Tocqueville who, as I have shown elsewhere, was deeply steeped in Burke's writings, should write the important chapter on the theatre in his *De la Démocratie en Amérique*, which we reprint fully in our Appendix I. Perhaps Alexis de Tocqueville was the last great European political philosopher before the age of specialisation became finally triumphant.

Yet there is one notable exception amongst our contemporary specialists: Lord Keynes, the great economist.[2] Perhaps he alone carries on the great European tradition that a social scientist must not necessarily confine himself to his *Fach*, as the Germans say. It is not just a *façon de parler* when we read in Lord Keynes's *Treatise on Money*[3] a remark on Shakespeare: 'We were just in a financial position to afford Shakespeare at the moment he presented himself. . . . I offer it as a thesis for examination by those who like rash generalisations, that by far the larger proportion of the world's great writers and artists have flourished in the atmosphere of buoyancy, exhilaration and the freedom from economic cares felt by the governing class which is engendered by profit inflations.'

---

[1] Cf. Burke, *Reflections on the French Revolution*, ed. by F. G. Selby, London 1900, p. 90 sq.

[2] While reading the proofs of this book I must say with profound regret that the following sentences appear now as an obituary notice.

[3] II, p. 154.

The flippant form of Lord Keynes's argument is obviously intentional, yet it should not deceive us. Behind it is a profound appreciation of the 'totality' of a theory of culture in which economics and theatre are linked together. In his more recent book on *The General Theory of Employment, Interest and Money* (1936) he makes the following trenchant comment, after having brought to life again the social and economic philosophy of mercantilism: 'No wonder that such wicked sentiments called down the opprobrium of two centuries of moralists and economists who felt much more virtuous in possession of their austere doctrine that no sound remedy was discoverable except in the utmost of thrift and economy both by the individual and by the State. Petty's "entertainments, magnificent shows, triumphal arches, etc." gave place to the penny-wisdom of Gladstonian finance and to a state system which "could not afford" hospitals, open spaces, noble buildings, even the preservation of its ancient monuments, far less the splendours of music and the drama, all of which were consigned to the private charity or magnanimity of improvident individuals.'[1] Against this theoretical background, Lord Keynes's programmatic and emphatic pronouncements as Chairman of the *Arts Council* can now be adequately understood.

I refer to his broadcast in July 1945 (Cf. *The Listener*, July 12th 1945): 'There never were many theatres in this country or any concert halls or galleries worth counting. Of the few we once had, first the cinema took a heavy toll and then the blitz. . . .' Lord Keynes declares that the Arts Council will attempt to help in the decentralisation of the dramatic, musical and artistic life of Great Britain. And with explicit reference to film he states unmistakably: 'How satisfactory it would be if different parts of this country would again walk their different ways as they once did and learn to develop something different from their neighbours and characteristic of themselves. Nothing can be more damaging than the excessive prestige of metropolitan standards and fashions. Let every part of Merry England be merry in its own way. Death to Hollywood.' There indeed, is a social theory expounded which embraces state and individual and their cultural activities as a whole. And only 'the whole', as Hegel taught us, 'is truth'.

The modern cinema has taken over the heritage of the universal theatre in the sense defined in the preceding pages of this chapter. Only the cinema has a mass appeal which can be compared with the classic theatre of Athens and the Roman circus. The modern

[1] *The General Theory,* etc., p. 362.

cinema alone has a universal audience. Yet where are the social philosophers to-day who reflect on the norms which guide and underlie the contemporary film?

We leave it—at least in Western Europe—to the financial holders of this most powerful Art-industry to decide what 'the public wants'. The only link between State and cinema consists of purely technical police regulations. The British Board of Film Censors is not a State institution though by virtue of its monopoly it has all the advantages of a State institution, except that of being free from any control of the House of Commons. It is guided by uncontrollable, vague norms applied by an unknown body of 'experts' appointed by the film industry itself; an institution which is entirely inadequate for its formidable task. The moral and spiritual code as applied by the Film Censors is hardly more elaborate than the Ten Commandments of the Bible. The complexity of our modern world problems has not yet communicated itself to those who decide what films we are allowed to see and in what shape.

Indeed, Augustine has written for our time. *Let the laws protect the rights of property and leave men's morals alone.*

Surely, the daily and weekly papers all have their film critics— and some of them may, and do, join our cry in the wilderness, but are we heard? Are we not regarded as cranks or unwelcome outsiders, as alien elements who only want an undue influence in matters of which we are not competent to judge?

In the meantime our children, our adolescents, a considerable proportion of the adult population of Great Britain are conditioned by those very few who hold the reins of the big exhibitor-circuits.

Only Soviet Russia has logically applied the Athenian lesson. There Art, Cinema, Society, and State are intimately related to each other. 'There is', writes a competent observer in *The Spectator* (July 6th 1945), 'an "organic unity" between the people and their art . . . and because the cinema is considered the most important of all the arts for the Soviet State, the significance of any developments reflected in Soviet films extends far beyond the field of cinematography.' The immediate relationship between audiences and film technicians which, for the cinema in Western countries, is non-existent, forms the substance of the Russian cinema. Children, adolescents and adults are not fed by fan-stories and star-hero-worship, they actually form a productive part in film creation and appreciation. Certainly the *blanned* centralised structure of the Soviet State does favour such a development, but its normative lesson should be studied and applied in Western countries. Only then may we be able to maintain a healthy and vigorous community spirit—the spirit and the heritage of Athens.

CHAPTER 3

The Elizabethan Theatre and the Modern Cinema

The sociologist who attempts to appreciate the universal audience of the modern cinema will do well to study historical audiences. *Quae sint quae fuerint.* . . . He will humbly, though perhaps not uncritically, and not without substantial reservations rely on the expert research of the historian.

There exists, perhaps, no better analysis of the Elizabethan theatre than Professor Harbage's book on *Shakespeare's Audience*, published by the Columbia University Press in 1941. I am not at all certain whether this important study is well enough known to the general reader in this country. It has been difficult to maintain cultural relations with the U.S.A. in recent years and it is, perhaps, imperative for us to make ourselves familiar with a considerable number of outstanding books which shipping space, trade restrictions, or U-boats prevented us from reading. The process of sifting will last some time.

Professor Harbage is fully aware of the inherent difficulty of any investigation of historical audiences—past and present. For he writes: 'If we could mingle with Shakespeare's audience reincarnate, its secret would prove no more penetrable than the secret of audiences now. What occurs within the minds and hearts of some thousand men and women is not casually revealed: an audience—almost any audience—is as difficult to appraise as the human race itself.'[1] And yet in reading Professor Harbage one is inclined to believe that, under his guidance, we get a better knowledge of the theatre-going public in Shakespeare's time than we have so far been able to acquire of our contemporary cinema audiences.

Certainly there was class antagonism in Shakespeare's London (Professor Harbage illustrates this admirably though he is not a Marxist), but in the theatres, he writes, 'the rights and privileges

---

[1] *Shakespeare's Audience*, p. 3.

of class melted before the magical process of dropping pennies in a box'.[1] The Elizabethan civic authorities had no democratic leanings. They were afraid that the crowds might disrupt the established order. 'Elizabethans had a very real fear of the potentialities of a crowd—any crowd. They were less used to crowds than we are, less adept at policing them, and evidently quite conscious of the degree to which privilege rested more upon precedent than upon any physical power to preserve it.'[2] We must bear this important sociological characterisation of two different historical crowds, the Elizabethan and our contemporary crowd, in mind, as we shall return to this point later on.

Out of an estimated population of London of some 160,000, Professor Harbage suggests that about 21,000 were, in 1605, weekly spectators of the theatres. In other words, 13 per cent of the population of London, or 2 persons in 15, went to the theatres each week. Professor Harbage submits these figures also as an estimate covering the whole period of Shakespeare's theatrical career. On the other hand, it seems probable that about two thirds of London's population did not go to the theatre at all. All the same the theatres in Shakespeare's time were able, according to Professor Harbage, to draw weekly attendances of 13 per cent from London's population.

Now how can the social structure of Shakespeare's audience be described? 'The wage earner of that time . . .' observes Professor Harbage, 'could go to the theatre almost as cheaply as his modern counterpart can go to the movies.'[3] Moreover, as the Elizabethan artisan had to pay proportionally much more for food, clothing, fuel—the necessities of life—he may have been willing to pay his penny the more readily. It would, therefore, appear arguable that 'craftsmen . . . with their families, journeymen, and apprentices, must have composed the vast majority of "groundlings".'[4] The next largest group in the London area was formed by the 'dealers and retailers'. A considerable number of them were wealthy, but the majority were ordinary shopkeepers. Professor Harbage then turns to professional men and officials. The teachers earned then somewhat less than the artisans; the lawyer's profession was then —as to-day—highly profitable.

The prices for the Elizabethan theatres 'were calculated as prices in general were not, to what workmen could afford to pay'.[5] Later on when the 'private' theatres raised the minimum

[1] *Shakespeare's Audience*, p. 12.   [2] *Ibid.* p. 14..
[3] *Ibid.* p. 56 sq.   [4] *Ibid.* p. 60.   [5] *Ibid.* p. 64

charge to sixpence, the great majority of the earlier audience was effectively excluded. The 'private' theatres thus became theatres only for the upper strata of British society, 'and the price inflation', remarks Professor Harbage, 'at the private theatres begat no second Shakespeare'.[1]

During the first half of the seventeenth century the tempo of capitalist development gathers momentum. The joint-stock companies, to give only one or two examples, considerably grow in number and in 1631 we hear of complaints, certainly not of an isolated character, that the wool weavers in Suffolk and Essex are 'so much abridged of their former and usual wages' (cf. Lipson, *The Economic History of England*, III, p. 258). Thus the modern industrial proletariat is being formed and the town *bourgeoisie* combines with the aristocracy to enjoy their new mastership of state and culture of which 'the glorious Revolution' is only a phase.

But let us return to the Elizabethan theatre. Can it be compared with our contemporary cinema? Professor Harbage finds the analogy poor. To-day the cinema follows us everywhere. In every town, in every town area, is a cinema with three performances a day. The mechanical reproduction allows for greater variation and exciting novelty. 'Elizabethans had to go to the theatres; the movies come to us.'[2]

Who stayed away from the Globe? And why? Moral and religious reasons were not negligible. But puritanism was not victorious until 1642. In 1580 we read these words: 'Seeke to withdrawe these felowes from the Theater vnto the sermon, they wil saie, By the preacher they maie be edified, but by the plaier both edified and delighted.'[3] You might have been a faithful parishioner in Shakespeare's London and gone, all the same, to the theatre.

Nor is it tenable, according to Professor Harbage's investigations, that women did not attend the theatres. Not only the 'light women'. Thus we read in 1614: 'These theatres are frequented by a number of respectable and handsome ladies, who come freely and seat themselves among the men without the slightest hesitation.'[4] Family parties, young men and their girls, husbands and wives went to the Elizabethan theatre. Last, but not least, come the students and their friends, and particularly the law students. 'A student at the Inns of Court was a well-born, affluent, university-educated young man. . . . He lived in a society devoted to

[1] *Ibid.* p. 65.　　　　　　　[2] *Ibid.* p. 66.
[3] *Ibid.* p. 69.　　　　　　　[4] *Ibid.* p. 78.

intellectual pursuits and well disposed towards *belles-lettres*. He must have made a good spectator.'[1]

Another important group among Shakespeare's audience consisted of the apprentices. Some of the guilds insisted on certain property qualifications of the boy's parents and educational qualifications of the boy himself. 'Many of them', Professor Harbage instructs us, 'had about as much formal education as Shakespeare himself.'[2] Neither the fact that the Elizabethan theatres were open only during day-time, nor their professional routine, prevented the apprentices from attending the plays. Generally speaking, the Shakespearian audience was strikingly youthful.

If we ask why so many people stayed away from the theatre, Professor Harbage suggests this as answer: 'Many people . . . did not care for plays. A dramatic and poetic age confers no universal taste for poetry and drama. Elizabethans could be Philistines, and thousands of them were.'[3]

Against the not inconsiderable number of scholars who have told us otherwise, Professor Harbage stresses the law-abiding character of the Shakespearian audience. 'It is probable that both the upper and lower classes behaved best when each was under the surveillance of the other, before the audience was split in two by the system of high-priced and low-priced theatres.'[4] A Shakespearian audience was noisy before the play began; it listened intently while the play was acted.

The inner mood of any historical audience is most difficult to describe. The Elizabethans had no doctors who analysed their dreams. Yet the following sentences, written in 1580, might likewise apply to Robert Taylor or any other contemporary film *beau*: 'The wilines and craft of the stage is not yet so great, as is without on the scaffoldes. For that they which are euil disposed, no sooner heare anie thing spoken that maie serue their turne, but they applie it vnto them selues. Alas, saie they to their familiar by them, Gentlewoman, is it not pittie this passioned louer should be so martyred. And if he find her inclining to foolish pittie, as commonlie such women are, then he applies the matter to himselfe, and saies that he is likewise caried awaie with the liking of her; crauing that pittie to be extended upon him, as she seemed to showe toward the afflicted amorous stager . . . Credite me, there can be found no stronger engine to batter the honestie as wel of wedded wiues, as the chastitie of vnmarried maides and widowes,

---

[1] *Shakespeare's Audience*, p. 80.   [2] *Ibid.* p. 82.
[3] *Ibid.* p. 83.   [4] *Ibid.* p. 110.

than are the hearing of common plaies.'[1] One must admit that even without Freud the Elizabethans were fine psychologists. They understood how to appreciate their own changeable emotions as roused and sustained by the theatre.

The ability to quote from the plays was widespread. Who would quote even a sentence from a contemporary 'moving picture'? The very name 'moving picture' seems to suggest that film moves so fast that words and sentences must pass through our minds like pictures. Whilst the Elizabethans sustained their attitudes and behaviour by the visions and memories of Shakespeare's plays; our contemporary cinema audiences have only empty songs to hum. (Some time ago I travelled from York to London. In my compartment were an enterprising young English lady and a few American soldiers. They sang film songs from York to London. They never repeated themselves. I was amazed at such memory and I reflected sadly on the future of the human race.)

The Elizabethan authors reflect also on the enigmas their audiences offer:

> *How is't possible to suffice*
> *So many ears, so many eyes?*
> *Some in wit, some in shows*
> *Take delight, and some in clothes:*
> *Some for mirth they chiefly come,*
> *Some for passion—for both, some;*
> *Some for lascivious meetings, that's their arrant;*
>
> *Some to detract, and ignorance their warrant.*
> *How is't possible to please*
> *Opinion toss'd in such wild seas?*
> *Yet I doubt not, if attention*
> *Seize you above, and apprehension*
> *You below, to take things quickly,*
> *We shall both make you sad and tickle ye.*[2]

Shakespeare had no quarrel with the groundlings. His contemporaries liked his plays, 'and the most fascinating of the plays now were the most fascinating then.'[3] Great art, as Marx already knew, is beyond class and time.

Professor Harbage confronts Elizabethan appraisals of Shakespeare's audience with modern appraisals. With regard to the latter, his interpretation is, if I am not mistaken, slightly contra-

[1] *Ibid.* p. 118 sq.   [2] *Ibid.* p. 124 sq.   [3] *Ibid.* p. 136.

dictory. 'Nothing we can discover', he writes, 'from examining their daily routine, their frugal expense accounts, and their quiet and sensible letters, suggests that Elizabethans, individually or collectively, were vastly different from us. Their nature cannot be deduced from the defeat of the Armada or the public hangings in Tyburn. We ourselves live in a spectacular age, without being individually spectacular.'[1] On the other hand, Professor Harbage asks whether ignorance was so crippling in the time of Shakespeare as it is to-day. 'Cannot one say', he answers, 'without casuistry, that when theory is fallacious the ignorant benefit by their enforced reliance upon observable fact?'[2] If this is correct, which I think it is, the Elizabethan audience would appear by no means to have been 'nine-tenth illiterate'. Professor Harbage gives revealing facts about the distribution of ten thousand copies of the reading primer, *The ABC and Little Catechism*, in the single year of 1585. It is important to realise that this Elizabethan empiricism, which expresses itself on its highest level in Francis Bacon's philosophy, is certain of its place in the world—and what may be beyond it. Though our complex industrialism in culture and life is apparently rational, we know less about the meaning and the machinery of things—natural and spiritual—that surround us than did the Elizabethans. We have lost ourselves in our own perfection. It is this fundamental sociological phenomenon which the American historian has in mind.

Yet he insists on the sameness of human nature—then and now. 'The range of feeling must have been the same. People still are compounded of heaven and earth: kind fathers are harsh creditors; decent folk exchange ribaldries; and ruffians rescue puppies. We need to know more about human impulses in all ages before we grow rash about the Elizabethans. *We need to distinguish between what is fundamental in human nature and what is superficial adjustment to environment* (my italics). Perhaps the whole range of impulses was more operative in the less comfortable age of Shakespeare and more apt to impress itself upon art. It is more accurate to say that the audience expected brutality than that they demanded and enjoyed it.'[3] I am not certain whether the distinction between the basic elements in human nature and the superficial adjustment to social environment can be maintained. I am inclined to believe that environment changes human nature, anyway in the long run.

In his concluding sentences Professor Harbage provides us with material for examining the relationship of the basic nature of the

[1] *Shakespeare's Audience*, p. 139. [2] *Ibid.* 147. [3] *Ibid.* p. 153 sq.

FROM THE RUSSIAN FILM 'LAND OF TOYS'

LAURENCE OLIVIER AS HENRY V

human being to its environmental structure, more fully. He returns to 'the analogy' of the Elizabethan theatre with the modern cinema. 'The moving-picture clientele is truly universal. . . . In theory, at least, it is to Hollywood that we should look for new dramatic triumphs. But, unluckily, the moving-picture clientele does not compose an audience at all. It does not participate in the creation of a play, and its influence upon creative artists is exercised through deputies not of its own choosing. The true audience of a moving-picture is a delegation of studio critics. Their difficulties are considerable, for the diverse elements constituting that humanity whose tastes they try to gauge form an amalgam in no one theatre but are distributed in complex patterns. It is little wonder that Hollywood's aim is confused. It is interesting to notice that Chaplin and Disney, the Hollywood creators who have permitted the fewest intermediaries to come between them and their public, are the truest artists and the most generally approved.'[1] The Elizabethan audience was a crowd sharing in a unifying experience. Our modern crowds are atomised and lack the organic structure without which art must lose its social function. It deteriorates either into *l'art pour l'art* or into empty 'entertainment'. An Elizabethan play which did not please had to be taken off the stage. A contemporary film—good or bad—is forced on the public through the irresistible power of the exhibitor circuits. The general manager of *one* modern cinema cartel may decide what 'the public' wants. The spiritual dictatorship of the modern cinema is more powerful than the dictatorship of Hitler because it is less obvious, hidden in the vast machinery of the modern large-scale industry. A French film critic, as a friend is kind enough to inform me while I am writing this chapter, extends my argument to the international aspect of the film industry. He writes: 'Nous assistons depuis plusieurs années, et le cinéma est la preuve, à la constitution d'un grand trust du cinéma. Si les gouvernements ne se penchent pas sur ce problème, si des mésures énergiques ne sont pas prises, dans cinq ou six ans le cinéma, moyen d'expression populaire et sociale d'une diffusion extraordinaire, sera entre les mains de quelques personnes qui domineront non seulement l'art cinématographique, mais encore la pensée des créateurs cinématographiques.' (Cf. *Spectateur*, Paris, June 6, p. 1 sq.) So it seems my observations do not warrant the expected objection that they come from an uninformed outsider.

Against this background I am not at all certain whether Pro-

[1] *Ibid.* p. 166 sq.

fessor Harbage is not too optimistic when he writes: 'A universal audience and an immediacy of relationship between audience and artist may be conditions impossible to recover. Even in Shakespeare's days these conditions were a felicitous accident.'[1] So far, I fully agree with him. But his further conclusions distinctly trespass on the historian's proper field: 'One truth remains by which we may be both warned and comforted: the human fabric has not deteriorated, and it is as vain to inveigh against our generation as against Shakespeare's. Under right conditions the "people generally" are still "very acceptive". Their capacity to respond to what is great and beautiful remains undiminished, if less frequently exercised. It was impossible to produce anything too good for the race in Shakespeare's day, and it is equally impossible now.'[2] Here again Professor Harbage separates the basic human elements from their environmental framework. Only the *synthesis* of both makes human beings into what they are.

You may object, of course, to my somewhat pessimistic outlook in respect of the future of *popular* art—has there not been a recent film *Henry V*? Indeed, this was a great venture, and one probably gives no trade secrets away in saying that this film was made *against* the resistance of the narrow-minded 'showmen' within the film industry. But the artistic courage of the small band of producers and directors broke this resistance down. To those who have watched the social composition of the audiences who came to see *Henry V* it was no surprise that it was a modern *universal* audience who enjoyed Shakespeare, now as ever. But does one swallow make a summer?

If we are conditioned to be passive, if our emotions and behaviour patterns continue to be shaped unchallenged by ever changing stimuli and excitements without substance, perhaps then very soon the human fabric will be such that no new Battle for Britain, no epic of Arnheim can be sustained, or that we grow weary of the arduous and humble struggle of our daily task and leave it to our masters to praise perennial economic freedom and benevolently to give us *panem et circenses*![3]

---

[1] *Shakespeare's Audience*, p. 167.   [2] *Ibid*. p. 67.

[3] I should like to draw here the reader's attention to the suggestive introduction to Edward Sackville-West's *The Rescue*, London 1945. There we read on p. 8: 'Radio is in fact susceptible of carrying far more *degrees* of dramatisation than the stage or the screen, because of the extreme flexibility of the medium and its wide powers of imaginative suggestion.' Indeed Radio *at its best* may be nearer to the Elizabethan theatre than the film medium could ever be.

CHAPTER 4

Impressions and Reflections on Children's Cinema Clubs

Between August 1944 and June 1945 I spent approximately twenty Saturday mornings in the Odeon and Gaumont British Children's Cinema Clubs. I always sat right among the children in order to be able to observe their behaviour, expressions and attitudes.

I took my assistants[1] with me in order to check my own observations. In addition, I took children (and their mothers), children whose educational and family background were intimately known to me. It is only fair to say that I saw only about 1 per cent of the Children's Cinema Clubs then in operation, but as my children's 'experimental stations' were situated in three different counties (Home and West Counties) with different social structures, it is probably admissible to draw certain general conclusions, particularly in view of the fact that these children's clubs are guided by strict central directives and are fed as far as films are concerned by two central offices with whose chiefs I had lengthy discussions. In addition, I had full opportunities of discussing with the local managers the whole range of problems which these children's shows present.

The child audiences of these clubs vary in size. They may amount to 1,200 children, sometimes to considerably less, but I would not be surprised if, once all these children's clubs which for safety reasons had to be stopped, are again operating, *several hundred thousand* children attend these shows every week—all the year round.

The children are enrolled free as club members, but pay sixpence or ninepence for every performance they attend. As such a large number of children is involved one would think that the State

---

[1] I owe much to my assistants, Miss I. Seresin and Miss M. McCrae, whose enthusiasm and patience have helped me to carry out these investigations.

would take an interest in these clubs. It appears that the Gaumont British Junior Clubs attempt to enlist the help of local educational authorities, but I was unable to obtain exact information as to the extent to which local educational authorities take an active interest in the management of the clubs. Some certainly do, some may be content to be only formally represented on a committee which has, like so many things in the film industry, purely a façade character. But it must be admitted that Gaumont British attempts to enlist outside expert help at least locally, though I have seen no evidence of such a committee where I have visited a Gaumont British Junior Club.

Contrariwise, the Odeon Children's Cinemas appear to be entirely run by the central office and the local managers. Some of the latter like the children's clubs, and if they like them show tenderness and understanding in dealing with all those problems which of necessity arise when large crowds of children gather together. Other local managers prefer to be strict. In these cases the children's clubs have no pleasing childlike atmosphere whatsoever, though the administration is orderly and correct.

There is another interesting difference between the Odeon and Gaumont British Clubs. Whereas the former appear to admit all children from four or five years upwards, the latter have a rule that only children from seven years upwards should be admitted. It is not surprising, therefore, that in the more proletarian areas the elder children take their baby brothers and sisters with them, which means certainly a great relief for those mothers who want to do their Saturday shopping quietly. But the children's cinemas are, to a certain extent, nurseries, and in my humble opinion children under seven should not go to the cinema at all, even if accompanied, except on condition that special films for the tiny ones are made, as I believe they are made in Canada. But such films cannot be made without the effective assistance of child psychologists who, so far, appear to be regarded by the film industry in Great Britain as non-existent.

Perhaps I should say now what is actually shown at such a children's matinée. Hundreds of children come in and see coloured slides on the screen, needless to say badly and crudely drawn. One says: 'It pays if you say thank you and please'; another, 'Odeon Billy wishes you not to push when you are waiting in a queue.' The children are also reminded that to wash and to comb one's hair is a good thing to do, etc. After that the club 'hymn' is sung:

ON CHILDREN'S CINEMA CLUBS

To the Odeon we have come,
Now we can have some fun,

. . . .

We are a hundred thousand strong,
So how can we all be wrong?

There is no club 'hymn' in the Gaumont British Junior, I am glad to say. I have not given the whole text, but I assure my readers it is not above the level of the four lines quoted. Now we listen to the club promise. In it the children promise to obey their parents, to be kind to animals, and to make this country 'a better place to live in'. This promise is crowned by the singing of the National Anthem.

I refrain from any comment except to say that it is regrettable that we have no I.C.I. song, or a Vickers song, etc. Most of our contemporary industrial problems might be solved if, as children, we were imbued by lyrical songs with loyalties towards the masters of industry and commerce.

Mr. Rank is president of the children's clubs and the children receive birthday greetings in his name.

Now the cinema proper begins, though in recent months cabaret artists have also been presented on the stage. You first see a Mickey Mouse picture, but not so often a genuine Walt Disney as one of his plagiarists who, as is well known, have copied only the technique but not the artistic taste of Disney.

A cartoon is followed by a full-length picture. Except on one or two occasions when good pictures like 'My Friend Flicka' have been shown, it would appear that either old westerns or old comical pictures (early Shirley Temple films and 'funny' comedies about ten or fifteen years old) are considered good, and what is probably more important *cheap*, enough for children. I have seen films of the type older than the familiar Tarzan pictures with animals almost killing human beings in strange cinema landscapes. Some of the children at such performances have been really frightened and horrified. My own son refused, after he and a friend of his—they were then nine—had accompanied me two or three times to these performances, to take a further interest in his father's sociological curiosity.

Last, but not least, come the serials, e.g., *Don Winslow of the Navy*. They are of American origin. I was never able to discover a coherent plot in these serials. A considerable amount of shooting goes on, with nerve-racking persecutions of the bad men who have kidnapped the beautiful, innocent blonde secretary. There is no lack of submarines (they are usually Japanese, and only 'recently' Nazi) being hunted down by aeroplanes, ships, etc., etc.

Undoubtedly these serials are, from the point of view of the children, the highlights of the cinema clubs, but they are pernicious in their psychological effects, leaving the children at a high pitch of expectation for the next week's show, poisoning their day-dreams and, by an utterly artificial unreality, influencing their play.

From time to time there are good geographical or travel pictures shown between the cartoon and the main film, but also Pathé shows. One I distinctly remember picturing the 'development' of girls' underwear, demonstrated by girls, of course. Here the children very clearly and loudly hissed. The local manager naturally, and I suppose successfully, reports such obvious mistakes to the central office, which is solely responsible for the selection of the film material, but in the meantime the pictures have been *shown*.

I have taken up the question of the utterly inadequate machinery of the central selection of the film material with those responsible for it. One person admitted to me, in the presence of my assistant, that he was by no means able to see all the films sent out or chosen for the local cinemas! Or I was reminded that the film material suitable for children was not enough. The latter argument is undoubtedly of great weight, but if there are not enough films suitable for children to go round, then why show objectionable pictures, objectionable from the point of view of the educationalist?

Moreover, the industry, or at least those who run children's cinemas, may say and have actually said: 'Listen, my dear fellow, we are here to provide entertainment and not education. In addition, we are making new children's films which will slowly replace those which you regard as objectionable.' To this I have answered, admittedly without the slightest success: It is *impossible* to provide entertainment divorced from moral and psychological norms. Even if you intend to give *pure* entertainment, the power of visualisation creates *moral* patterns. And at least as far as children are concerned, the State must supervise an industry which is obviously not able to see beyond its commercial horizon. Since the children's performances are being run as clubs, no outside adult person is permitted to attend without being carefully scrutinised. As neither the local management nor the central office seems to provide an *effective* selection of the film material, we leave several hundred thousand British children under an influence which is, to say the least, *very much* below the level of the definite rules and standards of the educational system. What the school builds up during the week *may* be entirely nullified on Saturday morning.

This is naturally not the intention of those who run the children's clubs. They have the best intentions, but the task they undertake is beyond their spiritual, mental, and technical equipment. In fact, they do not know what they are doing. The fundamental thesis (and purpose) of this book is not to attack individuals but rather to indicate that the film industry has reached a stage where the old 'showman' type, however well meaning he may be, must enlist the effective, not only the façade, co-operation of the social scientist, the educationalist, the psychologist, and last but not least, of the children themselves. And if it be not willing to enlist this co-operation voluntarily, the State must enforce it. Here, clearly, is a case where an economic monopoly creates under the cloak of 'free enterprise' mental attitudes which, in their present forms, are detrimental to the community as a whole.

What form such a supervision ought to take is obviously a question for discussion. Yet it would seem that the educational authorities should be responsible for a very thorough supervision scheme, served by full-time and qualified persons. *The State cannot shirk this task whatever political party may be in power.* The spiritual and mental health of a considerable proportion of British children is at stake. If the industry maintains that this would mean interference with private enterprise, it would seem justifiable to ask for appropriate *new* legislation, or at least of setting up a select committee in the House of Commons to investigate more fully the questions raised. It is clearly beyond the power of one investigator to cover such an immense field.

Another point in the argument against this point of view is that the new films produced by Mr. Rank's organisation might improve the present situation. But these films—with perhaps one exception—are, as films, hardly worth speaking of. They have been severely criticised by eminent film critics in the *News Chronicle* and in the series *This Week's Film*, by the B.B.C. I saw these films before they were shown to the public, and I also felt that they were futile, insignificant, though well-meaning. Only the best producers and directors should be concerned with making children's films, as is the practice in Soviet Russia. (See Appendix II of this book.)

My final argument is this: One may say: 'Do not those who select the material for the children's films rely on the 'U' certificates of the British Board of Film Censors?' This is certainly correct, but the Board itself does not appear to have expert knowledge of child psychology. I give an example. I recently saw a film, *Somewhere in Camp*, a film with a 'U' certificate. In this film a wife beats up her husband who has just returned from camp on unexpected leave, a scene which is hardly suitable for children. Or another soldier finds his wife with a 'lodger', and finally a scene is produced during which an old *viveur* looks for a housekeeper and the first gesture of the old gentleman when an aspirant appears is to search for details under his victim's frock. In five years from now such a film may be shown in our children's cinemas, not to mention the fact that some hundred thousand children have already seen it.

Perhaps one might be inclined to think that this was just an unhappy incident. 'You know all human institutions are frail' or some similar excuse may be brought forward. We do not criticise one incident, we criticise a *system*. Take, for example, a '*U*' trailer introducing the recent film *To Have and Have Not*, with Humphrey Bogart and Lauren Bacall as main actors. This film is very rightly certified 'A'. But it appears that the recent practice of the Film Censors is to provide 'U' trailers even for 'A' pictures. Now, I would like to see an educationalist in this country who would approve of this so-called 'U' trailer to this very 'sexy' type of film. You see, for instance, in this 'U' trailer, a kissing scene accompanied by a dialogue between the leading actors from which even experienced adults may have something to learn. (I saw this trailer in an ABC cinema in Norwich on August 7th 1945.)

To sum up: the constructive *potentialities* of these children's cinemas are immense. Given good film material, available in greater quantity than is now being used, given further an intelligent and responsible club management by experienced *youth* club leaders, these clubs could eventually become a real supplementary instrument for the civic education of our children.

The need and urge for entertainment can, and indeed *must*, go together with education. Any obtrusive moralising by films is abhorred by children—either in the form of films, slide, or 'club promise'. Many local managers would, I firmly believe, share my request for a speedy and revolutionary reform of the present state of affairs. But such a request is difficult to fulfil without the necessary pressure of the House of Commons, in view of the centralised structure of the film industry which runs such clubs. Our political scientists have dealt, it seems to me, too much with the 'new despotism' within the civil service, the 'new despotism' within modern industry may be more powerful and more dangerous, because it is under no public control such as the House of Commons ultimately exercises over the state civil service.

The permanent and higher civil servants of the modern large-scale industry, 'the managers', to use Mr. Burnham's phrase, are our real masters.[1]

[1] This essay was completed on July 1st 1945, four days *before* the General Election.

CHAPTER 5

Children and Adolescents and the Cinema

I. INTRODUCTORY

The following papers and documents were written and obtained at a fairly early stage of our investigations. (We publish them in the form in which they were submitted to Mr. Rank as preliminary reports.) We had distributed about 1,000 questionnaires in one of the Odeon Cinema Children's Clubs out of which 85 were sent back completed. We also received some 30 essays from secondary school girls about which we report at length.

We believe that the *selective* nature of the material obtained is sufficiently stressed. We felt we had to begin *somewhere*. It is for this reason that we used studies by contemporary psychologists (e.g. Arlitt and Murphy) rather arbitrarily. Until our contemporary psychology develops an adequate terminology with regard to the complex and subtle phenomenon of film, the sociologist will be forced to use existing psychological terms as approximations.

One last point: we were naturally also familiar with the related studies of the Payne Fund publications, but their entirely *quantitative* approach left us dissatisfied. So far as we found the Payne Fund studies useful for a sociology of film, we discuss the respective volumes of this series in separate chapters of this book.

II. METHODS

Even the most cursory view of methods to be employed in dealing with children's reactions to films must bear the following points in mind:

(a) The questionnaire, taken by itself, is not very satisfactory for children for several reasons; in our case, for instance, we found that, especially among the younger children (5—8 years), writing out the answers is difficult and tiresome, and very few of the children wrote more than a few words in answer to the questions. Also, we could not be sure whether the questionnaire was answered by the child himself or by an adult or older friend. But perhaps the most important objection to giving children questionnaires—and also to having them interviewed by strangers—is that they may write, or say, what they think is expected of them.

(b) We followed up our questionnaire by interviews with the children to whom we had given prizes for what we considered the best answers. However, direct interviews by strangers, we found, were also unsatisfactory as the children were shy and embarrassed. We hope, however, to get together a group of children whom we know and whom we will be able to interview in a less formal manner.

(c) Direct observation, as the third method, is useful as a study of behaviour which, in conjunction with informal interviews and, if possible, more essays written by children at school, should provide us with enough material in the first stages of this part of our investigation.

We think that these three different methods of observation will provide more satisfactory results than those of Mr. Ford,[1] who relies for his information solely on the impressions of cinema managers. While the latter can provide some useful information as to facts, we feel that as they are not trained social scientists their interpretations are not likely to be very accurate.

III. SOME OUTSTANDING PROBLEMS OF AUDIENCE REACTIONS

Before going more specifically into the question of the effect of films on children, it is necessary to study more fully the psychological mechanisms by means of which these effects are produced. This will involve such questions as, for instance, the relationship between the mental act of perceiving and the 'physical' act of perceiving—between *Vorstellung* and *Wahrnehmung*. The two processes are interlinked and any dissociation is artificial: 'All perception is the product of sensation . . . but sensation is also an aspect of perception.' (Gardner Murphy, *General Psychology*.)

In the cinema the film is presented to every member of the audience. But the sensation-perception mechanism is unique for each individual. What is perceived is unique in each case, but what is 'seen' is also unique. We can never see a number of objects com-

[1] Cf. Ford, *Children in the Cinema*, London, 1939.

59

pletely at the same time; when both eyes are used, retinal rivalry occurs—that is, two different impressions alternate in controlling the activity of the visual centres of the brain, so that a complete synthesis is not achieved. What impressions result will obviously differ in each case, but nevertheless it will be fascinating to study the individual, and if possible the group, differences of impressions. The objects chosen for selection will be those related to the fore-going scene—those that are important for each individual's particular interest in the plot. What is known about these general mechanisms has to be related to developmental child psychology. The development of perception is often retarded during the 'middle years' of childhood—that is, from five to eleven years; about 10·15 per cent of the school population suffers from a deficiency in visual perception, as distinct from weakness in visual acuity—that is, the intellectual part of perceptual development is retarded; reading difficulties are mainly due to this lag. Also, a deficiency in visual and auditory memory is frequently found. These facts show that the child's sensation-perception mechanisms are not by any means fully developed but are still in the process of developing during these years. Children's films, if they are to be fully understood, therefore, should be simple and take account of the experiences which the child is likely to have had, if he is to be helped in his perceptual development. Even if perceptual development has proceeded at a normal rate, a child's conception of the world is so very different from an adult's, since his needs are, and his experiences have been, different, that his 'impressions'—i.e. the perceptual synthesis—will differ fundamentally from those of an adult.

If a study could be made of the differences in selection which are made by each individual and related to an analysis of his social background, interests, and attitudes, we might be a step further along the road to solving our problems.

As far as children are concerned, it is thought that they see background and foreground separately. As considerable differences in development occur, it is difficult to say at what ages a more complete synthesis of perception is achieved, and most work that has been done on the subject deals mainly with infants. However, it is probably a fair approximation to say that until the ages of eight to ten such a synthesis, as far as background and foreground are concerned, is not achieved. This knowledge, if worked out by psychologists, might be used for establishing a new technique in the production of children's films. W. H. George has made a practical attempt to distinguish between the foreground use of the film for illustration, and the background use of the film for the direction of the imagination.

Apart from the problem of 'seeing' and 'perceiving'—another important psychological problem of audience reactions is that of memory. Memory, as Buehler points out in *The Intellectual Development of the Child,* is not merely the presentation of something already experienced, but a definite placement in the history of our past. What we remember, therefore, is obviously related to our past—we remember the things in which we are interested and which bear a relation to our life. Sometimes memory involves no exact placing, but merely a vague recognition. As far as children are concerned, the length of memory depends on how much the child was impressed at the time. A study of memory, and of the things remembered in a film, will give interesting indications of the effects of films, and of the role the film plays in the life of the public.

Examples can be given of some of the schoolgirls' essays; three girls chose *Gone With the Wind* as their favourite film, and the differences between the three accounts of the film are striking. One girl almost exclusively discussed the acting and casting of the main characters. The second girl recounted the story, picking out mainly the practical details of events, although Scarlett's personal history is also remembered, as far as practical details are concerned. The third girl mentions mainly the more profound implications of the personal relationships of the actors' characters—she describes not so much what the characters 'did', as what they thought, and relates the external events to the effect they have on, and the part they play in, the life of the characters.

Here, then, are three different assimilations of the film. The main points of the story as remembered and reproduced, give three quite different attitudes to the *same* film.

IV. EMOTIONAL RESPONSE

From the point of view of behaviour, a most striking example of the difference between child and adult reactions was furnished by our visits to the Children's Cinema Clubs. The children's enthusiasm was expressed in an altogether unmistakable fashion. In the two serial pictures, booing of the villain reached an almost hysterical pitch, and catching of breaths was audible during situations of tension, also exclamations of 'Oh!' when some ill had befallen the hero. The excitement of the children was, in fact, quite obvious, both during the performance of the films and in the intervals. Restlessness and boredom were expressed freely by moving about and chattering, usually during scenes of lengthy dialogue; children are very much more responsive than adults, on the whole, although there are, of course, exceptions. The child's stimulus-response pattern works more 'instinctively', and, as his behaviour patterns are not yet so fixed as those of the adult, many things will call forth a response.

The middle years of childhood, that is the years from five to seven and eight to eleven, are the most important from the point of view of the cinema, apart from adolescents, who must be left out for the present. Very young children, according to Susan Isaacs and most modern psychologists, accept though in varying degree Piaget's stage of 'egocentrism'. Here, the child is not yet aware of his separate identity from that of the rest of the world. This means that his attitude is subjective and there is no realisation of the separate identity of other beings; his playfellows are most often used to further his own ends. 'Clashes with other phantasies provide the first step in social development' (Susan Isaacs). This development continues throughout the middle years, combined with a lessening of earlier emotional intensity as these clashes continue and begin to be accepted. More independence is achieved, coupled with a greater reserve and more open hostility to adults as contemporaries. The child becomes a member of a group, which gives him greater security and makes him easier to live with.

The child during these years, then, is learning—'growing up'. But he is still a child, with the child's quick emotional responses, his sensitivity to impressions, his aggressiveness, his love of adventure due to a rich phantasy life expressing itself in play, and to his seeking and absorbing new impressions.

The attractions of the cinema for children can be said to be due to several factors. There is the pleasure taken in group-activity, due to a feeling of unity, of pleasure enjoyed in the company of others; Fleming deals with this aspect in *The Social Psychology of Education*. Dr. Miller, at the Conference on Children's Films at the British Film Institute in 1936, puts forward the view that certain situations presented in films, such as triumph of right over wrong and the punishment of the criminal, satisfy the child's aggressive tendencies.

He also stresses the importance of the child's identifying himself with the doer of heroic things: 'The imaginative or phantasy life of the child is largely occupied with the identification of the child with the doer of big and heroic deeds. Scenes of pursuit and conquest are the subject matter of phantasy which is again satisfied in films bearing on these themes. Not only is the aggressive motive satisfied, but enhancement of the self—or positive self-feeling is perhaps just as dominating an emotion'.[1]

Does the child distinguish between phantasy and reality? On the whole, it appears that after the first few years such a distinction is realised, although during the performance it is likely that a fairly complete process of self-identification does take place. However, during the early years the distinction between phantasy and reality is not always recognised and, as considerable variations in development occur, it is evident that younger children are frightened by things which would not affect an older child. It is essential, therefore, that films for younger children should be even more carefully selected than those for older children. For pointing out the importance of phantasy in child, and also in adult, life, we are indebted to earlier sociologists such as Lévy-Bruhl, and most modern psychologists. The child works out his phantasies in play, and in the first years, until five or six, according to Piaget, no distinction between 'real' and 'unreal' is made. The child's world is 'plastic'—he uses objects and people to express and reflect his interests, and these change frequently. The real world of the adults soon comes into conflict with the child's make-believe world. In the former, conflicts and unpleasant things occur; in the latter, the child is master and can do as he pleases. In the case of adults, the same conflicts in the real world occur also, and where these conflicts are not satisfactorily worked out he will compensate by building up a phantasy world—in extreme cases leading to schizophrenia.

The part which the cinema plays in the life of both children and adults in this respect is a fascinating study. The magical quality of many films obviously offers great opportunities for the phantasy life of both children and adults. Situations whose outcome is always happy provide compensation for the actual world with its struggles and difficulties.

But this is a more general question which does not properly come into this preliminary survey of children and the cinema.

The question of whether children have a stronger moral conscience or not is debatable. It is possible that they have, in those cases where the child is frightened by his elders' threats of what

[1] *Report on the Conference on Films for Children*, The British Film Institute, London, 1937, p. 18.

will happen to him if he is not 'good'. Piaget in *The Moral Judgment of the Child* distinguishes two types of moral feeling in children: firstly, that based on constraint, which is imposed by the teacher and parent; and that based on co-operation—the things learned in mutual co-operation with age-mates, that is, those involving an internal process of learning how to associate with others and making one's own rules. It is likely that children, through fear, the importance of which in child-psychology is very great, do feel strongly about moral issues in the first sense.

V. SOME PRACTICAL FINDINGS, AND SUGGESTIONS FOR PROVIDING BETTER FILMS FOR CHILDREN

The preferences of children depend, in the first place, on their experience of films, which in this country has been limited, with very few exceptions, to films which were produced for adults. As far as club performances go the same applies, apart from such films as, for instance, the *Chut the Kangaroo* series which, we believe, was produced as a children's film and enjoys an enormous popularity, according both to our questionnaires and to those presented by Mr. Ford to 150 cinema managers. Nature films are appreciated but evidently only when a story that 'moves' is attached to them. The educational type of nature film is not very popular—as one boy said, 'He didn't know nature was so jolly slow' (quoted by Miller).

According to the answers to our questionnaires, the great majority in both age-groups (5-8 and 9-13) prefer cowboy, war and Tarzan films—not very surprising since these are the main films that children see. However, while children will reply in a questionnaire that they like these films, it is perfectly obvious from attending one of the performances and from watching their behaviour in adult cinemas, that the greater part of the film bores them since it is impossible to understand the dialogue during a children's performance because of 'noisy offspring', as one of the older boys put it. But even if the dialogue were audible, much of it is boring to children, since it usually deals with occurrences in the adult world which are outside most children's interests and experience. Moreover, as must be concluded from Piaget's *The Language and Thought of the Child* (second edition, 1932), the various and distinct stages of the child's mental and perceptual development have an important bearing on his reactions to films. In this respect, prolonged case-studies by trained psychologists are *imperative*. Once such

DEANNA DURBIN IN 'THREE SMART GIRLS GROW UP'

DEANNA DURBIN CREATING FASHION AND BEHAVIOUR

studies are made, it might be possible to devise *guiding* principles for the production of children's films. Without such studies, children's films must, to say the least, remain haphazard, if not dangerous to the child mind.

Among the older, Shirley Temple and Deanna Durbin films become more popular. Cartoons are, relatively, liked better among the younger children, but mainly by girls.

Is the criterion of what films children like an adequate one for deciding what films they are to be shown? The answer is, *surely*, in the negative, since, as already pointed out, the preference or dislike is based on experience of films seen. At the moment, only the very worst types of films are shown to children: these exploit the child's love of adventure without offering him anything else except long dialogues which, for one reason or another, bore him. Surely his love of adventure and great curiosity and desire for new impressions could be utilised in order to stimulate interests that are a little nearer to the child's life than fantastic spy stories. Children are eager to learn about real things as well as imaginary ones; many children, in the answers to questionnaires and in the essays, mentioned that some particular film interested them because they had learnt something at school connected with it. One girl even said that she likes going to films because it helped her with her school-work.

There must be a long-term and a short-term policy as far as improvement in films for children is concerned. The former must be concerned with making *the best use* of existing films, a difficult matter, since distributors are prepared to rent to children's clubs only films that are not wanted for weekly performances. This means that films available for matinée performances are either very old or sub-standard—a most unsatisfactory state of affairs.

However, it is essential that a selection board should be established to decide on films that are suitable for club performances; on this board, only persons who are competent to make such a decision should sit. At present, the head of the Children's Clubs, who is responsible for the bookings for the 200 or more Odeon Children's Clubs in this country, sees only a small percentage of the films he books.

Some arrangement must be made with distributors about releasing newer films for children; this applies especially to Walt Disney's representative in this country.

The longer-term policy must concern itself with the production of special children's films and with the establishment of special children's cinemas as in Russia. The lines along which children's films should be produced must be worked out fully, but certain indications can be given here. Fairy tales and children's classics could be filmed, and much help might be obtained by making arrangements for showing foreign children's films in this country, especially Russian and Canadian, and studying them from the point of view of production. Many excellent children's classics and fairy-tales contain all the elements which appeal to children, but care would have to be taken not to represent scenes likely to frighten the younger children. In cartoons, for instance, close-ups of terrifying monsters are found to frighten children, also scenes of death and decay. Exciting scenes of pursuit, conquest, and fighting are not harmful, but lengthy scenes of torture and death or punishment of a criminal are unsuitable.

In conclusion, we should like to put forward the suggestion that the slides on moral virtue, shown at club performances, are perhaps unnecessary as well as extremely inartistic. The effect they are likely to have on the child's moral outlook is negligible: 'The good', as Piaget points out, 'is not, like duty, the result of a constraint exercised by society upon the individual. The aspiration to the good is of different stuff from the obedience given to an imperative rule . . . The rule of constraint remains external to the child's spirit and does not lead to as effective an obedience as the adult would wish.' The moral should always be given more indirectly, possibly 'by example', during a particular situation in which a moral is required.

DOCUMENTS

MY FAVOURITE FILM

1. A.B.

The sort of films I like best are historical films, which tell the story of some famous person. They tell about the life of the person. When the film is made the main facts are used but some small incidents are added. This does not spoil the film, but only makes it better because then one does not know all of what one is going to see.

The best film of this kind, I think was *Queen Victoria*. It was not just one film but the best parts of three films put together.

The film itself dealt with the reign of Queen Victoria. It was quite long and it was in technicolour.

The film showed how well faces can be altered, as one actress acted Queen Victoria when she was eighteen and when she was very old. Also the scenery in the film was lovely. I think of all the films that I have seen *Queen Victoria* was my favourite film and I would like to see it again.

2. S.G.

If anyone asked me what my favourite film was, I should answer, without hesitation, *Gone with the Wind*. My reason for choosing this film is not, as many people think, because of its exceptionally long run in town or because of its wonderful criticisms when it first came out.

When I read the book, although I had not yet seen the film, I thought Margaret Mitchell must have centred Rett Butler's part around Clark Gable, so alike in description were the two people. I cannot imagine any one else as the part.

Having seen the film *Adam had Four Sons* before I had read *Gone with the Wind*, when I actually did read the book, I could imagine no better Scarlett O'Hara than lovely Susan Haywood, and I was therefore frightened in case I should be disappointed in Vivien Leigh's portrayal of that part, thinking that the Southern accent would be too much for an English actress to cope with.

I went to see the film soon after its first arrival in London and I have never enjoyed sitting for three hours more than I did then. In case I should be bored I took three bars of chocolate with me but I was so enthralled with the film I forgot to eat them—a thing which has never happened to me before.

The casting of *Gone with the Wind* was, to my mind, superb. Leslie Howard was the perfect Ashley Wilkes as was Olivia de Haviland who played the part of Melanie, though I really thought she was *too* kind, *too* good to live, (which she didn't). This occurred to me in both the film and the book.

The part of Mammy was really excellently acted by a negress, who although I have seen her before, cannot recall her name.

The technicolour . . .

3. C.B.

I enjoyed the book *Gone with the Wind* a great deal so that when the film version of this book was produced I went with my parents to see it.

This film took three years to make and over a million dollars was spent on it. It was photographed in technicolour and played for three hours. Vivian Leigh acted remarkably well in the character of Scarlett O'Hara. Clark Gable also was just as I had imagined Rhett Butler to look and act like. I enjoy Leslie Howard's acting, but somehow he rather spoilt the picture in my mind of how Ashley Wilkes should be. Best of all I liked Olivia de Haviland as Melanie, she seemed to live in the part of the sweet and gentle cousin of Ashley.

The story is how Scarlett falls in love with Ashley who is to marry his cousin Melanie, as he is interested in arts and books and Scarlett whom he also loves, loves to have great balls and dances and they would clash if they were to marry. Then comes the war between the North and South Americans. The engagement party of Ashley and Melanie is broken up and Scarlett marries a young man, a cousin of Melanie named Wilkes. Both Wilkes and Ashley go off to the war. Wilkes is killed leaving Scarlett a young widow. I was very excited in the scene where Rhett and Scarlett are fleeing in a wagon from the town which the enemy has captured and set fire to, the technicolour of the burning buildings was simply glorious.

The story goes on to tell how Scarlett finds her mother dead on her return and her father crazy. The house and grounds are the background of the film and at the end of the film when she had married Rhett and he was leaving her, they showed you Scarlett thinking of her home Tara, and although her husband has left her, she still has Tara the home she loves to return to.

I thought it was rather a pity that they did not give the mother of Scarlett a larger part in the film as I liked the character in the book.

4. M.T.

When I am asked which film I consider is my favourite I immediately think of *Jane Eyre*. I have not seen it lately but all the story sticks in my mind far more than the majority of films.

Many of my friends say the film was far better than the book but others say it did not give a good picture of Charlotte Brontë's story. In some ways I prefer the original story without the alterations made by the studio which produced it. The scenes which I liked better than the original were the final ones, where Mister Rochester did not lose his arm, when his house was set on fire by his mad wife, as the book told us he did. Apart from this incident, the scenes were practically as I had imagined.

The actors and actresses, I thought were given rôles which they filled very capably. The part which Orson Wells played was cut out for him and it was a good return to the screen after having taken up directing, I believe. Joan Fontaine was too beautiful for the role of Jane Eyre when she was in the school as everyone seemed to think she was an ugly duckling. Margaret O'Brien made Adèle seem very sweet and real—more than Charlotte did in the book.

To start from the beginning of the film the child, Jane, was living with her Aunt and cousins but the boy bullied her a lot and she was disliked very much by all the family. Eventually her Aunt sends her to a school run by a terrible hypocrite named Mr. Brocklehurst. From the start she is singled out as a liar and very wicked child and is cruelly punished. She makes friends with a pretty girl named Helen. Helen is very delicate and after being made to walk round the courtyard in the pouring rain as a punishment, dies of consumption. Jane is left with only one other friend—the school doctor.

When Jane grows up she is offered a post at the school as a teacher but she refuses and answers an advertisement as governess to a little girl named Adèle. When Jane meets the child's guardian she falls in love with him, though she believes Mr. Rochester is going to marry a young woman, Blanche Ingram, who is only fond of his money. She leaves for another post and after some time believes Mr. Rochester calls for her. Jane returns to find the house burned, Mr. Rochester blind, but she marries him and gradually he regains his sight.

5. M.T.

The Scarlet Pimpernel

Introduction; comments on—: from book to film, choice of actors, personnal enjoyment, conclusion.

The Scarlet Pimpernel was an unknown Englishman who saved members of the French aristocracy from the horrible deaths of either torture, or the Guillotine, during the French Revolution. He, with a band of twenty friends formed themselves into a league and kept their identities a secret, even from their families.

Personally I enjoyed both film and book equally well. The book gave the reader more detail, while the film brought the scenery and costumes more vividly to the watcher's eye.

I think the choice of actors was exceptionally good as Lesley Howard played the role of the dreamy pleasure-loving baronet, who made himself a butterfly of society to hide his courage and sympathy for the illtreated French aristocrats.

Merle Oberon played the part of his beautiful, elegant French wife who held him in contempt for his seemingly disinterested attitude towards her suffering fellow countrymen.

I think I would have enjoyed this film better if it had been in technicolour. This would have shown the dresses and scenery up more vividly.

I think this was a well acted, interesting and slightly humerous play and I think that it would be a great pleasure if the Islington Studios would produce one or two of the Orczy Pimpernel sequels.

6. S.C.

When I saw *Gone with the Wind*, I came home with the impression that it was a marvellous film and I never expected to see another one that I like as much. So far, it is still my favourite film and I think I liked it because of its originality. Many famous stars acted in it and also as it was a long film you had time to catch hold of the spirit of it and you did not, as you do in some of the shorter films, come away with a feeling that you were not anything to the actors and feeling you were worlds apart from each other.

It started with Scarlett O'Hara as a young girl preparing for a ball and planning how she could trap Ashley Wilkes, a man of whom she was very fond. At the ball she discovered that he was engaged to his cousin and in her disappointment she accepted Charles Hamilton who proposed the same evening.

War was declared between the Southern and the Northern States of America and all the young men enlisted. Two months later Scarlett heard that her husband had been killed. She was left with a little boy whom she thought barred the way to her marrying again and so she rather resented his presence.

She left her home and went to Atlanta where she helped in a hospital for the wounded. There she met Rhett Buttler, a man who caught her fancy, but she could not make him propose. This naturally annoyed Scarlett, so when General Sherman approached the defences of Atlanta she seized the opportunity of returning home with Ashley's wife, Melanie, who had just given birth to a baby.

She found Tara still standing but the many fields were barren and there were no inhabitants for miles around. Her Father met her at the door and told her that her mother was dead and that her two sisters had been seriously ill and were just recovering.

Scarlett was badly in need of money to pay the taxes and so she made herself a new dress out of some velvet curtains and went to Atlanta. She happened to meet Frank Kennedy, an elderly man who had reached an understanding with her sister. He proposed to her and very soon Scarlett was Mrs. Kennedy.

Her husband was killed at a meeting of townsmen who had been caught conspiring against Sherman.

Shortly after this she met Rhett and this time he did propose. They had a rather unhappy married life and when their favourite daughter Bonny was killed when her pony threw her they parted.

Scarlett was sick with disappointment so she went to her beloved Tara and devoted herself to the cultivation of the cotton as her father had died some time before.

I think the attraction of the film for me was that we had learnt about the secession of the Southern States in History and I knew something about it. Everything including the scenery was very real and it was a very human and enjoyable story.

7. A.J.

I do not think I have a favourite film, but one I liked immensely which I saw recently was *This Happy Breed* by Noel Coward. I think I liked it because it was about ordinary people very much like ourselves and all their little ups and downs, also there was very good acting, especially by the people who took the parts of Mr. and Mrs. Gibbons.

The story begins with the return of Frank Gibbons after the last war, and he and his wife Ethel move into a house, complete with their three children Redge, Vi, and Queenie, whose ages are round fourteen. They also have living with them Ethel's mother Mrs. Flint, who is rather a grumpy old woman, Aunt Syl., Frank's sister, who is always complaining of being ill and who quarrels frightfully with Mrs. Flint, Edie, the maid, and a cat. This little family get on reasonably well together, in spite of Mrs. Flint grumbling and Aunt Syl. quarreling. We see Vi married happily to Sam, a boy she has known since childhood, and Redge marries Phyl, a girl he has also known for a long time. But while they are on their honeymoon Redge and Phyl. are killed in an accident. This tragedy seems to make Ethel much older and worried, but she has yet more worry, for Queenie, the youngest girl runs away from home.

So the story goes on, until 1939, just before the beginning of this war. Queenie comes home a better girl and is forgiven by her mother and marries a young naval officer who has been their next door neighbour for many years. Edie marries and leaves the Gibbons household, Mrs. Flint dies, Aunt Syl. becomes a spiritualist and annoys everyone, particularly Mr. Gibbons. Vi has two little girls, and Queenie has a baby boy, whom she leaves in her mother's care when she joins her husband in Singapore. The story ends with Mr. and Mrs. Gibbons leaving their house for a flat, complete with Queenie's baby.

Although I have not a favourite film, I enjoyed this very much.

8. K.B.

Although the ending was very weak and totally unsuspected, one of my favorite film's, if not the film I enjoyed most, was Noel Coward's *This Happy Breed*.

The plot was of an ordinary family of about middle class, between the years 1918-1939. The family consisted of mother, father—a demobilised soldier, two girls 'Vi' and Queenie and one boy 'Reggie', plus 'Grandma' and Aunt Silvia. Reggie at first, gets mixed up with a crowd of 'roughs' and comes home with his head bound up, after staying out all night. Queenie, the spoilt one, refuses to marry a sailor and leaves home to live with a man who has left his wife. Mother, refuses ever to have Queenie in the house again. Then Reggie marries and gets killed with his wife in a motor accident. Shortly after this 'Vi' gets married and goes to France for a honeymoon.

The sailor then finds Queenie in France, very ragged and dishevelled and brings her back and then mother receives her and the sailor marries her. Then the war comes and Queenie goes out to Singapore, leaving mother to look after the baby boy. And mother and father pack up and leave the house.

Although the plot is ordinary, the way the people acted was so naturally that it was very beautiful.

Some of the little things were immensely pleasing. I like the way they did not play soft music when news came that Reggie had been killed. The wireless was blazing away some jazz band, and it all came so naturally, not like it generally does in the films.

'Gran'ma' was typical too, so pessimistic and I loved it when Reggie's carriage was late, on his wedding day, and to cheer him up, she told him, how she knew someone who had been struck by lightening and that there was sure to be an accident. One of the most human things was however, when she found the cat, sitting on her feather boa.

Aunt Silvia thought she had a voice and it was comical to see the way father went into the kitchen, swiftly followed by mother, when she started to sing.

It was not at all funny, however, the skilful combination of humour, sadness and every day life made it unusual and very good, in fact thoroughly enjoyable.

9. J.W.

One of my favourite films is *The Way Ahead*. I liked it not only for the story of the film but also for the way that it paid tribute to our gallant soldiers, the orderliness and bravery of them, their thought for others and how they made themselves used to the army disciplin.

Other points that I particularly noticed were that the soldiers in civilian life had very different occupations, one was a stocker in the House of Parliament, another a manager of a big London store who spoke very grandly, two other young men were only troubling about their own comforts, one of these young men was a corporal at the end of the film. I enjoyed watching the men in battle train-ing, but I think when the men were shown crossing a river by swinging themselves along by a rope and one of the men fell off, it made the public laugh which I think altogether wrong as it seemed to ridicule the army in the eyes of the public.

I thought that the men being shown at home on leave was very lovely especially of the lieutenant of the company (who was David Niven) who was shown at home with his wife and little daughter fishing in the river, it was very sad when they all said 'goodbye' to their wives on the platforms before they knew that they were going abroad to French Morocco.

It was very tragic when they were hit by depth charges the men were so upset because they had to return to the Rock of Gibraltar, it was very sad and exciting when the company sergeant had his leg caught under a lorry in the hold of the ship, the ship was gradually sinking lower but at last they managed to free his leg.

When the men did eventually reach French Morocco the men were shown fighting against the Germans. After our men had been firing on the German fortress for some time a German officer told them to surrender but they did not.

10. E.F.

I think my favourite film was *My Friend Flicka*. This film, an animal one, had a different theme than the usual film of today. They are usually war or love, or the two mixed.

My Friend Flicka was a refreshing story of a boy and a filly he chose to be his own of all the horses on the ranch. The family from which the filly came had never been tamed. They were thought to be 'loco' or mad.

The film tells how the filly was gradually tamed, after throwing herself into a fence of barbed wire in a desperate attempt to get away from her captors. How after a long period of nursing she seemed to be recovering until one day she was found on her side with a half healed wound open again.

The father ordered the filly to be shot to put her out of her misery. The boy, however, managed to put off the shooting till early morning and went down to the pasture to say 'good-bye'. He found the filly lying in a stream that ran through the field, and he stayed all night holding her head out of the water.

In the morning he was found, stiff with cold, by the ranch hand who had been told to shoot Flicka. The boy was very ill for many weeks but when he was at last well enough he was carried by his father down to the pasture where Flicka lived. The filly had not been shot as the cold water running over her had taken the fever away. The film ends with the happy meeting of the two and as the book says leaves them to grow well and strong together.

11. B.R.

The most inspiring film I have ever seen was *My Friend Flicker*. It was not one of the films that you would see every day, and you know exactly how they are going to end.

It was about a little boy living in America who lived on a farm and whose Father reared horses. He very much wanted a foal of his very own, but, not being very brilliant at school was not allowed one. Although he had his own way soon enough, he having a mother who sided just a little bit with him.

One day his Father was going out to round some of the horses up and bring them back, but he was not allowed to go, owing to the fact that he had had a bad report and had to do extra work in the holidays. He was able to meet them on the way back and succeeded in scaring them and making them stampede.

After a little while he was able to choose a horse and he chose one that came from a very wild breed which did not please his father very much. He had this wild horse and the story continued to tell you how he tamed it. One of the important events being that it was very ill, and the boy was very ill, and they both nearly died. Anyway they almost died, but it didn't seem as simple as that when one was watching it on the screen. It ended up very happily although you did not know that until the very end.

12. D.F.

Although the film which I am going to write about was made a few years ago, I happened to see it, when it had recently been revived.

The title of the film was *Pygmalion* and it was based on the play by Bernard Shaw. It was considered to be the first successful play of his to be screened. I myself liked it for its witty dialogue, its polished acting and floorless production.

The story was about a very poor and badly spoken flower girl.

It happened that a certain proffesseur had suddenly found a friend of his from India. This friend had a bet with him, to see if this proffesseur could so train this very common flower girl, so as she could be passed into society within six months.

You are then shown how the proffesseur teaches her elocution, how and what to speak about when she meets people.

After a short while he brings her to his mother when a few guests have come for tea, Eliza, the flower girl while making conversation recites by heart, lines she had learned about in elocution. After the Proffesseur Higgins motions to her that it is time for her to go, she does so but not before she has shocked them first. The time draws on and the proffesseur arranges to take her now to a very important dance where he hopes she will be able to be passed as a lady. By this time she has entirely changed and makes a great success. He eventualy wins the bet.

13. S.H.

My Favourite Film—Pygmalion

When I went to see this film I did not know what kind of a film it was or what it was about. I knew it had been taken from the play by George Bernard Shaw and I was told that I should enjoy it.

I was lucky enough to arrive at the theatre so that I would see the film from start to finish. I was very impressed at the opening scene of a rainy night out-side the Covent Garden opera house and how Lizzy has an argument with a young gentleman who knocked over her flower basket. Professor Higgins who is soon going to be her tutor watches her very carefully and takes in all she says and does. The scene rapidly changes to the scene where Professor Higgins and his friend discuss the possibilities of training this flower girl Lizzy to become a lady and go to one of the famous balls which are held regularly in London. Professor Higgins who is a very well known and very good voice and poise educator thought he has a very good chance of training Lizzy, takes on a bet with his friend who is very pessimistic about the idea that he will be able to train her for one of the coming yearly balls.

Getting Eliza (as Higgins calls her) to come was the first difficulty Higgins had to overcome and this he manages with a little pressure on the part of Eliza. Also a little later Eliza's father comes along and demands his daughter or a payment which Higgins gives him without many questions. Straight away Higgins begins to mould Eliza's voice from a cockney slang very gradually into a good speaking voice. This is not good enough for Higgins he wants the voice to be perfect and you see him work on and gradually Eliza's voice gets to be a beautiful speaking voice.

14. P.S.

The Song of Bernadette is a film that has been classed as an epic, and although many people thought it was an extremely good film, others thought it was dull and uninteresting. Therefore there has been a lot of controversy about this film. I thought the film was excellent, and having read the book as well, I think the film was better than the book. Briefly, the story is about a young French girl, Bernadette, who has a vision of an extremely beautiful lady who is believed to be the Virgin Mary, but Bernadette always calls her 'the lady'. She has great faith in this lady, and although everyone in authority is against her she does exactly as the vision tells her. When Bernadette is twenty, she is persuaded by the Dean of Lourdes to enter a convent, and there she has to forget about the fame she had in the outside world, and she becomes a Sister. At last it is discovered that she has a tumour on her knee, and tuberculosis of the bones, She had, therefore, been in great pain for many years, and had never said a word. She was also suffering from asthma, but this was known by everyone. Then the nuns are positive that the vision was the Virgin Mary, and that Bernadette was a messenger of God. After a short while, Bernadette dies at the convent with a smile on her lips, because the vision appeared to her once again before she died.

I liked this film for many reasons, but mainly because I was able to relax and enjoy the film thoroughly, and not have to concentrate because the speech was indistinct, or the story complicated. The acting of the main characters was excellent, especially of Bernadette, her mother and the Dean of Lourdes. Therefore I could almost imagine myself there at the time the film was supposed to take place, and if a film can make you feel this, I think it has achieved its main goal, and this is especially true of historical films. Another thing I liked about the film was that it was different from other films, and also it made me forget the world outside for a couple of hours, and to place myself in a different world, where men were not always in a terrific hurry, and things happened in a leisurely way. These are the main reasons why I liked the *Song of Bernadette*.

15. S.B.

I very much enjoyed a film called *Journey Into Fear*. I also read the book and I thoroughly enjoyed it. It was about a man who had to go to a foreign country on business and how he was nearly murdered on his return journey. It was very exciting both to watch and to read. This man was sent back to England by a ship. He went to Turkey. Another wanted to kill him so to try and dodge him, he went over to France. One evening he went out and when he returned the murderer was in his room, and he fired at this man. He soon recovered and the next few days he decided to go back quickly to his home. He started on the boat and discovered that the murderer was on it. Luckily he had a pistol. The murderer kept on spying on him and took his pistol. His friend lent him one. This friend planned for the escape of the gentleman. The man was to be in a certain cabin by eight o'clock and stay there until his friend came for him. But when he went into the cabin he found his friend had been stabbed in the back. When he left the ship he was taken into a car and he expected that he would soon be attacked. Soon he was but he managed to kill two although he was badly knocked about and he made another unconscious. He just managed to escape from the other two. The book ends when he is in the train on his way to London. It was a thrilling story.

16. A.K.

I do not know that *The Song of Bernadette* is really my favourite film, but not having seen any other very good films for a long time, I think I can call it that.

The scene of the film is in Lourdes, a small French village. The heroine is the daughter of an ex-miller, M. Soubirous, and the sister of a girl Jeanne and two brothers. At the beginning of the story M. Soubirous is out of work and the family are only kept alive by the work of Mme. Soubirous who does washing. The time is February 11th 1853.

Jeanne and Bernadette attend the local school which is run by the Dean and a very strict nun. Bernadette suffers from asthma, and consequently is often absent from school and so at the bottom the class. Her worst subject seems to be scripture and she is very bad at her catechism.

One day she, Jeanne and their friend Marie are sent to fetch firewood. Bernadette does not cross the stream because of her delicate health. While she waits behind, she wanders to a small grotto where she thinks she heard music. As she stands there she sees a vision of a beautiful lady dressed in white, with a kind of holy light all round her. As Bernadette kneels the lady smiles at her and then vanishes.

On the way home she is very cheerful, and although carrying a heavy bundle of wood, and runs all the way.

Her parents and family do not believe her story. However the next week she again goes to the grotto at Marsepiells, and she is found there, very pale, looking as if she was dead. She says she saw the lady whom she promised to see again every day for fifteen days. However her mother had been nearly frantic with worry and forbids her to go again.

During the next few days she does not eat or sleep and finally her parents allow her to go. They and most of the villagers follow

Bernadette, and although they cannot see the vision, they kneel and pray.

The police do all in their power to stop them, but in vain. The people build an altar there, and go there daily.

Meanwhile M. Souribous had found a good job, and the family were healthier and better off.

One day the lady tells Bernadette to wash in and drink of the spring and eat of the plants growing by it. There is no spring visible so Bernadette begins to dig underground and washes herself in mud. However Mme. Souribous intervenes and drags her daughter away, fearful for her health.

Antoine, a young man desirous of marrying Bernadette, stays behind, sitting miserably on the ground. Suddenly he feels water on his hand, and looking down, sees a little stream of water coming out of the hole which Bernadette had dug. He rushed away to call back the villagers.

Meanwhile an old man who was half-blind, bathed his eyes in the water, and suddenly could see again.

17. S.M.

None Shall Escape! That was the title of a recent film, and also a warning to the free peoples of the world after the war. It takes the individual case of a Nazi war criminal after the war, being tried in a court of law. It is not a film that one could like, but there were many good points in the film, although it contained much to be criticised. It is certain that no war criminal will be tried in such a manner or in such a court. Also, to build up a story, many things were left by the film, in which the Nazis would have been absolutely ruthless. It did, however, portray in a vivid manner the inumerable crimes of the Nazis, and the danger in allowing even one of them to escape.

The film opens in a future war court, where the Judge announces that *Reichführer* X— is to be tried. He pleads innocent and wishes to act for his own defence, although he will not allow any verdict, as he, as a Nazi, does not recognise the authority of such a court. The first witness was the local padre from a village in Poland. As he tells his accusation, the scene is switched from the courtroom, back to the time of which the padre is telling. He is walking in the village square, soon after the Armistice of 1918 was declared, when he sees the accused man, then a German corporal, approaching with a missing leg replaced by a wooden one. He used to teach in the village school but he was German, he had to fight for Germany. Now he is back however, and the padre thinking it to be the will of God tells everyone that the corporal is not an enemy. The film here emphasizes the leniency after the last war shown to the Germans, and the vital mistake made.

18. T.S.

Now that so many purely fantastic films are being made I was very glad to see a true-to-life film which I thoroughly enjoyed—namely *The Sullivans*.

This, was I think, an excellently produced film about a mother and father and their five sons. It begins at the christening of the children, and takes you right along till their deaths. Some parts were extremely funny others—well, just everyday things that occur to all normal families containing schoolboys, and some parts were very moving, although even then, they were things that might happen to anyone in wartime.

The producer—I cannot remember his name—must have been a man who had at one time been just an ordinary working class man—living among such people as the film was centred upon.

One incident in the film I remember very clearly; the five boys —at the time the youngest was about five years old and the oldest about thirteen—'took' to smoking behind their father's back; when their father caught them they were each given half a cigar and ordered—yes, even the youngest!—to smoke them. After about five minutes they all felt so sick that they could hardly manage to get upstairs to the bathroom. Well some people might not find this so amusing but I have a small brother, and often he gets up to the same pranks as those boys!

Like most small boys, the five of them wanted to be sailors. The war began. What a chance for them. Oh!—but I forget—the youngest was married; just an ordinary attractive young girl but—how could he leave her—and his baby.

The day when he saw his brothers go, he had to go with them— they'd always stuck together—they mustn't break apart when the country needed them. All aboard the same ship one brother was injured; not even thinking of their own danger, the other four tried to get their brother off the ship which was sinking fast—but they weren't quick enough and they all died. The reason? Because they stuck together! Later a ship was named after them *The Fighting Sullivans*.

Some, may find that such a film is not to their taste, they want something . . .? but if more honest to goodness films, such as *The Sullivans*, which was or were supposed to be a true story, were made, I for one—and there must be others who think the same as I do— think that this would be a better world by far. Do you?

19. B.A.

I can always tell if I have enjoyed a film because if I have it remains in my memory. It may become a little blurred in parts and other parts may stand out in particular. There are several films that I have enjoyed so much that I would enjoy seeing again, one in particular which I saw several years ago, and was revived recently was *Goodbye Mr. Chips* from the book by James Hilton. Unfortunately I was unable to see it when it was revived, so my memory of it isn't very fresh.

The period of the story is the time before the last war about 1900, to about 1925 which was several years after the last war. Mr. Chips the hero of the story comes to the large boys public school as a master straight from college and has a difficult time settling down amongst the boys but he eventually succeeds in winning the heart of the school. His greatest friend is the German master, with whom Mr. Chips goes on a holiday to Switzerland. While in Switzerland he rescues a very beautiful woman and marrys her, bringing her back to the school with him as he is now housemaster. The boys are very fond of Mrs. Chips and are very sad when she dies in giving birth to a baby which also dies. Mr. Chips is very sad and devotes himself to the pupils of his school, to one boy in particular whose father was also Chips' pupil. Mr. Chips is now made head-master and then after some years as head the war breaks out and his friend the German master gets killed in the army. Several of the boys also get killed and the boy who was his special interest gets killed. By this time Chips is a very old man. What I think was the most dramatic part in the whole film was when Mr. Chips announces to the school the end of the war. The film begins with Mr. Chips as an old man sitting in a chair and then it goes back, at the end of the film we again find Mr. Chips in this chair and then a little boy comes in who is the son of the boy whose father got killed and the grandson of a boy who was Chips pupil. It is then discovered that Chips is dying and he remarks that he had hundreds of sons, they were all his sons although his only child died at birth. Faces of boys through the generations then reappear and they each say 'Goodbye Mr. Chips', and so the film ends.

Mr. Chips was brilliantly acted by Robert Donat with Greer Garson as his wife and Paul Henreid as the German master. The part of the boy of three generations was played by Terry Kilburn. The make up was very good and it seemed unbelievable that one man could look so young and then so old.

A COMMENTARY

This paper is a short analysis of the preceding nineteen essays by girls at a fairly small semi-state school in Hampstead; the essays were written during an English class; the subject the girls were given was: 'My favourite play or film'. Out of twenty-seven girls, nineteen chose to write about a film, the others chose plays and operas.

Behaviour

A perfect example of the effect of films on the behaviour of a boy of 14 was told us the other day: A youth-club leader was having a good deal of trouble with a fourteen-year-old boy, who was extremely unruly—his behaviour was aggressive, he would lie, and exhibit many other symptoms peculiar to the difficult period of adolescence. The youth-club leader went on vacation: when she came back, an astounding change had come over the boy: he helped her to take off her coat, got a chair for her, and was extraordinarily polite in his speech. Commenting on his changed behaviour, she jokingly asked him what had come over him; the reply was that he had been to see a film showing his favourite star, who had played the role of a gallant hero. The boy had decided to model himself on the star; the process by which this happened is likely to have been one of identification. During adolescence, a period of revolt against standards set by parents and teachers hitherto accepted, the young person is seeking for new standards of conduct and morals. Much is learned by imitation of 'heroes', where the hero embodies desirable qualities such as physical strength, in the case of boys, or beauty and 'poise' in the case of girls. This is largely the reason for the great popularity of such films as *The Song of Bernadette* and *Gone with the Wind*. Scarlett's actions are followed with the greatest interest, speculations are made as to what actress can best portray her, and the subtlest details in her relationships are noticed. For instance, one girl writes about Scarlett's relationship with Ashley Wilkes: 'The story is how Scarlett falls in love with Ashley, who is to marry his cousin Melanie, as he is interested in arts and books, and Scarlett, whom he also loves, loves to have great balls and dances, and they would clash if they were to marry ... at the end of the film, when she had married Rhett, and he was leaving her, they showed you Scarlett thinking of her home Tara, and although her husband has left her, she still has Tara, the home she loves, to return to.'

Another girl, discussing *Gone with the Wind*, says that she liked the film because she did not come away 'feeling you were worlds apart from the actors'. The main criticism made by children and adolescents is usually that they could not understand the film. For a film to be understood and liked in these years, the child must be able partly or completely to identify himself with the actors—that is, the film must be in conformity with the adolescent's experience. This seems to be the first requisite for the popularity of a film: that it offers scope for self-identification. The difference between children and adolescents in this respect is that children, up to roughly nine or eleven, tend to identify themselves with individuals. This is especially noticeable among very young children, when in their games they assume the rôles of 'mother' and 'father'; also, the great excitement during pursuit or battle scenes in which the hero is involved, points to a certain amount of identification. The adolescent's range of identification, however, is wider; it is concerned with filling an imaginary place in a social group. The child first accepts a rôle and a relationship offered by his immediate group, 'and gradually draws his own models from a wider range of possibilities. The fundamental task of growing up may be seen in terms of the need for defining a rôle for oneself which will give expression to one's own interests and capacities, and which will at the same time be acceptable to one's social group.' (Murphy and Newcomb: *Experimental Social Psychology*, p. 512.) From early adolescence onwards, the realisation of belonging to a larger group than home or school begins to be realised. The nation, the sense of citizenship, become important.

One girl, e.g., liked *The Way Ahead* 'not only for the story of the film, but also for the way that it paid tribute to our gallant soldiers, the orderliness and bravery of them, their thought for others, and how they made themselves used to the army discipline'. While children seem to like war-films mainly for the excitement of shooting, spies, etc., and boys often for the technical interest they take in ships and aeroplanes—one small boy next to us in the cinema the other day, sitting on the edge of his seat tense with excitement, whispered to himself the names of different types of aeroplanes appearing in the newsreel, oblivious to everything else—the adolescent already has a wider interest in 'our men' as belonging to a group which he—or in this case, she—recognises as one to which he also belongs.

The process of identification, then, is important especially among adolescent film goers. It is translated into behaviour on numerous occasions—as yet, we have not had a chance to observe such behaviour among adolescents. But the imitation of fashions, speech, and manners from the movies are well known; we know that imitation *does* take place—what we want to know are the differences in imitation that take place. For instance, among adolescents, how will a girl who goes to an expensive boarding school differ in her imitations from a girl of the same age who is already working? Here we come up against the difficulty of lumping all 'adolescents' together; working-class children tend to 'grow up' much more quickly than middle-class children—a girl of fourteen who is working, and possibly helping her mother to look after younger brothers and sisters, is obviously more mature than a girl who, like those who wrote the essays, goes to a progressive and expensive school all day, and takes little part in the running of the home. The social status of the adolescent must be taken into account when judging her attitude to life, and her reactions to films. For instance many of the girls under discussion had read *Gone with the Wind*, *The Scarlet Pimpernel*, and *The Song of Bernadette* before they saw the respective films. Many of them, judging by their style, read film criticisms before they went to see a picture. Their attitudes, therefore, can by no means be regarded as representative of a large majority. Having stated this limitation, however, it is still fascinating to study and, if possible, interpret their essays.

Emotional and Social Development

In our society, adolescence is a period of 'storm and stress', since full biological maturity is reached without accompanying recognition on the part of society of the adolescent as a full member. It is a period of conflicts between old and new loyalties, of emancipation from parental control, of new friendships, and speculations about 'fitting into' one's social group, choice of vocation, and so on. It is, also, a period when values and ideals are formed, and in this respect the cinema can be a powerful influence. By identification, widening of sympathy, and imitation, the adolescent learns to define his position in the wider world of the adult.

A period of conflict, then, is inevitable; but out of conflict arises construction—indeed, conflict is necessary for construction. What part does the cinema play in helping the adolescent resolve his difficulties—or does it offer him merely three hours of 'escape' from his problems?

The answer, as far as our group of girls is concerned, is clear when the films which they chose as their favourites, are considered. Three liked *Gone with the Wind*, three *The Song of Bernadette*, two *Pygmalion*, two *My Friend Flicka*, and two *This Happy Breed*. Other choices were *Good-bye Mr. Chips*, *The Way Ahead*, *The Scarlet Pimpernel*, *Queen Victoria* and *Jane Eyre*. Very broadly, these are all films with some kind of 'idea' behind them—only one girl, out of nineteen, chose a gangster picture about which, according to her description of it, she did not think at all!

This, we think, points unmistakably to the fact that 'middle-class' girls, at least, do *not* go to the cinema for 'dope'. It is true that these girls are only a small group, that they go to a progressive school, that, to judge by the essays, they receive encouragement from home to see the better type of film, and sometimes read the books, on which the films are based, beforehand. The criticisms are in many cases sensible, and the impression one gets from reading these nineteen essays is that this section of cinema-visiting adolescence will grow up into critical and informed adult cinema goers.

The question of the cinema as offering 'escape' has to be cleared up. A distinction has to be made between the psychological term 'escape mechanisms' and what is popularly known as 'escapism'. The former are defined by Arlitt[1] in this way: 'There is a series of mechanisms by means of which the individual may endure the situations or ideas which have produced a feeling of insecurity, and yet feel secure. These mechanisms . . . enable the individual to escape from the true pictures buried in the subconscious, (although) it must be remembered that we also defend ourselves from unpleasant ideas and situations of which we are wholly conscious.' Some of the most usual of these processes are projection, rationalisation, displacement, compensation, and day-dreaming. Escapism, on the other hand, is a vague term, often applied to actual actions,

[1] Arlitt, *Adolescent Psychology*, London, 1937, p. 67.

interests, and pursuits which are classed as escapist because they enable the individual to escape from facing the real world. But, as it is almost impossible to draw the line between active and 'escapist' pursuits, the term is too wide to have much explanatory significance. There are, however, different levels of interests and pursuits. One girl describes the film *Journey Into Fear* in the following manner: 'The man was to be in a certain cabin by eight o'clock and stay there until his friend came for him. But when he went into the cabin he found his friend stabbed in the back. When he left the ship he was taken into a car and he expected that he would soon be attacked. Soon he was but he managed to kill two although he was badly knocked about and he made another unconscious.' Her main interest is still the excitement of quickly-moving events, shooting, gangsters and the rest—she sums up by saying 'it was a thrilling story'; the description is still purely in terms of facts, without an attempt at explanation or correlation of the events. Her mental age is obviously below the average—she does not correlate events sufficiently and, amongst other defects, her vocabulary is limited. 'There is a definite correlation between ability of verbal expression and intellectual age' (Murphy and Newcomb). For the retarded adolescent this type of film is definitely bad, since it offers no stimulus to make an effort at perceiving more than appears on the screen as an exciting sequence of events. The events are not related to a fourteen-years-old's experience, but must appear to her as pure phantasy, quite unrelated to reality.

On the other hand, there is the type of film like *Bernadette*, and *This Happy Breed*, which does stimulate thought because it is related to the adolescent's experience and needs. In *Bernadette*, there is the struggle with authority—an aspect not overlooked by any of the three girls who wrote about it. One girl writes: 'Although everyone in authority is against her she does exactly as the vision tells her'—another 'the police do all in their power to stop her'. Other aspects like friendship, patriotism, and many others, are of great interest, and appreciated when shown in a film.

Realism

The reason given most often for liking a film is that it is 'real'; nearly every girl mentions the desirability of realism in films. Some examples are:

'Now that so many purely fantastic films are being made, I was very glad to see a true-to-life film which I thoroughly enjoyed—

The Sullivans . . . although some parts were very moving, even then they were things that might happen to anyone in war-time . . . the producer must have been a man who had at one time been just an ordinary working-class man, living among such people as the film portrayed.' Another girl, writing about *The Way Ahead*, liked the scenes of the men at home on leave, and their pre-war lives. But the most discerning remark is made by a girl about the scene where the parents learn of their son's death in *This Happy Breed*—'the wireless was blazing away some jazz-band, and it all came so naturally, not like it generally does in the films.'

The relation between realism and phantasy is a knotty problem. In so far as we all have ideals, we do very largely live in a world of phantasy, where the ideal is a goal towards which we strive in every-day life. But 'ideals should not be formed apart from reality' (Arlitt, *Psychology of Adolescence*, p. 196). The most difficult obstacle to reaching maturity in every one of its psychological aspects is the necessity for accepting the ideal as unattainable, but nevertheless not relaxing efforts to attain it. Phantasy means, very largely, wish-fulfilment, that is, in his phantasy the individual can attain his ideal; in this way he escapes from his problems. And in this way the film offers 'escape' (we have, unfortunately, come back to the same word, for want of a better one), in so far as ideal situations are presented, which provide material for the individual's phantasies. In so far as these phantasies cannot, even partially, be put into practice, they lead to maladjustment by becoming more and more remote from reality. In so far, however, as the phantasy is more closely related to life, it is a necessary stimulus to action by providing a wider horizon of experience.

One of our girls, at the end of her essay on *The Song of Bernadette*, says she liked the film because 'I could almost imagine myself there at the time the film was supposed to take place . . . it made me forget the world outside for a couple of hours, and to place myself in a different world, where men were not always in a terrific hurry, and things happened in a leisurely way'.

Here we have the appeal of the phantasy of the past; nevertheless, it is a phantasy presenting a very real and even profound feeling. During adolescence, traditional and parental values begin to be rejected, and values arising out of association with contemporaries tend to become of much more vital importance. In Germany, a study of 1,200 children between the ages of twelve and seventeen, made by Schaefer, revealed that at twelve, religious sanctions were the basis on which over half the children answered the question 'Why is stealing forbidden?' Of the seventeen-year-olds, only 10 per cent gave similar answers. Another study by Macauley and Watkins shows that up to about nine or ten, children's moral conceptions are fairly rigid and expressed in terms of immediate personal relations. After about eleven, however, attempts at more generalised moral rules are made—'from eleven years on, the children's ideas began to show an admixture of grown-up and conventionally recognised sins; but only in later adolescence do such "sins of the spirit" as hypocrisy and selfishness receive attention' (Murphy and Newcomb, *op. cit.*, p. 677).

Interest in wider moral problems is illustrated beautifully by one of the girls who describes the film *None Shall Escape*, dealing with the trial of a Nazi war-criminal. She ends her essay by writing: 'The film . . . emphasises the leniency after the last war shown to the Germans, and the vital mistake made; also (the film) portrays in a vivid manner the innumerable crimes of the Nazis, and the danger in allowing even one of them to escape.' While a younger child might, at the time he saw the film, be impressed by the political propaganda implicit in this film, it is doubtful whether he would absorb it in the way this girl has done; she has obviously thought about the problem of the Nazis, judging by her method of discussing the film.

The tendency to make independent moral judgments is encouraged by the fact that, in our society, moral standards differ widely among different groups; contacts with new groups, and different moral standards, necessitate choice between them. The cinema can play an important part in widening the child's outlook, by portraying the differences of moral standards. However, 'the change . . . from external authority as the guide, to guidance from within is not absolute but largely in degree, and varies widely between individuals. It is possible for an adolescent who has not been trained to make his own decisions, who has been controlled completely by the adults with whom he is surrounded, to be still in the pre-school period in regard to the need for external control' (Arlitt, *op. cit.*, p. 194). At the moment, the American and British film still portrays a decidedly traditional morality; for instance, in most gangster films the moral is that 'crime does not pay', but at least the causes for immoral behaviour are often shown, as in the *Dead End Kids* films. On the whole, however, it can by no means be said that the average film encourages the adolescent to make independent moral decisions; group and traditional morality is, on the whole, upheld. For instance, in *This Happy Breed*, one girl says that 'Queenie is forgiven by her mother', also 'she is found by the sailor in France, very ragged and dishevelled'—in other words, deviation from the family moral tradition is punished.

The Song of Bernadette is an exception in this respect; the internal nature of acting according to what one regards as right is stressed —but then, Bernadette has the advantage of external aid in the form of 'the Lady'.

Social Relationships

Friendships at adolescence become increasingly important; also, crushes and 'puppy-love' may increase after thirteen and fourteen. 'The meaning of intense love-friendships and crushes for adolescents is not yet entirely clear; they may reflect both the projection of the child's need for affection, and the sublimation of growing emotions that in another culture might have more immediate sexual expression' (Murphy and Newcomb, *op. cit.*, p. 644). The studies of small communities in New Guinea and Samoa made by Margaret Mead show that adolescents do not necessarily have to go through what is regarded in our society as the typical stage of great attachments for older persons. A good illustration of a 'crush' of an eighteen-year-old girl for an older man was given in a recent film, *This is the Life*. Especially among middle-class girls, the cinema plays an important part by providing heroes—and heroines—who can be worshipped from afar, where the segregation of the sexes in schools provides little opportunity for relationships with members of the opposite sex.

Among our group of girls, it is difficult to judge their attitudes correctly, since we have only their essays to go by for the present. It is, however, obvious that social relationships receive the closest attention; the story of the film is told mainly in terms of the relations of the characters to each other. Scarlett's numerous husbands, who marries whom and why in *This Happy Breed*, Jane and Rochester in *Jane Eyre*, are the main themes of the essays. The names of the characters are remembered with astounding accuracy, and since accuracy and persistence of memory depend largely on the degree of emotional intensity which accompanies perception, it is obvious that social relationships and the extent to which such relationships offer scope for identification, a subject already discussed, are the main attraction of the cinema for adolescents.

Friendships are, perhaps, even more important than the more intense relationships, although where the one ends and the other begins it is very difficult to say. On the screen, unfortunately, a great distinction is made between love and friendship—love being defined, almost exclusively, in terms of sexual attraction, and friendship in terms of affection. One girl said she 'particularly liked the film *My Friend Flicka* because it had a different theme from the usual films, which are either about love or war'. The other girl who chose *My Friend Flicka* (or 'Flicker', as she calls it) made much the same point; she wanted a film about real friendships. Tschernjawski, in his book on the film in Soviet Russia, quotes a boy of about twelve who, writing to the director of the Children's Film Studio, says: 'I should like to see in the cinema a good, truthful film about friendship . . . friendship is an important matter for all of us, from the time when children start to think seriously about what they are doing; a lot of problems appear then'.

Although we are aware that we have treated only some aspects of the effects of films on adolescent audiences, and these very summarily, we have at least dealt with what we regarded as the most important ones. We intend to go more deeply into the problems, which are here only indicated, by interviews and case studies. Above all, however, we are aware that we have dealt only with a very small social group—our main task will be the study of the lower income-group audiences, from children of the 'white-collar workers' homes to unskilled labourers.

NOTES ON INTERVIEWS

(1) *M.T.*—Age, nearly fifteen.

Family. Mother, father, grandfather, brother in the Air Force (cadet), training for engineering. Lives in house in suburb, about six rooms.

Grandfather used to take children to cinema; mother does not mind her going, rarely go together—parents don't go often.

Friends. Greatest friend P. (see 2), always go to the pictures together; does not belong to 'clique'—'in our form there are groups'. Sees a lot of P.—shares same interests.

Interests. Likes art best—she and P. do a lot of drawing together; 'craze' for 'glamour-girls'. Sent some drawings to brother's friend who is 'expert'. Also likes geography very much, history to a lesser extent. Apart from art and geography, does not think teachers think much of her.

Reads about two 'crime-books' a week, nothing else. No ideas about vocation—perhaps art.

General. Rather shy and awkward, fiddled about uncomfortably at beginning of interview. Very fond of P. who, though two months younger, is more sure of herself and more definite in opinions expressed.

Cinema. Reads critics in *News of the World* and *Pictorial* to get some idea about the film, also asks people. They usually go every Saturday afternoon, twice a week in the summer.

'I know it shouldn't be, but I usually go to a film for the stars.' Liked *As You Like It*, would like to see *Henry V* but doesn't think P. will like to see it.

Definitely dislikes unhappy endings—*Till We Meet Again* not liked because of it; cannot remember three other films recently seen, in spite of being asked two or three times. Would sooner go to the 'lighter' type of film. (But see her essay.)

'The only thing I notice at the beginning of a film, when the names of the people who made it are shown, is the costume designer.' Remembers fairly well different dresses that struck her —e.g. Deanna Durbin's 'Hungarian' evening dress in *His Butler's Sister*, Ginger Rogers' playsuits, etc.

Likes films about people; one of few war films liked was *Dr. Wassell*, 'because it's about a person—there always seem to be crowds in the others'.

Liked *This Happy Breed*, because it reminded her of people and situations in own life. 'My father and brother used to have rows, too, but they don't any more!' True-to-life story—the moral (sanctity of family life, etc.) apparently approved—e.g. quarrels not important, 'everything comes right in the end'.

Essay: Jane Eyre.

(2) *P.T.*—Age, about 14½.

Family. Only child; father in the Air Force. Often goes to cinema with parents when father on leave. Mother used not to like her going too often, but doesn't mind now. Would like brother or sister—'rather lonely without'.

Friends. Special friend M. (see 1); her form is rather 'starchy', everyone goes round in pairs.

Interests. Art—definitely intends to go to art-school, likes figure-drawing best; both she and M. regarded by B. (see 3) as 'good in drawing'. Bad at Latin and languages, likes needlework, 'might like cooking if I were very good'. Likes history, but doesn't like text-books—too old-fashioned; tried to get others at library but always out—'that discourages you'. Reads crime-stories, doesn't like school-girl stories, too unreal, rather silly—same applies to films about school and college life.

General. Fairly free and easy, not very shy, fairly definite opinions, intelligent.

Cinema. Does not particularly mind whether end of a film sad or not; likes musicals, *This Happy Breed, The Sullivans*, etc.—'true-to-life'. Did not like *Dragon Seed*, too dramatised; 'About two years ago I might have liked it; I went through a stage, as I suppose everybody does, of dramatising everything, but I don't any more. But then, I suppose, you get no pleasure from a film unless it is dramatic.'(!)

Likes 'ordinary things'; remembers mainly actors and the story of a film, e.g. liked *Fanny by Gaslight* and *The Man in Grey* because the same four actors, 'who go well together'.

Part of Mrs. Barbary rather shrewish—quite liked her but 'I suppose you were meant to like Phyllis Calvert, she was so sweet.' If in same situation as Mrs. B. would not act in the same way 'because she had a different upbringing'. But would not call her wicked—'I suppose she couldn't help herself'.

Saw *Jane Eyre*, wants to read book. Slightly disappointed in *Gone with the Wind*.

(3) *B.A.*—Age 16.
Family. Youngest in family; two older sisters, one brother, don't live at home.

Home in suburb, small house.

Friends. Belongs to youth club, sits on committee; girls and boys older than herself; no particular friend—friendly with all of them. Usually goes to cinema with these friends, often they go in a crowd.

Interests. Wants to do massage, interested and good in biology.

General. Quite mature, sociable, rather practical.

Cinema. Goes at least once a week, twice in the summer—'it's a source of enjoyment'.

Likes musicals, a film with a story, also 'classical novels', but especially 'films that go through a person's life'.

Films mentioned: *The Man in Grey*—the character Mrs. Barbary not really objectionable; 'She couldn't really help herself, she had the wrong sort of upbringing'.

Christmas Holiday—wrong part for Deanna Durbin—*Three Smart*

Girls unsophisticated, much better.

Three Comrades—'I suppose these things do happen', but rather unreal story; 'I hate to go away feeling "what a shame" '—doesn't like films that 'leave you guessing'.

Does not like American films (but most of the ones she mentions are American).

Notices different kinds of lettering at the beginning of the film. Talks to mother about clothes seen.

This Happy Breed—very true to life—mother and father often talk about the last war and post-war years, she gets same sort of impression. Colouring rather fantastic.

For Whom the Bell Tolls—not much in the story—not true to life—dull. (Main story is love-story, significance of the picture completely overlooked.)

Essay. Mr. Chips.

(4) *S.H.*—Age 14¾.

Family. Small house, furniture very modern; one older sister, 'very clever'. Mother used not to like her going to cinema too often, doesn't mind now. Sometimes goes with parents, discussions with mother and sister.

Friends. One particular friend, about same age, not at same school; doesn't see much of girls at school—most time spent with family and friend.

Interests. Likes maths. and science, wants to go to college. Reads a lot—classics, not much fiction, murder stories, but not adventure nor school-girl books—'They are too fantastic'. Works quite hard at school evidently.

General. Essay misleading; rather intelligent, logical mind; very bad memory as far as films are concerned.

Cinema. Does not go very often—about once a fortnight. Saw one Red Indian film recently, walked out in the middle. She has never been to the same film twice. Wrote about *Pygmalion*, read book after film. Noticed particularly the 'quick flashes' during tuition scenes. People could have lived, but action couldn't have happened. End of play better than film—it was peculiar Eliza should suddenly come back to professor after she had been so unhappy there; he did not treat her well—he did the whole thing for his own benefit, should have regarded her more, it would have earned him well in the end.

War films. Story of Dr. Wassell—'for once you did not feel that Gary Cooper was just Gary Cooper', actors so often are just actors, and you never feel that they really *are* the characters they portray. True to life film, the characters could have lived.

She liked: *For Whom the Bell Tolls*, but it couldn't have happened; again, she seems to mean mainly the love-story.

Jane Eyre—Thinks Jane had some idea of Rochester being married; only some parts could have happened—first part could. Rochester, for instance, would be sure to have told Jane about his wife as she was mad, otherwise perhaps not.

Liked *Things to Come*, but very far-fetched, utterly fantastic. Architecture very interesting.

Used to like Andy Hardy films, does not like them much any more!

Gone with the Wind—Scarlett acted all right towards ordinary people, but not towards her husbands; she acted according to her emotions—bad thing; very bossy.

The Young Mr. Pitt—likes historical films.

Madame Curie was very life-like—actor must have been really interested.

(5) *C.B.*—Age 14 years 11 months.

Family. Mother Austrian, father Polish—one sister (older), one brother (younger). Modern house; many relations (cousins, etc.) whom she sees a lot; have discussions on films, amongst other things.

Friends. Mainly family, has talks with brother about films, prefers older people—more interesting, more to learn.

Interests. Likes games, very good at them; at school, mainly history, geography, and Latin. Doesn't like school much, 'it's very tame'. Reads a good deal—novels, etc.

General. Very intelligent, progressive views.

Cinema. Mr. Chips—could actually *see* wife—in book she plays minor part.

Song of Bernadette—couldn't have happened—fifty years ago people believed that sort of thing, nowadays we are not super-stitious any more. Religion largely a matter of custom.

On the whole, prefers the cinema to stage because it is more real. Goes to flicks 'because there is not much else to do', good form of relaxation.

Rebecca—(main character) acted correctly, but he should not have married the girl in the first place if he were really fond of her —should realise she would be unhappy; nobody should kill any-one, 'it is in God's hands' (!)

Gone with the Wind—'I rather sympathise with Scarlett'—she was rather selfish, but did it all for Tara. 'She might have behaved differently if her mother had not died—should have acted according to what mother thought right, although mother can be wrong. To-day it's different—if I were her then, I might be the same.'

Does not like British-produced films; remembers one love-scene —'two people walk on a bridge, they say "I love you", and walk off again'. Thinks it would be more dramatic.

Does not like 'ugly heroes—although I suppose there are some'. Films have fundamentals of real life, but are over-dramatised. Likes more 'true-to-life' films once in a while, it's a change, but probably not always.

On the whole, prefers a book to a film—'you can use your imagination'; when she reads, she forgets all about everything, and has a picture in her mind.

Essay. Gone with the Wind.

(6) *J.W.*—Age 15.

Family. Mother, father; small house in suburbs.

Friends. No special friends, knows most girls in same form fairly well.

Interests. Likes chemistry, physics and maths. best—at one time wanted to be nurse.

General. Very shy, does not talk easily. (Rather dull?)

Goes to cinema about once a week, usually with one or two friends because she 'likes company'.

Main interest in actors and story.

Has seen mainly musicals and seems to like them best. Likes war-films. Dislikes love-stories. Sometimes reads criticisms in *Daily Mail*. Likes the cinema 'because you can sit back and listen'.

Films mentioned:

Atlantic Convoy—true to life.

Pride and Prejudice—wanted to see it twice—father portrayed well.

Wuthering Heights—Heathcote: 'quite a decent character', Cathy did not treat him well, 'it was a shame the way she turned round on him—she went in for money'. The brother's treatment of Cathy would have been justifiable if he had been her father. Remembers particularly the first scene of the traveller walking through the snow. Seen one year ago. *Lady in the Dark*—change from the ordinary type of film—liked the way it was filmed: interesting because 'it got into her dreams'. Remembers especially the dream sequence with the wedding-cake 'where she is going to get married'. Did not like the character portrayed by Ray Milland, did not like his manner; 'I don't think he really loved her'. Seen about six weeks ago.

The Lodger—liked the 'feeling of mystery'.

Essay. The Way Ahead.

(7) *P.T.*

Family. Small brother; mother present at interview—prompted, e.g. re *Madame Curie*, mother suggested that P. liked the film; on further questioning, however, it turned out that she found it rather boring. Whole interview, therefore, probably rather unreliable as mother was present.

Mother rather definite views—likes English, rather sentimental films; e.g. *Love Story*, *Mrs. Miniver*, etc. Also goes to shows, not necessarily 'straight' plays. Sensible woman, evidently gets on rather well with children on first impression. Six-roomed suburban house, comfortable.

Friends. Usually goes to flicks with one or two friends from school; no very particular friend.

Interests. Reading—novels because of films. Whole interview more superficial than others, did not talk very easily, fewer facts, fewer about herself.

'Why do you go to the cinema?'—'Well, I suppose to get away from everyday life.' Does not, therefore, like war-films; but liked *In Which We Serve*, because more 'true-to-life' pictures; how does that square with first statement? Says she likes documentaries, e.g. *Target for Tonight*, *Battle of Britain*, 'because they are interesting . . . not exaggerated'.

Likes Disney films—'would always go and see a cartoon'; *Fantasia*—'nice way of listening to music'—goes to concerts, and listens to the B.B.C.

Bernadette—'I wish it had been longer—it gave you something to think about'; very impressed by it—went to see it twice (Mother suggested—'I think you liked the acting'); parts mainly remembered: scene where Bernadette shows the nun the tumour on her knee; the nun in the chapel; the miller finds the stream. Last seen five months ago. Also read parts of the book.

Gone with the Wind—preferred book to film—'there was more in it'. But on the whole likes to see films, 'because you can sit back and watch it'.

Reads critics—*Mirror*, *Observer*, *Standard*; does not always agree with Miss Lejeune.

For Whom the Bell Tolls—liked guerillas, etc., but love story unreal.

Hotel du Nord—remembers very little, not particularly impressed.

This Happy Breed—some things more suited to being treated in a realistic fashion.

Too many films made after books!

Between Two Worlds—very indistinct, doesn't like that.

(8) *A.K.*—Age 14.

Family. Only child, lives near P.S., same sort of background.

Friends. Special friend (P.S.), and a few more whom she does not know so well.

General. Rather 'reflective', 'black and white' opinions; fairly slow, but by no means stupid.

Goes to cinema about once a week; less often in the summer (almost all the others go more in the summer, mainly because of black-out in the winter).

Choice of films: you go to a film '*if you hear* it's on the sort of thing you like'.

Likes historical films, and films 'made from books'. Not interested in stars, but mainly in the story. On the whole thinks she has seen more films made after books.

Films mentioned: *The Song of Bernadette*—unusual film; read book after film, would not have read book if she had not first seen the film—this goes for others as well!

Was convinced by the story—'if you actually see a thing on the film, I suppose it convinces you—if you just read a book, you might not have believed it'. Never wants to see Jennifer Jones in anything else.

Between Two Worlds—acting very good, it was 'different', 'made a change'; but 'not much story'.

Pygmalion—seen twice— 'lovely story, a change from the usual stuff'.

Lady Hamilton—'after I'd seen that, I got a pash on Nelson (meaning Laurence Olivier) for a few weeks afterwards'.

Essay. The Song of Bernadette.

(9) *S.M.*

Family. Brother, parents. Mother used to dislike her going to the cinema, does not any more.

Friends. A few 'special' friends.

Interests. Science, but especially modern history 'because it affects me most'.

General. Very lively, intelligent. Is producing an end-of-term play, spends much time on it.

Reads Ernest Betts in the *Sunday Express*; has not been to the cinema much lately, apparently because of lack of time.

Films mentioned: *Don't Take It to Heart*—'it was very different from the American stuff they dish out'; it was a bit slower and less sophisticated, which she prefers. She liked 'the way the earl wasn't aloof—it rather hits one on the head'; not like one's notions of the aristocracy—thinks it would be better if real life were more like that; thought the older people were better; thinks the aunt was a more representative member of the upper classes.

Pride and Prejudice—seen two weeks ago. Preferred book, as film not very real—'a bit too fancified', prefers 'realistic' film, but does not like documentaries.

For Whom the Bell Tolls—liked very much, 'it wasn't sloppy'— liked actors. It took a popular theme, civil war, and the treatment was not so hackneyed. The acting was dramatised, but the whole thing was much more likely than 'daring heroism'.

Essay. None Shall Escape.

FURTHER DOCUMENTS

THE SORT OF FILMS I LIKE

1. M.K.

When I go to see a film I really go to be entertained more than for anything else. I don't like to see an unrealistic film, I prefer a good story about something that could really happen.

The best and most realistic film that I have ever seen was *This Happy Breed*. It was a very good example of the every day life of an ordinary Brittish family. The people in it were not all beautiful with lovely frocks, etc., they were perfectly natural and ordinary. The house they lived in was an ordinary house such as you might find anywhere in England. I liked this film very much because it was so real.

One day we went to see another film called *Once Upon a Time*. We did not know anything about it and we never would have gone if we had. It was a story about a caterpillar that dances. The story was awfully silly and it just did not seem to make sence. The acting was not very good. I was so bored through that film that for the first time I was glad it finished.

Charles Boyer whom I saw in *Murder in Thornton Square* is a good actor, at least he is good in that film because he is rather wicked and not so sloppy. I think sloppy films with a lot of stupid love-making in them are horrible.

A week ago I saw *Rebecca*. That was a lovely film. I don't know whether I was not the least bit disappointed because I had expected such a lot after what people had said about it. I don't think films should be boosted up to such an extent that when you go to see a film you expect to see something wonderful.

I went to see *The White Cliffs of Dover* a few weeks ago and I did like that very much. It was just nice. A good story, good acting, and quite realistic. It was rather sad but I didn't mind that.

These are some of the sort of films I like and dislike. I like going to the pictures very much and I think that a film with a good senceble story is the best.

2. M.S.

When I went to the cinema a few weeks ago, I saw a film which was called *The Hound of the Baskervilles*. The acting was good, but in every scene in which the people were out of doors, there was a very heavy mist, even at mid-day. I have seen two or three films in which the moors (Dartmoor, etc.) were the background, and in each one, it has been very misty all through the film, and made everything seem unnatural.

One film that I liked very much was *The Sullivans*. In it, were five boys, and one saw them grow from little boys into men. It was very funny to see them as boys, especially when their father saw smoke coming from the shed, and when he opened the door, found them all smoking. Right from the beginning, if one of them was in trouble, the others helped him. Finally, they were all reported 'killed in action'. In some parts it was a bit too sentimental, but otherwise I liked it very much.

3. N.K.

A few weeks ago I saw a film called *Lady Hamilton*. The two main parts were played by Vivien Leigh and Lawrence Olivier. They have always been my two favourite English actors, and I think always will be. The film was based on the life of Lord Nelson (from the age of thirty). In some parts of the film the scenery and acting was very mediocre, and yet in other parts the acting was magnificent. Other films that I have seen and liked are *Rebecca*, *Wuthering Heights*, *Jane Eyre*, *Song of Bernadette* and a few more.

I like these kind of films because they are telling a story all the way through, and they nearly all have very good actors and actresses in the name parts.

When I went to see the *Song of Bernadette*, with a friend, sitting next to me was a lady, who, whenever there was a sad part would sniff heartily or go 'T, Tut, T' or say 'what a pity', or 'Poor little thing', which rather spoilt the film for me. However I did enjoy the film immensely, even though it was rather morbid in parts.

Fantasia was another film which I enjoyed very much because I enjoyed the music in it.

4. R.H.

I go to the pictures quite often and even though I like the music, dancing, and colour of the musical films, I think the films that I enjoyed as a story, and which I liked best were not musicals but films based on clasical or good books. Fore instance *Gone with the Wind* was a film I shall never forget and even if it was shorter than the book it portrayed the characters nearly as well. *Rebbecca* was another film which was very good and which I enjoyed immensly, the book I have been told (I haven't read it) is not as good as the film. *Song of Bernadette* was a film where I think most of the acting except that of Ann Rever and Jennifer Jones and a few others was weak but the film, supported by these few good actors was good on the whole. I liked it (and also cried a bit). *Pygmalion* was also a very good film which I enjoyed. Of the more comic films I liked *I Married a Witch* in which there was very good acting and it was genuinely funny, the chief characters were acted by Veronica Lake and Frederick March. I don't care for Walt Disney films in general except for *Bambi* and *Snow White* which were very good, I hate Donald Duck and Pluto, etc.

Even though I always like to see the good films especialy when I have read the book, and I remember them for a very long time, I often go to musicals. I usualy go to see the dancing and the dresses, but I am getting rather sick of Carmen Miranda who always dances the same kind of dance, and also of Aline Faye who sings with a very melancholy look on her face, and always seems to be jilted.

On the whole I think that it is worth it to go to the pictures sometimes, because unless one is very fussy there is always some film to one's taste.

5. D.F.

I like and generally enjoy a film that has a good story to it, not a silly, sloppy film that has to much of this kissing and cuddling in it. Mind you, I do like a bit of love story but not a lot of it. The kind of love that is shown by action. For example *Rebecca*. There was a story behind it. Laurence Olivier who married Joan Fontaine at the beginning of the film, was very much in love with her, but he did not show it by cuddling and kissing, he showed it by his actions and the look on his face, although he used to get angry and make her cry, but it was not because she had done anything wrong, but that she kept on reminding him of his previous wife Rebecca, who she thought he loved, but he really hated her as she was in love with another man, and also she was trying to blackmail him.

Greer Garson is one of my favourite film stars. Others are Margaret Lockwood, Joan Fontaine, Phyllis Calvert, and a few more. The men are Walter Pidgeon, George Mursky, Dennis Morgan, but not many more.

Lassie Come Home was a very lovely and yet pathetic film. Roddy McDowall is a very good little actor. Another of his films was *My Friend Flicka* which was also a sad but lovely film.

6. V.J.

I like especially films about the life of people. I think it is nice to see the way they behave in their homes and to study their character. I prefer the story of someone who actually lived rather than a made up story. A film which I have seen and liked was the one of Handel and how he wrote the *Messiah*. Although it is a long time since I saw it I can still remember it. A recent film I saw was *Song of Bernadette*. I liked this very much. It delt a lot with her life round about the time she was sixteen and I think Jennifer Jones acted the part of a simple peasant girl very well. She had a very quick wit however and I think this was rather exaggerated after the simple home and uneducated parents she had.

I liked also the story of *Fanny by Gaslight*. I think it was a very real story and it had many touching scenes.

I also enjoyed *Tom Brown's Schooldays*. Although I like the whole life story very much I think the part where the person is about twelve to eighteen is the part I like most.

7. M.W.   *This Happy Breed*

A few weeks ago I went to see this film, which I enjoyed immensely. It was in good technicolor and by that I do not mean the awful, bright American technicolor that so many films are in. The acting was very natural and really like ordinary family life. There were sad as well as humourous parts in it. The bit where George V died was very well acted. The film shown with it was one of these terrible cowboy films which are so popular nowadays. It was so utterly boring that I nearly went to sleep in the middle of it. You would see a cowboy say to another, 'We must catch Black Joe', and then they would go off on horses and you see them galloping round and round for about five minutes. After this there would be another short interlude, when two or three people were shot, and then off they would go again. It does seem a shame that they have to put such rotten films on with such good ones.

I think it was worth the money to see *This Happy Breed*, for it really was a very good film.

8. E.K.   *Little Lord Fauntleroy*

I saw the film at a very third rate cinema, where arrangements were very bad, but still I liked it. The story is natural and the characters were, on the whole well played. You could sympathise with Ceddie, when he had to part from his mother, and feel with the Earl his pride in Ceddie. And the finale, with Mr. Hobbs in England, changing all his ideas about English aristocracy is really amusing. I prefered the book, of course, because there I could imagine my characters, and could imagine the atmosphere which somehow a film cannot get.

In general I detest films. I only go to see things like *Bambi*, and *Snow White*, *Fantasia*, *Pinocchio* and that class of films, and then I liked *The Scarlet Pimpernel*. Otherwise, apart from those, films bore me, and seem unreal, and glamorous in an unpleasant way.

If film companies would put on things like ballets, in colour, or more instructive films altogether then I would go more frequently, but as things are now—it is the theatre and concerts for me.

9. E.B.   *Films*

Most of the films now-a-days are trash, except for a few English films.

American films are to over done, and their coloured films are far too flashy.

Sweet Rosie O'Grady has hardly any story to it. It was based on the same lines as all the other films are made, only the stars where dressed up in nineteen century clothes. The same with *Once Upon a Time*, only this was more ridiculous than ever. This film was about a Dancing Caterpiller.

The films about American schools are just about as bad. All the boys and girls do, is sing and dance instead of work. *Pygmalion* was quite a different thing altogether, it wasn't flashy, the actors acted naturally, the story was pleasant, and there were really humerous parts. This film was British. American actresses are far too made up, its horrible to have to sit and watch masks acting.

Also they put a good picture on, with a nasty little film to fill up the programme.

10. A.S.

My favourite films are historical ones. I think the one I liked best of these was *The Scarlet Pimpernel* which starred Leslie Howard, Merle Oberon and Raymond Massey. It seemed an awful pleasure of the French people to go and watch people guillotined with such joy on their face even if the aristocrats were hated by the ordinary people of France. The best film I have ever seen, though it was not a historical one, was *Wuthering Heights*. I think all the characters acted superbly, especially Merle Oberon as Cathy. All the characters of the story were filled by filmstars who really looked so if they had stepped out of the book. I especially enjoyed this film as Merle Oberon is my favourite actress and Laurence Olivier my favourite actor. I went to see *Jane Eyre* and was very disappointed as I did not think the film was nearly as good as the book. Orson Welles acted very well but I did not think Joan Fontaine suited the part. The scenery in *Jane Eyre* was much the same sort as in *Wuthering Heights*. Another film I enjoyed very much was *Pygmalion* which starred Leslie Howard who acted excellently in it. Two films I am waiting to see eagerly are *Caesar and Cleopatra* which stars Vivien Leigh and Claude Rains, and *A Song to Remember* a film which is about the life of Chopin, and stars Merle Oberon and Paul Muni.

11. R.F.

A film is really for the enjoyment of the public and most of the public enjoys films. The type of film I like now is quite different from the type I liked two years ago but I think some of my views are still the same. I rather like the picture which makes you cry, but not too much. As I am the sort of person easy to cry I am easily pleased in that way. On the other hand a film with, say, Abbott and Costello can be screamingly funny but I don't think I would enjoy it more than a sad film. I always enjoyed Deana

Durbin's films when she used to be a girl at college but in *Christmas Holiday* I didn't think and like her half as much.

The usual films of young girls and boys I enjoy very much but beside that I think a good murder is very thrilling but a bit impossible, still most films are impossible.

Cowboy films are usually stupid but all the same I still get a thrill when 'Buffalo Bill' fights single-handed against hordes of red-skins calling and whooping madly.

Although many people think that Walt Disney's films are babyish I still enjoy them as much a my younger brother and sister. I even think my father enjoys them better than an ordinary film. *Bambi* I thought was lovely. The little woodland creatures and the old Prince Stag looked so different yet all seemed to belong to the fairy like scene. 'Dumbo' the elephant who could fly with the big ears I thought was very sweet and when he cried and the tears welled up out of his eyes well—I don't know, but may be I like cartoons best after all.

A FURTHER COMMENTARY

CHILDHOOD AND ADOLESCENCE

As a short supplement to the nineteen girls' essays, nine girls were interviewed in their homes; also, we received eleven more essays from girls in the Lower V—one year below the others. The average age is thirteen and a half in the latter group, and fourteen and a half in the former, although one of the girls interviewed was sixteen.

The tastes in films between the two groups are rather different. The essays on the whole, and particularly the opinions expressed, are more spontaneous among the younger group. Two of the girls have not much to say for most films—one says: 'Most of the films now-a-days are trash, except for a few English films.' Another: 'I detest films in general . . . (most) films bore me, and seem unreal, and glamourous in an unpleasant way.'

This girl only goes to see the longer Walt Disney films which she enjoys very much; two other girls admit in a rather shame-faced manner to preferring the Walt Disneys—shame-faced because of a vague idea that cartoons are 'babyish'. So one girl says: 'Although many people think that Walt Disney's films are babyish, I still enjoy them as much a my younger brother and sister. I even think my father enjoys them better than an ordinary film . . . I don't know, but maybe I like cartoons best after all.' Another girl admits to still being thrilled by cowboy pictures—'Cowboy films are usually stupid but all the same I still get a thrill when Buffalo Bill fights single-handed against hordes of red-skins calling and whooping madly.'

On the whole, this group of girls in the transition stage between childhood and adulthood are definitely still nearer the former than the latter, unlike the older group; their reactions are more *spontaneous*, opinions more clear-cut. Other films mentioned, however, are mainly the same in both cases—*Bernadette*, *This Happy Breed*, *Scarlet Pimpernel*, etc., with the one notable exception of *Gone with the Wind*; on the other hand, *Tom Brown's Schooldays* and *The Hound of the Baskervilles* are also mentioned by the younger girls, in addition to *The Great Mr. Handel* and one or two more 'historical films'. A change in taste as to the films liked is evident with increasing age, and is realised by the girls themselves; S.H., one of the girls interviewed, mentions a Red Indian film seen recently during which she walked out, but said that two years ago (*sic!*—she is 14¾ now) she enjoyed that sort of film. Another girl, P.T., saw *Dragon Seed* recently, which she disliked because it was too dramatised; she thinks that about two years ago she might have liked it, because 'I went through a stage, as I suppose everybody does, of dramatising everything, but I don't any more!' Another girl used to enjoy the *Andy Hardy* films very much, but they bore her *now*.

The differences between the two age-groups having been noted, we will now take the group as a whole and try to enlarge a little on a few points already touched upon in the previous paper.

The most important point is that of 'reality' in the films; the question one involuntarily asks on reading the girls' essays is not only do these girls prefer 'realistic' films, and if so, why, but the much more complex one—what precisely do they mean by a 'realistic' film? That there has been a very decided movement towards what Margaret Thorp calls 'intelligent realism' in the cinema has, by now, become a platitude; the British film *This Happy Breed* is a good example of the 'new spirit'. It is also noteworthy that it is the most quoted film in our essays and interviews, always liked for its 'realism'. (This, incidentally, is also evident from our returns of adult questionnaires.) By taking the camera into the family's kitchen, dining-room and back garden, as the background to 'a story of a family that could happen to anyone' (to quote one of our girls), this film achieves one requisite for realism; the kitchen, dining-room, and back garden are those of the majority of British film-goers; here is a background which is within our experience, which we therefore call realistic. A second requisite for recognising a situation as realistic is breadth of outlook, which involves such qualities as sympathy, imagination, and partly, perhaps, curiosity; something can be recognised as 'realistic', even if outside our experience, if we imagine ourselves in such a situation.

The first type of judgment is illustrated, as already mentioned, by the girls' opinions of *This Happy Breed*. Another example is *The Sullivans*, of which one girl in each group described a scene where boys are caught smoking in the wood-shed by their father; she says: 'Some people might not find this so amusing, but I have a small brother who often gets up to the same sort of pranks.'

The second type of judgment is shown by a girl who, describing *The Song of Bernadette*, says: 'I could almost imagine myself there at the time the film was supposed to take place, and if a film can make you feel this, I think it has achieved its main goal.' From imagining oneself 'there at the time' it is only a small step towards judging a film to be realistic—as another girl said during an interview, 'If you see a thing on the film, I suppose it convinces you—if you just read a book, you might not have believed it'!

This last sentence brings out beautifully the impact of visualisation of the film—how could one disbelieve, for the duration of the film at any rate, what is actually presented in all detail before one's eyes?

Another point which is worth while mentioning here is the question of the relation between literature and film. As Margaret Thorp points out, the film can stimulate interest in literature; and already has considerably done so; quite a number of girls said they read a novel, e.g., *Rebecca*, *Jane Eyre*, *Pride and Prejudice*, etc., *after* they had seen the respective films; one girl even said that she could never wade through a whole book unless she had seen the film first(!). Others will read a novel *before* they go to see the film in order to know what it will all be about. However, we found that the more reflective and imaginative girls preferred, on the whole, most books to the films made from them: the latter type of girl prefers to use her imagination and create her own characters, an active occupation; the mentally more lazy prefers to 'sit back and enjoy herself'. Another girl even said that 'somehow none of the films made after books managed to quite catch the spirit of the book'. The essential difference between seeing a film and reading a book is one of passive and active recreation; however little effort is made when reading a novel, some effort there must be; in the film, little effort is needed to grasp what is being represented in a visual shape.

As already mentioned, films play an important part in the phantasy life of the individual; instances are known where scenes from films have been mentioned by patients while under psychoanalytic treatment. A few girls said they sometimes dreamt about films, but could give no instances.

Many of the girls said they liked 'realistic' films as a change, when questioned, but did not know whether they would like to see them all the time. It must be realised that the 'better' films mentioned are very few in number, that all the girls, or nearly all of them, go to the cinema once a week, and that the majority of films seen are 'glamourous in an unpleasant way'; and, although the evidence goes to show that these films are barely remembered consciously over a number of years, when seen regularly once a week they are bound to have a deep effect.

A few concluding remarks about the moral aspect of films. The incessant patriotic propaganda in most war-films is not liked by the more discerning girls; one girl preferred *For Whom the Bell Tolls* to most other war-films—she found the film more convincing than 'heroics'; *Dr Wassell* and *The Way Ahead* are the only other war-films mentioned as being liked. Here, of course, we must bear in mind that the group of girls under discussion represent only a specific social section of British society as a whole. It appears that the girls are sick to death of war-films as a whole; about two of those interviewed said they 'did not mind' them. The way in which the moral of a film can be conveyed by the film is shown strikingly by one girl, who said about *Don't Take It to Heart* that she 'liked the way the earl wasn't aloof... it rather hits you on the head, though, and changes your previous notions'. Her previous notions, on further questioning, apparently were that earls *were* aloof in real life. On further conversation, she decided that the aunt was definitely a better representative of the upper class—but the immediate reaction, as can be seen, was that 'earls aren't such bad people after all'.

It would be interesting to make an analysis of the 'moral' of a film, show the film to these girls, and try to ascertain how far this moral has been absorbed by them by means of a very simple questionnaire. One of the Payne Fund studies worked out a similar test, also testing the persistence of effects by giving another questionnaire six months after the film was seen. Their results they found to be positive, but their methods have come in for a good deal of criticism lately.

Our girls, on the whole, like 'good' films, and remember them to an extraordinary extent. But they nevertheless go to the 'lighter' films and enjoy them, such as musicals, light comedies, etc. They have come to accept the fact that a film like *Bernadette* is turned out once in a blue moon, but that most second-raters are nevertheless enjoyable. One thing, however, is certain: they will not swallow rubbish, since their standards are being set by the few better films of each type.

CHAPTER 6

Children and the Cinema—(*continued*)

. . . nothing psychological is truly measurable (in spite of useful fictions used in intelligence and similar testing).

J. T. MacCurdy, *The Structure of Morale*, p. 128.

DOCUMENTS AND COMMENTARIES

We continued to apply our essay method. This method has the advantage of giving our contributors a free field in which to express themselves. There was no guidance given except what was implied by the title. The strait-jacket of the questionnaire method was thus successfully avoided.

The following twenty-two essays were obtained from the same school in Hampstead as the preceding ones in Chapter V. Yet the contributors are on the average not older than 12½. They definitely belong to the child age. Their parents are probably mostly members of the middle class. The children are well looked after. It would appear that many parents or mothers accompany their children to the cinema.

Various points *clearly* distinguish these children from the other age groups. They are all less plot-conscious, or rather they still have language difficulties in describing a plot. (Essay 12 is in this respect of particular importance.) The preference for technicolour films, as is evident from Nos. 1, 2, 9, 16, 22, is also striking. Perhaps we do not know enough yet about colour preferences with regard to film, but I am inclined to believe that children *up* to the age group under discussion generally prefer technicolour films, because, if I may put it tentatively, their rationalising mechanisms are still undeveloped. (If I am not mistaken those among adult cinema goers who have little or no formal education tend to show the same preference for colour-films. Colour takes the place of dialogue or of a complicated plot. To what extent colour corresponds particularly to child emotionalism, I am unable to say, but I would not be surprised if there is such a correspondence.)

Another point which is characteristic of this age group is the love for animal pictures. Here Nos. 8, 9, 10, 12, 15, 20, 21 are relevant. One girl (No. 12) makes a particularly delicate and fine point.

Fright, terror, nightmares are mentioned in three contributions (in almost 15 per cent of the essays obtained). The reader will do well to remember that this information was volunteered (Nos. 7, 10, 21). Considering the class origin of the girls and their educational standard, it is safe to say that the experiences of fright, terror, nightmares, as a *direct* result of film are in children of another class origin considerably more numerous. (I shall submit more detailed evidence on this point in vol. III of this series.)

It is also important to realise that the children under discussion see mainly 'A' pictures. This habit they share with British children of all classes. The amount of mental maladjustments resulting from this, is in my opinion immeasurably serious, whatever the film industry may say. It would therefore appear *imperative* to revise existing legislation, so that children—say under 14—are not allowed to see 'A' films whether accompanied by adults or not. If they are admitted, the cinemas should then be heavily fined.

The variations in taste of these 12½ years old girls is considerable. They are on the verge of becoming individuals. Evidently an intelligent sensitive film appreciation through film classes (either in the schools or through the B.B.C.) could strengthen their individual tendencies before these are crushed by the impact of the typified mass-standard of film, once they take their lives in their own hands.

Finally, there is a last common striking note in our documents. Seven girls express themselves against 'silly love scenes' (see Nos. 5, 7, 8, 11, 14, 17, 19). They know love will come to them—one day. But for the present they resent instinctively as impudent what one day will be their innermost secret.

DOCUMENTS

1. R.E.

First, I will write about the sort of films I like.

I like, best of all, historic films. The first one I can remember seeing was *Queen Victoria*. It was about her lifetime. But having seen it so long ago, I cannot remember very much. One incident, however, remains clearly in my mind, and that is how even after her husband's death she used to pour out tea for him each afternoon as if he was actually there.

Then comes *Lady Hamilton*. This was about Nelson and Lady Hamilton (who was the wife of the British Ambassador of Naples and a friend of Nelson's). They loved each other and so many exciting incidents occur. It is told by Lady Hamilton in a prison for stealing in France. She relates it to a fellow prisoner and also explains why she is brought to such a low state.

Then I like technicolour films such as Sabu ones, sensible tropical island ones, Gypsy dances and carnivals, and animal films such as *My Friend Flicka* and best of all *Lady in the Dark*. I liked the first ones because of the story as well as the colour, *My Friend Flicka* because of the pretty way it was told; and *Lady in the Dark* because of the wonderful colour schemes and the dresses! But I will describe none of these as it is too hard, instead it is best if people go to see them for themselves.

Then I enjoy any Magaret O'brien films, such as: *Journey for Magaret* and *Lost Angel*. The first dealing with a sweet little girl in a tall pixie-hat having a charming time with a kind gentleman; she has lost both her parents in the blitz and with a little boy in the same condition finds herself in America to live happily ever afterwards. The second is about being lost in New York and having several delightful adventures wearing all the while a sweet little tyrol hat. At last she is rescued.

Then I like all Walt Disney films except for *Pinnochio*, and all cartoons except Mickey Mouse and Donald Duck which seem to be getting a bit tedious for me. Also I used to like Shirley Temple, but have not seen them for a long time. Then I liked a film of an American club of young girls (about fifteen or sixteen years old) who collected autographs of film stars. Unfortunately I cannot remember the title or any of the actresses. Also I enjoyed *His Butler's Sister* with Deanna Durbin who sings most wonderfully a Russian song. I cannot, however, clearly recall the contents. Then I saw a film with Ginger Rogers when she dressed up as a little girl in a train to avoid paying the full fare. It was very amusing.

As for serial films, I like one about an American family; and the other about a group of children, including a little boy with a deep, very growly voice, who have many adventures. They too are very jolly.

Next, I enjoy, good war pictures, such as, *In Which We Serve*, *Pied Piper*, *Mrs. Miniver* and *49th Parallel*. The first is about a ship and five men in it who are hanging on a life belt when it is torpedoed. It relates certain incidents they can remember while waiting to be rescued. But it mainly deals with the life on a big ship in wartime. The second is about an elderly gentleman, who, while fishing in France, the Germans come, meets two children whom he is to take along to England, while travelling along he has many adventures, and meets almost every other minute some more children whom he takes along very unwillingly. At last they are seen on a boat going to England. The third is about a typical English family life in the 1940-41 blitz. And 49th Parallel is about some German spies who while travelling in Canada get less and less in number till even the last is caught. All these four films are very good indeed.

Then I like films based on novels. But as I know so many I will only attempt to describe one at all. The others are: *Madame Curie*, *Blossoms in the Dust*, *Gone with the Wind*, with Vivienne Leigh, *Pygmalion* by Shaw with Leslie Howard and Wendy Hiller, *The Three Sisters* with Bettie Davis, *Fanny by Gaslight*, *Random Harvest*, *Jane Eyre* with Joan Fontaine, *Suspicion* and lastly *Pride and Prejudice* with Greer Garson. This is about the Bennet family and their five worries. These worries are their daughters whom they do so wish to marry off. In the last scene these daughters all are either just married or just about to be married. The whole is very amusing, particularly the anxious mother!

As for actors that I like they are without being in any particular order as follow: Charles Boyer, Bettie Davis, Greer Garson, Walter Pidgeon, Magaret O'brien, Deanna Durbin, Monty Wooly, Mickey Rooney, Judey Garland, Anne Stevens, Coleman, Noel Coward, Leslie Howard, Ginger Rogers, Joan Fontaine, Vivienne Leigh, and Wendy Hiller.

All these are the sort of films I dislike, Murder films such as Sherlock Holmes or any other crimes films; crimes films such as Johnny Appolo and so forth; thrilling war films such as *Dragon Seed*, of underground movements (with a few exceptions); bad piano and concert playing; stupid fighting ones, with soldiers and muddles and silly love; cartoons only Mickey Mouse and Donald Duck; Jazz music and particularly Carmen Miranda and night clubs in films; cowboy films.

But this is all I can possible say tonight or otherwise I would have enough to publish a whole book on films!

2. C.F.   *My Favourite Film Star*

Greer Garson is my favourite film star.

She has something so charming about her, her face is full of beauty and sweetness, and her personality, seems to be all that is good and kind.

When acting in a film, she really lives her part. I admire her very much. Perhaps it is because she is English and of the same nationality as myself.

I cannot help feeling, that I would rather see her act in an English film more often than she does, for I think that our film production could do with such a humane person as Miss Garson, as well as many more like her.

I believe she has kept her real name, although I would not be certain on that point, for the majority of Hollywood stars change their names for screen purposes.

What I mostly like about her is, her natural manner with no affectation about it. She looks good-natured, but definitely she does not seem weak-willed in fact I think, quite the opposite.

Greer Garson married the young man who took the part of her son in *Mrs. Minnever* for which she won the Academy Award, her husband's name is Richard Ney.

I think on the whole she is a very sincere actress.

3. H.G.   *Comparison between Theatres and Films*

I do not know wether I am to be considered lucky that I happened to have a wireless on when the Brainstrust was discussing the subject on which I am going to endeavour to write about.

First the cinemas good points.

One is always sure of being able to hear and see what is going on. Whereas in the thatre you are not, unless one is very near the stage, a position which is not very suitable because one can see the actors and actresses make-up.

In wartime the theatre is apt to be drab and the costumes look as if they have seen better days, also in the films one does not expect colour, unless it is in Technicolour which is very pleasing to the eye in days of war.

Once I was in the pictures seeing a film in Techni-colour called *Best Foot Forward* with Lucille Ball it was lovely, and the warning went, it was a very heavy raid, but I was much to interested to think about it.

I do not think that the theatre could get one, so concentrated in programme, to forget about it.

Unless one is fond of comedy the theatre can be very boring, if the artists are not good. But films must be good or at least good enough to pass the critics (who allows the films fit for the public).

Plays are not too bad in theatres, but are also apt to be boring.

Last year my sister took my mother and I to see *Arsenic and Old Lace*. Mummy hated it, but would not tell my sister so because it may have hurt her feelings.

Mummy hated it because (a) She could not hear properly and only caught snatches of the conversation; (b) She was bored stiff, because all they seemed to do was open and shut a box by the window.

I like plays, and during the examinations I went to see *The Lisbon Story* it was a very spectacular show, and we had a very good seat, which makes all the difference.

In the cinemas it is warm and not so draughty as theatres.

In the theatre one is seeing the thing actually being done, and every thing is more or less real, where as in the cinema, one is seeing something that has been practised to perfection, and if one is seeing what I term a THRILLER! one knows that if somebody in the picture has been killed he or she is not really dead.

So . . . on the whole I think pictures are better, most of them come from Hollywood and America has all the best stars and I do not think the english film star has a chance.

In the pictures the story has been picked out and the unnecessary parts cut and the best parts brought out, and in my opinion the films are infinately better than the theatre and if not in your opinion, better, they are very good entertainment, and I don't know what a lot of us would do without them.

4. H.K. *Films I Have Seen*

I think that some films are really very good and worth their money, while some are just trash, like those with Abbot and Costello and Laurel and Hardy. There is nothing to these films because they hardly ever come from books.

I do not really enjoy films which have too much singing and dancing but there are some exceptions for instance, *Spring Parade*, that was really loveley and we all enjoyed it.

My special reason was because Deanna Durbin played in it, and she is my favourite singer, she really sings very well.

I especially liked *Dragon Seed* which was based on the novel *The Good Earth* with Chatherine Hepburn and Turhan Bey. It was about the chinese and it showed their everyday day life and when the Japs came. When I saw the *Seventh Cross* with Spencer Tracy, I thought that there was to much German in it, I think that they aught never to put foreign languages in films only English.

I can put much more down but I am afraid that my homework period is over.

5. P.M.

Of all the things I hate, I hate films with lots of kissing and love most. The films I like best are those with lots of murders and secret passages and moving panels, or a very funny one with Tommy Trinder, Tommy Handley or George Formby. Two of the best murders I have seen were *The Cat and the Canary* and *One Body Too Many*. The best funny picture *Sailors Three* with Tommy Trinder in. *The Cat and the Canary* and *One Body Too Many* were similar both were about wills of eccentric men who made conditions to them, in both cases somebody murdered the lawyer and saw the will, if it was not to their advantage they would try to stop the conditions being fulfilled. *Sailors Three* was about three sailors who managed to get into all sorts of trouble at last they got drunk and boarded a German ship by mistake. I think that there are too many love films now, all about the same thing and as untrue to life as possible, giving people wrong ideas about it. Although what it is really like to be in love I do not know, and I do not want to know yet. War films I do not like so much they are mostly very sad about people losing their relatives, and friends. One of the best war films was *In Which We Serve* it was wonderful. That is my idea of films, but many disagree with me.

6. Y.J.

I am very fond of films and I think they are an enjoyable entertainment. I can go to the pictures and really enjoy myself. Some people may disagree with me and say films are silly. Some of them are but I think on the whole they are very good.

My favorite type of film is a true story of war especially about the R.A.F. I went to see *Target for Tonight*, I thought was wonderful. I went away and I saw it there again. The way in which it was made was what I admired, and I like to think we are able to learn a little about what the men of the R.A.F. are doing for us.

The other type of film I like is a crime. It takes you away from the thought of war, which sometimes does get one down (war I mean). I rather like 'The Saint' films staring George Sanders as the Saint. It gives one a thrill when the hero is caught and you think there is no way of escape for him, then far away you here the drone of an American Police Car drive up outside and you heave out a breath of relief.

The Walt Disney Cartoons are quite good, but I would never go crazy on them. He is certainly very good but I think it frightens the children dreadfully when he draws those awful witches of his.

One of my many favorites was Lesley Howard, I thought it was dreadful the way his life ended. His best film was *The First of the Few*, where he took the part of Mitchell the designer of the Spitfire. The story is told by the Test Piolet who is first to fly this new plane, which every-body thinks will never fly. Lesley Howard plays his part marvelously.

I am not very keen on the films in which there are dozens of well known stars. I cannot think of one on the spur of the moment but I know there have been a few.

One of the actresses I cannot stand is Bette Davis, when she gives that smug smile of hers I could do something crazy.

I like Don Ameche very much. His acting is very good indeed.

A film I enjoyed very much was *Yankee Doodle Dandy*. James Cagney was very good. In it he tells the story of his life from where he is born to the time he is telling it. He is not just telling the story to thin air, he is supposed to be telling it to F.D.R. This film I also saw twice.

James Stuart (who is now in the Army) was a star who I liked very much. I like Will Hay to a certain extent, but after I have had too much of him I think he is very silly.

A very good picture I saw was called *The Immortal Sergeant*. Thomas Mitchell plays the part of sergeant. Another very good picture was *The Way Ahead*. This is a story about an officer who has been in another company, and expects his men to be as good as his old lot. One day while out on manoeuvres they get very tired and shirk it. After that when they were in Africa at the end of the story the officer always remembers that day and their motto becomes 'remember the manoeuvres'. The officer is played by David Niven who is another of my favorites. He is a fine actor.

Some of the films I think are silly, are the films that have no back-ground to them. The sort of films that are based on some silly Love-story. I like a love-story in which there is some sense and a bit of a thrill in it.

You can enjoy a film better if the seats are soft and comfy and the atmosphere is not too hot. In some cinemas the atmosphere is so hot one feels quite sick. That is really off the point but I think it makes a difference to the film.

I am not very fond of the Nazi Gestapo pictures because I think they are one side of this dreadful war we need not see. They are marvelous acting but I think they are not needed. One I am think of is *The Hitler Gang.*

Glyns Johns is very popular with most people. She is a really Welsh girl. Her father is very good too. The last film I saw them in was *The Halfway House. The Pied Piper* was very good film. The Pied Piper was a man who went to Germany to fetch some children. On the way he gathers more and more. The piper was played by Monty Woolly. I enjoyed it very much.

Bing Crosby heads my list of favorites. I like his singing it seems to be so different from every-body-elses. His two best films were, *Holiday Inn* and *Going My Way. Holiday Inn* was very pretty indeed. In *Going My Way* he played the part of a clergyman in New York.

The Song of Bernadette, was very well acted. Jenny Jones was Bernadette. I thought the Virgin Mary whom she saw in her visions, was much too made-up. Our Lord's Mother was only the village carpenter's wife.

Another film I enjoyed very much was *Till We Meet Again.*

7. Y.L.

I go to the films about once every fortnight, and I only go to it if it is worth while. I can't bear sob-stuff. Another sort of film I loathe are jazz and swing films. For instance, I went to a news theatre about a month ago, and one of the short films showed a band, and one of the singers was so funny, that everyone was absolutely roaring with laughter. I laughed so much that I was nearly crying. A man in front of me choked from laughing, and he had to go out of the theatre.

As I have said before, I don't like love and sob-stuff. It not only amuses me, but it also bores me stiff. When two people kiss each other and keep like it for about ten minutes, I think I have reason to be bored.

Once I went to the pictures on a Saturday afternoon, and there were two women behind me. One of them was telling the other one all about the film, and also keeping a running commentary going. It got to the pitch when I felt as if I wanted to tear her hair off. My mother, who had come with me got in such a temper that she had to tell the woman to be quiet (in I am afraid a rather rude way). I am interested in historical films, and also murders. I am afraid to say that I am very bloodthirsty. Murder films affect some people, so that they have nightmares. That has only happened to me once. I had been to see a film about a detective. While a man who was a dealer in gold, was sitting with his back to a window in his house, a pair of hands came through the open window, clutched him round the neck, and finally strangled him. The man let out the most awful shriek, which went right through me. That night I dreamt I saw someone sitting in front of the window, and a pair of hands came up behind him. I rushed up and clutched the hands. The man who had tried to strangle the other man chased me all through the woods and goodness knows what, and when he caught me up, and was just about to strangle me, I woke up. You could not imagine how very relieved I was, at that particular moment to wake up. I was very surprised with myself, as I had never had a real nightmare before. As you have gathered from this essay, I like historical and detective films, but not love.

8. M.I.

The films I like are very mixed. I like historical films because I think they are interesting (and perhaps because I like history).

I like dramatic films (especially if they are gruesome) because they fascinate me. I need not like the story but if I like the acting it is very enjoyable. I was fascinated by the *Man in Grey* because the acting was good and James Mason was so ugly and menacing, and Margaret Lockwood was so convincing as the villainess.

Comedies and Musicals I like if there is not much cuddling and kissing in it.

Although I like films I prefer plays because they are more real. (I don't include pantomime as a play.)

I think my favourite actress is Margaret Lockwood because she is so realistic. My favourite actor is Monty Wooley because he acts very well. He was very good in *Pied Piper*, the story of an Englishman who taking two children to the safety of England from occupied France finds children joining on to his two charges and finally takes a German officer's Jewish neice.

I think Stewart Granger is good and he generally is leading man to Margaret Lockwood. Patricia Roc is a new actress and as a jealous actress she is very convincing.

Deanna Durbin has a good voice but she has had not many good parts lately. *King Arthur was a Gentleman* and the other film *Miss London* I thought were nice films being very funny and yet not too funny. Arthur Askey is amusing. Jack Train is a very good impersonator.

Max Bacon was very funny with his funny mistakes.

Greer Garson gave a good performance in *Madam Curie*.

Margaret O'Brien is the nicest child actress and very clever.

Shirley Temple is not an extremely good actress but very charming to watch.

Ida Lupino acted very well in the *Hard Way* but I don't know if she is a very good comedy actress.

Rita Hayworth and Betty Grable though being good dancers are not good actresses. I do not like Betty Grable very much.

Gene Kelly is quite good as well.

I like Walt Disney's films (*Bambi*, *Dumbo* and *Snowwhite*) but not the Mickey Mouse and Donald Duck cartoons. I think why I like the films better than the cartoons is because the animals are so sweet.

9. M.B.   *My Criticism of Films*

On the whole I like most films.

I like the films adapted from Conan-Doyles books. They are about Sherlock Holmes, who is a detective, and Doctor Watson, Holmes's helper. Two very good films of them are *Sherlock Holmes Faces Death* and *The Hound of the Baskervilles*. In *The Hound of the Baskervilles*, which takes place near a wild and lonely moor, somebody lets out a hound which is nearly mad with hunger, and this hound is often the cause for some exceedingly perilous happenings.

I like murder films. I also like the Saint pictures and the Falcon pictures. They are both detectives but I do not think either of them are as good as Sherlock Holmes.

I like films in which Bing Crosby stars. I thought he was very good in *Going My Way*. In that he sang 'Three Blind Mice' as a round with some boys. In this same film was a clergyman, with whom Bing Crosby stayed, he was played by a new star, who I thought was a very good actor. His name is Barry Fitzgerald.

I like most funny films. Especially if any of these people star Arthur Askey, Charlie Chaplin, Will Hay, Bob Hope and Bud Abbot and Leo Costello and many more. I like funny films about the army and the navy, especially if Joe Sawyer takes the part of a sergeant.

I like Fred Astaire but I don't think he has very good partners.

I like History films, for example *Lady Hamilton*, Lady Hamilton was in love with Nelson. It showed you the Battle of Trafalgar. Lady Hamilton was played by Vivien Leigh and Nelson was played by Laurence Olivier. Both are very fine actors.

I like animal films such as *My Friend Flicka* and *Lassie Come Home*.

I hope many more such films will be made. I think Roddy McDowall is very good in this sort of film.

I like true films about the Army, Navy and Airforce. Of the army I liked *The Immortal Sergeant*, I think, the best airforce film I have seen is *Target for Tonight*, a film which I liked and was mostly about the navy was *We Strike at Dawn*. Some other good films are *Gung Ho*, *The Way Ahead* and *Coastal Command* and *The First of the Few*.

I liked *Women Coragous* which was about The Womans Auxiliary Ferrying Service. Sometimes I like *The March of Time* which is a monthly programe.

I like cowboy films but the trouble is the stories are all so much alike. I also enjoy films like *North West Mounted Police*.

I prefer technicolour to ordinary black and white.

I like Nelson Eddie and Jeanette Macdonald together. Eddie Cantor and his goggly eyes makes me roar with laughter.

I do not like sloppy films.

I do not like films in which there are too many bands. I did not like *Sensations of 1945* because it had about six jazz bands and there were also some negroe singers which I detest.

I like a film to have a fairly possible story. I do not like all singing and dancing and no story.

One thing I do detest, which is not really about the films themselves but about the cinema, is little boys who make rude remarks and keep hissing and booing at things.

(Time taken, 1 hour 45 mins.)

The Films I Like and Dislike

10. L.C.

I am not very fond of films as a whole. If I do go however I like films about animals and the Wild West. Also I like funny films. I do not like sloppy films. I went to see *Madame Curie* and I liked it very much as it was true. I do not like murder films as they make me dream. I hate jazzy films. I think Walt Disney spoils his films by having some nasty parts in them. I especially like horse and dog films.

11. J.C.

Some films are very nice, but others are not too good. I like films like *Wing and a Prayer* which was about a carrier unknown which is called X because in case the name would be letting out Information to the enemy. This picture was about the adventures of the men on the carrier and their feelings. There were no women in this film. I think women sometimes spoil the film. The women in the film *Ladies Courageous* did not spoil the film at all. But I think it would have been a much better film without the love part.

The sort of pictures I don't like is where the heroine meets the hero and they do all sorts of silly things and then something happens then they part and at the end they usually kiss. *Life Boat* was a very good film spoilt by the fact there was not very much story to it, you only saw the funnel of lines disappearing beneath the waters, and at the end the men and women in the lifeboat just get up and shout 'A Ship'—'A Ship' and the words 'The End' appear on the screen.

Cowboy films are nice, where they keep to cowboys and indians but when they make a girl start kissing a man it becomes spoilt. War films are usually very good I liked *In Which We Serve* very much with Noel Coward the star in it. I also liked *Sahara* with Huphrey Bogard as star, there were no women in it. Some love pictures aren't too bad, but when the people start kissing everybody else it makes me feel sick. I often wonder if the men ever get nervous breakdowns with all those women kissing them? If I was one I would.

In some films the men have to carry women for a long time, I expect the women must be awful light in weight or the men very strong. *For Whom the Bells Toll* was a good film, their wasn't very much love in it and Gary Cooper and Ingrid Bergman did behave sensible in it.

I like comedy films or least some of them if they have a good laugh in them.

12. J.H.

I very much enjoy going to the pictures. I do not like animal films (not because I do not like animals) but quite the opposite. I never go to see animal films because they are generally sad. *My Friend Flicker*, *Lassie Come Home*, *Home in Indiana* are among the films which I purposely avoided because of this. I particularly like war films like *Guadalcanal*, and *The Navy Comes Through*. I also like films like *Pride and Prejudice*. In which Greer Garson and Lawrence Olivier starred.

Greer Garson is my favourite film star and I like Gloria Jean and the new star Jane Powell also. I do not like the Andrew Sisters (to put it rather vulgerly), they get on my nerves. I do not like much to see a film that is all one thing all the way through. I like a little of laughter and music half of the time in a serious picture. I like an occasional murder but I do not like them too often or to blood-thirsty. When I go to the pictures it is a sure thing that I will like the news better than the actual pictures. Mummy never allowed me to go more than once a week but I thoroughly enjoy it when I do go.

(30 minutes.)

The Films and the Stage

13. B.B.

The films of to-day have improved from the earlier ones, in various ways. The earlier films were silent and only in two colours black and white. Where as to-day we have a Talkie and some films are produced in technicolour. One film I enjoyed very much was *Good-bye Mr. Chips*, although when I was younger I admired Waltz Disneys films and Shirley Temple.

I prefer the Theatre to the cinema. The plays and pantomimes I have seen, such as *Lambeth Walk* and *The Merry Widow* have seemed very real and entertaining. I also enjoy variety acts, where you can laugh at comedians, hold your breath when Jugglers throw half a dozen plates up at once, and feel excited at other thrilling events.

Altogether I think the theatre is more entertaining than the films.

Films

14. E.J.

I have not seen many films recently, but, the last I saw was *This Happy Breed* which was an English film, I like English films best although some American ones are quite good.

The type of film I like best is a serious or humerous films. The stars I like in humerous ones are George Formby, Arthur Askey and Charlie Chaplin and Tommy Handley, films I have seen and liked starring two of these were *Bandwagon* and *It's That Man Again*. Stars in serious films that I like are Anton Walbrook and Sally Grey who were in *Dangerous Moonlight* a film which I admired very much. Another film which I liked was *Pride and Prejudice* which I saw at the Classic Cinema in Brent Street Hendon.

Films I do not like are ones with too much love in them. Personally I think they are silly because I think there is nothing in the film except softness. Stars that I do not like are Charles Boyer, Clarke Gable and some ladies I do not like are Judy Garland and Shirley Temple.

Films I Like to See

15. T.H.

The films I like best are historic. I do not mind romance with a story or murder behind it, but I am not very keen on films like *Greenwich Village* with Carman Miranda. Films like this are like concerts which go too far with jazz.

The best historic films I have seen are ones that have lovely Maureen O'Hara as the star. Films like *The Black Swan* a story about pirates and the dashing Henry Jones who was made governer of Jamaica. When he was made the governer he gave up being a pirate so did his followers, but some of the gang became mixed up with another great dashing pirate who was owner of the ship *Black Swan*. It ended with the death for the owner and the marriage of one of Henry Jones' men and Maureen O'Hara. Another film starring Maureen O'Hara is *Buffalo Bill*. A story about Red Indians and their hatred to the Palefaces.

I love murder films. Films with mystery always the unexpected man or woman being the murderer. *One Body Too Many* is very good. It is a murder with comedy, romance and Mystery mixed up together. It is about a man who had died and left a will to his two nieces, nephew, cousins the butler and the palour maid. If his body is buried other than where the Stars will shine on him, the will would be reversed. Only One person knew where it was but he had no intention of trying to reverse it. Nearly everybody except one niece (who had been warned to leave the house but did not) tried to reverse the will the result was two murders and two attempted murders which did not succeed. The murderer, being the man that had only a dollar entitled to him according to the will, met his end, by falling off the top of a tower (when he was trying to escape after being found that he was the murderer) thousands of feet into space to end on a precipice with horrible crags and rocks.

The only thing, I think spoils some of the films, is the love of too much jazz. I think it spoils films which otherwise would be quite good.

I like Shirley Temple films, I don't think they are quite so good now. The best one I have seen is *The Little Princess*.

Animal films are lovely, I think, such as *Lassy Come Home*. It is a story about a collie dog, who loved his home and his little Master. Storys of horses are nice.

16. C.H.

I do not go to the cinema very often but when I do, I like either a slapstick comedy or an educational film. I like a comedy because as well as being entertaining it gives an amusing thought afterwards. I do not like gangster films because they are silly, and seem to me not true to life, though the same thing applies to comedy, it is amusing.

Of educational films *Henry V* was the best I have seen, it was true to Shakespeare's play, beautifully coloured and very well acted with Laurence Olivier playing the part of the king, he also produced and directed the film, which seems to me to be a very fine effort. This film teaches us history as well as Literature and the speech and clothing of the time. This has made me want to see more of Shakespeare's works.

I have often enjoyed films starring Sonja Henie as she skates so beautifully. I also enjoy musical or dancing films.

My Likes and Dislikes of Films

17. A.D.

There are many films that I have not seen, and I am just going to try and criticise the ones that I have seen. I have seen *Bambi* and I like it very much, because it is pretty and interesting. If the speaking were in plain English it would be very nice, but in American slang you can't hear what they say, and it's a nuisance, because you can't conscentrait on the film if you are trying to listen to the words very carefully, which is very difficult. The films all about people dancing with nothing on, are very silly because they just haven't got any story at all, so are love films about girls calling sailors whome they don't know at all 'my darling' or 'my sweetheart', because it is very insinsere. I don't mind the ones about really truly love, not gushing.

There are some very good films going round. *The Song of Bernadette* and *The Great Dicktator* are two of these, but the name of Bernaddete is quite spoilt by being Americanised. But we have to put up with it because it is in the fashion.

Time taken, three-quarters of an hour.

Apology. Note. I am afraid it is untidy because I am writing with a crossed nib because all my others are at school.

CHILDREN AND ADOLESCENTS AND THE CINEMA
My Views on Films

18. J.G.

I like Comedies, Musicals and Thrillers.

The Cat and the Canary was a thriller and a comedy. Some of the musicals I have seen are *Yankee Doodle Dandy* with James Cagney, *My Gal Sal* with Victor Mature and Rita Hayworth, *For Me and My Gal* with Judy Garland, Gene Kelly and George Murphy.

One very good musical, that I remember very well was *Show Business* with Joan Davis, Constance Moore, George Murphy and Eddie Cantor.

One of our best comedians is Tommy Trinder but in one film, he made, he was wasted and that film is *Champagne Charlie* which wasn't at all good. Last week Mummy, Daddy and I went to see *Green-eyed Woman* with Rosalind Russell and Fred Macmurray also *Twilight on the Trail* with William Boyd, which was a Western. About six months ago I saw *Gone with the Wind* with Olivia de Havilland, Vivien Leigh, Clark Gable and Leslie Howard, when Leslie Howard's plane crashed we lost a very good actor and producer.

Some films are very creepy such as *Rebecca* with Laurence Olovier and Joan Fontaine, who is a sister of Olivia De Havilland.

Ginger Rogers is a good star, but one film she made, was really awful, it was called: *Roxie Hart*. *You Were Never Lovelier* was good but I still think Fred Astaire is better with Ginger Rogers and not too good with Rita Hayworth. *Kitty Foyle* was very good; Its cast was Ginger Rogers, James Craig and Dennis Morgan. There is a great rage in America over Frank Sinatra, but I think Bing Crosby is a much better crooner.

Most of Bing Crosby's films have been the 'Road' series, such as *The Road to Morocco* and *The Road to Zanzibar*. Bob Hope is also in these films.

Random Harvest was a very good film its stars were Greer Garson and Ronald Colman.

Greer Garson has also starred with Walter Pidgeon in, *Mrs. Miniver*, *Blossoms in the Dust* and *Madame Curie*.

America has a very good actress named Bette Davis, who has been in many films. Some are *Now, Voyager*, *The Three Faces*, *The Great Lie* also *The Bride Came C.O.D.*

Well these are my likes and dislikes.

I go to the films once a week, mostly on Sunday.

Time taken, 30 min.

125

19. S.L.

I like the films generally but sometimes after seeing a picture I come away feeling that I have derived no pleasure or enjoyment from it at all.

I do not like seeing cowboy films and American Gangster films because there is always such a lot of shouting that I can't really hear what is being said or done.

I like Detective stories best. Some grownups say to me, 'Oh! but a little girl like you shouldn't like such gruesome things'. But I do all the same and when anything exciting happens I always sit tensely and watch and listen eagerly.

Love Stories? Yes I do like them as long as they are not too sentimental. What spoils a lot of love stories is when the lovers get over dramatic in their words and actions. When this happens the picture loses a good deal of its charm.

At almost every picture that I go to Jazz is played. Most people like jazz but I can't seem to enjoy it. I think that a good deal of it is rather cheap and it is not always appreciated by everybody. I dislike it intensely when girls with elaborately painted red lips come onto the stage and sing in deep quivery voices; I just can't enjoy it.

I would not call myself a 'film fan', but I do appreciate a good film when I see one.

Three Films I Liked Very Much

20. H.B.

I saw these films a long time ago, but I think they are the ones I liked best.

The First two are historic films, and they are of one person, as a boy, and as a man. The person is Edison, who invented electricity. The one as a boy shows him making experiments, and frightening his school master, how he invented the morse code, and how a little girl friend of his was in an express train, and he knew there was a broken bridge ahead, so he blew morse very loudly, on the whistle of a following train, and so saved the whole of the express train. It had its funny parts, and the parts which showed the costumes on a horse, and the milkman with a jug, and the dresses of his sister and mother. His father was very particular as to how he shouldn't put his hands in his pockets!

The other film of him as a man, shows all the hardship and danger he went through, and how poor he was, and how he tried hundreds of different threads for his electric light. You see him pulling out a hair from a workman's beard! You also see his great laboratory, and how fond his men were of him. Last you see the streets lighted up for the first time, and how angry are the gas people, when they know he has succeeded by using a cotton for his light.

Other films I like are animal films, the one I am going to write about is called *Bambi*. It is, I think, the best Walt Disney film yet.

Bambi is a little deer. He grows up in the green forest, and has many little friends, including a rabbit, and a sleepy old owl, who fluffs himself up when praised. The rabbit showes him how to slide, on ice in winter and he suddenly sits down, with all four legs stretched out, and he has quite a job to get to land again. One day he loses his mother, and sees his great, splendid father, the prince of the forest. He falls in love with his cousin, and fights a stag, and wins. A fire starts, with a hunt at the same time, he jumps an enormous quarry, to get away from the hounds, and meets the fire the other side. His father rescues him, the fire goes, and you see them, father and son, standing on the top of the cliff, then the father walks away, and Bambi is left, the Prince of the Forest. It is a lovely film.

21. V.A.

The sort of films I like: biographys, comedies, stories of animals.

A Biography

Madame Curie Is the life story of Madame Curie and her great discovery of Radium. She was Polish by birth but went to Paris to study Science. After many years of experimenting, hard work and many disappointments she discovered radium.

I liked this film because it was a true and interesting story. It showed the little ups and downs of life well.

A Comedy

Gold Rush. Was the story of the rush for gold in Alaska. It was sheer nonsense which only appeals to some people. My taste in funny films is that the actors make me laugh with their antics and not with their conversation. I find that the older styles of dancing and songs are more to my liking than the up-to-date jazz and crooning.

Animal Pictures

Lassie Come Home. The story of a dog that was very true to life.

A remark which impressed me a lot, was the remark of an old tinker when speaking to Lassie. He said 'They say that men are more clever than dogs, but dogs understand the language of men, men do not understand dogs.' The picture had beautiful scenery of Northern England and the Yorkshire Moors. Any other dog pictures suit me as I am very fond of dogs.

Examples of Films I Do Not Like.

Murder Films.

The Glass Key. A film that was very far fetched, and very creepy. If I see creepy films I have bad dreams, walk and talk in my sleep and cause a disturbance in the night. So I very seldom see murder films and therefore can write little on such films.

Some War Films.

I do not like some war films because once you have seen one example the rest are the same, like *Lifeboat. This Above All.* The exceptions are films which are true to life such as *Target for Tonight, One of Our Aircraft is Missing* and *Western Approaches*. Films like *Lifeboat* annoy me. It starts with Tallulah Bankhead sitting in a lifeboat after being torpedoed, with her dress clean and not torn. Her hair still up, her make-up still on and other absurd things. A man swims to the boat and he is covered head to foot with oil. These things I do not like.

Bands and Music

I do not like the American jazz bands in films. It is not music at all but just a horrible row.

My Favourite Film Stars

Greer Garson, Robert Donat, for serious acting. Charlie Chaplin and Arthur Askey for funny films. Susannah Foster and Nelson Eddy for singing.

Films and Plays
22. M.C.

My favourite film is a historical film, I saw a very good one once called *Queen Elizabeth and the Earl of Essex* all about the Tudors, Bette Davis was the Queen and Errol Flynn, the Earl of Essex.

Robin Hood was also very good, with Errol Flynn again as 'Robin', both films were coloured.

Three very good films this year were *Pride and Prejudice* with Greer Garson, and Laurence Olivier, also *Jane Eyre*, and *2,000 Women* with Phyllis Calvert who is my favourite actress, and actor Errol Flynn.

I prefer coloured pictures, to ordinary ones, and I am hoping to see *Western Approaches* which is all about the navy, as I like naval pictures.

One half-holiday Mummy took me to the West End where she had previously booked two seats, for *Tomorrow the World* starring the two child actors 'Angela Glynn' and 'David O'Brion', it was very good about a German boy a Nazi who went to his Uncle in America, and he was still a Nazi. His cousin (Angela Glynn) he hit over the head as she discovers he was spying on her father. But it ended happily.

Naturally we did not confine our investigations to the Hampstead children. We also made extensive experiments in North Paddington. Here the essay method was only partially successful.

We had distributed about 800 guidance sheets in an independent cinema in North Paddington. This theatre has a child attendance of about 1,000 on Saturday in the early afternoon. The majority of the children are of proletarian origin. Though we had proposed to give prizes, and the Manager co-operated with us wholeheartedly, the result of our competition was disappointing.

We obtained not more than six returns.[1]

[1] Our guidance sheet was framed thus:

COMPETITION

THE Management of this Cinema wants all boys and girls between the ages of 8 and 15 to take part in a competition. You are requested to write an essay of any length on the following subject:

'*The Films I Like and Dislike, and Why*'

It is important to give your reasons for liking or disliking any films you have seen.

A First Prize of 10s. 6d. will be given to one boy and to one girl.

A Second Prize of 5s. od. will be given to one boy and to one girl.

A Third Prize of 2s. 6d. to one boy and to one girl.

Please add on top of your essay:

Name, Address, Age, School, Occupation of father or mother, Nationality.

Return your essay to the Manager of this Cinema, who will get in touch with you if you have won a Prize.

The judging will be done by *Film Research*.

However, I shall give three answers out of these six as they suggest several important points when one compares them with the contributions of our secondary school girls:

1. P.G., aged 11 years.

The Films I Like and Dislike and Why

One wintry day I went to the pictures and saw the film *The Sullivans*. For some reason I liked that film, because it was sad and one wonders what is coming next. The part I liked best was the begining when they were children. It was exciting to watch them grow up into five men and one girl and their parents grow old. Their acting was very good. I also saw in the papers once that it was true.

The film I disliked was *Hail the Conquering Hero*. It was very silly and should have had more natural experience in it. The stars were alright but Eddie Bracken could have been a stoway from the Marines and have been landed on an Island with invasion troops and saved somebody's life and won a medal and then come home as a hero and be elected Mayor. Then it would have been more interesting.

2. G.W., aged 13 yrs.

The Films I Like and Dislike and Why

The picture I like best is the *Eve of St. Mark*. Why I like it is because it has fighting in it. I like fighting pictures.

The picture I dislike is *Rose-Mary*. I dislike it because it is so much singing and Romance.

3. J.K., aged 13.

Father soilder. Nationalit Engish 'The films I like are Tarsons disert mystery Because Johny weadusmother Played in it and gave me action and thrills. and I like westom apohrost to Because it was a truth film.

To begin with the 11-years-old girl P.G. She is definitely very near to our $12\frac{1}{2}$ years old secondary school girls as far as her mental and emotional attitudes and standards are concerned. She may even be more mature in the sense that she knows more about life as it is.

The documents by the two boys who both are 13 show not only class differences with regard to their origin if compared with the secondary schoolgirls' essays, but, what is more important, they reveal a difference of educational standard which is so obvious that no further comment appears necessary. And yet these two boys represent in all probability a not negligible percentage of our cinema-going youth. How can their minds resist the emotional temptations films offer? How can they become appreciative of life, its obligations, its beauties, its disappointments? They are 'movie-made', even before they begin to live.

Another experiment was undertaken with a North Paddington L.C.C. Junior School. We obtained about 100 essays on the subject *The Films I Like* from two classes (boys and girls) of about 10 years. We analysed the essays, but found we could not incorporate them in this book, having asked already for too much indulgence from our readers and our publishers. The essays show a distinct preference for technicolour films (expressions like 'pretty', 'nice', occur almost in every contribution). There is also a marked lack of plot-consciousness which I venture to explain by the early stage of language-development of these 10-years-old children who have mainly workers, clerks, employee or lower middle class people as parents. Piaget has, I think, admirably described the structure of the child's thought in his great book, *The Language and Thought of the Child*. I take the liberty of quoting for the convenience of the reader who may not have the book at hand some of the relevant sentences:

(1) 'It (the child's thought) is non-discursive, and goes straight from premises to conclusion in a single intuitive act, without any of the intervening steps of deduction. This happens even when thought is expressed verbally; whereas in the adult only invention has this intuitive character, exposition being deductive in differing degrees. (2) It makes use of schemas of imagery, and (3) of schemas of analogy, both of which are extremely active in the conduct of thought and yet extremely elusive because incommunicable and arbitrary. These three features characterise the very common phenomenon called the syncretism of thought. . . .'

'Now childish ego-centrism seems to us considerable only up till about 7 or 8, the age at which the habits of social thought are beginning to be formed. Up till about $7\frac{1}{2}$, therefore, all the child's thought, whether it be purely verbal (verbal intelligence) or whether it bear on direct observation (perceptive intelligence),

CHILDREN AND ADOLESCENTS AND THE CINEMA

will be tainted with the consequences of ego-centrism, and of syncretism in particular. After the age of 7 to 8, these consequences
of ego-centrism do not disappear immediately, but remain crys-
tallised in the most abstract and unmanageable part of the mind,
we mean the realm of purely verbal thought. In this way, a child
may cease between the ages of 7 and 11 to 12 to show any signs of
syncretism in his perceptive intelligence, i.e., in those of his thoughts
that are connected with immediate observation (whether these are
accompanied by language or not), and yet retain very obvious
traces of syncretism in his verbal intelligence, i.e., in those of his
thoughts that are separate from immediate observation.'

M. Piaget explains the term syncretism thus:

'Children therefore not only perceive by means of general
schemas, but these actually supplant the perception of detail. Thus
they correspond to a sort of confused perception, different from
and prior to that which in us is the perception of complexity or of
forms. To this childish form of perception M. Claparède has given
the name of *syncretistic perceptions* (Arch. de Psych., Vol. VII 1907,
p. 195), using the name chosen by Renan to denote that first "wide
and comprehensive but obscure and inaccurate" activity of the
spirit where "no distinction is made and things are heaped one
upon the other" (Renan). Syncretistic perception therefore ex-
cludes analysis, but differs from our general schemas in that it is
richer and more confused than they are.'

This does not, of course, mean that there are not children of the
respective age group who are further advanced in their language
development. Furthermore, we must bear in mind that the essay
method is also hampered by the profound difference between
speaking and *writing* (*Eine Rede ist keine Schreibe* writes Lessing). This
applies not only to our children's essays. It also applies to later
parts of this book and the reader is very often asked to read as it
were between the lines. Another difficulty with regard to the essay
method is the psychological structure of human memory. We have
not overlooked this difficulty. There are interesting examples of
'Rationalisations' and other memory phenomena to be found on
the pages of this book. But we refrained from drawing attention to
those documents as we are primarily interested in the *sociological*
structure of film reactions.[1]

[1] Cf. F. C. Bartlett, *Remembering*, Cambridge 1932, and Blackburn, *Psychology
and the Social Pattern*, London 1945, where on pp. 43 sqq. a very useful summary
of the present stage of memory-psychology is given. A psychologist who under-
takes to study film-remembering will do well to bear in mind that the pheno-

Having realised this intrinsic difficulty in our child experiments, we chose to use a lengthy questionnaire, used in its original form by Professor Blumer in a slightly changed form, adapted to British children (this questionnaire will be found in Blumer's *Movies and Conduct*, pp. 208 sqq.).[1] The questionnaires were filled in during school lessons and show a high degree of accuracy. Only one class (42 boys and girls) completed the questionnaires.

Yet, before I discuss some of the more relevant results of these questionnaires, I print the following two essays from two of the children of the same class whom I had taken with me to see the film *Henry V*.

Hazel writes: *Henry V* is a very interesting film. I think that whoever trained the horses must have been a very clever person or persons whichever the case may be. I think the part I liked most was the battle. At first I could not tell the difference between the two sides but gradually I learnt by the different kinds of flags. The film was one of Shakespeares plays. It was all about an English king who had been insulted by a French king. The English king then said he would declare war on France if the French king did not give up his crown to Henry the English king. He wouldn't. Henry then declared war on France. At first the French were winning but in the latter part of the fight the English were winning. They won. Henry then married the daughter of the king of France.

Peter writes: *Henry V* is very good and and interesting . . . I think the actors must be very good ones and must have been a great task to the houres and men while they were being trained to keep walking and galloping. I think the battle was the hardest scene to act and I like it best of all and the courtship of the king of England with Katherine second best the humorous scene when kink Henry V was reading pieces of paper on which were written all sorts things all about France and her rights I liked third best and now I will write about the battle. The English archers got out their sharp knives and banged in a trunk of a young oak sharpened them up with their sharp knives and the sharpened oak trunks were used to trap the French horses so that knights on the horses backs would fall to the ground and because of their heavy armour they would die. They were placed like this the artchers were behind the knights. The English Yoman fiered a swarm of arrows but the French

menon of identification or *participation mystique* will make the memory-phenomena undoubtedly more complex.

[1] We reprint ours as Appendix V.

knights got behind the English Bowman they fled but near the end of the battle the French defeated.

Both children are intelligent. Hazel, I am sure, shows more school diligence than Peter, but the latter may possibly have more innate abilities. Hazel's father belongs to the employee class; Peter's father is an 'intellectual', the writer of the present book. While Peter's observations are subtler ('all sorts of things about France and her rights'), both children are unable to record (and perhaps to understand?) the full meaning of the play.

Now to the questionnaires. To repeat, the children are 10 years old. Out of the 42 children, 5 children admit that they visit the cinema twice a week, 3 go three times. All the others, except one child who goes once a month, go once a week.

The questionnaires reveal, too, that only 6 children are content with their one weekly visit (3 boys and 3 girls). The boy who goes once a month and whose first three preferences are in this order, historical pictures, educational pictures and cartoons, is also content with his monthly visit. Yet 16 children who go once a week would like to go twice (6 boys, 10 girls); 11 children would even prefer to go three times (2 already go twice, 1 actually goes three times already, the remaining 8 go only once a week—3 boys, 5 girls). 6 children express the wish to be able to go four times a week (but of these 4 go once, 1 three times, 1 twice—2 boys, 4 girls). Finally, 2 (1 boy, 1 girl) would like to go five times.

It is gratifying to learn from our documents that all children except one have to ask their parents for permission to go. The importance of this fact can hardly be over-estimated. For if this should be a sociologically representative statement, which it well may be, it would tend to indicate that through a vigilant and energetic process of parental education (through press, radio, adult educational classes) parents might be taught what films their children ought or ought not to see.

This leads us to the thorny problem of the child's film preferences. Our questionnaires enabled us to prepare the following three lists of preferences:

List of First Preferences

	Boys	Girls
1. Cowboy Pictures - - - -	******	—
2. War Pictures - - - -	—	—
3. Love Pictures - - - -	—	*******

	Boys	Girls
4. Detective Pictures	***	***
5. Cartoons (like Walt Disney's)	*	*****
6. Ghost Pictures	***	******
7. News Reels	—	*
8. Serials or Follow-up Pictures	—	—

(I suspect this group of children is not familiar with serials.)

	Boys	Girls
9. Gangster Pictures	*	*
10. Documentaries	—	—
11. Comedies	*	—
12. Historical Pictures	*	*
13. Musicals	—	**
14. Educational Pictures	—	—

List of Second Preferences

	Boys	Girls
1. Cowboy Pictures	*	*****
2. War Pictures	*****	*
3. Love Pictures	—	*
4. Detective Pictures	***	*****
5. Cartoons	*	****
6. Ghost Pictures	**	******
7. News Reels	—	—
8. Serials	—	—
9. Gangster Pictures	*	—
10. Documentaries	—	—
11. Comedies	—	*
12. Historical Pictures	—	*
13. Musicals	—	**
14. Educational Pictures	**	—

List of Third Preferences

	Boys	Girls
1. Cowboy Pictures	***	**
2. War Pictures	*	**
3. Love Pictures	—	*
4. Detective Pictures	**	**
5. Cartoons	*	****
6. Ghost Pictures	**	*******

7. News Reels	-	-	-	-	**	—
8. Serials	-	-	-	-	—	—
9. Gangster Pictures	-	-	-	**	—
10. Documentaries	-	-	-	*	—
11. Comedies	-	-	-	*	***
12. Historical Pictures	-	-	-	*	—
13. Musicals	-	-	-	-	—	***
14. Educational Pictures	-	-	-	—	**

These preference tables appear to show a distinct difference in film taste between boys and girls.

The *first* three preferences of boys are—Cowboy Pictures (6), Detective Pictures (3), Ghost Pictures (3); whereas girls express their *first* preferences in this order—Love Pictures (7), Ghost Pictures (6), Cartoons (5).

The liking of ghost pictures, though less marked in boys, needs perhaps a word of further interpretation. Moreover, it must be noted that, apart from the first preferences, ghost pictures appear with 6 marks in the *second* list of preferences, and again with 7 in the *third* list. I suspect that the ghost pictures with our 10 year old girls (and boys) assume the function which the 'fairy tale' had in our youth. The fairy tale is characterised by its lack of reality[1] which corresponds to the vivid phantasy life of children up to a certain age limit. It is only fair to say that I am by no means certain of this interpretation. I merely offer it as a suggestion to psychologists for further investigation.

Another possibility of getting at the children's film taste is by listing their answers to question 23 of our questionnaire. They are as follows:

What Kind of Film would you like to have made?[2]

1. A film which has Deana Durbin in it and George Formby that what I would have liked made. (Girl, first preference ghost picture.)

2. The films I want are the news reels. (Girl, first preference, news reels.)

3. Musical films. (Girl, first preference, musicals.)

4. A sad film. (Girl, first preference, detective pictures.)

[1] Cf. Karl Buehler, *Die Maerchenphantasie des Kindes*, in *Abriss der geistigen Entwicklung des Kindes*, pp. 93 sqq.

[2] I regret to say that our question is somewhat marred by its ambiguity.

5. Cowboy film called *The Famous Cowboy Joe*. (Girl, first preference, cartoons.)

6. I would like a cow boy film that lasted for six hours. (Girl, first preference, love pictures.)

7. A Detective film like *The Hound of Basivile*. (Girl, first preference, detective pictures.)

8. A film of Walt Disney's. (Girl, first preference, cartoons.)

9. A sad film called *When Will the Happy Life Come about a poor family*. (Girl, first preference, cartoons.)

10. A Murder film. (Girl, first preference, gangster films.)

11. *Gone with the Wind* which had Clark Gable in it thats what I would like to have made. (Girl, first preference, Historical pictures.)

12. One from the stories of the *Arabian Nights*. (Girl, first preference, ghost pictures.)

13. I would like a musical film with dancing in it. (Girl, first preference, love pictures.)

14. I would like a film with a lot of music in it (Girl, first. preference, love pictures.)

15. I would like to make a Cartoon about Donald Duck. (Girl, first preference, cartoons.)

16. I would like to make a Murder film. (Girl, first preference, detective films.)

17. I would like to have a film made with a lot of dancing in it. (Girl, first preference, musicals.)

18. One of Shirley Temples films. (Girl, first preference, love pictures.)

19. A Cowboy film from Roy Rogers. (Girl, first preference, ghost pictures.)

20. A very funy one, and it must have some very pretty girls in it. (Girl, first preference, love pictures.)

21. I would like a film of somebodys Life. (Girl, first preference, love pictures.)

22. The Film *Bambi* in Technicolour. (Girl, first preference, ghost pictures.)

23. I would like a ghost film that would last 3 hours. (Girl, first preference, ghost pictures.)

24. A Walt Disney Film. (Girl, first preference, detective pictures.)

25. A Happy-go-Lucky film with dancing, singing, and funny bits, sad bits, happy bits and some of my favourite film stars. (Girl, first preference, cartoons.)

26. I would like to have a musical film made in technicolour. (Girl, first preference, love pictures.)

27. A Detective film. (Boy, first preference, detective films.)

28. I would like a long Walt Disney's Cartoon made. (Boy, first preference, gangster pictures.)

29. A Tarzan Film. (Boy, first preference, detective pictures.)

30. I would like a nice Detective film. (Boy, first preference, detective pictures.)

31. A good film of the prehistoric ages to the present. (Boy, first preference, historical pictures.)

32. I would like a Cowboy film with Roy Rogers acting. (Boy, first preference, cowboy pictures.)

33. Comedy. (Boy, first preference, ghost pictures.)

34. A Cowboy Picture. (Boy, first preference, cowboy pictures.)

35. The Life story of 'Winston Churchal'. (Boy, first preference, comedies.)

36. Walt Disney Cartoons. (Boy, first preference, cartoons.)

37. I would like to have a Walt Disney film made. (Boy, first preference, cowboy pictures.)

38. A cowboy. (Boy, first preference, cowboy pictures.)

39. Gipsy Wildcat. (Boy, first preference, cowboy pictures.)

40. A funny ghost picture with Monty Woolley acting. (Boy, first preference, ghost pictures.)

41. I would like a cowboy film to be made with all the famous cowboys in it. (Boy, first preference, ghost pictures.)

42. A cowboy Picture. (Boy, first preference, cowboy pictures.)

Taken altogether, 26 answers out of 42 are in conformity with the children's first preferences, i.e., more than 60 per cent. When the second preferences are taken into account, the degree of conformity is higher. (There may also have crept in a certain amount of involuntary inaccuracy on the side of the children in view of the 'abstract' character of No. 3 in our questionnaire.) So much about our children's taste for films.

To our question, *'Have you seen any film which made you want to be really good?'*, 15 children have answered 'yes' (4 boys and 11 girls. The whole class consists of 25 girls and 17 boys). It is interesting to note that proportionally more girls admitted the 'good influence' of films.

The films which had good influence are worth listing:

Boys	Girls
Queen Victoria	*A Tree Grows in Brooklyn*
—no film mentioned	*Hollywood Canteen*
Since You Went Away	*Jane Eyre*

The Great Mike	*Meet Me in St. Louis*, (three times)
	Since You Went Away
	The Underdog
	If I Had My Way
	No film mentioned

The 'goodness' lasted 'two hours', one day, a few days, one week, a month. It must also be noted that most of these pictures are 'A' pictures. Only two out of our 42 go by themselves to the pictures, 20 in company of their parents, the rest with friends (boys with boys, girls with girls), brothers and sisters, or in one case with other grown-up people.

Another interesting point is the admission 'that films make boys or girls do bad things'. 12 children—almost 30 per cent—gave to this question a definite yes. I list their answers:

> Steal (girl)
> Steal (girl)
> Answer their mother back (boy)
> Steal (girl)
> Fight—steal—run away (girl)
> Hurt somebody (girl)
> Thieving (girl)
> Fighting (girl)
> Stealing (girl)
> Break into a shop (girl)
> Break into houses and steal things (boy)
> Thieving (boy)

> No comment necessary!

This must be compared with our other question: '*Do you think that films make boys or girls do good things?*' Here 22 said outright *no*. The other 20 suggested that films cause the following good deeds:

> Feel they would like to help their mother (boy)
> Going errands for people (girl)
> Help your mother more (girl)
> Help a poor person (boy)
> Go home and help mother (girl)
> Not specified (girl)
>   "   " (girl)
> Not to steal (girl)

Help their mothers (girl)
Help their mother (boy)
Help other people (boy)
Be kind to humans and to animals (girl)
Help other people (girl)
Help an old woman (boy)
Behave themselves (girl)
Be kind to people (girl)
Not specified (boy)
Good deeds (girl)
Helping a blind man (girl)
Pull the fire bell in case of fire (boy)

9 children answered 'yes' to *both* questions whether films may induce children to do good *and* bad things; 6 maintained that films make children do only bad things, whereas they answered in the *negative* the question whether or not films make children do good things. With 8 children it is just the other way round.

We refrain from further exploitation of our questionnaire. What we intended to prove, the direct moral influence of pictures, has been proved. The children themselves have had their say. Their answers should be a warning and a challenge.

Emotional responses of children to films have been investigated experimentally by American psychologists.[1] They used galvanometric devices to *measure* emotional responses. It is of importance to stress that the authors' conclusions, though entirely based on a quantitative approach to psychological problems, are in complete conformity with our own findings.

They consider that 'scenes of danger and conflict incite strong emotions among children of all age levels'. And further: 'These motion-inciting emotions must be suppressed to a considerable degree . . . this experience may be considered as questionable for the health of the child.' As a consequence the authors suggest that certain types of pictures ought not to be shown to children, adding significantly, 'providing such restriction is made by understanding critics.'[2]

The authors agree also with what I have called the decreasing plot-consciousness of film reactions: 'The younger the child the more he appreciated and emotionally responded to the separate

---

[1] *The Emotional Responses of Children to the Motion Picture Situation* by W. S. Dysinger and C. A. Ruckmick (The Payne Fund Studies, 1933).

[2] *Ibid.* pp. 114 sq.

items in the film and the less he appreciated or even assimilated the continuity of the story, to say nothing of the moral or ultimate outcome of the picture'.[1] This fact can hardly be over-emphasised. 'The isolated episodes . . . repeatedly stood out in attention and in emotion. *The story as a whole had little or no effect* (My italics) . . . Consequently, we have no right to expect that very young children or even adolescents will make the same synthesis of a motion picture that the adult does.'

From this it is evident that the detailed facts given above about the amateurish way in which films are being released and distributed to child audiences must claim the most urgent attention of State and community, if the moral health of youth is not to be wantonly ignored and further undermined.

For who would dare to contradict the American psychologists when they write: 'An exciting robbery, an ecstatic love-scene, the behaviour of a drunkard, and the like cannot be toned down by the moral situation at the end of the picture when the episode is justified in terms of the hand of the law or the retribution of an outraged Providence. . . . The ultimate outcome of the story, the moral that honesty is the best policy, the assumption that the way of the sinner is bad, are adult generalisations. . . . Even if the picture clearly depicts this outcome it very seldom strikes the attention of the younger generation with anything like the force that it does the adult mind.'[2] Nor have Messrs. Dysinger and Ruckmick, writing in 1933, omitted to anticipate the future development of the screen. For they prophesy with only too much justification: 'When the pictures are finally shown in colour . . . and when the stereoscopic effect of tridimensional perception is added . . . *an irresistible presentation of reality* (our italics) will be consummated. Even as they are now, however, the moving and talking pictures in their present vogue carry a tremendous sanction. When, therefore, a psychoneurotic adolescent, for example, is allowed frequently to attend scenes depicting amorous and sometimes questionably romantic episodes, the resultant effects on that individual's character and development can be nothing but baneful and deplorable. From this extreme example there are, of course, all varieties of deviation. . . .'[3]

I have nothing to add to these sentences, except that I read Messrs. Dysinger's and Ruckmick's most valuable study after this chapter had already been written. This summary of its main conclusions was added to it as a postscript.

[1] *Ibid.* pp. 116 sq.   [2] *Ibid.* p. 118.   [3] *Ibid.* p. 119.

CHILDREN AND ADOLESCENTS AND THE CINEMA

Was ist das Allgemeine?
Der einzelne Fall.
Was ist das Besondere?
Millionen Fälle.

GOETHE, *Maximen und Reflexionen.*

An additional Page from my Case-Book

This chapter was written in August 1945. Now, eight months later, while I am reading proofs of this book, I am adding a few observations in order to bring the subject-matter under discussion to the level of my present knowledge.

I have continued to observe Hazel and Peter. Both children have been with me to the National Gallery or we went together to Hampstead Heath. Hazel is a constant playmate of Peter. Both children play together several times a week in our house. I am also thoroughly familiar with the social (and home) conditions of Hazel and of both children's progress in school. I have discussed the latter matter with their headmaster and their class mistress. Peter's spelling is still very bad, but it is nevertheless likely that he will go to a Grammar School. Hazel will go to a girls' High School. (Both children have passed the common entrance examination for secondary schools.)

Bearing in mind this background, what is there to say about the children's cinema-going? Peter is still not very enthusiastic about cinema-going. He does not go oftener than once a month or once every six weeks. We go together and I choose the film we see. He has seen *Nous les Gosses* which has been certified by our competent film censors as an 'A' film, *Peter the Great, La Mort du Cygne*, and *The Last Chance*. With regard to the last film the following point struck me. When we came to the cinema, the film had already been running for perhaps twenty minutes. When we had seen the whole of it, the little one insisted not only on seeing the beginning, but also on seeing the whole film again from beginning to end. When I discussed the film with him, I discovered that even though he had seen the film almost twice, he did *not* understand the *full* story. The child mind observes only episodes, sequences, or at best a simplified version of the whole. The reader must remember that this case deals with a child of higher than average intelligence. It would, therefore, appear that our remarks about the remoteness of adult abstractions—the good moral end of the majority of films—entirely fails to reach the child's mind.

Peter perhaps liked the Russian film *Peter the Great* best as he is profoundly interested in history. He wanted also to know how the film compared with the 'real' history of Peter the Great. We had read a fairly good children's book about the subject long before the film was shown. After we had seen the film, I read to the boy the relevant pages from a reliable and competent history of Russia.

Another point is worth noting. Some weeks ago Peter objected to my wife and myself going out together. As he had never objected to this before, and as he was fairly insistent, I stayed behind, went to bed with him at 8 p.m. and used a psycho-analytical method to find the cause for his anxiety. For this it was: after about two hours I had traced his fright back to the film *Of Mice and Men* which we had seen together some six months ago. I must admit that I should never have taken the child to see this film, but as I had no idea about the film beforehand my action may at least appear understandable. The child was frightened through seeing the very realistic strangling scene which occurs in this film. He felt relieved through our 'conversation', thanked me, and now again stays by himself when we go out together though this does not happen oftener than once a week. The reader may see how very difficult it is to say in advance what psychological maladjustments may and *do* arise from films.

Let us now consider Hazel. She goes every Saturday to the cinema. Her favourite films are 'thrilling' films which she prefers to 'funny' pictures. She has recently seen with either her grandmother or her father: *The Wicked Lady*, *The Spiral Staircase*, and *Shock*. Hazel obviously likes these pictures. Hazel is undoubtedly a much more 'rationalised' child than Peter. She is not frightened (or rather she says she is not) by the various strangling scenes in *The Spiral Staircase*. Straightforward murder is all right. What frightens her are 'eerie' episodes, dark corridors, wind and rain. She told me the other day that two days after she had seen *The Spiral Staircase* she was frightened to be alone in her bedroom, she kept 'thinking' of the dark corridor, but tried then to think of the 'funny' picture which was shown together with *The Spiral Staircase*. Further inquiry evidenced that the poisoning scene in *The Wicked Lady* has similarly occupied her *Einschlaftraum*.

A week later Hazel saw the film, *Leave Her to Heaven*. She did not like it very much as there was only *one* thrill: when the evil heroine drowned her husband's crippled younger brother. This girl of eleven years perfectly understood the scene when the same heroine threw herself down the stairs in order 'to destroy the baby she was going to have'. These are Hazel's very words when I asked her to relate the story of the film.

There must exist tens of thousands of Hazels in this country, not to mention the United States of America. Hazel is by no means a highly-strung child. The social conditions of her case allow *strict* and *valid* generalisations, though I am unable to say whether 100,000 Hazels are similarly affected or merely 99,999.

I should think that no state can afford not to take notice of these social facts, however unpleasant and inconvenient they may appear to the film industry.

CHAPTER 7

Movies and Conduct

Since the time when the film began to establish itself as one of the principal forms of contemporary entertainment, many books have been written about its general significance—as a new art form, as an instrument of propaganda, as a fascinating and complex industry, and as a sociological factor. It is with this last aspect of the cinema that we are concerned here, and it is one which has received the least serious attention hitherto. Passing references to the cinema as an important influence, especially with regard to children and adolescents, have been frequent enough, and it would be untrue to say that writers on sociological topics have failed to recognise this vital new factor in their analyses of the contemporary social *milieu*; but there is a great dearth of detailed empirical evidence in most of the comment which has so far been put before the public. Opinions, often violently phrased, have been voiced in favour of and against the cinema's popularity, but the arguments put forward have in most cases been unsupported by facts.

There is one notable exception to these strictures: a study published in the U.S.A. in 1933, in the Payne Fund Series *Youth and the Movies*. It is by Herbert Blumer, Professor of Sociology in the University of Chicago, and is entitled *Movies and Conduct*. Professor Blumer's aim, as given in his introduction, is 'to ascertain the kinds of influence wielded by motion pictures on conduct, in so far as these can be determined from personal accounts'. His method is to present rather than to evaluate the evidence, and his commentary on it is chiefly elucidatory.

The material which he uses is extracted from 'motion picture autobiographies' secured from a body of 1,823 young Americans of varying race, colour and religion. 634 of these were obtained from university students, 431 from college and junior college students, 583 from high school children, 67 from office workers, and 58 from factory workers. In order that the authors of the documents should be willing to write freely of every aspect of their film experiences, it was arranged that their work should be submitted anonymously, and it was further impressed on them that a full, frank and unexaggerated account was necessary if the scheme were to show any valid results.

In some 60 or 70 cases male university students were interviewed six months after sending in their papers, and additional material obtained in this way was useful as a check on the earlier written statements. In no case was any important discrepancy revealed.

The writers were not required to answer specific questions, and so the material produced was likely to be more spontaneous than if it had been solicited by means of a formal questionnaire. The recurrence of certain attitudes is very marked and has provided a basis for the division of the material into sections each dealing with an outstanding theme. No attempt was made to discover whether there is any significant difference between the reactions of the different economic levels of society, and this may possibly be regarded as a deficiency in the book.

In the groups which are represented there is, however, a very great uniformity of response, and this is particularly interesting in view of the fact that the districts from which the collegiate writers were drawn were as diverse as New York, North Carolina, Arkansas, and Illinois.

There are, of course, reservations which must be made in applying the conclusions which may be drawn from Professor Blumer's evidence to audiences of British children and adolescents. In some respects the average American child seems to be considerably more sophisticated in its reactions than the average British child, and there is perhaps a greater tendency in America for children from different social groups to conform to certain standardised patterns of behaviour.

This can be illustrated by the similarity of response to films in persons as socially distinct as the negro schoolboy and the white college student. Such a degree of common ground would not be found in a comparison between the attitudes of, say, an English Council School child and one educated at an expensive public school.

Yet there is little doubt that a considerable amount of Professor Blumer's findings are true of all children irrespective of material background, and it is these parts of his work that are of the greatest interest for the British reader.

Play and Imitation by Children

One way in which the cinema has influenced children in this country as unmistakably as in the U.S.A. is in determining the form of many of their games. All children delight in make-believe and impersonation, and they find in films a wealth of material which they can use in this kind of play. Obvious examples are the imitation of cowboy, Red Indian and gangster situations. Professor Blumer quotes a schoolboy who, after seeing a film of the violent action type, would regularly re-enact the picture with a group of playmates who also had seen it. A schoolgirl of sixteen writes that she would frequently dress up as the heroine of a film she had visited, and try to persuade her brothers to play the rôle of her admirers. Re-enaction of love scenes is common among girls, even those of twelve or thirteen years, whereas boys tend to prefer scenes of fighting and police arrests, shootings, escapes, etc. It was noticed, too, that the rôles of gangster, robber, etc., were as popular in areas with a low rate of delinquency as in areas where the rate was high. The numerous examples quoted by Professor Blumer of film influence on children's play indicate a very wide variety in the forms which it takes, and that the influence is very generally felt is shown by the fact that, out of 200 boys under twelve, 75 per cent admitted playing at impersonation of film stories, and, out of 70 boys aged twelve to fourteen years, 60 per cent made a similar admission.

This raises the complicated problem of the significance of play in the life of the child and in the formation of the adult. Although children appear often to be entirely absorbed in whatever they are playing at the moment, they can, however, change from one rôle to another with the greatest ease, and this may indicate that the play-acting does not make a very deep impression on the personality. On the other hand it is likely that the continual imitation of the stereotyped characters of the screen will produce somewhat standardised conceptions of life in the mind of the imitator. This will apply particularly in cases where information gleaned from the cinema is not supplemented by other kinds of knowledge—for instance from reputable literature, conversation of intelligent adults, etc.

Since the publication of Professor Blumer's book in 1933, many studies have appeared on the subject of children's play, one of the most important being *Play in Childhood* by Margaret Lowenfeld (Gollancz, 1935). On the question of whether the behaviour of the child influences the conduct of the adult, Dr. Lowenfeld writes:

'Modern dynamic psychology, however, has suggested that certain elements of a child's nature and outlook do not change, in the process of growth, into adult versions of those elements, but persist unchanged in some part of the mind and form the ultimate background to all adult life'. The importance of this statement with reference to those children whose minds are stocked with film imagery, and with little else, is obvious. In her conclusion Dr. Lowenfeld makes this interesting observation on children's play: 'Play is to a child, therefore, work, thought, art, and relaxation, and cannot be pressed into any single formula. It expresses a child's relation to himself and his environment, and, without adequate opportunity for play, normal and satisfactory emotional development is not possible'. If one accepts this statement in the case of the film-nurtured child, one is forced to conclude that many people to-day must interpret their world largely in terms of film material.

Imitation by Adolescents

In the play of children there is a large element of make-believe, and the impersonation of a character from the screen is to the child an end in itself—a pleasant pastime which has no practical aim in relation to the affairs of everyday life, whatever longings it may awaken in the player's imagination.

When, however, we observe the forms in which film influence manifests itself in adolescents, we are at once aware of a much more conscious and deliberate use of screen material as a means of furthering the designs of real life. It is, of course, impossible to make an arbitrary distinction between the semi-fanciful 'dressing up' of older children and the more serious copying of film styles in clothes, hair, etc., among girls in their teens, but there is nevertheless a marked tendency for the adolescent to seek in the cinema patterns of behaviour and dress which he or she can incorporate in ordinary conduct.

That this type of film influence is very widespread among adolescents is indicated by Professor Blumer's examples. These suggest that the main motive behind the imitations, whether of clothes, mannerisms, or methods of love-making, derives its force from the universal need of the adolescent to make a satisfactory adaptation to the adult world, and to conform with the standards of behaviour of his social group. There is, moreover, an indication in some of the accounts quoted that these standards are themselves considerably modified by those exemplified on the screen.

One of the most obvious influences is in the field of dress, hair style and personal mannerisms. One nineteen-year-old college girl appears to have based her whole wardrobe on ideas taken from films, and there are numerous instances of the appropriation of details such as jewellery, new ways of using perfume and accessories in general.

In fact, out of 458 papers by high school students, 62 per cent admitted imitations of this or a similar kind. The witnessing of films dealing with society life creates a desire to emulate conduct of the actors in such settings. Thus one girl of fifteen would watch intently the behaviour of the women at table—how they sat and talked, what gestures they used, and so on. Men, too, show this trait, as for instance the college boy of twenty who learned from the cinema the right way to touch his hat, and take a lady's arm.

Much 'trying out' of screen manners in private before the mirror occurs before some of the imitators employ the new effect in public. This is particularly true of girls who wish to acquire some facial expression of a favourite star, but it extends to ways of sitting, walking, and even of crying!

There is, of course, a good deal of the method of 'trial and error' in this kind of imitation. If a trick or mannerism does not produce the desired effect or, even worse, is ridiculed, it will be quickly abandoned. In some cases, too, the opposition of parents will necessitate its rejection, as when one girl startled her family by adorning herself with an ankle bracelet. Sometimes, however, the lesson learnt from the screen is a valuable one, and may lead to a girl's acquiring better deportment, an easier social manner, and a general *savoir faire* which, though it may not be based on an ideal way of living, is yet useful in helping the beginner in life to accommodate himself or herself to the accepted behaviour patterns of the group.

Perhaps the most striking way in which young people use motion pictures as a guide to living is in their relations with the opposite sex. We prefer to use in this context the term 'guide' rather than *imitation*, because it seems to us that in the sphere of instinct-reaction it is *participation mystique* which may be interpreted as the mechanism of the guiding function. (To what extent *participation* also underlies the imitation of fashion, hair style, mannerism, is difficult to say. We are inclined to see in all forms of 'imitation' an element of *participation*.) Love in all its aspects is of supreme interest to the adolescent, and it is at the same time an unexplored territory of which they have so far had little experience. They are thus highly receptive to films which exhibit love-making, especially if they can derive from them any hints as to how to proceed in their own affairs. This may be partial explanation of the intense popularity of stars who specialise in the more elaborate kinds of courtship.

That quite young girls and boys are interested in love scenes in films, and like to re-enact them among themselves, or at any rate try to copy the techniques employed, is indicated by the numerous extracts from the motion picture autobiographies which Professor Blumer quotes. Thus one sixteen-year-old girl writes—'What movie does not offer pointers in the art of kissing? I do not think it is surprising that the younger generation has such a fine technique' —and there are many more extracts in this vein, the ages of the writers ranging from fourteen to twenty-two years.

It may be desirable at this point to mention again the possibility that a similar set of papers from British adolescents would show a less 'sophisticated' outlook. This would, we think, certainly be the case in the higher income groups, and even among the working classes it is improbable that the borrowing of 'love techniques' from the screen would be quite such a conscious art as it appears to be among young Americans. But this does not mean that the emotional effect on the British filmgoer would be any less powerful: it is simply that the American adolescent tends to attach greater importance at an early age to its relations with the opposite sex, and is sufficiently articulate to be able to describe its experience in a more sophisticated language than one would generally expect to find in the average adolescent of fourteen to sixteen in this country. This raises, naturally, the much wider problem to what extent 'national audiences' differ from each other, not only child or adolescent audiences. It is true that Hollywood has set itself certain universal film norms which are meant to provide a common 'human' denominator for any rational audience. Obviously this type of 'internationalism' is deceptive. A real and genuine internationalism could only be established by an untempered distribution of national films (French, Russian films, etc., etc.). Only in this way could the various 'national publics' appreciate and understand the profound differences of their respective societies—and of the films they produce. Must we say that a Russian girl kisses differently from a British girl and wants to be kissed differently— in spite of Hollywood's insistence on this point? In the long run it is likely that the direct 'imitation' of specific details of conduct which is so recurrent in Professor Blumer's material, is a less important type of influence than that which has a profound or disturbing effect on the emotions of the individual concerned. In the one case the observation of film behaviour leads to extrovert activity which may or may not be harmful: in the other the deeper layers of personality are affected, and the emotional life of the individual is involved to a much greater extent. This aspect of the subject will be dealt with more fully later on.

Day Dreaming and Fantasy

Up till now we have been considering the influence of the cinema on the external life of children and adolescents, and it is clear that this form of influence is of frequent occurrence. There are, however, other ways in which the individual may be affected by films, and one of the most important of these is in the provision of material for day-dreams and fantasies. It is, of course, true that the inclination to build imaginary worlds is inherent in the psychological make-up of certain types of people, and also that a stimulus for such activity is to be found in books, music, etc., as well as in the cinema. It is nevertheless a fact that the very nature of the film medium, with its power to facilitate the identification of spectator with actor by technical devices such as the close-up, its freedom from the limitations of time and space, and above all its extremely vivid presentation of life, can be a more potent inspirer of fantasy than any other variety of art or entertainment yet created. Moreover, we suspect that the visual experience of film arouses more violent reactions within our instinct world than for instance, the experience of reading. We say we 'suspect', because we do not know enough about this phenomenon—yet.

The adolescent is particularly prone to indulgence in day-dreaming and, out of Professor Blumer's 458 motion picture autobiographies from high school students, 66 per cent on a conservative estimate acknowledged this experience as a result of seeing films. Among children, too, there was similar evidence, and in studying the influence of films on impersonation it is often difficult to say where overt play ends and fantasy begins. As Professor Blumer points out, day-dreaming is in a sense an internal playing of rôles. Thus the child who plays at being an airman or a gangster may at the same time picture himself as actually performing the deeds of such characters. One boy for instance saw a Tarzan film, after having read the Tarzan books, and he relates how he would lie awake at night thinking of the heroine of the picture, and wishing that he could live the same kind of life. This kind of reaction would appear to be far more common than is supposed by people who believe that children live mainly on the plane of action rather than of imagination. Out of 1,200 papers from Chicago children of elementary school age, over 50 per cent stated that their day-dreams were influenced by what they saw in the cinema.

In the higher age groups the tendency is even more conspicuous, and the fantasy is generally unaccompanied by any overt activity, and enjoyed for its own sake. Thus one girl writes: 'Day-dreaming was my chief pastime and I can trace it back to being aroused and stimulated by motion pictures. I'd picture myself the wife of a star, living in Hollywood and all my friends envying me my handsome husband. But no one ever took him away from me; he was always faithful to me'.

Another girl states: 'The pictures I saw became the chief source of subject matter for day-dreams. I would lie awake for hours after going to bed day-dreaming. After seeing an especially good show I have gone off to bed especially early to get those dreams started'.

A high proportion of the fantasies described are concerned with wealth, luxury, social ambition and success of various kinds. Among the daydreams indulged in by the girls from whom Professor Blumer drew his material a big part is played by glamorous stars like Rudolf Valentino, and there is a perpetual recurrence of the desert background and the sheik who carries off the beautiful white heroine.

It is important to remember in this connection that from 1934 onwards the whole tone of motion pictures has been considerably modified by the requirements of the Hays' Code, much of whose force derives from an influential American body known as the National Legion of Decency. The Hays' Code is actually a set of principles 'to govern the making of talking, synchronised and silent motion pictures'. It covers a wide range of subjects, from surgical operations to the display of the American Flag, and the vetoes which it imposes are of a severe and far-reaching kind. In general it can be regarded as having a function similar to that of the British Board of Film Censors. As may be expected, the Code is stringent in its treatment of the sex element in film, and it is probable that some of the pictures which excited Professor Blumer's students could not have been issued in their original form after 1934, when the Hays' office really got under way. The following extracts from the Code are relevant to this aspect:

"2. *Scenes of Passion.*

  (a) They should not be introduced when not essential to the plot.

  (b) Excessive and lustful kissing, lustful embraces, suggestive postures and gestures, are not to be shown."

It is quite common for the dreamer, male or female, to imagine himself or herself in the place of the hero or heroine of a particular film. Sometimes the story of the film is re-enacted in the mind of the dreamer, without personal modifications: in other cases the dreamer uses the situations presented in the film merely as a starting-point from which he or she creates an entirely new fantasy moulded to the individual's own tastes and experience. The latter type of dream is obviously more subjective and is liable to play a more significant part in the dreamer's emotional life. The danger is that fantasy may eventually become so interwoven with thoughts about real life that the dreamer can no longer separate the one from the other, and ability to cope with everyday problems is vitiated.

It is a notable feature of the majority of day-dreams that they deal with experiences which are generally frowned on by society. Unfortunately, Professor Blumer deliberately excluded material which dealt with sexual life and conduct, although he states in his preface that the evidence shows film influence in this field to be considerable. He does, however, quote one or two examples which serve as an indication of how this type of influence works. This is from a girl of eighteen: 'I have had dreams of practically every phase of life, worked out in every imaginable way. I've had all sorts of young men as lovers. From an American to an Egyptian, and back'. Another extract comes from a paper by a boy of nineteen, describing his reactions to a film in which sex was stressed: 'Often before I would fall asleep, while lying in bed, I would live through the part of the man under such conditions and I derived pleasure from it'.

A very interesting example of how an individual can build up a whole fantasy world from film material is quoted in *The Education of the Emotions,* a book by Margaret Phillips. In this case the individual is a schoolmistress with a university education, which perhaps makes particularly significant the violent form in which the cinema influenced her life. It appears from her account that she had been fascinated by films from early childhood on, and from the age of twelve years. She stated that she lived 'completely under the aegis of a film star'—a Japanese star of the silent days, with a screen personality of a markedly sadistic type. At this period the girl regulated every detail and moment of her daily existence according to what she imagined would be the will of her hero, who seems to have combined for her the qualities of childhood bogey and adult lover. Many of her fantasies then were concerned with flagellation. Later, during her career at university and in her first teaching job, the cinema was to her a means of escape from a world where intellectual pursuits were paramount and pleasure as an aim of life was disregarded. Finally she came to live in London, and here at last her real life was sufficiently satisfying to make dependence on a dream-world unnecessary, and she began to go to films purely for entertainment. She nevertheless continued to make direct use of the cinema in her actual life. For it was in its friendly and relaxed atmosphere that she found her lovers, and when on one occasion a love affair ended unhappily it was to the cinema that she repaired for consolation and sat there every night for five weeks, partly in the hope that she might encounter her lover and be reconciled to him under the influence of the special mood which cinema background can create.

Not enough is known at present about the function of daydreaming in life for us to be able to say how far the fantasies stimulated by films may affect the general conduct and outlook of the individual. There are in existence two conflicting schools of thought on this phenomenon. According to the one school, the day-dream has a useful social purpose in that it acts as a safety-valve for emotions and impulses which would be harmful if allowed uninhibited expression and which, if entirely repressed, would tend to create a neurotic condition in the individual. It is, in fact, a form of compensation which helps people to put up with monotony and frustration in their daily lives. The other current view of day-dreaming is that it is resorted to by people who cannot cope with the problems of reality, and who turn to fantasy as to a drug, which will at first appear to make them happier but will eventually undermine their morale altogether and sap any further attempt by them to re-order their lives. Neither of these theories has been proven, but the application of either to the question of the day-dream inspired by films can suggest interesting lines of thought.

Finally, it must not be overlooked that frequent indulgence in fantasy may create or encourage desires and inclinations, and that these may possibly be expressed in actual conduct, should a suitable opportunity arise.

Fear and Terror inspired by Films

The next four sections of Professor Blumer's book deal with different aspects of one type of experience which he calls 'Emotional Possession'. This condition, which is well-known to students of behaviour, results when feelings which are usually restrained are stimulated to such an extent that the individual undergoes some diminution of his power of self-control and behaves in a manner which is a departure from his normal conduct. Such a state can be induced by intense absorption in a film: the mind becomes so obsessed with what it perceives that for the time being it is swayed by impulses and emotional currents which it would ordinarily be able to master. The experience is usually a temporary one, but in certain cases it may leave an indelible impression. This is perhaps particularly true of emotional possession by fear, which we shall now consider.

Judging from the accounts collected by Professor Blumer, it is a very common occurrence for young people to be frightened or horrified by certain types of films or episodes from films. Children are particularly susceptible to this kind of reaction, but it is not unusual in adolescents and adults. Nor should one assume that these experiences are only to be found among American film audiences. Fright, horror, nightmares cause serious psychological maladjustments in a considerable number of British filmgoers too, as will become evident in a following chapter of this book and particularly in Vol. III of this series. It seems imperative to us that children or boys and girls under fifteen or perhaps fourteen should be forbidden to see 'A' films at all, whether accompanied by adults or not. In addition, the censorial practice of *The British Board of Film Censors* needs the most searching scientific investigation with regard to its competence in estimating the effects of films on people as a whole. The effect on the child varies from an instinctive covering of the eyes to nightmares and even to quite serious emotional disturbances. It happens sometimes that a young child is alarmed when it first sees a motion picture, even when the subject of the picture is not of a terrifying nature: this is due to the strangeness of the film medium, with its amazing power of persuading the spectator that what he sees is actually taking place. An adult may consciously surrender to this persuasion, while yet retaining a greater or lesser degree of intellectual or aesthetic detachment; but for the very young child who has had no explanation of how the cinema works, the experience is apt to be disconcerting.

This type of fear is, however, one which might conceivably be prevented in all but the most sensitive children if parents took the trouble to prepare the child in advance by impressing on it the make-believe character of the cinema. In any case, familiarity would soon achieve a similar result.

Much more significant is the fear which is occasioned in children who are accustomed to cinema technique by incidents on the screen which are in themselves horrible or terrifying, or at least may appear to the children to be so.

Out of 237 younger school children questioned on this point, Professor Blumer reports that 93 per cent said that they had experienced fright while watching films. Among the 458 high school accounts, 61 per cent refer to similar experiences.

One type of film which seems to be particularly liable to induce intense horror is the kind which presents something monstrous or supernatural. One account after another refers to films like *The Phantom of the Opera* (original version), *Dr. Jekyll and Mr. Hyde*, *The Gorilla*, and so on. The last of these seems to have been outstanding in this respect: its theme is that a scientist transfers the brain of a dead murderer to an ape, and the animal then proceeds to perpetrate the crimes which the murderer would have committed had he lived. The idea of the mixture of human and animal has some particularly horrifying effect on the mind, as does also the idea of a semi-human machine. One boy of nineteen describes how he saw as a child a film in which a young man kept a machine endowed with life in a mummy case, and was throttled by it in a dark room. The boy went home after the film in 'a perfect paroxysm of fear', and for many years had a distrust of being alone in the dark. He continues: 'Strangely enough, it was never the thought of something natural that frightened me, such as a man, a burglar, for instance, but it was the fear of something entirely outside the physical field. For the same reason I have never yet been able to feel comfortable among the mummies in a museum, and I instinctively look at them with revulsion and disgust'.

The most common result of seeing films of this kind is nightmares and a fear of sleeping alone. One girl saw a film about a mountain feud which involved numerous tortures and killings, and she states that for two or three weeks she continued to be so frightened that she would not be alone.

Enquiry was made of 47 children aged seven to nine as to what objects in films alarmed them: the answers covered ghosts, phantoms, devils, gorillas, bears, tigers, bandits, grabbing hands and claws, fighting, shooting, falling or hanging from high places, drowning, collisions, fire, flood, etc. All these objects appear week after week in the children's clubs as they are run at present by the organisation of Mr. Rank. Expressions of emotion during the show included nail biting, grabbing one's neighbours, hiding eyes, screaming, jumping out of seat and even getting under seat. After the show some of the children would run all the way home, avoid dark streets, be frightened by shadows and so on, and they would also be afraid to leave the window open, would look under the bed and behind chairs, and would want a light in their room or someone to sleep with.

Although in many cases the emotional condition induced by frightening films lasts only a short time and the incident which gave rise to it is forgotten in a few days, there are instances where the effect is more enduring. Thus one girl retained a permanent horror of lunatics from having seen a film dealing with a crazy woman of homicidal proclivities. Many examples could be given of children who have developed a neurotic fear of the dark as a result of mystery films of one kind or another. *Dr. Jekyll and Mr. Hyde* seems to have had a potent influence in this direction.

It is interesting to note that, in spite of the fact that the terrors experienced by children in the cinema are often of an acutely painful intensity, yet there is a large number of children who enjoy frightening pictures. For instance, out of a class of 44 young school children, 38 stated that they had been frightened by motion pictures, and 31 of the 38 admitted that they liked these pictures.

Where, however, the fear aroused is so great that the individual feels a compulsive need to take special precautions for his safety, and suffers from delusions about non-existent causes for alarm, it can hardly be supposed that any pleasurable sensation is not heavily outweighed by the sense of insecurity thus created. Frequently, too, the child or youth is aware of the absurdity of his fears but is unable to dispel them by reasoning. Thus one girl who had seen a film containing a horribly disfigured creature in a mask, continually imagined the man to be hiding somewhere in the dark, behind a door—and she writes: 'I tried to dispel this crazy idea by calling myself silly, but it did not work. I don't like to write about it now because if I recall the picture too vividly my imaginings may begin again'.

It is this condition of emotional possession, wherein the ordinary common sense of the individual is overpowered by an irrational but uncontrollable impulse, that is the most important aspect of the experience of fear in connection with films.

Sorrow and Pathos

A condition with similar psychological features to that noted in the examples of possession by fear may be induced by pictures which portray overwhelming pathos. Everyone is familiar with the type of person who invariably weeps at any sad or touchingly sentimental scene in a film, and who seems to enjoy the process. But there are others who make energetic efforts to hold back their tears, but are unable to do so, and these people may be said to be in a state of emotional possession. Their emotions have swept over the ordinary barriers imposed by common sense, and they have temporarily lost control of themselves.

The kind of pictures which seem to have a particularly powerful effect on the emotions of pity, sympathy and tenderness are of the type of Al Jolson's *Singing Fool*, where the situations tend to be pathetic rather than starkly tragic.

Difficulty in controlling the expression of emotion aroused by a picture of this sort was acknowledged by 39 per cent of the 458 writers of the high school documents. The proportion of boys unable to control their tears was lower than the proportion of girls.

An interesting by-product of the reactions of some individuals to films of the dolorous type is a desire to 'be good'. Feelings of remorse, self-abasement, self-criticism are stirred up, and resolutions are formulated to ensure that the situations portrayed in the film may not arise in the individual's own life. As Professor Blumer remarks, this attitude may be compared with that which follows a religious conversion. Generally, of course, the experience is forgotten fairly quickly and the resolutions are not put into practice. But occasionally the impression made by the film is so powerful that the effect of it is lasting. Thus one girl who had seen *Over the Hill*, whose story dealt with a mother deserted by ungrateful children, resolved that she would never treat her own mother in this way—she writes: 'I don't believe that the effects of that picture will ever wear off'.

Love and Passion

Perhaps this is the most powerful form of emotional possession— at least in the case of adolescents. After witnessing a film which portrayed a love scene in a stimulating manner, a boy or girl may feel a desire for a similar experience in real life. Here again we see the conflict of impulse with inhibition, and the frequent relaxation of ordinary controls when attacked by irresistible surges of emotion. The practical result may be a willingness to behave in a way which the individual might not have done had he or she not been emotionally prepared by the film. Often the reaction is of a very mild type—the boy may hold the hand of the girl beside him and exchange glances, and both may become more sentimental towards each other than usual. This type of reaction is characteristic of the 'calf love' of some young people and is not of a violent kind. In some girls the witnessing of romantic love pictures induces merely a vague longing for some kind of romantic adventure. In others the love scenes may produce considerable excitement, and a distinct vicarious pleasure. One girl described how she was at a cinema with a girl friend, and when the hero kissed the heroine 'we thrilled in ecstasy'. She had identified herself with the heroine, and so, when a group of rowdy boys made fun of the incident in question, she felt that it was like a personal affront. After the picture was over she allowed herself to be picked up by a boy whom she had seen and admired in the cinema. This is her account of what happened—the influence of the films can be detected in the style which she employs, as well as in the episode itself: 'I had known it all along, from the moment I had seen that perfect embrace in the movies; I had felt that this would happen. He had parked in lover's lane, his arms were about me, persuading. To my bewildered mind there came two thoughts; one, "Mum said 'Don't kiss the boys' "; the other, "What harm can it be? It is beautiful." So I struggled no longer; and I learned the charm which before I had only dreamed of.'

Even where the thrill derived from love pictures is entirely vicarious and does not lead to any direct action as in the above case, it is likely that the repetition of such experiences may play a big part in moulding the individual's ultimate attitudes to love situations. The vicarious enjoyment of love pictures appears to be very common among girls of high school age—67 per cent of them admitted this type of experience, as against only 41 per cent of the boys.

When, however, we turn to the more acute forms of emotional possession by love and passion, we find that on the question of whether love pictures made them more receptive to love the proportion of boys and girls is the same. Instances of the more violent types of reaction are quoted below:

Female, 16 years. 'Seeing such scenes has made me more receptive to love-making; before, I didn't like it and thought it silly, but the movies have changed my ideas.'

Male, 17 years. 'By viewing one of those intense love pictures, I get a burning sensation within to perform those things which I see done on the screen, and I must admit that in doing so I get a great deal of pleasure.'

Female, 22 years. 'Going out with boys after a romantic love picture I would let them kiss me.'

It is interesting, too, that many boys and girls observe this kind of influence in their companions. Thus one youth states that a girl whom he kissed after taking her to a love picture told him that the only time when she had difficulty in restraining herself from kissing was after a show of this type. In fact, some young men deliberately use films as a means of creating a responsive attitude in their companions. Here the influence of films on conduct is being consciously recognised and utilised. One youth writes: 'I generally pick the movies we attend with that point in mind . . . the girl's emotional state can be regulated and used to what may be either advantage or disadvantage.'

It is clear from the material which Professor Blumer quotes that in general the emotional possession induced by love pictures constitutes an attack on conventional social restrictions. In some cases the relaxation of inhibitions may be quite temporary, but in others, where the film has made a very deep impression, the individual may be led to alter his mode of life completely, or to seek experiences which he would not otherwise have sought.

Thrill and Excitement

This form of emotional possession is more prevalent among children than adolescents. Everyone has at one time or another observed how absorbed children become when a 'thriller' is being exhibited, and how apt they are to give expression to their over-stimulated feelings by shouts and cries, or even physical movement. This kind of behaviour is particularly noticeable at children's matinées when an instalment of the serial picture is in progress. There is tremendous excitement whenever the hero or heroine is in danger, or is rescued, and particularly when any kind of fight takes place. Groans accompany the successes of the villain, and sighs of relief are heard when the peril is past. One investigator has observed that little attention is paid to scenes which do not contain

CELIA JOHNSON IN 'BRIEF ENCOUNTER'
An unglamorous great actress

ROBERT TAYLOR·GIVES A LESSON IN LOVE-MAKING

an element of danger and that discussion of earlier fighting scenes goes on during the sequences which show the happy ending. The child's own view of the serials is given in the following extract by a boy:

'Perhaps the earliest type of motion picture that I can remember is the serial. This old type of thriller, usually consisting of ten parts, was shown every Saturday at the neighbourhood theatre. All the children of the district used to attend, and then followed one glorious week during which each scene of the episode was enacted out in our backyards. We had grand times playing "lion men" and Tarzans. During the showing of the picture itself we used to be worked up to a terrific high state of emotion, yelling at the hero when danger was near, hissing at the villain, and heaving sighs of relief when the danger was past. The serial was nearly the sole object for going to the movies for me and for most of the children in the good old days when I was seven or eight years old.' These very same serials, as has been shown above, are still being used in British film matinées for children.

The characteristic feature of the serial is that it stops abruptly when suspense is at its height, and instead of the child being left in a state of tranquillity it is keyed up during the whole of the subsequent week, and is brought to the same condition again by the next instalment. It is impossible to say definitely what permanent effects this perpetual state of suspense may have on the child's mind, although it seems certain that these effects are of an important kind.

Some of the excitement which is noticeable during a children's matinée is, of course, created simply by the fact of there being a large mass of children together, each of whom tends to be infected by the tension of the rest. A high degree of emotional possession is, however, very evident, and may be observed in the behaviour of children after leaving a picture of the 'thriller' type. Many declared, in response to enquiry on this point, that in these circumstances they felt adventurous, daring, and even 'tough'. Usually the feelings are of short duration, as in the other kinds of emotional possession which have been considered, but while the mood is on the child may be prepared to do things from which he would normally refrain. In some cases the acts thus committed may be of a delinquent type.

It is clearly incontestable from the evidence which Professor Blumer brings forward that films can and do create states of emotion which some individuals have some difficulty in controlling. The vivid and skilful presentation of life, in which the screen excels, captures the imagination of the spectator and, by stimulating his impulses and weakening his power of self-discipline, makes him more susceptible to whatever tendencies to anti-social behaviour are dominant in his particular case.

It has been stated that the condition of emotional possession is usually short-lived and that the mind generally settles back into its former state after some time has elapsed, but the return is probably never quite complete.

Emotional Detachment

In cases of emotional possession the individual is, as it were, at the mercy of the picture. No part of his mind remains free to criticise what is happening to the rest of it, or to prevent him, from the outset, from allowing himself to be carried away by the appeal of what he is witnessing. There are, however, people who by one means or another have acquired an ability to approach a film with a certain awareness of what it sets out to do, and who are consequently less likely to succumb to its spell than is the more naive and unself-conscious person.

This attitude of emotional detachment is to be found consistently among the highly educated minority, who are accustomed to observing and analysing their own reactions, and who can, if they wish, submit to or reject the appeal of a film at will, and even while submitting are fully aware of the fact, and so immune from the consequences. There are, however, less subtle approaches to be found, which yet involve a certain resistance to obvious emotional attacks. These occur in people who are not necessarily of the intellectual class but who have a sophistication of outlook which makes them unwilling to be 'carried away' by a motion picture, particularly if it be of the sentimental kind. Such an attitude is often acquired because the individual observes that it is prevalent in his own social group, and his desire for conformity is apt to be stronger than his personal tastes, should these be contrary.

Another way in which a detached attitude to films may be acquired is through an accumulation of real-life experience which runs counter to the versions of reality portrayed on the screen. Or it can be created to a certain extent by instruction from parents or teachers who can point out that much of what is shown in films has little to do with reality and must not be taken too seriously. Similarly, increased knowledge of the technical aspects of film production is likely to make an individual less likely to be profoundly affected by the pictures he sees.

Among children, too, it is quite common to find one age group ostentatiously despising what it revelled in a few years before. This does not necessarily mean that the original response has really ceased to operate, for the attitude of scorn has probably been adopted for social reasons, but it does mean that the emotional effects will be less pronounced.

It should not, however, be forgotten that however emotionally detached people become, they may still use the material of motion pictures for the purposes of imitation, and may even be better equipped to do this by virtue of their freedom from absorption in the action itself.

It does, nevertheless, seem possible that the more intense forms of emotional possession induced by films could to a great extent be avoided if a more detached attitude could be developed in the mass of the people who go to the cinema. The creation of such an attitude is helped by open discussions of films between children and adolescents and their instructors, as opposed to unqualified condemnation by the latter, and would if successful prove to be a more positive method of dealing with film influence than the negative method of censorship on which we have to rely now.

Schemes of Life

In addition to having a significant influence on the emotions and personal behaviour of many children and adolescents, the cinema may also be a determining factor in the creation of the individual's general outlook on life—his plans for the future, his ideas as to what kind of life is best, and his conception of the ways in which people of different backgrounds from his own conduct themselves. In many cases the films portray a kind of society with which the spectator is himself unfamiliar, and about which he has often no other source of information. Thus whatever views he may have on these alien modes of existence will be based on what he has seen in the cinema. It may happen, moreover, that he is led to compare the life depicted on the screen with his own life, to the disadvantage of the latter, and the result may be dissatisfaction, unrest, aspirations, ambition, and so on. Some individuals work out the desires thus created in day-dreams and do not seek to transform their own lives in any way, whereas others may be inspired to try to alter their way of living to something more akin to the ideal which they have built up from film material. Where there is a tendency to positive action of this kind, it may have the effect of strengthening the individual's ideals and arousing praiseworthy ambitions, but it may also have the effect of making him ready to give way to anti-social temptations, if by so doing he can achieve his aim.

Among children it is evident that motion pictures play a big part in stocking their minds with certain types of imagery, often of a stereotyped kind, which they use automatically to interpret situations in real life. This is illustrated by the appearance of film motives in children's games, which has been discussed already, and also in their school essays and short stories. Older children, particularly high school girls, often appear to think entirely in terms of the cinema world. They read avidly the magazines devoted to film gossip and decorate their lockers with cuttings from these publications. Many keep scrapbooks, and in general devote much time, thought and conversation to film topics. This attitude can become so engrained that the reading of fiction is accompanied by visualisation of the story as it might be screened.

One very important aspect of film influence on ideas is the way in which individuals form stereotyped and sometimes false conceptions of certain nationalities, occupations, social groups, and so on. Thus many children acquire a horror of the Chinese as a race, as a result of seeing mystery films in which the villain is a China-man. Similarly, strong notions may be developed about subjects like war, the life of the wealthy, and other aspects of society commonly presented in films.

The power of such conceptions lies in the fact that the original presentation is of a highly convincing and persuasive kind. The images are, moreover, simple and unequivocal and therefore all the more readily assimilated.

It sometimes happens that institutions of other aspects of social life, whose prestige is generally unquestioned, may be treated in a film in a manner which may weaken the spectator's respect for them—an example of this is the way in which certain films depict the police force as amusingly inefficient. The result may be to set up a confusion or conflict in the mind of the observer between his habitual attitudes and those implicit in the film, and if this happens often enough and over a wide range of subjects, his whole system of values will be shaken or distorted.

Many pictures are concerned with the activities of modern youth: these are generally presented in a highly coloured way which may well teach the young members of the audience to wish to do likewise. One of the most conspicuous examples of this effect is in connection with the relations of parents and children. The adolescent boy and girl see a film in which the young people are allowed an enviable degree of freedom from parental control, and their resentment of restrictions on their own liberty is heightened. Thus one girl of sixteen writes: 'Of course, the movies made me want to rebel against my parents' supervision.' And from a boy of seventeen this: 'The movies have made me dislike restraint of any kind. They have also made me dislike work.'

A similar reaction can be seen in the case of pictures dealing with love. Many young people in fact acquire most of their information on this subject from films. Thus one girl of seventeen writes: 'I learned something about the art of love-making and that bad and pretty girls are usually more attractive to men than intelligent and studious girls.' And another girl of sixteen writes: 'I think the movies have a great deal to do with present-day so-called "wildness". If we didn't see such examples in the movies, where should we get the idea of being "hot"? We wouldn't.'

Films which show young people leading free and luxurious lives amid romantic settings are liable to stir up a certain amount of restlessness among those whose own circumstances are markedly less exciting and attractive than the ones presented on the screen. Thus 22 per cent of the writers of the 458 high school autobiographies admit having experienced dissatisfaction with their homes as a result of seeing motion pictures. It is an interesting fact that the percentage of girls who acknowledged this influence was twice as high as the percentage of boys. This may be partially explained by the greater degree of restriction which some families continue to impose on their daughters, and which would accordingly make the latter more receptive to the appeal of the gay life portrayed on the films. Thus one sixteen-year-old schoolgirl writes: 'I think that girls should be treated the same as boys by their parents. They should tell their folks where they're going but shouldn't be kept on a strict time limit.'

A film which seems to have had a very widespread influence on the adolescents from whom Professor Blumer drew his material was one called *Our Dancing Daughters*. This picture was apparently a kind of apologia for modern youth, and purported to show how too strict an upbringing may produce the very results which it is seeking to avoid. The moral was seized on joyfully by those who felt that it could be applied with justice to their own cases—'I think parents should take a lesson from that picture. I wished that mother had seen it. Maybe she would not be so strict on me if she had seen that picture.' Another rather important aspect of this particular film is that it appears to have given the impression that a considerable freedom of conduct may be justified or at any rate accepted if it is accompanied by strict adherence to a code of fair play and sportsmanlike behaviour. This is a good example of the way in which films can have a confusing effect on values by appearing to sanction a whole way of life by concentrating attention on one favourable feature of it.

Another type of film which has a tendency to develop and give content to new schemes of life is that which deals attractively with travel abroad or with various kinds of career, especially a college career. Life at college is generally presented chiefly from the angle of its social activities and opportunities, and many boys and girls get from films the impression that it consists of little else. Among the high school documents as high a proportion as 51 per cent indicate that their authors have experienced a desire to go to college as a result of seeing pictures which present it in an exciting way.

It is interesting, however, to note that, with the exception of the desire to go to college, ambitions inspired by films appear in less than 7 per cent of the documents. Occasionally one finds an instance of a film creating an urge to become a dancer or a musician, or even a lawyer, but such cases are comparatively rare. This observation does not, of course, refer to the desire of young children to become cowboys, detectives, airmen, etc., as such desires, though frequent enough, are almost invariably ephemeral, and have no material effect on the ultimate plans of the individual concerned.

The type of influence which any individual may receive from a given film may, of course, be determined to a certain extent by his or her personal idiosyncrasies and general social experience. In this way a picture may elicit from one spectator a response which would not be found in the audience as a whole, and which could scarcely be anticipated by those responsible for making the film. This can happen if a situation in the picture recalls some event in the observer's own life and seems, therefore, of special significance for that person. Thus one girl whose engagement had been broken was strongly moved by pictures whose stories resembled her own.

What we may call a specialised approach to any particular type of film often results from conditions of a less personal character, as for instance age, race, cultural background, and so on. This is illustrated by the variety of reaction produced by a film like *The*

Birth of a Nation; the individual response in such a case tends to be simply a reflection of his customary social outlook.

Another powerful type of influence can be exerted by films with religious or semi-religious themes. The effect is often very similar to that produced by films in which sorrow or pathos are dominant, and is manifested in a temporary desire to be 'good'. We have recently been confronted with a number of pictures of this kind, notably *The Song of Bernadette* and *Going My Way*, both of which have been extremely popular. It has been suggested that this popularity is connected with the emotional conditions created by war, and there may be some truth in this view, but a very deep impression seems to have been made also by pre-war religious pictures such as *King of Kings*, *The Ten Commandments*, etc. Although generally such impressions are transient, if they happen to reinforce an attitude or inclination already present in the individual's mind the result may be of some practical significance.

Conclusion

It would seem uncontestable from the evidence which Professor Blumer brings forward, fragments of which have been quoted above, that motion pictures may affect conceptions of life and initiate schemes of conduct. One reason for this is the extensive range of topics presented in the cinema, many of which are new and fascinating material to the average filmgoer whose experience is generally of a limited kind. If as a child he goes to the pictures regularly and sees there aspects of life portrayed in a particular way, he will naturally form his views of those aspects of life from the screen images, unless he has access to other sources of information which would act as a corrective or antidote. And, since in films the extremes are often depicted as though they were the norm, he will tend to acquire a distorted vision of life, if he is not sufficiently astute to realise that much of what he sees is intended simply as 'entertainment', and does not provide an interpretation of reality.

In this connection it is very important to bear in mind that the people who wrote the accounts on which Professor Blumer bases his study were in the main of a sophisticated and comparatively cultured class. This may not be altogether true of the high school children, but it certainly applies to the university and college writers. The point is that even among these people the influence of films is clearly very strong, and it is difficult to avoid the conclusion that in the much larger class of filmgoers who are less self-conscious, less sophisticated, less detached, and less well-informed the effects must be still *more* marked. In trying to form any estimate of how far, and in what ways, a particular type of film will affect a particular class or section of society, it would clearly be necessary to know something of this general background, social code, and degree of experience. But it can be said that though the types and intensity of influence may perhaps vary from class to class, age group to age group, in men and women, and so on, yet in one way or another films may do a great deal to provide patterns of behaviour, to stimulate the imagination, and to determine conceptions of life. They are a much more important factor in the contemporary social scene than is implied by those who regard them merely as a means of temporary escape from the harshness or drabness of everyday existence. To many people the film appears to be an authentic reflection of life, and to question the values which are implicit in its presentations would never occur to them. These values are, moreover, strangely confused, and it is very rarely that a film attempts to provide a consistent outlook: in any case, the guiding principles of conduct implicit in one picture will be replaced by a different code of behaviour in another picture, and the impressionable spectator becomes more and more bewildered.

It must here be admitted that since the publication of Professor Blumer's study in 1933 there has been a considerable sprinkling of films which do present a more or less adequate picture of aspects of contemporary society. In this category fall films such as *Mr Deeds goes to Town*, *The Little Foxes*, *Grapes of Wrath*, and of course recent British films like *Good-bye Mr. Chips*, *The Way Ahead*, *This Happy Breed*, *The Gentle Sex*, and *The Lamp Still Burns*. But the fact remains that a very big proportion of the current output still has as its primary aim some form of emotional stimulation. This in itself must inevitably lead to a degree of emotional exhaustion in the child or adolescent, irrespective of whether the kind of stimulation involved is of a harmful kind or not.

It may eventually so blunt the individual's powers of emotional response that he is incapable of any sensitive reactions in real life. In any case, regular over-stimulation of the more violent feelings and impulses cannot be of any positive value and may in many instances be definitely harmful.

CHAPTER 8

The Content of Films

Earlier volumes in the Payne Fund series *Motion Pictures and Youth* established beyond question that the attitudes, emotions, and behaviour of children and young people are influenced by the cinema. Mr. Edgar Dale's study, *The Content of Motion Pictures*, goes a step further and aims at analysing the *content* of motion pictures, taking for its material the bulk of the motion picture output in certain selected years.

One inherent difficulty, which the author notes in his preface, is that different individuals do not react in the same way to the same stimuli, or as Mr. Dale puts it, 'content is a function of the individual who views that particular picture.' It is, however, a fact that most persons are so conditioned that there is a sufficient degree of similarity in their response to make the findings of a study of this kind valuable. In the case of children and young people of very diverse age groups and levels of experience, a more specialised enquiry is necessary, but, as a means of obtaining a broad idea of the various stimuli to be found in films and of the manner of their operation, the technique employed by Mr. Dale would appear to be adequate.

As no comparable attempt to isolate the essential ingredient of motion pictures has been made hitherto, the first problem of the author was to evolve a valid method for tackling his material. He decided eventually to make analyses of three different degrees of intensity. The most comprehensive but least detailed method he applied to 1,500 films in all: 500 from the year 1920, 500 from 1925, and 500 from 1930: this meant that he covered practically the entire output of feature films from the major companies in those years.

The aim of this first analysis was simply to classify major themes, and the material used consisted of written précis of the stories of the films. It was clear that only a rough indication of content could be obtained in this way, and that questions relating to the more subtle influences of films through their tone, atmosphere, etc., were left unanswered.

Mr. Dale therefore selected 115 pictures from the years 1929, 1930, and 1931, and subjected them to a more intensive analysis, using this time trained observers who personally viewed the films, and reported on them by means of a specially prepared schedule, having first acquainted themselves with the plot of the film by a perusal of the critiques in the daily papers. The schedule which they used was designed to secure information on the treatment accorded by films to various aspects of life and society. The following are typical headings from the nine main categories: 'Nature of American Life and Characters', 'Crime, Delinquency and Violence', 'Relations of the Sexes', 'Depiction of Underprivileged Peoples'. Each main category was sub-divided, so that under 'Nature of American Life and Characters' we have these sub-headings: A. Home, B. Education, C. Religion, D. Economics, and so on, there being 16 sub-headings in all. These in turn were further analysed into special aspects, for instance, a sub-heading, 'Industry and Commerce,' is developed thus:

1. The nature of the portrayal of industrial and commercial activity.
2. Goals of characters engaged in industrial activity.
3. Method of distribution of goods.
4. Nature of portrayal of owners and workers.
5. Nature of the management of industry.

This type of schedule is, we consider, too statistical in its approach, and its wealth of categories would tend to distract the investigator from perceiving the more fundamental value-patterns of a film. What is really important to the sociologist is the discovery and isolation of the implicit attitudes of a motion picture, the general assumptions on which are based the conduct of the characters and the treatment of the situations of the plot. To a certain extent the schedule does seek to comprehend these more intangible issues, but there is a danger that a too meticulous adherence to its terms of reference may produce only a neat set of details on various unrelated topics and fail to acquaint the investigator with the basic texture of any particular film or group of films.

A certain difficulty was experienced in selecting the 115 pictures for this 'second-level' analysis, as it seemed desirable that they should form a truly representative sample of the cinema fare then being offered to the public. For instance, it appeared that more weight should be given to films which had proved to be outstanding box-office successes than to pictures which were poorly attended: but the attempt to achieve this grading had to be abandoned on account of the inaccessibility of reliable information as to box-office returns.

Mr. Dale obviously ran into the same difficulties as we did while our investigations were proceeding. Box office statistics have been flatly refused to us. It would have been of interest to have been able to compare our sociological method with a statistical method, though I do not think we lost much as we were able to obtain enough verbal evidence from local managers with regard to box-office returns in order to check *our* findings. (We had no interest in improving the box-office returns of the film industry.)

Eventually the selection of films for the analysis was made quite at random, with a roughly appropriate proportion from each major producing company. When, however, a classification was made of the 500 pictures released in 1930, it was found that the proportions of each main type were more or less the same as the proportions of types in the 115 films chosen for the analysis.

The chief deficiency of this second level of analysis is that it fails to present the total context of any situation which it discusses. It was, therefore, decided to employ a third method of analysis which should aim at giving, as far as possible, the entire content of a number of films. Dialogue scripts were, accordingly, obtained from the producers for 40 pictures, and these were used in conjunction with the schedules prepared for the 'second level' analysis. The procedure was as follows: a number of trained observers, one or two per film, familiarised themselves with the dialogue script before viewing the picture. They made stenographic notes during their attendance at the cinema on all aspects of the film not covered by the dialogue script, i.e. detailed descriptions of clothes, settings, gestures, facial expressions, approximate age and economic status of the characters and so on.

Immediately after the show they 'rewrote' the film in the form of a narrative, based on a combination of the script and their own notes, with precise indications of every change of scene. These reviews provided a 'verbal description of what competent observers say has occurred on the motion picture screen': this, in Mr. Dale's opinion, is a fair definition of the phrase 'motion picture content'. He adds, quite correctly, that to describe the content of a film is not the same thing as to be able to predict its effects on an audience, and that any judgments he makes in the course of his book regarding the possible influence of certain types of motion pictures on children and youth are merely inferences from the evidence before him, and are not conclusions based on a scientific investigation. The reader is urged to work out his own interpretations of the data, by relating it to the findings of other investigators who have studied the actual reactions of children and adolescents to films.

Towards the end of his introductory chapter, Mr. Dale summarises the aims of his study in this way: 1. 'to devise a technique for analysing the content of motion pictures'; and 2. 'to discover by this technique what the content of motion pictures has been'. To the reader of 1945 the words 'has been' will suggest a more serious doubt as to the continued applicability of Mr. Dale's findings than to the readers of 1935, when his book first appeared. Even in 1935, many features which characterised the typical motion picture successes of the years 1925-31 were fast disappearing, and indeed the whole tone of the cinema was in the course of transformation. This break was occasioned to a considerable extent by the operation of the newly established Hays' Code, but it was probably caused, in a more fundamental sense, by a general reaction in public opinion of which the Hays' Code was only a symptom, and which must be explained in terms of sociology. Between 1935 and 1945 many more striking developments have been apparent in the unformulated but widely influential *Weltanschauung* of Film, this implicit outlook which binds together the typical motion pictures of any 'period'. Moreover, in 1936, the Hays' Code was considerably amended, and this inevitably affected the films produced between that year and the outbreak of war in 1939.

The type of film which served merely as a setting for the antics of an exotic vamp or *femme fatale*, and which was, in its general feeling, a throwback to the decadent romanticism of the 90's (e.g. Aubrey Beardsley, Wilde, etc., in other medias) had, by the late 30's of this century, almost disappeared from the cinematic scene. This trend is exemplified by the fact that the last representative of the type, Greta Garbo, abandoned the siren rôles which had made her famous and began to make light comedies—e.g. *Ninotchka*.

The qualities which films now appeared to strive after were speed and slickness of action, wisecracking dialogue, and whatever is connoted by the American word 'cute'; all of which was in striking contrast with the languorous, hot-house atmosphere of the epics of the vamp era. The *coup de grâce* may, perhaps, be said to have been administered by the films of Mae West who actually burlesqued the vamp type, to the delight of the public which had in all probability been entranced a decade earlier by what they now saw ridiculed.

As one would expect, simultaneously with the decline of the vamp occurred the eclipse of the romantic heroes, usually of Latin origin, of whom Rudolph Valentino was the prototype. Mystery and intensity ceased to be the characteristic qualities of the male film star, and a more typically American and 'manly' type of hero began to dominate the screen. But while 'sin', of the exotic variety beloved by the late romantics some decades earlier, was losing its belated popularity with the cinema public, there was a marked increase in the exploitation of brutality as a major motion picture theme. This tendency is clearly shown in the appearance of the gangster film, which became one of the principal types of film during the middle 30's, but which was less frequent in the years immediately preceding the war, and is now, in 1945, an almost extinct species.

During the war a high proportion of the film output has, as was natural, been devoted to war themes, many of which involved similar emotions to those excited by the old gangster, which suggests a possible explanation for the shelving of the latter. But if we exclude essentially topical films, by far the most common type would appear to be now the Technicolour musical. We have no statistical backing for this view, but it is evident that producing companies bestow their most frantic publicity on this type of picture, and it is the stars who feature in them that seem to epitomise the film world for the public of to-day, just as the stars of the vamp films and of the gangster films were household words in other years.

What emerges from this very brief survey of recent cinema history is that the proportion of any particular type of film to the total output is continually changing. Now, in Mr. Dale's book the bulk of the information and conclusions are based on the structure which prevailed in the period 1920 to 1931, and it is accordingly impossible to apply his findings to the present-day scene. The most valuable part of his study for us is, in our opinion, the technique of research which he evolved and which he describes in great detail. This technique for isolating the content of motion pictures is as valid to-day as when the book was first published, and might be used with very important results on the films of our own decade.

For it seems to us that only by a sociological and normative analysis of film will it be possible to raise the standards of film appreciation. So far, film analysis has been left to the professional film reviewer who mainly reports only about his *personal* preferences. (Naturally there are exceptions: there are some film critics who do their best to analyse 'the meaning of film' in relation to its audience. But they are rather the exception than the rule.)

Perhaps we should illustrate the point we make by a concrete example. Take the recent film *Blithe Spirit*, which is reviewed in the *Monthly Film Bulletin of the British Film Institute* in Vol. 12, No. 136, in the following terms:

GREAT BRITAIN. *Blithe Spirit*—Comedy.

Novelist Condomine invited medium, Madame Arcati, to his Kent home for an evening séance. His first wife, Elvira, materialised, to the scorn, annoyance and confusion of his second wife, Ruth. Ruth enlisted the aid of Madame Arcati to send Elvira back to the 'other side'. Elvira arranged a car accident to kill Condomine so that he could be with her. But Ruth was in the car and it was Ruth who was killed. Condomine, exasperated by the presence of two ghost wives, decided to leave his home and them; but they had manipulated the car again—and he joined them as a shade almost as soon as he drove off. Here is another brilliant demonstration that Coward's sense of cinema is as shrewd as his sense of theatre. With a strong team in all departments he has created a swift-moving, beautifully produced farce which gets a laugh with its first provocative line and does not flag right on to its last irreverent shot. Colour and production men are worthy allies of the lively, swinging, travelling camera of Ronald Neame. Harrison could not have been better cast as Condomine. Constance Cummings and Kay Hammond are in the rôles they created with such success and polish on the stage. Margaret Rutherford gives Madame Arcati tremendous gusto, and, with generous help from the property department in massing occultist paraphernalia, gives us some of the most bizarre pictures the screen has presented.

SUITABILITY: A, B, C.   K.F.B.

It is interesting to note that this film is even being given a C-Certificate which means 'films to which parents can take or send their children in the knowledge that they contain no scenes or characters likely to frighten or disturb children'. But will children —let us say up to an age of $9\frac{1}{2}$ years—understand the farcical character of this film: will they not be profoundly disturbed by the appearance of ghosts? Moreover, will not other age groups—

from 10 to 14 years—be taken in or become influenced by the cynical attitude towards married life? Our questions show that we entirely disagree with the Film Institute's verdict about the film.

In our film-diary we have written the following note about *Blithe Spirit*:

Here is a film which, from the point of view of acting, direction, and general technical achievement is superb, but whose implicit outlook is completely out of touch with the main currents of thought and feeling to-day.

It is not as if the film were genuinely escapist—then it would have to stand or fall by its success as pure entertainment: the fact is that in *Blithe Spirit* we are confronted with an expression of values which pervades every line of the dialogue and the treatment of every situation of the plot. These values are essentially negative; they involve an attitude to life which is brittle, egotistical, and thoroughly cynical. It is true that such a spirit was prevalent between the wars in certain sections of English society, and that to this extent the film does reflect reality. But what one deplores is the way in which the situation is accepted without criticism, without detachment, without irony, as though it were the desirable norm, for to-day as yesterday.

If the play could have been presented in the film as a kind of 'period piece', there would be no grounds for complaint, but the world which it portrays is, perhaps, too near us, in time if not in feeling, for the average person to be able to view it in this way.

One cannot, therefore, help wishing that so much brilliance in production had been devoted to a theme more worthy of the great days in which we live, and that Mr. Coward's sparkling trifle had been left for a time when it could be seen in perspective for what it is.

We do not seek a quarrel with the British Film Institute. On the contrary, we only intend to show that even the Institute, which has done so much to raise the standard of film appreciation, is so uncertain of the critical norms it applies.

The problem of the value patterns as implicit in films appears to recur again and again on these pages. Clearly this is only one problem of a sociology of film among very many others of similar urgency. (Not all of them are discussed in this book.) For example, take the art *form* of the cinema in relation to the theatre. It is true that we discussed (*see* particularly Chapters II and III) the cinema in relation to the Greek theatre and the Roman circus from the point of view that all three had and have a universal audience, but we did not ask the question to what extent and why is the modern 'amusement' art a *form* of art which appears at the same time everywhere: in France, Germany, America, Soviet Russia, and the East; in China, Japan, and India. This is not only a phenomenon of the ultimate victory of a technical and industrial civilisation, for the national characteristics of film in any country, including, for example, China, are distinct—in spite of Hollywood's 'internationalism'. Is it not possible that the *form* of the cinema is *also* a further phase in the art-cycle which is characterised by the stages of epos, theatre, novel as we find it in all European societies?[1] All these art structures are related to specific social patterns in a continuing process of 'democratisation'. Why do they arise everywhere?

It is not possible to answer this question within the compass of this book, yet it is precisely the answer to such a question which may provide the adequate ramification and perspective for a sociological appreciation of film.

I found a significant confirmation of the immense vistas of a film sociology in Albert Thibaudet's brilliant *Histoire de la Littérature Française* (Paris 1936), where we read the following remarks in his concluding paragraph: 'Le jeune auteur, plus que de la littérature, s'inquiète aujourd'hui du cinéma. Consciemment ou inconsciemment, l'influence de l'art nouveau s'est insinuée dans une partie notable de la littérature dramatique d'après-guerre. D'abord le cinéma, soit l'art du mouvement, a fourni au spectateur moyen un champ d'entraînement, il s'est habitué à des perceptions plus rapides, ce qui a permis à l'art dramatique de déblayer: le théâtre des jeunes auteurs ne vit plus dans la même durée que le théâtre des anciens auteurs, et les dernières traces des longues expositions ont disparu. En second lieu les jeux de physionomie ont remplacé ou éclairé le dialogue. Enfin il y a certaine recherche de la qualité et de la nouveauté qu'interdisent au cinéma des considérations matérielles, la necessité de s'adresser à un gros public, et surtout au public de province: c'est au théâtre, infiniment plus souple, plus affranchi des matérialités de machinerie, même d'argent, qu'il appartient de faire fructifier littérairement le capital du vogue du cinéma.' (p. 563).

Obviously the great French critic writes with the French literary scene in his mind. Paris is for France the traditional centre of art. All the same, he clearly has realised the new rapidity of the cinema which forces us to quicker 'perceptions'. 'Physiognomy' has largely taken the place of the subtle expression of the actor. In short, the

[1] Cf. R. M. Meyer, *Die Weltliteratur im 20. Jahrhundert*, Berlin 1913, pp. 220 sqq.

JENNIFER JONES IN 'SONG OF BERNADETTE'
A rare example of a profound religious experience on the screen

PHYLLIS CALVERT IN 'THE MAN IN GREY'

PHYLLIS CALVERT IN HOLLYWOOD STYLE

durée of the cinema is different from that of the theatre—with all its deep repercussions on us. Perhaps the author of *The Decline and Fall of the Roman Empire* would say of us, too, that we have become —spectators.

Only if one envisages such a horizon of a sociological film appreciation, can its importance and scope be adequately understood. A discussion of the problems of 'content of motion pictures' cannot be isolated from these and related problems.

To return to Edgar Dale who, in another volume of the Payne Fund Studies, has examined the problem of *How to Appreciate Motion Pictures* (Tenth edition, Macmillan, New York 1938). There we read: 'A new point of view regarding the place of motion pictures in our scheme of living must be developed. At present motion pictures are only made for personal profit; they must be produced to fit the needs of the people. Many of these needs are satisfied by laughter and gaiety and joyousness, which erase our worries. Other needs relate, however, to the abolition of war, to a new point of view regarding crime and punishment, to the more satisfactory distribution of wealth, to a deeper insight into the problem of a democratic government . . .' Mr. Dale writes these sentences in a handbook for American high school students. They may be applied likewise to British students of the cinema.

But pressure through group or individual appreciation is not enough. 'If producers', writes Mr. Dale, 'are not making motion pictures the seeing of which you can honestly regard as a worthwhile leisure activity, then you should demand that such pictures be produced. You represent a group of intelligent movie-goers, trained in the appreciation of pictures, and you have the power to influence the future of motion pictures. If producers discover that there is a demand for the finer pictures, they will make them. The demand must be first created, however, and you are the logical persons to do it.' I believe Mr. Dale underestimates the financial and propaganda power of the film producer. Education in film appreciation must be combined with state supervision of the commercial children's cinemas and also with the establishment of a public distributing corporation along B.B.C. lines. By such a combined effort it may be possible to safeguard the spiritual health of the nation.

CHAPTER 9

The Adult and the Cinema

Strong counter-measures are indicated against theorists who damn the personal document with faint praise, saying that its sole merit lies in its capacity to yield hunches or to suggest hypotheses, or that the mental operations brought to bear upon the single case are merely a matter of incomplete and inadequate statistical reasoning. Although these points of view do reflect the prevailing empirical climate of our times, they fail to express more than a small part of the value of personal documents for social science. Properly used, such documents anchor a discipline in the bedrock of human experience, make the most of the predilective value of the single case in the normal process of human thought, exploit the ideographic principles of reasoning, and aid in meeting (more adequately than can unaided actuarial methods of work) the three critical tests of science: *understanding*, *prediction*, and *control*.

GORDON W. ALLPORT in *The Use of Personal Documents in psychological Science*, Social Research Council, New York 1942.

1. INTRODUCTORY

We began our studies of British adult audiences with unique advantages. Mr. Arthur Rank had given us facilities to visit any of the Odeon Cinemas in this country. We talked to managers, assistant managers, their secretarial staff, doormen, usherettes. Moreover, we sat amongst the audiences and we distributed questionnaires in theatres. The managers were almost without exception extremely helpful and there can be no doubt that if their experiences could be pooled audience reactions research would profit considerably.

All this gave us an invaluable background for forming a sociological appreciation of cinema audiences. In conjunction with those questionnaires which were distributed through the cinemas, we handed out the same questionnaires to people in all walks of life.

In addition, we kept a selected group of people whose lives and social circumstances were intimately known to us under constant observation. We sent them to see specific films and recorded their reactions and impressions.

Thus considerable material was collected. Yet I resist the temptation to publish this material or some parts of it, for several reasons.

First, I believe an investigation of this kind presupposes a thorough understanding of the psychological and sociological mechanisms of film reactions. Second, however considerable or weighty our material may have been, we were not able to cover wide enough *regions* in order to be sure that the material obtained was really representative. Third, while the investigations proceeded, we were never certain how long we were to be allowed to work with the given facilities. We had first agreed with Mr. Rank to work for a trial period of four months. After they had elapsed, we were granted another six months to continue our work. Before this half-year had passed, the technical and financial facilities were withdrawn as the investigations were thought to be of 'no practical use to the film industry'.

Naturally, I anticipated such a decision. Five months before Mr. Rank decided to stop our work as far as his theatres were concerned, I had approached the Editor of *The Picturegoer* who very kindly allowed me to use his paper in order to obtain film-reaction material.

From the beginning of our investigations I was convinced that a quantitative and purely statistical method would not produce any satisfactory results. A study of Professor Blumer's book, which has been discussed on preceding pages of this book, confirmed my conviction that only a *method of case studies* might be able to provide us with reliable patterns for a sociological appraisal of film reactions.

Moreover, before I had accepted any financial support for this investigation from the film industry, I had looked out and searched for psychological literature which might give us help and guidance in our work.

This search was disappointing, as our contemporary psychologists and social scientists appear to have neglected the cinema to an extent for which I have no explanation to offer.

Only from two psychologists have I received much help and encouragement. The majority of our contemporary psychologists pay hardly any attention to the cinema. When they do, they confine themselves to generalities. Take, for example, Jung, who in his book

Modern Man in Search of a Soul, which was first published in 1933, writes one sentence on the influence of the cinema: 'the cinema ... like the detective story, makes it possible to experience without danger all the excitement, passion and deliriousness which must be repressed in a humanitarian ordering of life.' In this single sentence, it would seem, the eminent psychologist takes the 'aggressiveness' of human nature for granted, an assumption which presupposes an 'anthropology' which I cannot accept. Jung also stresses 'the ideal of internationalism or supernationalism which is embodied . . . in the cinema. . . .' Both statements seem to me highly superficial and problematic.

Mr. Loewy, a distinguished Czech scientist, whose book *Man and His Fellowmen, Modern Chapters on Social Psychology* appeared when our investigations were already well under way, comes to just the opposite conclusion: 'Pictures, whilst satisfying the psyche for two hours, operating after the fashion of alcohol or a sedative drug, may drop into the mind the additional seed of the desire for the unattainable, instead of solving the difficulty'.[1] And what about Dr. Jung's idea of internationalism? As long as the majority of distributors and exhibitors refuse to show us Soviet films whilst they take delight in showing us every third-rate American detective film or musical, no healthy internationalism nourished by film can be said to exist.

Last, but not least, I should like to refer to Miss Margaret Phillips' book on *The Education of the Emotions through Sentiment Development*. This book was published in 1937. We have already referred above to a representative protocol which Miss Phillips reproduces. Here follows her general comment: '. . . dramatic art may serve that compensatory purpose which has by now become so familiar to us. It may offer experience not on another level but, occupying another area, than that which one's own life occupies; it may satisfy in fantasy needs still of an urgent, personal, instinctive kind, but which are deprived of satisfaction in actuality. In the eyes of many the art of the cinema is specially adapted to meet this need, and my most representative protocol of this type does, in fact, describe a sentiment of the cinema. The object of the sentiment is life, as lived either in actuality or on the screen. The latter may supplement the former, but there must be no change of quality, no artistic transformation. The cinema must provide more and more intense emotional experience of the same kind as real life

[1] I reproduce Dr. Loewy's important psychological interpretation of film in Appendix III of this book.

supplies.' Miss Phillips, too, accepts I think, the reality character of the film experience. And indeed a close perusal of the protocol she gives as an example, shows that film may become for people a part of their sexual life.

It is important to note that Miss Phillips refrains in her book from any quantitative conclusion with regard to the representative character of her protocol material.

We have strictly adhered to the same policy and leave it to the believers in Gallup poll or mass observation to work out numerical formulas, an enterprise which we did not feel competent to undertake.

Our protocols which now follow in their original form were obtained in February 1945 through *The Picturegoer*. (Only names and other obvious indications to endanger the anonymity of the authors are being withheld.)

The following questions were put:

Your help is requested.

A lecturer at the University of London has asked for your assistance.

He is conducting an investigation regarding film audiences.

He would like you to answer two questions:

1. Have films ever influenced you with regard to personal decisions or behaviour? (Love, divorce, manners, fashion, etc.) Can you give instances?
2. Have films ever appeared in your dreams?

In answering both questions name the films.

You may write to your heart's content. There is no limit on wordage and the best will be rewarded by a guinea, ten shillings, and two prizes of five shillings.

The University lecturer asks particularly that you should state your age, sex, nationality, profession, and profession of parents.

Naturally, all correspondence will be treated as confidential.

2. DOCUMENTS

1. Mr. . . . .

Being a regular reader of *Picturegoer* I have decided to enter your contest not in the hope of winning a prize but in the hope you can or know of someone who can help me to realise one or two of my ambitions. I have enclosed a photo of myself in the hope it will be returned.

First I will give particulars of my parents and myself. I am 28 years, height 5 ft. 9½ in., weight roughly 10 stone, Religion Roman Catholic, Strict T.T., Grey eyes, Auburn hair, Brownish complexion. Slim build, health moderate teeth bad. Not extra strong, could nearly be classed as a weakling. Plain appearances. Quiet disposition, very refined, Politeness a speciality. I could honestly say I speak International English; as we in the province of...... have always had the reputation of speaking better English than the English themselves.

Profession. Unemployed. Shop Assistant, Grocery and Provision and light Hardware trade. I have done some light farm work too, I have never attended a dance and have no talent in the line of music. I have the gift of the gab as it were I like reading. Pictures, I have played Golf, Croquet, cards, some tennis, the profession of my late parents, Mother, a domestic servant, Father, Grocery, horse van driver.

Ambition No. 1. To get to Hollywood and to get small parts in films even insignificant ones. I would be happy even if I had to draw the dole some of the time.

Film Remarks. The film entitled 100 *Men and a Girl* starring Deanna Durbin seen by me about 7 yrs. ago have being the result of my second ambition I fell in love with Deanna Durbin and my love has grown for her every day. It is not just calf love or a passing infatuation but its the real thing. I follow all her films and one film of hers seen recently made me sad: *Three Smart Girls Grow Up.* I felt rotten over the trend of the picture and would much prefer to have sacrificed Jackie Coopers love affair. The entire crowd were disgusted with the finish, I am happy now D.D. is free from Vaughan Paul and it is my ambition and hope that one day I will be able to get to Hollywood and make my love known to her and I hope even though I am only an Irish peasant without financial or other mean to make the grandest star in Hollywood my wife, its all I live for and I would be ever grateful if you would send her my photo and letter. I wish her to know of my two ambitions as perhaps she could influence her Company to give me small parts, also I wish to tell her if ever we are married it will not be one for the divorce court to wreck, but one of happiness. One of honour and we will never double cross our promise to our Creator but will keep our vow until Death do us part. Glamour is not everything but peace, happiness and the love of God. Mutual respect for each other. Moral Religious and Political aspect, so give my love letter and photo to Deanna, I am a sentimentalist and cried sincerely when I seen *Men of Boys Town* also *San Francisco* I eat the American style with my knife and not fork, also films no one in particular have been responsible for my present refined manner. I have adopted the manners of the stars. Films and reading have been responsible for a lot of my Education.

2) Films have never appeared in my dreams.

I don't expect to win a prize but I do hope you will send my letter and photo to Deanna Durbin you can send all this letter and I will be very grateful to you, tell Deanna it is not necessary to marry another star or person of position, love comes to the humblest.

P.S. Nationality of my parents and I is Irish.

2. Miss . . .

Looking through a recent issue of the *Picturegoer*, I read that you want some assistance, so here goes:

Some films have influenced my personal decisions, for instance, the films that Donald O'Connor or Mickey Rooney are in. I often wish that England could have Colleges and Drug Stores, like those in their films. America seems to be a country of fun and games, and I feel discontented when I think of it. On the subject of love, the boys always seem to run after the girls, and find someone to introduce them, before they dare speak to them, but the boys in England never wait to be introduced, they just whistle, and if the girls don't turn round, they think you are 'snobs'. I often wish the boys would treat us as Donald O'Connor treats his girls. I also wish we could go back a few centuries, and the ladies wear beautiful crinolines, and gentlemen wear Cavalier clothes. I am not always discontented after seeing a film, because sometimes I come out of a cinema, with a feeling of utter satisfaction. For instance, after seeing a 'Murder' film, I'm thankful that I'm not involved in a 'Murder', and all the pictures of Japs and Germans torturing I appreciate my freedom.

In answer to the Second question, I remember one instance, that I ever dreamt of a film. It was the film of *Gone with the Wind*, it kept on haunting me, I enjoyed it very much, but if I had a chance to see it again, I would not go. Every night for about a month, I used to wake up and find myself thinking about it. It was not because my favourite film stars were in it, because Clark Gable nor Vivien Leigh aren't on my 'favourites' list. I also wondered what happened after the end, I used to imagine that when he met her again, he would want to go back with her, and sometimes I imagined that Leslie Howard would go with her. Now, whenever

I think or talk about it, I quickly change the subject, as it will start haunting me again.

Age. 16 yrs. old, eldest of four.

Nationality: Born in London.

Profession: Clerk.

Profession of Father: Member of His Majesty's Forces now abroad.

Profession of Mother: Home work.

3. Miss ...

I saw your request as to the effect of films on the public.

As to your first request about the influence of films on people, I do not think it makes any difference in regard to love and divorce, but as to manners and fashions I think it does especially to woman. I have copied many styles started by Hollywood stars.

As to question No. 2, as regards to films appearing in dreams, I have found that they do, but only in certain films.

If I go and see a musical, I am interested in it, as long as I am in the cinema and maybe afterwards I tell my friends whether I liked it or not, but I would not go home and dream about it.

Then there are other films, love stories, gangsters, etc., they leave very little impression, and I think no more about them.

Lastly there are the films I do remember, ones that are very well acted or very sad, or grim. One film I dreamt about was *Song of Bernadette*, now I did not like this film to a great extent but there was something in it, the poverty in which the girl lived and the way in which she died. Then there was *Madam Curie* which stood out.

Now to get a different type of film one I can't help remembering e.g. *Hitler's Children*: a brutal film about a young couple's love under the nazis, there is so much torture in this it to became a nightmare rather than a dream, the same with *The Cross of Lorraine*.

A totally different type of film was Bing Crosby's *Going My Way* which ended so sadly with Bing leaving the place and people he loved to help a poorer parish.

I have heard the girl next door (she is 14) say she dreams of film-stars but it is usually after she has just come home from the pictures, and then it is usually some nice looking star such as Tyrone Power, Denis Morgan or Robert Taylor.

I think films influence people in other ways too.

Films such as the story of Amy Johnson make me feel I want to fly. I have always had an urge to fly but seeing this film made me positive.

I have read in film books that it was going to the films such a lot that made Van Johnson positive that he wanted to be an actor.

I noticed that you wanted some details about the writer of the letter.

I am 17 years of age, female, born in Britain (Essex) of an Irish Father and American Mother. I work as secretary to the headmaster of one of our local schools. My mother was a clerk and my father an engineer.

4. Mr. . . .

Re your article in the *Picturegoer* asking picturegoers two questions regarding our reactions to motion pictures.

The first one is, to me, a difficult question to answer. I myself am a film enthusiast and have seen scores of films covering almost every type of entertainment devisable, but never yet have I been moved by a tense or emotional scene, in any shape or form.

Although the acting is sometimes of a very high standard, I sit in the comfort of the cinema, knowing well, that the film is, in a way fake, and that the actors aren't actually experiencing or have not experienced, most of the rigourous and dramatic scenes presented on the screen.

These in my opinion would demand the services of a superman, but, bear in mind, this is not the case in every picture.

For instance, my favourite film is a comedy, not a slap-stick affair as presented by such as the 'Three Stooges', but a film starring comedians such as Bob Hope.

These pictures create a good laugh and leave their impression on me for a long while, giving me many a moment silent laughter when reminiscing to myself.

But as regards these films having ever influenced me, I define them as a pleasant, non-sensical form of entertainment.

(The films mentioned below are the Jon Hall and Maria Montez series).

I will make a confession though, There *is* one kind of film that leaves me spell-bound and that is those films featureing the tropical ilses, such magnitude of colour and scenery, coupled with splendour on a magnificent scale.

When watching these, I seem to forget the present world, in which I am living, lost in a kind of spell that is enchanted by the impression of my being actually there.

No doubt this has affected me, for it is my ambition some day, to see for myself the actual place, if there were any, where these films were shot, purpously to view the scenery, and see if the spell that is cast over me in the cineama takes effect on the actual setting.

Had it not been for the films I may never have been the witness of such awe-inspiring spectacles.

That is all I can say about question one.

Question two is quite easy to answer because only once has film appeared in my dreams.

This may seem peculiar to you but it was soon after seeing a film starring my favourite actor, Humphrey Bogart.

The dream did not actually concern the film itself but the actor, Humphrey Bogart.

I dreamt I met him personally and had the honour of conversing with him.

This vision presented him as a calm common homely sort of person, and I am of the opinion that he *is* what I dreamt.

I presume the reason of this dream is that my flare for films of Humphrey Bogart causes him to stand out in my career of picture-going.

You'll notice that my reactions are based on male stars.

The astounding fact is, that female stars, whatever way they are presented on the screen, do not impress me.

I don't know the reason for this but if films were presented without women I should not be in the least affected.

Those are my answers to your questions and although they may sound fantastic, they are absolutely true.

Age nineteen,
Male,
British,
Manual Worker.

5. Mr. . . .

In answer to your request for letters from readers re. Have films ever influenced you with regard personal Decisions or Behaviour love divorce manners fashion my answer is yes.

I am learning to play the piano and when I hear music which is written for picture such as that lovely Melody 'Irish Eyes are Smiling' from the picture of that name it makes me want to study music more (?) and also when I heard the voice of Dick Hayes I wanted to learn singing.

Now the second word behaviour takes me back to that picture *Lady in the Dark* in which you will remember Ginger Rogers throws a paper weight at Ray Milland and later apologises in a very charming manner this also brings in the word manners.

Well now think of that British picture *It Happened One Sunday* remember the fun they use. Well, *Lady in the Dark* teaches you your manners the Americans have a very nice way of showing you but the British picture is teaching you how to swear. A picture can be good without this fun. For wisecracks American pictures certainly show you Fashions but where is British fashions, Stars are always smart I should certainly like to go to a Dance in Evening Dress with a young Lady in a long dress.

And now the second question: Have films ever appeared in your dreams.

Yes. One night I dreamt that Edward G. Robinson was in a room with me and that he had hold of me by the throat trying to murder me because I was insured. I think that brings in the picture *Double Indemnity*. Well I hope these questions will help you.

6. Dr. ....
  1. Influence of films on behaviour—
Such films of the beautiful open air, semi-nudes, glamourised sex affairs as

> *Escape to Happiness* (Mediterranean)
> *Autumn Crocus* (Switzerland)
> *The Blue Light* (Dolomites)

have almost persuaded me to escape from professional work, social convention etc to take up painting, travel and have amorous adventures (finance and discretion unhappily prevailed).

Lady in the Dark (after reading *Arrival and Departure*) showed me that physical fulfilment matters more than professional success. *Mark of the Vampire* I'd give anything not to have seen.

  2. Films in dreams—
Not individual films, but scenes of infantile memory and infantile biological fantasies sometimes appear as seen in a film—as the first of baby brother (horror) or identification with royalty.

  Personal data.

Age 42 (look and feel 32)

Nationality—Scottish but mother Shetland (and they mature late and have menopause at 60)

Profession—Medical

Profession of parents—father a lawyer (family military for generations)

Class—landed gentry but impoverished.

Had 180 sittings with Freudian analyst. Eldest of 2 children.

Type—narcissus and mildly paranoid.

7. Miss . . .

1. I can truthfully say that films have influenced my behaviour in many walks of life. Not in love or divorce, for I don't consider myself old enough to be involved in serious decisions regarding these—and sincerely hope I shall never be faced with divorce! But as regards manners and fashion, my answer is a definite 'yes'. Let us begin with fashion. Without being egotistical, may I say that my figure and face closely resemble those of Deanna Durbin. Having decided on that point several years ago now, I proceeded to study Miss Durbin's actions, personality, and deportment. Not that I would allow any one's personality to influence my own, but I have found several instances in my life, where, faced with a decision, I thought to myself 'I wonder what Deanna would have done (or said) had she been placed under similar circumstances'. And this invariably led to my thinking the position over calmly and (I think) sensibly and being well pleased with the forthcoming result.

Regarding actions and deportment, I have watched Miss Durbin closely. The way she held her head as she was introduced to guests at her coming-out party in *Three Smart Girls Grow Up*; her graceful yet determined walk; her whole posture—these have influenced me greatly, and, I am sure, all to the good. As regards fashion, I model the majority of my wardrobe on the clothes Miss Durbin wears. I pride myself they suit me, and therefore I feel confident in myself (for surely you know how much nice clothes go towards a woman's poise and mannerisms!) Naturally, I do not copy the more, shall I say, 'elegant'? fashions of Miss Durbin—they would look out of place and inconsequential under the circumstances in which we live. But not only has Miss Durbin aided me to make my début as a 'woman of the world'. Other films and film stars have helped me too. *Going My Way* made me realise more fully what an awe-inspiring and magnificent thing is religion—as did *The Song of Bernadette*. *Gone with the Wind* (as one example) showed to what great lengths a self-centred woman will go to satisfy her wretched self, and I thereby resolved never to let myself be eaten into by self-complacency. *Claudia* illustrated how a girl can rely too dangerously on her mother—and how, in the end, she gained independence. *Love Story* signified how great love can be between man and woman. All these films, and many more have, in some small way, moulded my character. It is interesting to note that the latter is an English film, and does not embrace the usually fiery type of American romance. I could continue to list 'influential' films far into the night, but hope these I have mentioned will prove sufficient to your needs.

2. I must be honest in answering this question, although my reply is far from exciting. You see, I have never dreamt about any films at all. I sometimes wish I could! But very often I find myself (only in my dreams—unfortunately!) talking and mixing with film stars. Perhaps this personifies the impression movies make on some people? As I am sure they do. It would indeed be an empty world for me and many others if films were suddenly to disappear from the face of the earth.

Particulars you require—

Age—19. Sex—Female. Nationality—British. Profession—Shorthand Typist.

Profession of Parents—Father—Office Clerk. Mother—Housewife —formerly Secretary.

8. Mrs. ....

The University teacher's question was a very interesting one.

I have been going to the cinema since about 1930. With the help of the *Picturegoer* I have chosen the more or less worthwhile films but as yet they have failed to influence me in any way.

The Cinema has the power to influence the people. Of that one is sure. There are so many Betty Grables and Rita Hayworths trotting about.

The films could be a great influence for the good of mankind in future. The Camera is a powerful instrument of taste and could be the means of helping people to understand home and foreign affairs by showing us, how the people of the world live and under what conditions and so on.

During the war it is not necessary to show pictures of bombing and fighting. Most people can imagine the battles only too well. And many know the sound of bombs coming down. After the war, however, it would be a good thing for these photographs to be shown they could influence people who had not experienced war against starting another.

Films such as *Love on the Dole* could also help towards turning the public mind to the help of others less fortunate than themselves.

I would just add that I do sit and sigh for the kind of clothes Ginger Rogers and Lana Turner wear and would also be influenced by the Hollywood home with the pretty curtains and marvellous white kitchens if Mr. Dalton would let me be.

Age 27. Married. Librarian.

9. Miss ...

You ask have films ever influenced people. I would say frankly, no. For instance: The film, *Road to Frisco*.

Ida Lupino. The part was defiantly (definitely?) too far fetched. No woman in thier (their) right sense of mind would think of murdering a perfectly good husband for a ordinary truck driver. Which I think gave Humphrey Bogart an understanding part. Also Ann Sheridan.

In my dreams I have often seen myself play a part such as *Cover Girl*. Rita Hayworth. As I myself am a dancer I too see a possibility of someday making a carrear (career). But Gene Kelly defiantly (definitely) not a lover. But a perfect dance partner.

I hope you understand. It is just my view of what the actors take the wrong part.

I am—Etc—Female.

Age, 18 yrs. Born. Oct. 1926.

English. No Father, Mother. Both English.

I am a dancer. (Ballroom) seven in family. Mother a dressmaker. Two sisters. Tap dancers.

10. Mrs. ...

The film that made a profound impression on me is not by any means a current one but one nevertheless that has remained in many people's memory like myself. To wit *Sorrell and Son* at the time of seeing this film which starred 'J. B. Warner' I was in 'Domestic Trouble' and feeling very morbid and miserable also extremely sorry for myself, after seeing *Sorrell and Son* I came away from the Cinema with a sense of shame and made up my mind to be more courageous, independant and understanding.

The part of 'Sorrell' impressed me so much—such a strong character he had—noble and self sacrificing in spite of his continuous ups and downs and not troubling about false Pride which enabled him eventually to arise above all obstacles.

I tried to do the same—in fact did and found my many vicissitudes gradually disappearing and so feel grateful to the film *Sorrell and Son* and the actors who made it possible to impress an individual.

Age 50—Housewife and Part Time Red Cross Worker.
English—(Parents deceased) Mother was a School teacher. Father Registrar Births and Deaths.

11. Miss . . .
A film which influenced me greatly into a way out of my troubles was *The Song of Bernadette*. It showed faith, courage and endurance, Bernadette had to endure many criticisms, sneers and great physical pain, but she had the courage to go on and an unshakeable faith in her beliefs.

This particular film helped me in this way. I loved a man very much although my parents objected to him, I still went around with him, because I loved him so much I could not bear to ever think of staying away from him.

Eventually my dreams were shattered in one day when I found he was only having a game with me, he no longer wanted me, that I was just another girl in his life. I was so upset I wanted to take my life that day. My mother knew I was cut very deeply so she asked me to go to the pictures, the picture was *The Song of Bernadette*. I didn't think then, that I should feel differently afterwards. I begun to realise as I watched the picture that the way out was to have faith in God to ask Him for courage to go on with my everyday task as Bernadette did. She endured great pain but she triumphed over all in the end, and peace rested with her, I knew if I asked God for strength and courage to overcome my difficulties I should find peace also. I can now say I have done so, Faith, Strength and Courage is what everyone needs during these very trying times especially for those who are bereaved through enemy action, they need *The Song of Bernadette*.

Age—19 yrs. Sex—Woman. Nationality—British.
Fathers Profession—Machinist.
Mothers Profession—Housewife.
My Profession is Machinist.

12. Miss . . .
There is no doubt at all that films have influenced me from a very early age. In fact, the influence started on 10th March, 1916, the night before I was born. Had my mother not gone to a cinema then, and laughed immoderately at a comedy she saw, I would have been able to start life at least three weeks later than I did.

One of Shakespeare's heroines says a star danced when she wa:
born. I should like to know what antics Mamma's star performec
in the comedy she saw, but she has forgotten.

However, after making my appearance a trifle too soon, I wa:
kept so busy growing curly hair, getting teeth, and learning tc
walk and talk, that I had to refrain from further film going till I
had reached the age of three years. By this time my father, a
carpenter, was no longer with us, and I was sufficiently mature tc
be aware of this, and also of the fact that although my mother,
grandmother and myself were all British, I differed from them in
being 25 per cent Scots as well. In order to give the rest of the
personal data asked for, I will take this opportunity of mentioning
now that I went out to work as a Shorthand-typist when I was 16,
and I still follow this occupation, only for the last three years it has
been done in the W.R.N.S. My mother has never had a profession,
other than the very strenuous job of looking after house and family.

Well, at three years old, I saw the first film I am able to remember, which was a serial called *The Brass Bullet*. At the beginning of
each instalment a big bullet and a long bright flash used to zip
across the screen, and I always watched out for this. Then I got a
little older and we saw some horrific films about Sherlock Holmes,
and one frightened me so much that although not yet of school
age, I was influenced to make my first personal decision with
regard to films. I decided to stay home with my grandmother and
be read to while Mamma went and saw the frightening things.

Presently my courage came back again and we saw one movie
a week, including most of the Rudolph Valentino successes. When
I was about 7, I used to act being 'The Sheik' in the back garden
with my little playmate who had parents on the stage. She used to
like me to be very strong and silent while she did a dance for my
delight. When I was between 10 and 11, I was allowed to go twice
a week to the pictures, the second time usually being by myself.
I developed a taste for foreign silent films, and often used to see
stories that nowadays would be considered too advanced for young
people. Those were the days—when a sixpence could be laid out
like this—3d. for Cinema ticket, Sweets 2d., and bus one way 1d.

By this time I had chosen some film favourites for myself, first of
all two pretty blonde actresses, one American and the other British,
who acted in gay comedies, and then I wavered for years between
Ivor Novello and William Boyd. In those days Ivor often used to
move me to tears with films like *The Lodger* and *The Rat*. He did
suffer so beautifully. William Boyd was a more cheerful type, and

made me that way, too, I think, even when at the age of 14, I started on a strict slimming routine, inspired by the screen fashion of painfully slender heroines. I called a new puppy I had, 'Skyscraper' after one of William Boyd's films, and I started writing from memory the stories of all the William Boyd pictures I had seen, including dialogue, when talkies came. I made my mother take me to London as a special treat to see *The Leatherneck* which was the first Boyd talkie, and my first talkie, too.

Now, in spite of being quite 13 or 14, I reverted to being frightened by a film again—this time *Dracula*. For months after seeing this I refused to sleep without a light, which I kept on my bedroom mantlepiece in front of my film star's signed photos. Postcards of film stars, movie magazines and theme songs for piano playing were heavy items in my pocketmoney budget.

Only once so far, can I remember copying a movie fashion, a rather nice sailor collar worn by Marie Wilson, a Warner Bros. feature player, in a film where she was acting the part of a scatter-brained typist. The healthy habit of gargling I learned from films, after seeing Conrad Nagel in a silent film where he was the husband of Myrna Loy. *Rigoletto*, the first opera I saw, was the result of hearing Grace Moore sing a song from it in one of her pictures, but I didn't like *Rigoletto* and it was about eight years after that I discovered opera properly for myself.

All kinds of dancing appealed to me, and after seeing Fred Astaire tap-dancing in *Follow the Fleet* I went to 'Dancing to Health' classes, learned quite a lot for myself, and still sometimes do small parts in amateur shows.

I have noticed that amusing books and plays make me laugh more heartily than screen comedies, but on the other hand I can cry more readily at a sad film, afflicting book, or grand opera, than I can at plays.

I don't believe films have ever influenced me to the extent of going by them for guidance in matters of love, manners or divorce; not yet, anyhow. I am told by my mother, and have some slight recollection of it myself, that when asked, as a little girl, what I would do if she died, I said 'Oh, I'd put a wreath on your grave and go to the pictures!' but I think I was just being contrary.

If I had money and time enough for a course of psycho-analysis, I am sure I would be tempted to have a course of treatment like Ginger Rogers and Bette Davis did in their respective films *Lady in the Dark* and *Now Voyager*, but I don't think I really need it.

My dreams are not usually about any films, but sometimes in

them I find myself behaving more or less naturally with some actor or actress, though the ones I meet in my dreams are not as a rule ones I care about when awake. None of my dreams are in the monochrome some authorities say dreams are made of—it's technicolour for me.

I cannot give titles of any films I've dreamed about, even though I've sometimes been considerably disconcerted to find I am apparently in a cinema that has a screen at both ends, with two films running simultaneously. It's been so hard, trying to look at both of them at once.

13. Mrs. ....

When I saw *Jane Eyre* I was taken with the great love of Jane for Rochester—even when he was in a terrible state, her love did not falter. I decided to love my husband like that whatever he did to upset me. I have, and in consequence his love for me has grown, and he has become more faithful to me. Whenever I find myself tired and nervy, and most irritable, I think of Jane, and her love and sweetness and desist. That film helped me more than any sophistry could have done.

I saw a film *In Which We Serve*, I often have dreams in which I am in the icy water clinging with frozen fingers to the side of the upturned boat. In my dream I am never saved, but sink down, gasping to the bottom.

Age, 49. English; Housewife.

Father a schoolmaster, mother housewife.

14. Miss ...

My answers to your two questions in *Picturegoer* Feb. 3rd are as follows:

(1) I am a very regular film-goer and have been to the cinema at least once a week since I was three weeks old. My average now is twice a week.

Fashions influence me more than anything else on the screen. I am quite skilfull with my fingers and make most of my own clothes. With a fashion book one only sees a dress, skirt or coat, but on the screen a star presents a whole ensemble. Therefore a better idea is obtained as to whether the style presented is practicable or suitable only for dressy occasions. It prevents a *faut pas* (*faux pas*) in accessories. One small error in judgement and an outfit is ruined.

For example, in *Laura* a recent film, Gene Tierney wore a striped short coat, tied with a belt at the waist, worn over slacks.

I thought the idea smarter and more practicable than a dressing gown or housecoat. Technicolour influences me as regards colour schemes. To quote a recent example, the brilliant reds and purples in *Kismet*. I had never dreamt of wearing purple until now (my colouring is dark).

I prefer films which deal with real people—biographies. They prove how a person will struggle and fight for an ideal, and whether it is worth it or not. Such as *Louis Pasteur*; *Emile Zola*; *Madam Curie* and particularly *The Story of Dr. Wassell*.

Films do not influence me very much as regards Love. I have very definite ideas on that subject and am not easily influenced. There are certainly not many screen heroes whom I would care to possess as a lover or husband. I do believe in divorce though. To my mind it is absurd for a couple to carry on together, if they are hopelessly at cross-purposes. Of course where children are concerned, it involves deep and serious thought. I think this subject is treated too flippantly on the screen, such as *Marriage is a Private Affair*.

However, I am influenced as regards etiquette. The type of clothes to be worn at different social functions; the correct and most interesting method of laying a table for a dinner. The correct wines with different meats and fishes; the correct use of cutlery.

All this can be learnt much better by keen observation of a film than merely reading from a book.

I think that children could be educated better by films—educational, of course, and especially prepared, not the incorrect Hollywood editions. (I am referring to history here.) A far better method and more interesting than learning solely from books. Films can present subjects in a more intriguing way. History and Geography can live, instead of being a succession of dates and rivers and towns, etc.

As regards the portrayal of children, films go from the sublime to the ridiculous. They are presented as precocious brats, such as the 16 yr. old child portrayed by Ann Gillis in *Meet the Stewarts* or stupidly good-natured, but still managing to come through with flying colours as acted by Jimmy Lydon in the 'Henry Aldwich' series. I think that Mickey Rooney and Judy Garland, and Cecilia Parker, and the rest of the 'Hardy family' are as true to life as possible in a film. Their types of homes, and ways of living in the 'Andy Hardy' series often make me very envious.

In films the good-looking hero invariably wins the good-looking girl (to quote any film). While I think that in real life it seems that a handsome man picks a plain girl and vica versa. (The logical reason for this occurence seems to me that one partner can then enjoy the limelight unchallenged and always have a permanent devotee!)

(2) Films very rarely appear in my dreams, unless they present an idea that appeals to me strongly such as the clever dancing of Zorina in any of her films, or the skating of Sonja Henie in any of her films; or arouse a deep emotional feeling such as the *Story of Dr. Wassell*.

A lone star can appear in a film occasionally. Usually the same one—Nelson Eddy. I don't suffer from repression, but I have liked him from the day he first stepped onto the screen, and his place in my affections has not yet been usurped or even threatened. Blonde men hold more attraction for me than a dark man ever could. (I myself am very dark, but fair-skinned.)

A nightmarish situation will often penetrate a dream, such as *The Cat and the Canary*. Or a very lively film will make me feel brighter in myself and a dreamless sleep usually follows; or if I dream, it is to go through all the actresses antics myself. To quote any gay musical such as the 'Broadway Melody' series, or *Step Lively* etc.

I can attain the limelight in a dream, which I can never hope to do in real life.

I can also win a hero in a dream, which certainly wouldn't happen in real life.

Born 1921. British nationality.
Profession. C.I.A. (Government Inspector)
Fathers profession—Engineer.
Sex. Female.

15. Mr. . . .

I felt I had to write to you in responce (response) to the announcment (announcement) in *Picturegoer*.

A few days ago I had a dream in which appeared a scene from *Sahara*.

The scene was the one where the German plane is brought down, and the Nazi Pilot is captured by Humphrey Bogart, and four others, odd, since I saw the film some twelve months ago.

The Song of Bernadette remained in my memory a long time after I had seen it.

It brought me closer to the church and all it stands for. Maybe it was the acting, I think it was the whole picture itself, anyhow

too (to) my mind it was the best film I have ever seen—and I go to the cinema three to four nights a week—every week.
(Male, British, age 17, non-profession)

16. Mr. ....

Reading the *Picturegoer* one day I saw in your column that you were inviting readers to give their views on the effects of films on character and moral disposition. So being a very ardent fan, and thinking myself quite a critic I decided to send you my opinion which I hope will be of some use to you.

I am 28 years of age, British, sex—male. I have served 9 years in the Hotel trade, from a page-boy to a waiter. The war years took me into the engineering trade. My father spent most of his life in the theatrical world. Mother was a chorus-girl. So you see that I have some relationship with the acting profession, which possibly accounts for my being an awful dreamer and sentimentalist.

Up to the age of 14 years, due to my fathers work, I saw a lot of the stage, which made me always appreciate a good show. Then, when I started to work I began to see quite a few pictures each week, and these made a very great impression on me. Through the passing years there flowed before my eyes countless visions of beautiful scenes, and wonders of this universe. Of the peoples, their way of living and fight against nature, their character, and temperament. Stories from the Bible, and History book, from the classics of our time, were brought before us forcefully, vividly, in all their glory. Truly this was something realy (really) amazing, that the stage could never produce, even in small measure. And what variety, one could listen to the best the world could offer, for a fee of a few pence.

The great picture, *All Quiet on the Western Front*, showed to me the horror and futility of war. It imprinted on my mind a picture that no book or talk could analyse to my young mind.

'Ramon Navarro' in most of his films (*In Gay Madrid*) was a great influence of my trying to be chivalrous, polite, and understanding to women.

The many *Crime Does Not Pay* films have shown me to appreciate, and respect the law.

My early life was a period of moving to different apartments culminating in the death of my mother, and it is only of late that I have started to enjoy the love of the family, and intimacys (intimacies) of home life. But before that I would catch glimpses of that atmosphere in films such as *Skippy*, the 'Deana (Deanna)

Durbin', and last but not least, the 'Hardy Family' series. These, I can assure you are of the pattern that I would like to shape my family life. I definately (definitely) think that indirectly the films have been the greatest medium for consolidating and strengthening the bonds of social welfare in the homes, throughout the world.

Again as far as morality is concerned they do much good. I think I am a normal type of fellow. I like a certain amount of fun. Especially now and then to indulge in courting, and having a kiss or hug, which is only natural. Well I have seen me in this mood going to see a good, sound emotional film like *The Song of Bernadette*, or of a lighter vein, *Hold Back the Dawn*. This type of film makes a very profound impression on me with the result that I come out of the pictures with an entirely different perspective towards the girl, of having a better respect for her. This of course is only temporary, but deep down the memory still remains to be revived, so you can see what an influence films have on me.

Yes I believe that films have taught me much of what I respect and appreciate today. I only wish the film industry would realise what a potent weapon they have for the propagation of world understanding and everlasting Peace.

17. Miss . . .

With reference to Question 1: 'Have films ever influenced you with regard to personal decisions or behaviour? (love, divorce, manners, fashion etc.)

(1) When I was younger, people often teased me about my mouth, saying how very large it was. Naturally I grew very conscious of the fact and used to feel that everyone noticed it and when introduced to anyone I felt quite certain that they were thinking of it and would point me out to others as 'the girl with the large mouth'.

About 1937, when I was 13, I saw the film *Wings of the Morning* and there was something about the way Annabella moved her lips that fascinated me. When I got home that night I tried doing it myself i.e. speaking like her. After a bit of practice I was convinced it made my mouth look smaller, so I kept it up. It didn't alter my voice at all, merely drew my lips more together at the ends so nobody noticed the change then.

Whether or not this had any effect I am unable to say, but from that time onwards I ceased to think of my mouth being extra wide and nobody has since pointed the fact out, nor have any of my more intimate friends noticed this, *but* my mouth is definitely smaller and I could send photographs to prove this.

Possibly the reason is that in growing up one's features alter slightly or perhaps I made myself believe that by imitating 'Annabella's mouth' my mouth would automatically in time become smaller.

That, I think is the only thing that has directly influenced me.

There are several catch phrases which I now use, from films. Two chief ones in my case being 1, 'I am in no position to demur' (?) (meaning to disobey), from Mickey Rooney in a Judge Hardy film, this is sometimes my reply when asked to do something I do not particularly wish to do but know I must.

The other 2, 'What watch?' ('Ten watch',) 'Such much?' from the conversation of the old German would be English couple in *Casablanca*, used frequently when I ask someone the time.

I don't think that these however have much to do with the question.

Films of great men and women have always impressed me, notably *Stanley and Livingstone*, *The Magic Bullet* and others of a similar nature but they haven't influenced me, they have usually left me with a 'good', satisfied feeling of life.

So much for Question 1.

Question 2: 'Have films ever appeared in your dreams'.

I go to the cinema about 3 or 4 times a month and regularly dream every night, but have never had a dream with anything clear from a film in it.

I once dreamt I was stabbed in the throat by a Russian in an Underground passage, which somehow I associate with a film I saw in 1936 or 7 about some prisoners of war digging a tunnel and escaping, but the dream was probably due to too much cheese at supper.

I had a very vivid dream some years ago about Deanna Durbin, when she was at the peak of her career. I thought she was wonderful and used to travel 20 or 30 miles to see her films and always read all I could about her. I dreamt I was invited to her house and remember seeing a white wooden fence in front of the house and being introduced to her mother and father and dog 'Tippy'. I forget now what we said in the dream or anything else about it now. At the time it seemed very real and natural and not at all extraordinary.

Age: 19 yrs. Sex: Female. Nationality: British.
Occupation: Clerk-typist.
Parents Occupation: Mother—Domestic and Prison Wardress.
Father—Station Master on S. Rly.

18. Miss . . .

I am a shorthand-typist in an office. I get very bored with it and wish I was experienced enough to enable me to get a post as a private-secretary, But it seems that'll have to wait. My mother is a housewife, and my father is a merchant, he deals in various lines and is independant.

I am very fond of films, and for the past two years, have developed a 'pash' for Bette Davis. I have not tried to copy her in any way, as I think it would be an impossibility to do it successfully.

I have dreamt of her a few times. I often think of her, and my thoughts usually wander to how I should ever have the chance of meeting her. I really get some of the most fantastic notions, but however although I realize that, I still like her very much, and the thoughts still persist in coming. I am not like this over any other star, and rather envy them all.

I love to talk about her to other people, and especially to people who like her also.

Whether I get a prize or not, I should like you to answer this, and tell me whether I am wrong in this, or whether it is a natural thing. Please tell me anything you can about it.

19. Miss . . .

At first I thought this question seemed easy, because I cannot remember a time when films did not form part of my everyday conversation and affect my whole outlook on life. But although there are many logical down-to-earth plots and true-to-life backgrounds in films today, I do not think any of them have ever influenced a decision of mine.

Even fashions, passionate love scenes, and educational 'shorts' have not made such an impression that I am conscious of it; but I still think that, although it may be indirectly, films definitely influence most people who visit the cinema more than twice a month.

The books and plays I have read after seeing the screen adaptations are innumerable. These include *Quality Street* (except for *Peter Pan* I had never read J. M. Barrie before), *Fire Over England, Show Boat, Jamaica Inn, Man in the Iron Mask, Mr. Deeds Goes to Town, McLeod's Folly*—(James Cagney in *Johnny Vagabond*), *Yank at Oxford* and these are only a few.

It is really interesting to be able to imagine a flesh-and-blood character rather than the shadowy image created by the author's ethereal description.

Music, of course, owes much of its popularity to films. By merely listening to various people whistling in the street it is easy to guess which film is on at the local cinema.

Here we had *Irish Eyes are Smiling* last week, and consequently there were many repetitions of the theme song being whistled from Monday to Saturday.

In remembrances of childhood days films also have a certain significance—to me at least. The first time I ever went to what was known as the 'second house' (when there were no continuous programmes) I saw *Red Waggon*, and although the memory of the film itself is anything but clear it is always connected with the thrill of 'staying up late' experienced at that time.

Altogether, even if only in these unimportant instances, it seems that films have an influence on my life, although perhaps just occasionally.

The second question is less difficult, as I have quite frequently dreamed of films and film stars.

The most vivid dream of all was about the *Seventh Cross*, just after I saw it last December—perhaps because I was so impressed by Spencer Tracy's really 'inspired' performance. The dream was not disconnected, but continued—as in the film itself, with a harassing sense of danger, until the final escape of Spencer Tracy, and the sea washing against the ship in which he was going to sail.

There was another dream quite recently, not so clear and about no film that I remember, but the scene was a wide plain (perhaps a prairie, but with distant pine trees, a shining stretch of water and hills) with a wild looking tribe of Indians led by Anthony Quinn—about to attack Gary Cooper and another man whom I did not recognise, Gary Cooper, of course, escaped, and was next seen with Claudette Colbert on a ship, sailing down a river which was likely to break its banks at any moment.

I have also dreamed of Betty Grable in *Sweet Rosie O'Grady*, and, years ago, of Katherine Hepburn in *Little Women*, but the majority of the dreams are less vivid than those mentioned.

Age 22. Sex, Female. Nationality, English.

Profession, Insurance Clerk.

Profession of Parents, Father—Water Inspector.

Mother—Home duties.

20. Miss . . .

Dreams: Recently I dreamt a part of the film entitled *Maddona* (Madonna) *of the Seven Moons*. The only connection of the film was the Sign of the Seven Moons. I don't know exactly as its some time since I've seen it. I saw it when it first came to be released. I never dreamt any other part of the film at all at least I don't remember. It was just the sign the thing she drew with her lipstick on the Mirror. What broke my dream was that when glancing at the evening papers at the amusements and seeing the Letter '7' imediatly (immediately) thought 7 moons and I remember something about it. All I can recall doing in the dream is that I kept drawing the Sign on Something as 'Miss Calvert' did in the film. The strange part is why it come in my dream if you can call it a dream as it is the only thing I remember about it. I kept seeing the Sign continually and each time I saw it it got bigger each time. I can't remember even how it ended yet, there was no other connection with the film. It was just the Sign of the Seven Moons. It was funnier still when a Couple of Days later I should read the Editor's Column a piece about whether or not anyone had dreamt anything of films.

2. The film that stood out in my mind was the film *Jane Eyre*. It reminded me of a lot of things Home, as my Mother was in the same Condition as Orson Welles first wife was. But I could see the agonies of the Husband in the film being tortured by the memory of his first wife still living and in that condition—and kept under lock and key, from the outside world, trying to conceal the tragedy from the outside world. It reminds you of a prison a Dungeon. Horrible. The fact of Jane Eyre entering his life made him live again. But he could not shut out of his mind (his first wife) and she was still living—and the Law forbids any man to remarry while his wife is still living, no matter the circumstances. My Father may have wanted to remarry but my Mother has been away 9 years now, and my Father Has never wanted to remarry my (mother?) went when I really needed her. I missed her more than anything. Now I find while I'm in the Forces, I get miserable at times and you feel you could go to a Mother tell her how you feel. Not like going to your Commanding Officer a lot of Help they give you. But the strange thing is I can't remember much about my Mother and what she was like. I seemed to forgotten everything. I sincerely feel sorry for anyone that had a Mother and lost her at an early age. You feel it most then. I've met girls that don't seem to care anything for Home. They take it for granted. They'll realise one day wot (what) they've missed of Home. That picture brought back a lot of things especially of Home. In that Childs life of *Jane Eyre* it could really happen. There is only one wish I'd like to

fulfill. That is to take my Mother out on a rest or vacation. Buy Her things and give Her a wonderful time and make up for all the things she Has lost. But thats a thing I shall never fulfill because I can't see my Mother ever being well enough on this earth. It was the part of where his wife was mad in the film that brought it all back to me. Not a pleasant thing you would say but I dont mind it as so far (?) I'll not completely forget her. But when you dont see Her you are apt to do so. It upsets me too much to go. Thats the reason I dropped of (off) going. Seeing her looking so blank and not knowing me I felt I was powerless to do anything. But one important thing is I like to remember Her. As she was. Not as she is. Hope I Havent Bored you by writing this. Its the only film thats ever brought it to mind and a lot of Memories.

P.S. Hope I've not put to (too) much of a personal side in this letter.

Sex: Female. Age: 23. Nationality: British.

Profession: Art in civil life. Tele-typist in the Service.

Father: Now in Leather Manufactures.

Mother: Art. Not professionally.

21. Miss ...

(1) *'Have films ever influenced you with regard to personal decisions or behaviour? Can you give instances?'*

On the first reading of the question I should certainly say 'no', but on further thought, I should say to an extent 'yes'.

With regard to setting an example in fashions films tend to show quite a large amount of influence on women, particularly with regard to hair styles, when one considers the number of Greta Garbo bobs, 'Maria' cuts, Peek a boo bangs, and Colbert fringes one meets in the streets; also clothes, as quite a number of styles are often displayed in windows with stills showing the frock, etc., as being worn by so and so, in so and so; and in the height of their career, one saw rows and rows of Shirley Temple and Deanna Durbin clothes for children. Yes, I think one can say in the matter of fashion films have influenced women to quite a large extent though whether it is for better or worse is rather doubtful. I cannot see however, that in this respect it has affected men at all.

Though I should not imagine the immediate influence of a film is often felt, it may make itself felt in time, as they certainly tend to make you think, and a decision arrived at later may subconsciously be the result of something seen on the screen. Also films dealing with a problem, such as *Blossoms in the Dust, Boys Town,*

The Good Earth, and *The Primrose Path*, all bring different aspects of life before you, and afterwards you start to think about it, 'To Start you Talking' in fact. After seeing a travel film about Sweden, I wanted to know more about that country, and borrowed some books out of the Library describing it. Also after seeing any famous novel on the screen, *Vanity Fair*, *The Little Minister*, *Wuthering Heights*, *Pride and Prejudice*, etc., if it isn't one I am familiar with, I want to read it, for whereas on the shelf it might have looked a bit heavy and rather dull, with Greer Garson as the heroine and Lawrence Olivier as the hero it seems entirely different. Though having seen the film first you tend to take their interpretation of the author's ideas instead of your own, as you can see the film stars as the character all the time.

In the more serious matters of life, Love, Marriage, Divorce, etc. films often tend to show too flippant an aspect, by making divorce appear too easy, and as too frequent an occurrence in normal life, though whether this has anything to do with the growing number of cases at the Divorce Court sessions, is I should imagine, rather open to speculation. This point is illustrated by such films as *Casanova Brown*, *Marriage is a Private Affair*, *Escape to Happiness*, *Made for Each Other*, and *Midnight*. Though this type of film is usually of the comedy type, and is not meant to be taken seriously, also the circumstances that arise, and seem to disrupt the marriage, would not often be likely to occur in normal life.

As films have to get through a whole story in rather a short time, it is only natural that characters have to get to know one another straight away, and thus do away with more formal introduction (James Brown and Jean Heather in *Going My Way*) and this in turn is copied by most young people today. But on the whole film stars polite manners (Charles Boyer) or their opposite (Gary Cooper in *Bluebeard's Eighth Wife*) do not seem to have much effect on the average young man, which in the latter case is perhaps just as well. As one mother once said, she didn't mind her daughter copying Marlene Dietrich, or Greta Garbo, but was there ever any hope of junior turning into Robert Taylor about the house?

Yes, films have definitely come to stay, and as your mind will probably retain a small amount of what you see on the screen, I should imagine that it is only natural that you are influenced by it when you come to make a decision, but let us hope it will not be a case of 'The evil that men do lives after them, the good is oft interred with their bones'.

(2) *'Have films ever appeared in your dreams?'*

My answer to that question is definitely 'yes'. A few years ago I was a very keen fan of Claudette Colbert, and in the first flush of infatuation could think of little else day or night. As I went to bed thinking of her and the latest film I had seen her in, it was only natural in my dreams, they should both appear.

Any film I enjoy I tend to live over again afterwards, and then in my sleep I see it again. Not as a continuous film, but snatches of it, with yourself generally in it, on awakening you couldn't definitely say of what you had been dreaming, but you are left with the impression it was the film you saw the night before, or one of your favourite stars' films. These are very pleasant dreams, but all films do not produce such pleasant thoughts, particularly war films such as *Bataan*, *The Story of Dr. Wassell* etc. And I know of one child who after seeing *Mrs. Miniver* was so terrified by the air raid scenes, that she woke up three or four times during the night screaming with terror.

Sometimes for no apparent reason you dream of a film, a part of which you very much enjoyed and subconsciously retained in your mind; or an odd sentence heard, or picture or cutting, seen during the day, may recall a film to your mind for a moment, and then in your sleep it will come back to you again. Any film I have enjoyed will do that for me, say *Top Hat*, or *Goodbye Mr. Chips*, films you do not enjoy or just bore you, you tend to forget very quickly, which is probably just as well.

Age 22. Nationality, British. Occupation—shorthand typist. Father—Insurance Claims Inspector. Mother—teacher.

22. Mr. ...

An ardent filmgoer since the early days of Cinema I can recall no instance of a film encouraging me to make any important personal decision. I was, however, inspired during adolescence by the antics of the late Douglas Fairbanks, snr. I tried to imitate his personal mannerisms and emulate his athletic prowess in the mistaken belief that I could, so achieve an extra strength and self reliance—(at the time I suffered from exaggerated feelings of inferiority).

Since those days, I have never consciously desired to imitate anything admired in others, on the screen.

Whereas my early cinegoing was largely a matter of 'escapism', to-day choice has supplanted habit. What concerns me now is enjoyment through interest, not escape through fantasy. I now

seek interest through appraisement and analysis. The appreciation
of good acting, imaginative lighting, interestingly authentic decor
and wardrobe, evocative 'cutting', the expressive use of sound and
dialogue—in short, seeing films 'whole' motivates my present day
picturegoing. It is the content and manipulation of a film that now
interests me and not merely that a film can provide a temporary
escape from a reality which is, in nine cases out of ten, largely
self-created.

Having grown up with the Cinema my understanding and
appreciation of it has matured just as the Cinema has, in many
ways, itself matured. It was during the pre-talkie period of the
so-called 'Golden Era' of German and Swedish production, that
I first became aware of the *real* possibilities inherent in the film as
an art, and a mental and cultural stimulus. The notorious *Cabinet
of Doctor Caligari*, for instance, excited my imagination because, for
me it opened up new vistas of a fascinating and undreamed of
significance.

'Caligari' is said to have changed the whole outlook of cinema,
and I believe that it *did*.

I will admit that my first impressions here were largely bound
up with childhood wonder and excitation experienced through
Grimm's fairy tales. I think 'Caligari' re-created for me those
perhaps rather unhealthy delights, connected somehow with fear,
i.e. the fascination of weirdness, dark forests, witches, hobgoblins,
magic, sinister castles, and, in fact, the frighteningly suggestive
in general.

And yet it was *through* such films as *Caligari*, *Waxworks*, *The
Student of Prague*, *The Golem*, *Nosferatu* (*Dracula*), etc., etc. that I
was subsequently to acquire a more objective understanding of
what artistic and constructive film entertainment could mean.
They gave me my first insight into the true potentialities of
Cinema.

To-day, I visit films less often, and when rare and culturally
valuable ones such as *Citizen Kane*, *Earth*, *The Grapes of Wrath*,
etc. do become available I try to see them as often as possible
before they disappear—possibly for ever.

In answer to your question regarding fashions and manners, it
is obvious, and especially with regard to women, how greatly the
screen has influenced and encouraged consciousness of and interest
in personal appearance and behaviour. Women have learned the
value of attractive clothing and make-up in the development of
poise and self confidence, or at least a sense of it, for I notice that

people influenced by such things frequently fail to adopt them with any real degree of success.

Misapplication, resulting in artificiality rather than attractiveness seems all too often the inevitable result. Finger nails and hair 'do's' are not necessarily indicative of character or self reliance, or even of good taste.

Personally, I cannot say that I have been influenced in any way here. I believe that *real* poise and self confidence result from an objective rather than a subjective attitude to life. I would far rather be my natural self (at least as far as I am capable of being), than a second rate edition of some movie idol I admired, or might happen, faintly to resemble.

Love and divorce do not apply to me. For one thing I have never really *been* in love, and for another I do not believe that the screen exercises so much influence with morals as seems generally to be supposed.

So now to dreams. I believe that few people dream about the films they see, but I can recall (though of necessity, only partially) dream experiences the content of which included the Cinema in one form or another, although I have never dreamed of any particular film. When I have dreamed about Cinema, the building itself seems always to have been included. Sometimes it has been curved in shape, (which is when I have been *inside*), and sometimes square, and rather aggressively strong looking, (and then I have been *outside*). Recognising, in my limited understanding of Freudian psychology, that 'shape' has significance in dreams, I draw, or imagine I draw, the obvious conclusion here. I have also dreamt of meeting 'stars' personally, and having them regard my criticisms of their work and of Cinema in general as something to marvel at.

I certainly do feel that the Cinema can and does exercise considerable, and probably far reaching influence on individual psychology, and mainly in the sense that many filmgoers tend unconsciously to identify themselves with pictured characters and emotional situations. More briefly, many of us see ourselves in the movies we like.

I think, for example that it is possible to read into films the things we would really like to *do* and *be*. But are the things we enjoy *really* projections of the hidden truths about us? I cannot arrive at a decision about this.

I do think about it, but I really do not know. I would very much like to determine just why I believe my initial reactions to say

Caligari, or *Warning Shadows,* or perhaps *The Street* or *The Last Laugh,* would not be repeated were I able to see them again to-day.

I might still enjoy them as museum pieces, and in a nostalgic sort of way, but would, somehow be unable to 'recapture the first fine careless rapture'. This overlong letter must now end.

I hope you will gather at least something from it that is worthwhile to you. I expect there are many things I have failed to remember, and probably from your own point of view the most important ones of all, but, on the spur of the moment, it is the best I can do in the time at my disposal. I have tried to be truthful about it, but how often can one be *satisfied* that one has succeeded in being *really* truthful? As a psychologist, you will probably arrive at a much truer solution to this problem than I myself am at all capable of achieving.

Age—44. Sex—Male. Nationality—British. Profession—Shopkeeper—(now in costing office of war factory).

Profession of Father—Builder. Mother—originally a court dressmaker.

23. . . .

On perusing your two questions, my immediate answer for both was in the negative. But then I began to think—perhaps films had influenced my life and personality unconsciously. I am a very ardent filmgoer. Before I became so keenly interested in the cinema I was a shy, retiring person, and very quiet: could never think of anything to say. The cinema taught me that shyness was unattractive, and that loquacious, communicative people got the most out of life, especially popularity. So I changed (let it be presumed unconsciously). I became more easy in my manner, more loquacious, and I made many more friends. Of course all this may have had nothing to do with the cinema—after all it was the period in which I was growing up. Still we'll give it the benefit of the doubt.

Having never had a love affair I cannot pass an opinion. But if I ever do fall in love—and I believe most people do at some time or other—I should want my love to be of the type as portrayed by Bette Davis and Paul Henreid in *Now Voyager,* sincere, all consuming and regardless of all that stood in its way. I call that true, lasting and perfect love.

Sensual love, on the other hand, cannot be ignored—men after all are merely educated animals. This type of love was shown most delicately on the screen by the torrid romancing of Hedy Lamar and Richard Carlson in *White Cargo.* That film taught me that

GREER GARSON IN 'THE VALLEY OF DECISION'

If you are as pretty, clever and kind as she you may easily marry the son of a steel magnate even though you are a housemaid

PAUL HENREID AND BETTE DAVIS IN 'NOW VOYAGER'

even sensuality is an art. As for fashion and manners, I can honestly say that the screen has not touched me in these ways. I'm 'me' and I'd never copy such petty things from anyone else—not even the most glittering star.

So if the cinema has influenced me at all it has done so unconsciously, and never 'bothered' me in the slightest.

I dream often, sometimes vividly, sometimes obscurely. A dream that reoccurs is a scene from *Gone with the Wind*—the one where Scarlet O'Hara falls down a steep flight of stairs. In my dream I see Vivian Leigh hurtling down, clad in that vivid red gown. When she reaches the bottom and is still, I go to touch her and find the red of her gown is of blood. At this point I usually wake up with a horrible sense of morbidity.

Again, sometimes I dream I see Joan Crawford's face as it appeared in *A Woman's Face*—one side disgustingly disfigured. This dream fills me with a strong sense of apprehension and fear, and I wake up with a cold brow.

Otherwise I cannot think of any other 'film' dreams that startle me—and anyway, one has to dream of something.

These are the desired facts:

Sex—male. Age—24. Nationality—British.

Profession—Farming.

Profession of Father—Farming.

Profession of Mother (before marriage)—nursing.

24. Miss . . .

I hope that the following may be of some assistance to you in your research.

My sex: female. Age: 20. Occupation: Student. Nationality: Australian. Parents' Nationality: French and Australian. Profession: Accountant (unless travelling can be called a profession, before marriage my mother had none).

On a few occasions I have dreamed of films. Once, after seeing a horror production, *The Werewolf of London*, I had nightmares in which fear of the 'monster' predominated. My brother and a friend, both aged 9, who saw the film were similarly affected.

L'Orage with Charles Boyer was the first French film I ever saw, and at that time I thought the star better in this than in any American rôle. It was an intensely dramatic story. Anyway, whatever the cause, I dreamed entirely in French that night (I should mention that I speak the language fluently). I do not know what I said, or to whom, but I remember thinking that I was talking a great deal.

If films have influenced me at all, I think it must be from the artistic point of view. I notice and admire all the harmonious settings, especially in Technicolour pictures. Even the make-up of stars (I do not use any myself) or the ugly legs camouflaged with designed stockings, etc. For a clearer example I mention *Blood and Sand*, in which the brilliant colours were so impressive as to be mentally refreshing. Possibly because I am more used to sunny climates.

As a contrast, *Fanny by Gaslight* was so dull in theme and setting that I lost patience and condemned a public that could like such a film. I now dislike all the stars who appeared in it.

With regard to more personal influences, fashion, etc. My answer is 'No'. Although I have known several English girls who have admittedly copied movie stars in many ways, but we (i.e. the family) concluded that it was because they had unimpressive personalities.

I venture to suggest that were you to conduct a similar research in Australia or South Africa (that is, if my experience is at all representative) you would find people were much less film conscious. No one desires earnestly to 'see the stars in the flesh', or to go to Hollywood. If they want to go anywhere it is to England. Despite the unglamorous, unattractive presentation of the country on the screen. May I offer the opinion that this is because in the Dominions our lives are more social, and active, leaving less time for day-dreams.

I trust that I have not been too prolix.

25. Miss . . .

I am 17 years of age and will be 18 on August 24th. I am of British Nationality, and a member of the female sex. My father's profession is that of a Gent's Outfitter, and my Mother has no profession except that of housewife. Having given the information requested I shall now proceed.

In answer to the second question as to whether 'Have films ever appeared in your dreams'—my answer is definitely in the negative.

The first question is rather more difficult to answer. If someone should ask me whether films influence my behaviour with regard to any personal decisions I should be called upon to make, either in love, divorce, manners, fashions, etc., I should answer on the spur of the moment 'Most emphatically not', but on thinking my answer over, I have come to the conclusion that it would not be strictly true. To a certain extent, and perhaps to a very minute degree, my subconscious mind is influenced by a film which had made a deep impression on my mind. But that impression, I can definitely state, would not in any way influence my personal decisions or behaviour. The reason why a number of people go to the pictures, is not only to be entertained, but because they want to escape from their own world into a world of unreality, romance and make-believe, where such things as Income Tax do not exist. Films offer this escape—an escape from reality. However, an intelligent person realises that life is very much different from that presented on the screen, and therefore one is not influenced by such films. However, there are exceptions, and it is to these exceptions that I refer. Occasionally one sees a film which consists of more than just laughter, glamour and romance. To give a specific example the type of film to create an impression, was one which I saw some time ago entitled *Thunder Rock*. Nevertheless I am informed that this film was considered a failure, and was considered too 'interlectual' (intellectual) for the masses. I'm afraid that on that point I disagree and I can only add that the mentality of the average person must be very low if the only type of film which appeals to them is one in which there appears numerous pretty girls and a certain amount of display of the female limbs. The type of film which I have given as an example is the only type which could personally, make an impression on me. Please do not think that I despise the other type of film—that would be incorrect! People go to be entertained, and most films provide this entertainment, but I cannot help but think that it is indeed regrettable and unfortunate that this type of film should make an undesirable impression on the youth of to-day. Girls are, I believe, more inclined to imitate the various film stars and their mannerisms—more so than boys. The result is that a large proportion of girls are influenced to such an extent by what they have seen on the films that the thoughts which are mainly in their minds are namely: the opposite sex, sex appeal or sex allure, how to cultivate it, and love, and therefore their decisions and behaviour is governed to a great extent by what they have seen on the films.

However, I find I have somewhat deviated from my original point which is to state that films have no influence whatsoever with regard to my personal behaviour. Some films I have seen may create an impression but under no circumstances are they applicable to my personal behaviour and decisions.

26. Miss . . .
On reading your article in the *Picturegoer* I decided to give you my views on both questions.

(1) Yes *The Lady in the Dark*, not so much of the dreaming part, but how she always was a second fiddle when a young girl.

It reminded me so much of myself. The way Johnny (I think that was his name) was dancing with Ginger Rogers telling her how lovely she was, telling her she was the kindest girl he'd ever met, and then he said she was a better girl than his other girl friend.

Then his other girl friend came in just said she was sorry for something and he went out to dance with her leaving Ginger Rogers outside on the terrace without saying a word.

I turned away at that just to remember myself being in the same position as Ginger Rogers, several times before I saw that picture. Only of course my own friend being the girl who came in every time to spoil anything I ever thought I had.

I've often wondered whats wrong with me, and thought how I should like to see myself as others see me, so I could know what was wrong, and then check up on the things that are wrong, and so become a little more confidant in myself.

So now I have decided after seeing that film, to do the same as Ginger Rogers (or Liza Elliott as she was called in the picture) did, go about being kind to people, not to take things too seriously, and not to have any fancy clothes, just to be smart and plain as she was, to see if that will help me at all. Many people like me, boys like me for a friend but that isn't love.

In the end of *Lady in the Dark* three men loved her, but I havn't got to the end yet, thats to come.

(2) Yes I have *Rebecca* was the film, I dreamt I was going through the gates Joan Fontaine went through in her dream in the beginning of the film, up the drive to Mandaley.

Afterwards I should be by the sea in my dream, near Mandaley (Manderley), watching the waves dash up against the rocks.

Then I should feel giddy and fall over the edge of the rocks, having the sensation of falling I woke up never reaching the bottom. I've had the same dream twice, and I don't know how long they last, but thats all I dream about *Rebecca*, if they last half an hour.

The Purple Heart I've dreamed about too, but that's just because its horrible and it played on my mind all night till I dreamed about it.

Just the same things happen though, were (where) they cut off one man's hand, and cut another man's tongue out, and all the rest of the horrible business.

Its these sort of pictures you dream about mostly the ghostly and weird ones.

I am 18, Typical English, Clerk.

Father—Surface Foreman at a Colliery;

Mother—ordinary housewife.

27. Miss . . .

Have Films Ever Appeared in Your Dreams?

Yes, films have often appeared in my dreams.

I think films are a wonderful medium of entertainment, one which we should think about a great deal. When I see a beautiful film, as when I see a beautiful play or hear a lovely piece of music at a concert or on the radio, I like to think about it by myself and when I go to bed I dream about them.

For me to think about and therefore to dream about a film, it has to be one of the first class or else to be very unusual. The acting must be good, the voice arresting for me to see or hear them in my dreams. I never dream of slapstick comedy, or even a thrilling murder. When I see a film it may interest me during the couple of hours I am in the cinema, but I may forget it promptly on leaving it. Sometimes, however, I see a film which I like very much, one which I could see again perhaps, on the way home from the theatre I think about it, and at night, asleep, certain scenes will come back to me. Perhaps it will be a line spoken by one of the actors, maybe a glance or gesture.

I can always remember, when I was a child seeing *The Great Ziegfeld*. In those days it was considered spectacular, and in my dreams for many nights afterwards I dreamt of the revolving stage, the glamourous (glamorous) girls and those lovely dogs. In those days too I used to see Shirley Temple a great deal. At night I used to re-live her adventures and unhappy moments. Wonderful things like films have a strange impression on a child's mind, and now that I am seventeen, films still have a great fascination for me.

I went to see *The Man in Grey* some time ago, a picture which I found thoroughly enjoyable and stimulating. At night I kept seeing the terrifying look on James Mason's face as he beat Hester to death. I could not get it out of my dreams for some time.

After I had seen the picture *The Great Waltz*, I did not dream of scenes or people but of the haunting Strauss waltzes. It was the same with *Love Story* when parts of the Cornish Rhapsody appeared in my dreams. Also *The Great Victor Herbert* and *A Song to Remember*.

A week or so ago I saw *Madonna of the Seven Moons*. I enjoyed it and thought about it quite a bit. When you think about a thing a lot before going to sleep, it is likely that you should dream about it. But no! For some reason or other I kept hearing Patricia Roc say when she saw her mother—'It isn't possible, no one could be so lovely'. While on the subject of split minds, I always remember going to see *Dr. Jeckyll and Mr. Hyde* on a foggy night, and having the most terrible nightmare afterwards. I kept seeing the face change from good to bad and vice versa.

After seeing *Blossoms in the Dust*, lilies kept appearing in my dreams. The night after seeing *Since You Went Away* the scene in the hay was re-lived in my dreams.

Rebecca was one of the best films I have ever seen, and therefore quite natural that I should think and dream about it a lot. I often saw in my dreams Joan Fontaine's shy face. And in many of my dreams I saw Laurence Olivier's expression when he told his wife about Rebecca. I heard that wonderful voice saying: 'Do you think I killed her, loving her; I hated her.' It was a wonderful piece of acting.

I think the film I dreamed about more than any other was *Gone with the Wind*. I could see it over and over again and still dream about it. How often did I dream I saw Vivien Leigh as Scarlett O'Hara climb the stairs at Twelve Oaks after telling Ashley that she loved him, she was so proud, so beautiful. How often did I see her treading her way among the wounded in Atlanta. And I could see Melanie's face when she was so ill. A scene I shall never forget was of Scarlett on her return home, standing in the desolate garden and saying 'As God is my witness, I'm never going to be hungry again'. You could not see her face only her silouhette (silhouette).

I dreamed of her also standing in the windy orchard almost at the end of her tether. I saw over and over again Clark Gable's eyes as she fell down the stairs. I dreamt I saw Scarlett entering Melanie's party, in her red dress and her head up, ready for anything. I saw the sweet smile of Bonnie, Mammie's disapproving face, and Gerald's expression as he opened the door to Scarlett.

The scene I saw most was the last one where she lay on the stairs thinking everything she loved most in the world had gone, and she heard the voice of her father, Ashley and Rhett coming to her telling her that Tara was left. I saw her stiffen and say 'After all, tomorrow is another day'. What a lovely ending for a film!

I could go on for ever telling of all the films I have dreamed of, but it would take too long. Films take my mind off things and I can always relax in a cinema. They make me forget this world and live in another. Therefore I like to dream of good films and sometimes I dream that there were more good films to dream about. Don't you?

Have Films ever Influenced You in regard to Personal Decisions and Behaviour

No films have never influenced me in the big moments of my life, only in the small things such as clothes. They do influence my manners and behaviour to a certain extent.

I do not think that what is seen on the screen should have an effect on our personal decisions. After all things that happen on the screen do not always turn out as they do in real life. What goes on in the mind of a script writer cannot always be correct. He is only human.

Films definitely have an influence over me as far as dress and hair styles are concerned. When I saw Gene Tierney wearing a very pretty costume in *Laura* I decided to have it copied. Last week I saw *Madonna of the Seven Moons* and I saw Patricia Roc in a very nice coat which I would like to have made. I hope, too, soon. Films take a lead in fashion and therefore it is only natural that women should copy them.

Films also have an influence on hair styles. When I saw Veronica Lake in *This Gun for Hire*, I tried to copy her hair style. However it did not suit me.

I have not had the luck to go to the Royal Academy of Dramatic Art, but most film stars (if they act and not just look glamorous) have. There they learn to walk, to sit down, to take a coat off and to speak. So to a certain extent I try to benefit by their good points. I shall never look like Vivien Leigh but that is no reason why I shouldn't copy her walk and the way she sways her hips. I shall never act like Greer Garson, but I still try to laugh like she does. There is a right way and a wrong way of holding a cigarette; they do it the right way on the pictures and when I begin to smoke I shall do it like Katherine Hepburn in *Philadelphia Story*.

Having been brought up well and having had a good education, I know good manners and how to behave, and therefore I do not need to be shown by actors and actresses on the screen. In fact more often than not the manners on the American Pictures are atrocious.

Nearly every film has a love interest and if I let them all influence me when I fall in love, I should be in a nasty mess. They contradict each other too much. I do not mean to be heroic, but if I had been in Bette Davis's position in *Dark Victory*, I would not have let the man I love marry me. I think it unfair to both of them. The same in *Love Story*.

Films generally have a happy ending. Life doesn't always. Therefore I will not let a film influence me in my dicisions (decisions). Behaviour yes, because we all like to be something we aren't. Many films are about the eighteenth and nineteenth centuary (century), when manners and the way of life were different. We cannot copy their way of living but we can benifit (benefit) from their good points. When I lost someone very dear to me and I felt the most miserable person in the world, I thought of some of the courageous people I had seen on the screen, and I felt better. I thought of Scarlett O'Hara in *Gone with the Wind*, and all she went through. And I thought of the courage of the soldiers in *The Way Ahead*. They suffered much more than I did but they never lost face.

If I was ever enclined (inclined) to do anything really wicked, or perhaps contemplated murdering someone (which I certainly do not) I should be influenced by some of the really good thrillers I have seen on the screen. There it has been rubbed in that Crime does not pay. Not even very cleverly concealed crime as in *Double Indemnity*.

'We should learn by other people's mistakes' is a well known saying, and so I let the screen influence me in some ways. If a person does something wrong in a film, I should not put my head in the fire by making the same mistake.

Age—17 years. Profession—Junior Clerk. Nationality—British (London). Sex—Female.
Profession of Father—Furrier.

28. Miss . . .

I am writing to answer your questions as I have found that films in certain ways do affect me, as it decides me in fashion but to me love and divorce are yet to seem very unreal on the screen. One film decided me however, it was the film *Lady in the Dark* wherein Ginger Rogers disliked certain things for unknown reasons and dreamed of things she longed to do and dared not until explained by a doctor which were childhood memories grown into an inferiority complex it was like seeing my own thoughts and fears on the screen although somewhat varied, when I had seen this film I had a good laugh at myself for these things now seem stupid and I think there was really nothing for Ginger Rogers to worry about, so why should I. Films have on several occasions appeared in my dreams, not the actors or actresses, it is always people I know and they have been the people in the film but I have acted differently which I think is due to when I see a film the thought is always running through my mind that I wouldn't have said or acted that way, this film was *Dark Waters* and in my dream I didn't run out to the trouble but just 'phoned the police, it is always dramatic films that I dream about. I have explained how films affect me, my age is 20 years and I am conscripted to a munition factory my nationality is English, my mother is a housewife, my father a night supervisor.

29. Miss . . .

I cannot answere (answer) naming the films in question 1. but quite a few have influenced my clothes but not the others.

As for question 2 I can name quite a lot, but first I'd like to explain why I dream about films. Nearly always before going to sleep I tell myself a story made up by myself about school, hospital or a guardian, etc. (sometimes I get so interested I do'nt sleep for ages!) Other times I remodel a film I have like(d) to suit myself and put myself in it. Funnily enough they are nearly always English films I dream about, not because I don't like American ones, but English actors fit in better with me!

During the last year I have dreamt about *The Man in Grey*, *Rebecca* (I know that's a US one), *Headline*, *Pimpernel Smith*, *49th Parallel* and *A Canterbury Tale*. Not about all the film just sceans (scenes) from it.

1. I am 21. 2. Female. 3. English. 4. Firewoman. 5. Mother Norwegain. 6. Father English. 7. Mother's profession: none. 8. Fathers Mining Engineer.

P.S.—I can't spell.

30. Mr. . . .

No. 1. The remake of the *Constant Nymph*, tells you how a young girl in Pigtails falls for an older man than herself, who is a composer. The same thing has happened to me. It was last year when I went to a big job, in the Isle of Man, My Landlady had a beautiful Daughter, who was no more than 16, she was also in pigtails, and she fell head over heels in love with me. I tried to avoid her, but couldn't, until I came across to England again, she still writes to me, I am not a composer, but I am a great lover of music, any kind of music, I sometimes make up little tunes in my head, I think it is a coincidence. Well, to get to the next question.

No. 2. Yes Mr Lecturer, do you remember a film called, *The Farmer Takes a Wife*, with Janet Gaynor and Henry Fonda. Well I dreamt one night of that film, there I was, looking through a wooden fence, than all of a sudden Janet Gaynor is there looking at me, and then I woke up, I can recall another film, *Blood and Sand*, which co-starred Tyrone Power, and Linda Darnell, I got my chest burned, although it wasn't serious. Well I dreamt one night of *Blood and Sand*, when the famous Matador Tyrone Power gets gored to death, then all of a sudden I woke up, and soon discovered my chest was sore alright (all right), not from a Bull's horn, but from that burn I had at work. Well Mr Lecturer thats about all I can say.

I am 26 years of age, (Male) I am a 3rd Class Cook. I am a Scotsman, Mother is a native of Ireland, My Father is Scottish, My Mother was a nurse before marrying my Father.

My Father got killed after the last war, he was a Soldier, he never had the chance to make a proffession (profession).

31. Master . . .

In my opinion, the cinema has a great influence on public opinion, and fashion, a great number of films influence the everyday experiences of filmgoers. For instance, a hat, worn by a film star, is copied by the people of my town. This was much more apparent before the war. The hats of Ginger Rogers were seen among crowds on a market day. With regards myself clothes of film stars have had little effect on me. The way a film star buttons his coat may have caught my eye. Perhaps, the greatest influence on my own fashion is the way Gary Cooper or Brian Donlevy brushes his hair. I would say films have a great influence on fashion, and I would say Ginger Rogers has the greatest influence, espicially after *Follow the Fleet*.

If a film is of a serious nature, it may cause you to take important decisions. This depends on whether your mind is pliable. The decision of Michael Redgrave in *Thunder Rock*, to return to Europe and the world, and to continue the struggle, influenced me to quite a considerable extent. It made me continue in taking an exam which I hoped to take, but I was not sure about the exam before I saw the picture.

In another way, the film of J. B. Priestley's book, *Let the People Sing*, influenced me. This film made me feel it was worth struggling for your ideas. I was about to give up playing my violin, but this film changed my mind. I would say definitely that films influence people in taking important decisions.

Occasionally I dream about a film. This is generally when the film leaves an idea in your mind unsolved. I dreamt about *Song of Bernadette*, after I saw the film. This was because the film left me with the idea, 'did it happen.' In my dream it happened.

I am English, my father is a lecturer in Sociology. Aged 15.

32. Miss ...

1. Yes, particularly *Sergeant York*. (Gary Cooper) This film, produced with exquisite attention to detail, moved me considerably in two ways. (a) I am unable to accept Christianity, as mercy (vicarious atonement) seems to me unjust. I'd like to be a Christian; after I saw *Sergeant York* I was able to pray, after a gap of years. That was last April and I still have a confidance in 'providential care' a resignation to fate, which has brought me unworried through many difficult months. (But I'm still not a Christian)

(b) Several long-short stories were ready in my mind but I had not been able to bring myself to getting them down on paper. In the four days following this film I got the longest (9,000 words)— of an individual's search for belief—down on paper. Two others, on allied themes, came later, and they are now touring the publishers. I *know* they are good! Their length is unfortunate, but that is the way they came.

Note: Much as I admire Gary Cooper, it was Alvin York's honest faith and refusal of easy money that moved me, not fan worship.

2. No, never.
Age: 39. Sex: female.
Nationality: Scots.
Profession: Housewife and Writer.
Parents: Ironmonger and Housewife.

33. Miss ...

In regard to your request for information as regards the average film audience I am writing the following examples of how some films have influenced my conduct, hoping they may be of some use to you.

1. Until five years ago I took an average interest in music, but never listened to it seriously. I liked the effect of incidental music in films. While seeing *The Great Lie* I was entranced by the music, but I thought, 'Oh its incidental music. It was beautiful, but I shall never hear it again, because incidental music is very rarely published.'

Later I discovered that the music featured in the film was actually Tchaikovsky's Piano Concerto No. 1 in B flat minor. Because of the effect made on me by the beauty of this music, I gradually came to take an interest in symphonic and classical music in general. Nowadays one of my regular joys is listening to the symphony concerts featured by the B.B.C. on Sundays. I don't think many of the highly emotional films would have nearly so much effect without incidental music, but I suppose there are hundreds of people who disagree with me on this point. Sometimes I try to memorise the incidental music in films and write a rough sketch of it for piano. It seems such a waste of beautiful music, that you hear it in a film and then it is so quickly forgotten. Such films as *All This and Heaven Too*, *Marie Walewska*, *Juarez*, *Lady Hamilton*, and *Elizabeth and Essex*, have made me read a good deal about the characters represented in films.

People and events in the past come vividly to mind on seeing the films and reading the books, and give me immense pleasure.

I always go to see films on my own. After seeing a really good dramatic film I like to go off on my own for a walk, and think the various scenes over. I don't like to come in contact with people. They seem to intrude on my enjoyment of bringing to mind the excellent acting I had just seen.

Films such as *Dark Victory*, *Now Voyager*, and *Watch on the Rhine*, among many others, affected me in this way, and later I wrote out the dialogue as near as I could remember it. And now if I wish to relive the scenes in any of the films, all I have to do is to read over my writing.

The greatest wish of my life is to meet Bette Davis. It was on seeing her in *The Sisters* in 1939 that made me take an interest in films.

In my estimation, acting such as hers is beyond all praise, but if I could ever meet her, and try to tell her even a little about how much her acting means to me, I should be the happiest person in the world.

The fashions in films have no effect on me, because they are usually specially concocted for use in the studios, and are for everyday use, quite unsuitable. Hairstyles need constant professional attention if they are anything like the elaborate affairs featured by stars in some films.

2. I have never dreamed about films, but I have dreamed about individual personalities in films.

Age—18 years. Sex—Female. Nationality—British (Scotch).
Profession—Cashier. Profession of Mother—Housewife. Father is
dead.

34. Mrs. . . .

Your questions—(1) Have films influenced you with regard to
personal decisions or behaviour? (2) Have films ever appeared in
your dreams?—interest me very much.

I consider I am an average type of woman in every way. Age
forty (young in ways and looks though!) and am the daughter of
a Bank Clerk and a French woman. I am the mother of a little girl
of ten, and also have a little war orphan boarded on us by Dr.
Barnado's Homes. My husband, ten years older, is a Surveyor and
we visit our local picture houses twice a week (paying once and one
invitation) I am of a serious type of mind and prefer true films or
travel to musicals and 'love' stories. My war work is invoice clerk.

The only conscious effect of films I have noticed is that I so
admire the smart, well dressed and groomed actresses, that I often
try to make my *very* scant supply of clothes look as well as theirs.
Not the ultra fashonable (fashionable), but the sensible, comfortable garb. I have very successfully made several hats by cutting up
mine and remodeling (remodelling) them from films.

Regarding dreams. Only once have I drempt (dreamt) of a film,
or rather film actor, but then I am far to (too) sleepey (sleepy) to
dream and cannot remember doing so more than about twenty
times in my life!

This dream was during the time my husband was away on war
work and after seeing a George Murphy film—(I cannot remember
which). He was making violent love to me at some beautiful house
near a river! I like Mr. Murphy's acting and think him a versitile
(versatile) and clever man, but nothing more than that and I am
sure *photographs* however real, could never give me feelings other
than interest and pleasure of *sight* only.

However, my husband is quite different and seems to have a real
affection for several of the actresses we see. The Actors have no
effect other than interest, for him and I have never noticed him
copying them in any way of manner or dress; but how very different
from our little girl!

Although she is only ten, she copies all the *best* traints (traits) in
dress, 'hair do's' (as she calls them) and, for a very short time,
manners of the actresses! I am sure I could tell what star she had
seen, even if I had not been to the film with her!

She has marked likes and dislikes for men stars and often 'spots' extras who she considers will become stars often correctly!

The little Orphan seems too thrilled with the whole thing to do more than watch intently, and make a few remarks after the performance, but little critisum (criticism).

35. Miss ...

Personally I find a good movie story enriches my memory and have proved that the cinema has educated the community and films have gained far more recruits for literature than the stage ever succeeded in doing.

Also recently when the whole world looked dark after a particularly trying week of hard work, I dropped into a local cinema to see *Cover Girl*, I left feeling amazingly refreshed, tackled the necessary household duties, and then—I made over one of my very old dresses (inspired by a dress worn by the star) arranged my hair à la Hayworth, and faced the world with new pep! And thanked my lucky stars I was fortunate to be living in this film-mad generation.

36. Mr. ...

I have dreamed very little about films, but there is one which stands out very much in my memory, and that was the all negro film *Stormy Weather*, which I enjoyed very much in seeing, and in dreaming!

I must confess that I am a 'Swing fan', and therefore films I like seeing best, are ones in which there are famous bands.

Why don't 'British Film Studios', make films featuring our own British bands? Too many of us with an interest in Jazz, and Swing music, the Jazzmen, and bands of this country have never had the chance to see them in films.

In America, quite a number of films are centred round famous bands, such as, Tommy Dorsey, Harry James, and Kay Kyser, etc., etc., and as you know these films have reached the top place for entertainment, and is now widely popular in Britain. Though Swing music has its critics, it certainly has admirers, especially among the younger generation throughout the country, which undoubtedly must run into millions.

For example take the visit to this country of eminent jazz and entertainment personalities, such as Dinah Shore, Bing Crosby, Artie Shaw Orchestra, Fred Astaire and Major Glen Miller and the American Band of the A.E.F. The welcome these American stars received in this country was tremendous.

Therefore I think that if British bands, vocalists, and personalities were featured more in films these films will move forward to a new and greater era of popularity, and would receive enthusiastic audiences everywhere.

My age is 18 years, am British subject. My profession is a waiter, my parents are Restuarateurs (Restaurateurs). Male Sex.

37. Miss . . .

I should like to answer the two questions put forward in last weeks *Picturegoer*.

To the first one I can reply that films have most certainly influenced my life. I am 19 years of age, and until I started work at the age of 16 led a very retired life. Consequently my chief idea of life was formed on what I saw at the pictures and what I read in books. I couldn't understand why people weren't as polite, as tasteful and as kind as I saw them in films. Consequently I lived in a constant state of disillusion until I learned a little more sense. Have films been a good or bad influence? Well on the whole, I think definitely more good than bad comes from films. Admittedly, certain types of girls make what they see in some sorts of films, an excuse for rowdy behaviour and heavy make-up, but then, I honestly think that these girls wouldn't be very much different if they had never seen a film in their lives. People blame most bad things to the influence of films, but that is unwarranted. There is more good taste in clothes than there used to be, and this is only because they have the constant example of good clothes before them on the screen.

As for myself, well I have been influenced in many ways. All films influence me in clothes. This is only to be expected in a girl. Most films show good manners—and also show how to behave in hotels and similar places, which is a help to people who seldom travel, when they do visit such places.

I will say this, that morals have not been badly influenced in films. Films compare very favourably with modern books when it comes to the question of morals. School-mates gave me more unpleasant ideas on love than films ever did. In love, films have definitely shown me what I want. I think that the happy companionship and love shown in such films as *Mrs. Miniver* is the ideal of everyone. Perhaps they make us expect too much in our boy-friends, but there, once more, common sense must come to our aid.

In conclusion I will say this. In films, like all things, one must be prepared to pick out the best things and reject the poor things. This way, films can only influence for the good.

2. In reply to the second question, I can definitely say that I seldom, if ever, dream of films. I dream a good deal, and being rather interested in Dunn's theory, take a good deal of notice of what I dream. I have never had a nightmare following any of the 'Horror' films, and have only once dreampt (dreamt) of being mixed up in any shooting. Admittedly, it is very difficult to draw a line, as films are very muddled and impossible things at the best of times. However, I have never knowingly dreampt (dreamt) about a film after seeing it.

Here are a few facts about myself. I am 19 years of age, a girl, and English. I work in an Accounts Department as a Book-keeper and Wages Clerk. My father is a Motor Engineer, and we live on the outskirts of a largish seaside resort. I hope I may say that I am intelligent, and take a very great interest in modern progress.

38. Mrs. ....

In your issue of *Picturegoer* of last week, you asked if any picture (film) had influenced any decision. Well I most certainly think they do, I will relate you mine. I am the mother of three daughters, a widow, and had brought up my children, as I thought, in the proper way, however one, like very many more, in this present war, formed an attachment for a married man, and left me. No one can imagine what a blow this can be. I was very bitter and felt I would never forgive her, I went to see the film (*Dear Octopus*) and a scene in which the same sort of thing had happened, the daughter returns penitent, the mother forgives her with the words that impressed me. (She would rather lose a conviction than a daughter) which changed my views.

I am 50 years of age.

39. Mr. ....

With regards to your enquiry about films influencing persons I have found that some films definitely do.

I found that the film *Between Two Worlds* did influence me in my personal decisions.

Before I saw this film I felt very depressed at times, so much so that I even considered committing suicide. I felt that life wasn't worth living, and that little daily disturbances worried me to distraction. But after seeing the film I had an altogether different view point. I saw what happened to those who did commit suicide.

WOMAN IN LABOUR FROM 'FORGOTTEN VILLAGE'
*A great film which was not passed by the British Board
of Film Censors for adult film-goers*

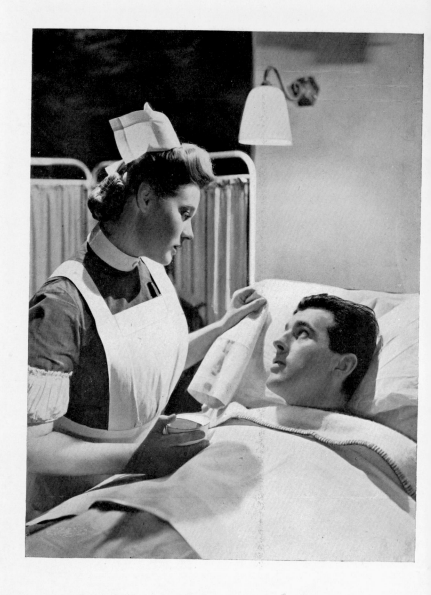

STEWART GRANGER AND ROSAMOND JOHN IN
'THE LAMP STILL BURNS'
An 'A' film which ought to have been certified as a 'U' film

They were never able to have complete rest or even a peaceful one. They would never be allowed into Heaven, they would just drift aimlessly in space with their terrible thoughts.

I then thought very seriously about it all. So you can see that one film did make a person change their mind.

In answer to your second question, as to whether any films have appeared in my dreams.

I was once dreaming of an air raid when suddenly Greer Garson seemed to appear. It was in the air raid scene in *Mrs. Miniver*. She vanished as quickly as she appeared.

This happened quite a long time after I had seen the film.

My age is eighteen. I am a male, and my occupation is an assistant in shop. My nationality is British. My father is deceased, but he was a Blacksmith, and my mother is a housewife.

40. Miss . . .

You wish to know my reactions, if any, towards films as regards behaviour, love affairs, personal outlook etc. Yes, films do have an effect upon me, some more than others and certain films become fixed in my mind for quite a length of time. Most, of course, depends on how well the characters are portrayed by the various actors, and how true to life, my own perhaps, the film is.

I tend to be a superstitious person and so the film *Flesh and Fantasy* had a distinct effect on me in the respect that it taught me a lesson. It consisted of three stories, the first I shall omit because it was not connected in any way with the lesson.

The second concerned 'mind over matter', and showed how a certain thing, if allowed to prey on one's mind can end fatally as was this case.

The third centred round belief in dreams and fear mingled with belief that those dreams might occur in real life. Each story showed eventually that the person concerned was a victim of over-imaginative powers which were beginning to take the upper hand in my life, but it taught me a lesson and a very valuable one.

Another film which had an effect on me was *The Moon and Sixpence*, a film based on the life of Gauguin the famous painter. My interests in art are very great apart from the fact that Gauguin is one of my favourite artists.

His ambition, determination to get what he wanted and his very unsettled ways impressed me very much, insomuch that I determined to achieve my ambition and become an artist also. Not to be the same as him, an artist, but something more, for the love of art itself and for the joy one can gain by expressing one's feelings in paint. It was a wonderful film and it impressed me greatly.

Films concerning the nursing profession are those which I also react to. Partly because I was a nurse myself and partly because I have a great admiration for the nurses and their wonderful profession. Films like *The Lamp Still Burns* and *Four Girls in White* impressed me very much. I could live the parts along with the nurses and I had a sort of yearning to return to the work. A feeling of nostalgia regarding my past experiences crept over me, although it was only at the time and when I left the cinema the feeling disappeared.

Another film I remember seeing when I was 16 which also had a great effect on me was *I was a Criminal*. It was the story of a criminal who was really a good-hearted sort, and his little son. Both characters were beautifully portrayed. I was so carried away by the film that I wrote out as much of the script as I could remember—I have kept it to this very day. I do not know quite whether it was the plot of the film or whether my mind was, at that time, filled with childish fantasy and love of adventure—but the film remained in my memory for as long as I can remember.

My reaction to animal films is that of tears because I have a very great love for those creatures. In films like *My Friend Flicka* and *Lassie Come Home* my sympathies were all towards the animals—I laughed when they were happy and cried when they were in trouble. But everyone's reaction to animal films is the same, I suppose and I find that those sort of films will produce sighs of sympathy and tears of sorrow from even the hardest of persons.

I have given you, then, to the best of my ability those films to which I react most.

In the majority of films I study every detail—movement, gestures, expressions (which if I happen to like—I find myself resuming unconsciously), clothing, hairstyles and make-up. I have copied hairstyles and sometimes clothing, which have appealed to me in films. But soon I find myself returning to my own individualistic hairstyle, when the novelty has worn off.

Everyone, I think has some sort of desire to act at one time or another—and I am no exception. I have seen a film; a part has appealed to me; I have made a point of remembering the lines—I find I can do that most successfully—and then I have acted the part at home. Sometimes making up and dressing-up to the best of my ability.

Such films were. *Nurse Edith Cavell* (nursing again); *Jane Eyre* and *Christmas Holiday*. These are only three—where I tried to play the part 'Anna Neagle' played in *Edith Cavell*; Joan Fontaine played in *Jane Eyre* and Deanna Durbin's 'Abigail' in *Christmas Holiday* which was very dramatic—all three were for that matter— which shows that dramatic acting appeals to me most.

I think, then, I have given you as many examples of my reactions etc. as I can.

A good many films have been recorded in my dreams and I am one of those persons who has innumerable dreams in the course of a night.

Films which have no effect on me consciously are those which I dream about. Such are *Bride of Frankenstein*; *Journey into Fear* and *Ministry of Fear*. Perhaps it is my adventurous spirit taking the upper-hand again. My subconscious mind carrying out those things which I should like to experience consciously.

I am continually playing the part of the person who is in the midst of danger in the dream. For instance, Ray Milland's part in *Ministry of Fear* and Joseph Cotten's in *Journey into Fear*. The only difference is that in the dream I am a female. That of course is only natural, considering it is my sex. At certain parts in the dream I found it very difficult to make my legs move when I was being chased.

I frequently dream that I am a ballerina and many scenes concerning ballet in films I dream about, seeing myself as the principal ballerina. Such films were—*The Goldwyn Follies*, where I danced the ballet which Vera Zorina danced. In *Forian* I undertook 'Irina Baronova's' ballet in the court scene, and more recently I saw the film *Lady Let's Dance* and shortly after I dreamed I was executing the same ballet 'Belita' had done in the film. Not to perfection, because dreams are never really as intricate as that, but enough to know, when I woke, that it was the ballet from that particular film I had been dancing.

Aviation films have rather a queer effect on me in dreams. I cannot give any names of particular films because most of them have been war films. I have a very great fear of heights and after having seen a film shot in an aeroplane thousands of feet up, where one can just see the ground below, I have the most fantastic dreams. I am flying through air—without aeroplane or anything, mind you, seeing the same distant ground as I had in the film. I am not afraid in the dreams very much to the contrary—I seem to be enjoying myself immensely—soaring up and down in the weirdest manner.

I have given you again my dreams and the films about which I dream to the best of my ability.

I might add, by the way—that most of my dreams are recorded in black and white—although the ballet scenes as far as I can remember were in, shall we say, technicolour.

Age, Twenty. Not married.

41. Mr. ....

Question 1. I believe the moulding of my career has been affected by films I have seen, not inconsiderably. Having always been imbued with the desire to learn and study continuously, several films have given me added encouragement, those springing to mind readily being *Repent at Leisure, Young Tom Edison, First of the Few, Television Spy, Invisible Man Returns, Pygmalion, Down Went McGinty, The Doctor Takes a Wife, Disputed Passage,* and most important, *Madam Curie* of more recent date. I have yet to see the importance of the cinema as an educator, expressed in print. By that I mean 'ordinary' films. I regard films as part of my education and choose films accordingly.

Question 2. Yes, twice. A 'ghost' film seen when young terrified me in dreamland for many nights following, and *Madam Curie* has turned up several times recently to inspire me! I am a male English student of aeronautics, my father being in the building industry. Age 22.

42. Miss ...

In answering the two questions in your Feb. 3rd Issue of *Picturegoer*, I find the answer to question No. 1. is yes in one instance only, that I was copying the hair-style of Ginger Rogers in *Lady in the Dark* with the long pageboy bob and sides sweeping up.

And to question no. 2—Yes I have dreamed of Pictures I have seen. For instance, *The Return of the Scarlet Pimpernel, Four Feathers* and *The Man in the Iron Mask.*

I am a sixteen year old British girl, a Chemist's Assistant, and my father is a Police Officer.

43. Miss ...

As a keen film fan for many years two films have had an influence on my character and life, one being *Going My Way* and the other *Madam Curie.* Both these films are sincere and as far as I know true to life. In my opinion the Theatre and Cinema can do a lot to educate and uplift the minds of the Public at the same time giving the Public what it wonts (wants): Entertainment.

Thanks to the medium of the screen we have learnt the life of a great Heroine, Madam Curie, who shows an example of courage, self sacrifice, Love of Humanity, and ultimate good.

Going My Way is spiritually a lesson in patience, and control of a great mind. For instance when the old priest discovers he is no longer in charge of his Mission, and again the destruction of his Church, his life's work. Yes these films have had a lingering effect on me personally, to say nothing of the consumate (consummate) art of Barry Fitzgerald.

Given this opportunity may I venture to suggest a few subjects that would be appreciated by the Public.

Lives of Dr. Johnson, Abraham Lincoln, Mr. Peeps (Pepys), Balzac, Beethoven, Wagner, or for an English atmosphere, Thomas Hardy.

(No personal data were given.)

44. Mrs. . . . .

I am 51 years of age, Belgian born of Dutch Parents, British by marriage for 32 years.

I have directed a dressmakers establishment for 20 years until 1943. A client came to me some years ago. This lady wanted an evening gown, could not find a style in my excellent fashion books. She wanted an impressive one, as she had seen a few days before, in a film called *Pygmalion* by Bernard Shaw. It was seen in the ballroom scene in this film. I went into town to see this film, about a month later, I had an exact copy of this gown for my client. Some years back I saw a film called *Scarface*. The Shooting in this film was so calculatedly brutal, that I dreamt many nights of this shooting afterwards.

I have dreamt many times of passages in films, that made a strong impression on me.

I have also copied, many times, good hints and sometimes, whole frocks or suits seen on the films. I have at the moment a frock, I have copied from a model I saw Adolph Menjou's wife wear, in a film, the name of which I have forgotten. I am also of the opinion that should certain happy or reverse passages, in ordinary people's lives, be taken for films, they would show the real home atmosphere and so interest more, also educate more, than at present is the case.

45. Mr. . . . .

Films on the screen generally have not made so much an impression or influenced me since 'sound' was introduced. The days of the silent screen I should consider far more beneficial all round. Take *Intolerance* as an example—No picture has impressed me since —for 20 years with one exception *The Four Feathers* and that— thro' being acted *True* and in the Native Locality. I have lived in the Orient travelled and worked with them—therefore have an understanding and appreciable (appreciative) mind. I should consider the part played and acted by John Clements *superb* and his best. Other Pictures appreciable and somewhat impressive are *Lost Horizon* (with Ronald Coleman as Chief Actor)—*Broken Blossoms*—featuring Emlyn Williams and Dolly Haas—*The Good Earth*—Paul Muni and Louise Rainer and the latter's FINE acting in *The Great Waltz* also *Goodbye Mr. Chips* with Robert Donat and Greer Garson.

To my mind the screen will not and never can replace the legitimate stage—in the latter the actors appear in person before the audience—and the 2 are 'in touch' so to speak—and the per- sonality presence—and charm—or otherwise—makes a contact with the audience—which the best portrayal on the screen with all its Technique practically perfect—can never hope to do. Consider for instance the Operas and Operettas of Gilbert and Sullivan? *Haddon Hall, Iolanthe, The Gondoliers* and *The Yeomen of the Guard* as an example would it not be a 1,000 times more appreciable to *see* and listen to the actors—and hear the music naturally very ably rendered rather than artificially.

The screen of to-day is really *noisy* and appeals to the taste of certain classes who need to sit and listen to something distracting and diverting from their hum drum daily round and/or too lazy to or unable to perceive True Art—and appreciate FINE Music.

No—Films have not appeared or figured in my dreams—I have 'visions' sometimes and only a slight effect of one scene occurring in *Lost Horizon* seemed to intrude and this—over 12 months after I had seen the above—and I had not been to the 'Pictures' on the day preceding.

I have been soldier and sailor—(mariner) too—am possessed of great will power am not easily impressed or moved—when I 'turn in' at night—I forget the days happenings—this is not possible with every one of us and only to those who LOVE Nature—and understanding—and an understanding of the Creator—as you may guess I am a Man—age 57—profession—Chef at sea—now Land- scape Gardener—Father—long decd. Solicitors Clerk Mother— decd. Nurse before marriage.

46. Miss . . .

In answer to your first question, 'Have films ever influenced you with regard to personal decisions or behaviour?' I say what kind of films? *Marriage is a Private Affair* type of film showed a happy ending but it showed that to make life turn out that way a family must be understanding and a fellow must wait after his wedding and let his wife have a good time with her past flames while he minds the baby. No matter how considerate a husband no such thing should be allowed. That film answers No. As for *Mrs. Miniver* your answer is Yes. It encouraged many young girls to get married and cling to what happens to be the present and to look with courage to the future and take from life what it gives them. The kind of films where a girl or fellow plays hard to get makes some of its audience think they'll try it but often the one who should do the chasing isn't willing to chase. Then comes disaster.

As for myself though I think films of the right kind, can influence people's lives a lot. For instance I'm a shop assistant and often I've longed to tell customers off but thought 'the girl in the film didn't get nasty she remained polite'. So lucky for some people the film did good. Women in uniform on the screen often make me feel I'd like to join the Ferry Pilots (Anna Neagle in *They Flew Alone*). Then came *Gentle Sex* which encouraged many girls into the A.T.S. But the wrong kind of films make our minds go haywire and though the films have happy endings, the examples we follow, don't. For instance, musicals! when the girl has both career and her man when in fiction it works out but not in life usually.

So the answer is 'yes' usually.

No. 2 Question. Have films ever appeared in your dreams? Yes.

Often I see a picture and if it's good keep thinking about it but I remember seeing two films *Lloyds of London* and also *Yankee Doodle Dandy*. In the latter I started dreaming of the war concerned and the last thing I remember dreaming about was the end of, by the fashions, this war.

Personally though I might have been thinking of the film and then began to wonder how this war would end, thus a dream. I also think that dreams often start and are actually based or led on by what you think about before you go to sleep.

I am 16, female. Shop assistant (hoping to be an actress!) English and Daddy works in an office old grey mum is just housewife.

47. Mr. ....

Having read of your investigation of film audiences I thought I would write to you. I am 18 years of age, and films mean a great deal to me, perhaps this is because I have ambitions to find film work for myself. I am at present employed by the L.M.S. railway Co. with whom I have worked for the past two years. I was born in Scotland and both my parents are Scottish. Some time ago I came to the decision that I wanted film work for myself, but finding such work in Scotland is impossible at the present time. I go often to the movies as it gives me the opportunity of watching other people act, and is always a little experience, films have appeared in my dreams sometimes I seem to be part of them, and sometimes scenes from different films appear for instance I had a dream recently in which I danced with Gene Kelly fantastic, I know, but that was the dream. Scenes from *Rebecca*, *Dark Victory*, *Now Voyager* and *Cover Girl* have appeared in my dreams, stars also appear these include Bette Davis, Spencer Tracy, Gene Kelly, Paul Henreid, Stewart Grainger and many others. Well I think that is all I can tell you about myself except that I am 5 ft. 9½ ins. tall, have blue eyes, brown hair, weight 10 st. 2 lbs.

48. Sgt. .... A.T.S.

Do films influence our lives—I'd often wondered, until this true, and very interesting instance (of which, as an A.T.S. I am very proud) became known to me. He was a wealthy man of 42, in a safe and certain post, and would never have been called up for active service. One day he saw the film *The Gentle Sex* and was so impressed by the fine work women are shown doing in it, that he became unhappy and discontented, convinced he was not pulling his weight. Overcoming difficulties put in his way he joined the Merchant Navy, and in a humble capacity, is now doing a fine job of work. So here's a bouquet to the *good* influence of films—a much rarer one than is generally deserved.

49. Miss ...

I am very interested to hear you are conducting an investigation regarding film audiences.

I am nearly seventeen, British, girl, I still attend school, my father is a manager at ——shop and my mother is a housewife.

I will try to answer your questions in order: first concerning the influence films have on behaviour.

In 1942 I saw for the first time Greer Garson and Teresa Wright in *Mrs. Miniver*. Since that day I have based my entire way of living upon them. I have lost many friends, hurt my parents and am regarded by all as completely foolish. I have made a large collection of photographs of them and have heard from both of them in the past.

At first I thought it was a 'pash' I had on them, as is common among young girls, but I found now that I live in an imaginary family and I have gone to terrible pains in building up my thoughts and putting them into action.

I have astounded my friend by being able to imitate their ways of speaking and by facial expression I have been able to make myself feel I am actually them.

I find that at every film of their's I see, it is not the story I follow but their actions, poses and most of all their eyes, which brings me to your second question about dreams.

I am not exaggerating when I say I dream about them three times a week, one night of which is *always* a Thursday (perhaps that is because of my having the *Picturegoer* on that day).

Usually I stand, in my dreams, in the same room as they are in a scene from any one of their films, sometimes they are all mixed up, one moment she is herself, the next 'Madam Curie', then 'Mrs. Miniver'.

Always I am in the background, following the story or trying to chip in, but always I am ignored as though I was invisible.

Once I was in a great Laboratory and I could see someone at the other end rubbing her hands as if she was in pain (Madam Curie suffered from burns while making Radium). I wanted to help but the harder I ran towards her the further away she seemed to go, when I awoke I was crying and had my hands tightly together.

To conclude my letter may I say that I am perfectly happy. Whereas my friend worries over her homework I find that by imagining that I am either of the two stars I can easily do mine.

Please excuse my writing but it is very late and I have been doing a great deal of work.

50. Miss ...

This letter is in answer to your appeal for help from members of the cinema audiences. I am a female, aged 17 yrs. 2 mths. and of British nationality. I am still at school at present, and I hope to enter into the teaching profession in the due course of time. My father is a bricklayer and also Secretary of a Trade Union, my mother is a housewife.

THE ADULT AND THE CINEMA

In answer to question one. I have seen many films and I have always liked to watch closely the women's manner of dress, or hair style. I may say that in many cases I have copied the styles but the most dominant film with regard to fashions were. Hair style. *For Whom the Bell Tolls.* Dress. *Now Voyager.*

And with regard to a film I have dreamt about I can safely name *The Corsican Brothers*, starring Douglas Fairbanks Junior and Ruth Warick. That film I dreamt about for many nights, and I remember especially that the death scene of Julian the twin brother of Mario was the piece I remembered most vividly.

With regard to dreams I have also dreamt about a serial film that I saw when I was the age of 11 or 12 years. That film was *Flash Gordon's Trip to Mars.* I can quite confidently say that I remember practically all of that film until a few weeks ago and then I saw part of it again as a weekly serial at a picture palace in our town.

It served to refresh my memory on the parts I had forgotten and I am sure I shall think and dream of it for a good many more years.

I think the facts that made it stick in my mind for such a long time was that it was of a strange planet and the costumes were also very strange. The hero and heroine and party did perform many incredible deeds but what did annoy me was the fact that many people in the cinema when they saw the Marsians (Martians) in the film doing things that seemed slightly unnatural to us, laughed!

I regard everyone who laughed at that film as a fool! They have no foresight. They have no understanding, nor did they try to understand.

I think there is a possibility of our, one day, trying to reach Mars by means of a rocket ship, after all they are trying to reach the moon shortly, so why not Mars?

51. Mr. . . .

I am writing to you in answer to your Questions in *Picturegoer.* I am 15 years of age I am of British nationality, sex Boy profession Messenger.

Well I think Question one is yes. For instance, after seeing the film *An American Romance* I suddenly decided to be good natured and hard working. Now I find it is making quite a good effect on my work. I also think the second one is yes. Once I had a dream about war and selfsacrifice the film *A Guy Named Joe* Imediatly

234

(Immediately) came into my dream, and that is my opinion of your two questions.

52. Miss . . .

On the Subject of Films. They have influenced me a great deal. For instance the charm and personality of Claudette Colbert I try to portray as near as possible.

Her style of carrying herself and the way she holds a conversation with her deep cultured voice and vivacious manner. But the best thing of all is her fashion which is smart and sophisticated, of course in these hard times its hard to do but I try to be like her as much as I can.

In my opinion to like a character so much you can't forget it proves how hard the actress must act to make her personality stand clear in your mind.

There is one more star that attracts me and manages to play a vivid part in my imagination, naming Jennifer Jones who starred in *The Song of Bernadette.*

After seeing that picture I made a resolution to love all that was beautiful and clean in mind. Before I used to give my attention to pretty flowers etc, especially beauty in men and women. The picture definitely made up my mind not to be swayed in my opinions of people in their different characters and facial appearances.

Also the sensitiveness she played when she cried because she was forbidden to see the holy vision was very wonderful, and being a sensitive person myself I finally found myself crying with her. Pictures I have seen similar to that one have influenced me so much that I dream about them.

Which brings me to the next question.

One film of the dramatic kind called *The Last days of Pompeii* I remember dreaming about. When Marcus Aurelius played by Frederick March fought in the gladiators ring doing as the crowd bid him to do I was putting myself in his position and what I would feel like and the consequences were I saw it all over again in my dreams. Then when he was dying and Christ came to him telling Marcus to arise to him, that I dreampt (dreamt) about also.

The picture called *The Little Foxes* with Bette Davis co-starring Herbert Marshall also I had a dream about. The part where Herbert Marshall her husband who had been treated for heart disease had an attack and was left to die. My dream showed Herbert Marshall trying to climb the stairs to get his medicine and falling down on the stairs. I saw most vividly Betty Davis his wife sitting in a differant position to what she was in the film watching him and not offering to help the man. It was so real that I was dazzled when I woke up and found myself in my own bedroom. I have had dreams about many others but it would take the rest of my notepaper to write down every part of them.

My age is 19 yrs (Woman). Nationality British. Profession, Brushmaker, also I sing when I'm not very busy. My Father is a printer and My Mother the ordinary housewife.

53. Miss . . .

You asked do films ever influence your life. Well I think that they do especially technicoloured films. I have always wanted to write an article on films and here at last is my chance. I am a great film fan and they certainly influence me. In fact I do not know what would have happened if films had never been invented—I have never been in love yet but I wish I had the chance of playing the role of wife to such stars as Allan Ladd Van Johnson Denis Morgan or Gene Kelly, neither have I been divorced yet. but if it is as nice as it appears on the screen in such films as *Escape to Happiness* or *Old Acquantience* (Acquaintance) *Great Mans Lady* or *In This Our Life*, O.K., I do not think I should have put (as nice) in describing divorce as it appears on the screen, but it is so thrilling and exciting.

Next on the list is manners. Well I wish above all things to possess such charming manners as Phyllis Thaxter as she appeared in I think her only film ever released *Thirty Seconds Over Tokyo*. But I also like such mannerisms as Vivien Leigh, in *Gone with the Wind* or Irene Dunne's such understanding manners in *White Cliffs of Dover*.

And lastly Fashion. Well nowadays give any girl the chance to wear any of the mordern clothes that you see on the films nowadays. For instance in *Home in Indiana* June Haver wore some beautiful clothes especially a Red coat and hat trimmed with Lambs wool and in *Pin Up Girl* Betty Grable wore a nice cream lace dresse (dress) and a smart white suite (suit). of course you imagine yourself in them so much more if the film is in technicolor (technicolour).

Now to question of films appearing in your dreams. Well they do in mine allright In *Doctor Wassell* I dreamt I was fighting alongside of Gary Cooper and I imagined that I was a nurse like Claudette Colbert in *So Proudly We Hail*. and in *Stage Door Canteen* I was a Hostess. These are just a few and it may seem silly but I do not think you enjoy a film if you are not living with it.

Age 18. Sex. Female. Nationality English. Profession, Cashier. Profession of Parents. Engineer. Mother none.

54. Miss . . .

'You may write to your heart's content' states the *Picturegoer* and goes on to say 'the best will be rewarded by a guinea . . . etc.' That was good enough for me and I'm afraid it means another letter for you to wade through, poor lecturer!

It seems that before I actually start on films I must give you some details about myself. I am practically twenty. My mother was born in C. My father was born in L. He is Jewish but my mother is not. So far I myself have not taken up any form of religion—I have strong leaning towards Julian Huxley's Scientific humanism which if not actually a religion, has a strict moral code.

As for professions, my mother was a shop-assistant, and my father has had several jobs with commercial travelling taking first place. For the last nine years he has settled down in C. and become an insurance agent. I was a library-assistant. My job is now to help my father with his collection, as he is suffering and must not exert himself, so we are both insurance agents now.

Now to films themselves and how they have influenced me. Naturally if one goes to the cinema regularly one is bound to be influenced, if one is a woman, on matters such as dress and hair-styles. Every girl is brought up to 'make the most of her appearance' and to study the stars definitely helps .Thus I wore boleros, when I was fourteen or so, because Deanna Durbin did, and boleros were obviously youthful and becoming to girls of that age. If common-sense is used screen-dress can act as a guide to practical but becoming every-day dress. It is when fifteen-year-olds use Lamarr instead of Durbin as a model that things do not work out. I was forgetting that Deanna's grown-up now—Gloria Jean perhaps. I still get ideas from the films for styles for frocks and am not ashamed of admitting that fact, since Dolly Tree and Adrian should know more about dress than I do. I nearly had my hair cut as Ingrid Bergman wore hers, in *For Whom the Bell Tolls* but my hair is naturally wavy and at the last moment, I was too conceited to have it cut, because all my friends were saying 'fancy she's having all those waves chopped off'. Which shows how weak-willed I am sometimes. As for behaviour, I have always thought I would like to have Barbara Stanwyck's manner, I like her cynical, wise-cracking way, but I have never consciously modelled myself on her. I don't think any films in particular have affected my behaviour. Perhaps *Going My Way* made me a little more tolerant towards Roman Catholicism.

There is one thing though that has altered a lot of my life and that was a visit to *Rebecca* when I was fifteen. I remember at that time I had decided that Charles Boyer was THE answer to a maiden's prayer. But I sat through *Rebecca* and—Mr. Boyer *est mort*. *Vive* Mr. Olivier!

But because of a schoolgirl 'pash' I gained much. After all I was fortunate in my choice. Here was somebody who was not just another handsome hero but who really *changed* in every picture. Yet his dignity, mobility and expression of face, and beautiful speaking voice could give most of Hollywood's strictly glamour boys points. Even to-day, at my calmer nineteen I would still make an effort to see any film in which Olivier starred. Did I say starred? Nay, *acted* is the word.

He made me realise that acting is an art. I studied film players more closely. Soon I could claim honestly to prefer seeing Mervyn Johns to Robert Taylor.

Then I gained an informal education, too, and also a devouring love of the theatre.

I went to see all Mr. Olivier's films, they are usually above the average. Because of them I read *Wuthering Heights* and own my copy of *Pride and Prejudice*. I read a good deal about Nelson too. I also listened to Laurence Olivier's broadcasts. He read some air poems by Pudney, which I now own, once. That aroused my interest in modern poetry in general. He read *Maud* by Tennyson—I started to read Tennyson. He appeared in *The School for Scandal* and I read that. I read Raynal's *Unknown Warrior* because he broadcast an excerpt from that. I have read innumerable portions of Shakespeare, all thanks to Mr. Olivier. I was almost seventeen when I worked in the Central branch of the C. libraries. We had a large stock of books on the theatre. When I should have been dusting them or putting them tidy, I was usually flicking through them for bits of information about my hero.

Not surprisingly this led to an interest in the books themselves. I was soon greedily reading all books on the theatre particularly dramatic criticism. I now long to become a dramatic critic myself! I read all the press notices by Ivor Brown, Desmond MacCarthy, James Agate and Alan Dent that I could lay my hands on. I listened to any talks on the theatre that were broadcast. Simultaneously my interest in the cinema began to be subjective rather than objective. I now read nine criticisms of films every week. I did not go to see a film just because I thought the star was 'cute', I began to notice the names of directors.

Reading so much criticism made me take an interest in the art of criticism itself. I began to read book-reviews and my love for literature, which had always been strong, became stronger. Many people have said that because it's in my make-up to love films, books, and plays, as I do, I would have, had there been no Laurence Olivier. I, however, like to think it is all a justification for hero-worship and shall always say, 'Thank you, Mr. Olivier'.

Now to your second question which sounds like Freud. I shall probably reveal the most terrible things about myself! I have never had dreams of actual films but I have dreamed of stars.

Years ago I had a dream where I went cycling with Deanna Durbin and Joan, a friend of mine. I had recently seen a Durbin film *That Certain Age*, I believe or was it *Mad About Music*? Anyway Deanna and her school-friends were all on bicycles. Joan, my friend, used to cycle frequently, at about the time of my dream. Incidentally we were on the most intimate terms with Deanna in the dream. She was just an ordinary girl and not a film-star.

When I was fifteen and sixteen I had several dreams about Laurence Olivier. I was always very forward in them (entirely unlike myself in real life). One I can remember vividly was one where he and Vivien Leigh invited me to tea, and she told me quite firmly to lay off her husband.

Recently I dreamed I met Bing Crosby at a party. He made a great fuss of me and gave me some perfume. I don't know if this has any psychological significance.

My theory about all of these dreams is that they consisted of what I would like to have happened in everyday life, that is I would like to have had Deanna Durbin as a school-friend, known Laurence Olivier, and gone to a party where Bing Crosby was entertaining.

I realise I am young, naive and probably 'cocky', but I do genuinely love a story and to watch people acting. Therefore I love the cinema.

55. Mr. ....

On reading your paragraph 'Your help is requested, on page 3, of last weeks *Picturegoer*, I should like to state my views as shown on the following sheets enclosed.

Age—19.

Sex—Male.

Nationality—British

Profession—Clerk.

Profession of Parent—Housekeeper.

Question No. 1.

I am afraid this is rather hard to explain, but here goes:

I think films have helped me to rid myself of self embarrassment, for instance, supposing you fell or tripped up in an overcrowded street (and I have fallen plenty times in frosty weather) you would feel as though everyone round about was either laughing or looking hard at you. But this does not worry me, because all I do is think of the films, for if anything similar happens on the screen, no one seems to take any notice. Take another case, supposing, you came out one morning, and after boarding a bus found that you had forgotten to take off your carpet slippers for your shoes. I know you feel rather a fool, but just imagine you are on a film, where a man may board a bus with his shirt lap hanging from the back of his trousers. No one seems to notice this at all, I mean the people on the bus of course, whether this is because it is America, and no one seems to notice things like this, or whether this is just film fun, I don't know, but I pretend this sort of thing does happen over here, and it helps a terrific lot when you are in an embarrassing situation, believe me. Why not try it next time?

I am afraid I cannot mention any special film this has appeared in, as it seems to happen in most pictures.

Question No. 2.

I remember after seeing *Cover Girl* with Rita Hayworth, I dreamt one night I was in this film. I took part of one of the men's chorus in the scene. I think it was near the end of the film, where Rita Hayworth dances down out of the mist from some sort of man made mountain, the path leading round and round. I could see she was wearing one of the most beautiful gold dresses I had ever seen, it looked like the one she wore as the Cover Girl in the film. As she came down on the stage, she suddenly stopped in front of me, and then I began dancing with her, while the other members of the chorus looked on in dismay. I whirled round with her faster and faster, from ballroom dancing to Fred Astaire stepping, (I always wanted to dance like Fred Astaire) and to the tune of 'Long Ago and Far Away', Faster and faster, it was sure swell dancing with Rita Hayworth, probably the only chance I'll get, untill we danced back to the top of the mountain, and back into the mist. Then I woke.

I have never forgotten this dream, as it seems to be part of my ambition, in fact the day after I drew and painted a girl with red hair and the best I could of a gold dress, and now, every time I look at this picture, it reminds me of my dream, which was so life like.

56. Mr. . . .

As I am by profession, a clerk, and my father is a funeral director I have paid particular attention when these trades have been depicted on the screen and I can cite below a few examples.

Funeral parlours in gangster films showing metal caskets and funerals.

Vaults in American cemeteries.

Florists shops showing horseshoe wreaths etc.,

Coroners procedure in America.

Dissections rooms and mortuaries in the Kildare pictures etc. In some mystery films a morgue showing bodies in a huge refrigerated filing cabinet where a mere touch makes the shelf containing the body project from the wall.

And in the office category:

Newspaper editors offices showing glass sound proof partitions and office equipment.

Filing systems in the F.B.I. identification Bureau such as records and fingerprinting files.

The use of the dictaphone in *Double Indemnity*.

The use of statistical machines in a short film made by the M.O.I. about jobs for forces men after the war.

Office films in the Blondie series.

and a recent film about Washington showing production charts also records shown in the March of Time pictures.

I could go on forever like Tennyson's brook but I trust that this is enough from one guinea pig.

Please after all my trouble do not throw this in the waste paper basket. . . .

I have read a little Psychology and Philosophy and as I have been seeing an average of three films a week for twenty years I can presume to have a sufficient background of information to draw upon. . . . I know it sounds rather egotistical but I have noticed actors playing 'bit' roles whom I have mentally classed as a future success and my mental foreknowledge has been proven correct by general concensus of public opinion at a later date.

For instance Alan Ladd playing a walk on part in *The Goldwyn Follies*. I cannot recall the names of more than two dozen films at one time but I recently bought a film review in which were the releases for a year and I could tick off all those I had seen.

I can even tell by looking at the cast list the type of film I am going to see.

After studying films for so long I now use a certain discrimating filter of those I wish to see and those I dont.

In answer to the questions I have never dreamt about anything let alone films. With regard to the second question, Yes as for instances my chief feeling is plain admiration with a feeling of inferiority, at the efficiency and attention to detail by the movie producers. *Pygmalion* and *Pimpernel Smith* both inspired me to better my diction and be a calm and collected personality. This is attraction of opposites because I am temperamental and of a nervous disposition.

Now Voyager and *Lady in the Dark* made me want to free myself from inhibitions.

Flesh and Fantasy intrigued my philosophical instincts and suggested inquiry into supernatural.

I am not one of those gullible film fans who believe that a film actor or actress displays in real life the same characteristics as those they portray on the screen. In fact after so many years of going to films if I see the same player in a number of films I can distinguish between those inherent natural characteristics and those assumed for the role. I always enjoy homely films like the Hardy series, Claudia, and others.

A recent example of wrong casting in my opinion was Deanna Durbin who is I consider the screens perfect player for the role of a *nice girl* being cast as a rather loose character in Somerset Maughams film *Christmas Holiday*.

Recent articles in the *Filmgoer* referring to Miss Durbins marital disagreements have rather shaken my idealistic conception of this young ladies (lady's) nature especially at her age but as I quote above in this case it serves me right.

Part of the question is whether the films have influenced me with regard to fashions.

I must admit that study of the dress and manners of Ronald Colman. David Niven. Walter Pidgeon. Brian Aherne. Paul Henreid. Leslie Howard have improved my taste in such matters. It isnt wrong to emulate an ideal as long as one keeps the standard of perfection very high.

One thing which always strikes me is how an actor assumes the mantle of a doctor lawyer accountant designer without undergoing all the necessary studying and application to hard work. Perhaps this can be both inspiring and dangerous.

A lecturer in Philosophy from Durham University once told me I had a photographic memory that is I remembered things and facts he told me in visual form, if this is so and I can certainly remember films well, films if the subject matter is properly chosen, and the film was slowed down assists reception could become a valuable educational medium. *Going My Way* was a beautiful picture and the story, of two priests and their efforts to help their parishonners (parishioners) was a theme to which no one could take exception.

Light comedies and musicals particularly those of Abbott and Costello, Donald O'Connor, Bob Hope and the Ann Sothern 'Maisie' series are very relaxing and serve as a mental refreshment, that is light farces like *Standing Room Only* and even in these one can find much of educational value. That is the setting of the rooms, furnitures, fittings fireplaces and as in *Thanks for the Memory* how not to cook.

Some of Preston Sturges attempts to show social injustices while elaborate, show certain subjects up in a different light.

Lloyd C. Douglas books *White Banners* and *The Green Light* all serve this purpose that is to show different opinions.

As the film going public can be taken as a cross section of the community surely their opinions as shown at the box office represent a recognised factor of public opinion.

With regard to sex life this is perhaps overemphasised but not in an ugly light, the censors would not allow this. You may take all this as a defence of one of my favourite hobbies and no one who thinks anything of great literature can criticise a filmic presentation of some of it.

Random Harvest was a fine film showing the rehabilitation of a shell shocked man and his conquest of his disability in sympathetic surroundings a most moving film to me.

Lost Horizon gave a fine example of a 'Utopia'.

I once saw a film I do not remember its name in which Thomas Mitchell took the role of a Professor of Philosophy who had an incurable and fatal complaint and possessing no dependants decided that before he died he would rid the world of some person of anti-social tendencies preferably a blackmailer in an unsolved crime. When he came to the conclusion that it is not right for one human to set himself up as a judge of human conduct and life he gave himself up to be electrocuted. The moral of this does not seem obvious to-day although the story is obviously a trifle fantastic. But self sacrifice is not always fantastic.

Lost Angel shows the effect of Psychology on a child sheltered from the world.

Detective stories like the Thin Man series The Inner Sanctum series Ellery Queen Charlie Chan Crime Doctor. All the films make me feel as if I am solving a crossword puzzle or jigsaw and I am curious to see if my solution is correct.

Eternal triangles also make me wish to see who gets the girl.

One question which is often raised is whether films of criminals influence children.

In my case I think that films like *Double Indemnity* which show that crime does not pay in conscience value is a sufficient answer to this. The side of law and order such as *North West Mounted Police* also needs adventure and courage.

The *Petrified Forest* was a philosophical problem.

Great music inspires everyone and Paderewski in *Moonlight Sonata* elevated ones soul. *Goodbye Mr. Chips* also did this.

Appreciation of fine scenery in *Rose Marie Valley of Giants Captain of the Clouds*.

I once saw Chester Morris in the film *Blind Alley* showing Ralph Bellamy as a psychologist showing the mental condition which led to crime, that was heredity and environment.

Random Harvest showing a mans conquest of shell shock and rehabilitation.

Age 30 yrs. Sex Male. Nationality English. Profession Clerk.

57. Mrs. ....

The film *A Chump at Oxford* and *The Magicians* convince me of 'the funny side to one's nature'.

Tutor and *Rajah*—incongruous. Yet, who can deny that not only do these 'two' 'lower' forms of mankind imitate 'higher' forms of mankind through clowning, its this clowning that magnifies the artificial absurdness's of the two great influences—high and low. ('Art' carries a wonderful endowment) but its decided me that each one of us has a 'funny' double personality and that the APE is undoubtedly the forerunner I'm convinced.

Age (middle) Profession—Music Teacher Mother—Schoolteacher Father—ex-carding felt-maker)

58. Miss . . .

Pictures have always had a decided influence on my decisions and behaviour. The following is an instance:

About 7 years ago, when I was 16½, I saw a picture called *Peg O' My Heart* with Marion Davies. It tells the story of Peg, a young girl living in a little village in Ireland. She is charming, pretty and seems quite intelligent. However, she is left a legacy and one of the conditions re this legacy is that she goes to live with her Aunt in England. Peg does so (I am giving only a very brief outline of the story), and finds that her speech is wrong; her pronounciation (pronunciation) shocking; her clothes atrocious—in fact, everything about her is simply terrible! Yet—in the village: in her own surroundings: she was all right; or seemed to be all right! Well, that picture made me think!! You see, I lived in a little village with my parents, right up in the North. I had never travelled more than 15 miles from home, so naturally knew nothing of large towns or cities. But I began to think: 'In this village I'm all right. My speech is correct, as is my manners. I dress smartly. I can discuss many different subjects. There can't be anything wrong with me!! And yet if I went to a large town, would I be able to say the same? Would I?' That doubt persisted in my mind until I could think of nothing else. I had quite a good job, with excellent prospects—but I just couldn't settle.

At last, one day I told my parents I was going to go to London! My Father stormed, my Mother wept and my brothers and sisters stared at me as though I had gone mad! It was unheard of!!

But I was determined; so I packed my things and two days afterwards I left home (with exactly 28/- in my pocket, being too proud to accept any money from my Father after what he'd said). You will understand what a tremendous step that was when I say that my ancestors had always lived in that village. It was almost a tradition with them. In fact, my Father has still not forgiven me (he won't even write!) and I haven't seen my parents since that day. However, that is beside the point!

When I came to London, I was offered a job by a firm with a branch in X.—and I accepted. Of course, I had a lot to learn, but it was worth it. I have now a very good position and as you can see from the address, am still in X.—and I can truthfully say I have never regretted my decision. But I've often wondered since, if I hadn't seen that picture just what my life would have been. Probably the usual monotonous, uneventful village existence! And yet—would it?

Your second question re: films in dreams. Again pictures have played a very large part in my dreams; but there is one dream which keeps recurring—each time more vividly than before.

Many years ago, I saw the picture *Smiling Thro'* with Norma Shearer. One scene particularly impressed me: she is dressed as a bride and walks up the aisle to be married. In the middle of the ceremony there is an interruption and she is shot and dies.

Well, I dream I am dressed as a bride; am looking very, very beautiful and am walking slowly up the aisle (the centre of all eyes). Then the ceremony begins and, as in the picture, there is an interruption. Someone shouts 'Stop!', and a man appears holding a revolver. He points it at the groom and as he fires I rush to save him (the groom) and I am shot instead. I don't feel any pain, but sink slowly to the ground. My chief feeling is one of pride to think this has actually happened to me! As I recline gracefully, I manage to arrange my frock and veil to my satisfaction.

The wound over my heart begins to bleed and as the blood runs down I think 'It doesn't look nice like that. I must make it run in another direction', which I do by moving very, very slightly to the right.

Then I place my hands in a position where my beautifully shaped nails can be seen to their best advantage. At the same time I become deadly pale, and I think 'How well this pallor must suit me. My skin must look beautiful against the ivory of my frock and veil.' This thought pleases me very much!

Then I slowly close my eyes, thinking at the same time 'My lashes must cast dark shadows on my cheeks. The effect must be wonderful.' I find I am so curious to see the result that I have to open one eye to look at the other closed one, and find my lashes are about an inch long! I sigh with rapture!! Again I think 'I'm glad I have dark hair. It makes a better contrast'.

I have then an irresistible desire to smile, but check myself in time with the thought 'This is serious! I'm dying, so I really *mustn't* smile!! What would people think?' So I lie there and listen to the murmurs of the crowd: 'Isn't it a shame!' 'What a tragedy!' 'Such a beautiful bride!' 'And so young, too!'—etc., etc.

My dream usually ends there—the only difference is that some-times I wear a different colour or style of frock; or the groom is not the same. He may appear as someone in whom I may be interested at the moment; or his features may not be distinguishable. The man who shoots may appear as someone with whom I may be annoyed; or again his features, too, may not be distinguishable.

These instances I have mentioned are only two of many; there are numerous others, and my reason for writing is to prove that pictures *do* have a tremendous influence on the minds of young and old alike.

Perhaps, then, if Producers realise this we may have better pictures in the future!

Age 23½. Female. British. Profession: Assistant Accountant.
Profession of Parents: Father, Interior Decorator. Mother, none.

59. Miss . . .

Several years ago, when I was 18, I had rather an unfortunate love affair, in-as-much-as the man concerned was married. Put it down to my youth if you like, but I fell for the old story of 'not being understood by his wife' etc., and I must admit that I carried on with this with my eyes wide open, really believing that I was doing the right thing in relieving this man of some of his unhappiness, and that eventually he would obtain the divorce he was always mentioning.

My friends talked to me, and tried to point out the foolishness of it all, but still I continued to see the man.

However, during this affair, the film *Back Street* came to the local Cinema, and I went to see it, and I can quite honestly say that that picture was the only thing that made me realise what a mess I was making of my life; I even dreamed about it, but instead of seeing Ray Smith furtively living in a back street, I saw myself, and the unhappiness and even tragedy in which it would inevitably end.

I'm sure if I hadn't seen this film, I should have still continued seeing this man, still believing, as many more girls are probably believing, that I should one day be the wife of a man who belonged to another woman.

The very same week that I saw *Back Street*, I gave up this man, and went to live quite a distance away for a while, and now, years later, I have a job in which I am very interested, a good considerate boy friend, and an aim in life, and I often look back and wonder what I would have been doing if I'd continued with the other unfortunate business. Would I have been like Ray Smith, always waiting and hoping for a telephone call or the sound of his knock on the door, or would I have been his wife? I shall never know, but what I do know is that I am far happier now than I ever was then.

You can see from this, therefore, that a film did definitely have a big influence in my life, and did figure in my dreams.

60. Miss . . .

My environment is not what I would have it, yet I do not alter it. (This preface is not beside the point, it is necessary if I am to reveal at all accurately why certain films have affected me). Partly because my mother is unwell and would be lonely without me, partly because my Father means well, and doesn't realise that he and not I is leading my life, partly because I am afraid to go against him at home.

I was considered clever at school, passed scholarships to Secondary and Technical schools, but my parents wouldn't let me go. As a result I never had a passable education. I am studying English and elocution and one day I may make an authoress. I have the brains but not the education.

George Sanders who portrayed the artist in *The Moon and Sixpence* seemed to me to be in my position. Tied to a home, that was not a home to him, and to a wife who didn't love him for what he was but for what she wanted him to be.

He had the courage (I seem to lack it) to cast aside convention and pursue his course whatever the cost to himself or others.

The cost was not great the love he had for his last wife and the joy he got from his achievements made his tragic death seem worth while.

This film made me realise more than ever, never to ignore inspiration, whether or not I receive acclaim.

Son of Fury was not a brilliant film, the scene that interested me was the one in which Ben (played by Tyrone Power) is teaching one of the island girls how to eat with a knife and fork; she drops the food and exclaims I am stupid, Ben reflected and said he was the stupid one for trying to alter their way of life.

With all that they lack in culture, this film brought home to me, that the uneducated people are the happiest, providing their associates are equally ignorant.

Kings Row was the most perfectly acted film I have ever seen. The charactors that interested me were that of Cassie the insane daughter of the doctor who instructs Paris, a young student in his studies.

Cassie loves Paris, and he is devoted too (to) her, the way she acts make him aware that she is unbalanced, but he won't let himself believe it is anything that matters.

Cassie's Father Dr. Towers kills Cassie and himself, rather than see Paris ruin his life.

Paris knows that it was best, yet Cassie is always in his thoughts, and while walking by the river he momentarily mistakes a young woman for Cassie.

A romance springs up between these two, I believe that Cassie's soul was in harmony with his and he visualised it as this young woman.

When I saw *White Cargo* it revolted me. Not the immorality of Tondalayo who can hardly be blamed for it.

But the contemptous (contemptuous) way men seem to seduce and undermine coloured girls in a way that they wouldn't have the courage to try on European girls, and yet they are as much entitled to respect as we, I never really realised the havoc passion could cause until I saw this film.

More recently I saw *Summer Storm*, this was a strange film and vividly impressed me. What a fool Petroff was he knew he couldn't resist Olga, he should have killed himself too, when he killed her. Love goes beyond the earth I am sure and they would have been together.

Conience (conscience) is a terrible thing to live with, and he more than payed for what he did to Urbenin. Olga's death was a labour of love and though not justified was excusable.

What was so shattering, and yet this was the part that I can't forget, was the cynical ending, his dance card in the rubbish with the broken glass falling on it.

The Garden of Allah was a beautiful film. The story briefly is that of a monk who haunted by desires to see the world and experience love breaks his vows.

He meets, loves, and marries a lovely French woman with whom he travels the desert, he has found love but loses his peace of mind and feels evil.

Eventually his wife learns the truth and persuades him to go back to the monastry. This sacrifice made their lives more noble than they would otherwise have been.

When I was younger I believed in God, I never was particularly pious but whenever I comitted (committed) a sin, I always felt guilty and repented. I felt life was worth living, now sometimes I don't, I try to believe but its not always I can.

When I see such films as these I feel stimulated and sure that life is not the material thing it seems to be.

To be happily married is not nessasarily (necessarily) to be in love, most people are too shallow to experience a love such as these charetors (characters) did, but I shall try to find a life that is as spiritual as it is worldly.

If is (it) were not for these films, I see so little of life, that I should not be aware that the love you have for a brother is any different than that you have for your intended.

These films have made me realise that if I am too (to) take out of life I must probably pay, and I would be willing.

If I could but love and be loved, I shall be well content and not feel that I was born for nothing.

The films have all appeared in my dreams, but that is not remarkable, because I dream every night.

I am 18 years, a girl, and I help my Mother at home.

(Personal details for reasons of anonymity withheld. Parents working-class people.)

61. Mr. . . .

Being keenly interested in films not only for their entertainment value but also for their moral and spiritual reaction upon the average filmgoer I should like to take this opportunity of answering your two questions.

My age is 23, I am unmarried and as yet have had no serious love affair. Therefore in my case the question of films having any effect upon love or divorce does not arise but if it did I can answer you most emphatically that films would not influence me in any way and I enlarge that statement to cover any important decision I might make.

In the past when making an important decision I have often thought what some particular actor would have done in my place. In the film he would always make the right decision because he is governed by a story which says he will make it, but placed in my position with facts instead of fiction, his chances of making the right decision would be no more certain than my own. Consequently the influence is cancelled out and I am left with my own opinion.

With regard to religion there has always been the old controversy that the cinema is drawing people away from the church. My answer to that is that anyone who has been brought up in the doctrines of Christianity and professes to abide by them, would not allow his or her belief to be influenced by anything so trivial as a film and that any non-Christian would not suddenly start going to church if films ceased tomorrow. For myself I am and always have been a firm believer in Christianity and so far from allowing films to judge my Christian beliefs I judge films by those beliefs. However while on this subject I should like to make the tentative suggestion that the screen would provide an excellent medium for preaching Christianity providing it were done subtlely and not in blatant propaganda style.

From what I have written you will have gathered that where the important things of life are concerned I am guided essentially by own ideas or those of some older and wiser person but never by films or fiction of any kind.

There are however two small points in your question namely manners and fashion in which I am sometimes guided by something I may see in a film. For example I have always admired the quiet manners of Ronald Colman and although I do not go around emulating his every movement if a situation arises where a show of manners is necessary I conjure up in my minds eye what Mr. Colman, or it may be some other actor, would do in my position.

In fashions films have had a really big influence on me. Through films I came to prefer the double to the single breasted suit, through films also I choose the colour of my ties and suits and in general I have acquired a more appreciative attitude towards tailoring than I might otherwise have done.

In answer to your second question—I do dream about films but only in the same way that I dream about anything else that is occasionally and certainly not in any way to cause my sleep to be troublesome.

I hope I have satisfactorily answered your questions and it only remains for me to give you the details you asked for.

Sex. Male. Nationality. British. Profession—at present serving in the R.A.F. as a wireless operator, but before the war a Cost Clerk. Profession of Parents—My mother: none. My father an engineer.

62. Mr. . . .

1. Have films ever influenced you with regard to personal decisions or behavior (behaviour) (Love, divorce, manners, fashion, etc.) Can you give instances?

2. Have films ever appeared in your dreams?

In answering question one I have to go back a few years to the days when Rudolph Valentino was featured in *The Eagle*, *The Sheik*, and *The Son of the Sheik*. These films, as far as I can remember were the first to influence me in such a way as to make me ape the principal male star.

Every little detail was observed and noted, the play of the hands, the movement of the lips and eyes, and carriage of the body.

Valentino's attitude towards Vilma Banky in one of these pictures led me to act in a similar, but somewhat modified way towards a girl friend with satisfactory results.

In the first instance I became a little ashamed and disturbed at the reaction, but as the phase was shortlived it gradually ceased to worry me. I can only quote outstanding instances. I most certainly have been influenced before but not so strongly as in the cases mentioned here. Later in 1939, I saw *Juarez*. The influence exerted itself once more and I became a leader, a revolutionary, the very life-blood of the downtrodden masses. No mannerisms to be transferred here but the desire to become the orator and master of men.

And now, after seeing Ronald Colman in *Kismet* the effect is not so apparent and it has left me a little disappointed. Perhaps, a little later, other film may make a strong impression, I hope they do, it takes me away from this world for a bit.

A nil return must be made to question two as far as I am concerned. Films have never appeared in my dreams.
Age: 37. Sex: Male. Nationality: English. Profession: Clerk. Profession of parent: Storekeeper.

63. Mrs. . . .

Probably I am much too old to have my say, but here is my opinion for what it may be worth.

The picture which stands out the most vivid of all in my memory was *The King of Kings*. The man with whom I went was an ex-soldier of the last war; (He had lost a foot, and was rather 'off' religion). I recall so well the great hush that fell on the audience that night, and how it was asked that there should be 'No smoking'. We sat enthralled, and during the show, when the Saviour was shown as dragging along His Cross, my friend said something about *how much* he felt about it all, and *how* he wished he could have been *there* to have shown his reverence of Our Lord.

When we got home we discussed that film as we have never discussed a film before or since. We agreed that, for one thing, it seemed to correspond with the Bible story in *every detail*. I think that the greatest thing about it was that in no way had the Greatest Sacrifice of all been tampered with. *If it had* it would have been spoilt for any such as myself who believe (and am grateful for) the fact that Jesus Christ died for all people. AND FOR ME. I had loved Jesus before, but *never* with such intensity as I did after that film. To *see* it portrayed in pictures was I think, as I afterwards remarked, better than the finest sermon ever preached. And X my friend, to whom I put the question, 'Do you love Him now?' replied with great feeling in his voice, 'I do'.

During the last war I think it may have been, but one film I have never forgotten was called *Is God Dead?* Showing as it did the trails and trials of several families or persons who fancied that God must have deserted them, or was 'dead', as one guesses afterwards *each* peculiar circumstance was brought to a satisfactory conclusion, as left one in no doubt that God was very much 'alive'. I obtained great comfort from that film, and often since, when life has been particularly troublous I have remembered that film (More, than I have ever recalled either the *written word*, or the *spoken sermon*) and have gained courage from the fact that God is not dead. So much from the religious films.

To come to present days. No one could see *Mrs. Miniver*, or *Random Harvest*, to name but two, without being the better for them in more ways than one. Films of that category make one go home so much more determined to 'be good and let who will be clever'. And when one is tired of struggling for recognition in any kind of art, what picture can do one more good than, say, *Irish Eyes Are Smiling*? The scene in which the song writer (taken I presume from fact) bangs away at his own composition after so much discouragement, must surely give hopes to even the faintest-hearted amongst us. I know it, and other films of like kind, have always helped me greatly. If one dare say so, (when one is not at all great oneself) it gives one a kind of 'fellow-feeling' to see portrayed in story and picture form how the famous have had their struggles too. AND HAVE WON.

I have named but a few (simply because though I remember many films which have helped me spiritually, mentally, and psychologically I cannot recall their names) of some of the great 'pictures' of yester-year, and the present. And for fostering one's love of country never could I forget *Cavalcade*, and *This Happy Breed*. There was something particularly intriguing in *A Canterbury Tale*. Give us more of such films as I have named and the world is bound to be a better place to live in.

Age 56. Female. British, of British Parents.

64. Miss . . .

With reference to your article in *Picturegoer* films have never had an opportunity to influence me as regards marriage or divorce but they do influence me to some extent. After seeing *Old Acquaintance* I was very thankful for having a girl friend of the calibre I have and resolved to be a better friend to her. *The First of the Few* made me resolve to be more efficient at my work and to study more, whereas after seeing *Pride and Prejudice* I tried to be more sociable and pleasant with people.

I have never dreamt of a film but stars have figured in my dreams. The ones I can remember most vividly are Leslie Howard and James Mason.

I am 18 years old of British birth and parentage, work as a shorthand typist. My parents were both clerical workers.

65. Miss . . .

Age, 21. Sex, Female. Unmarried. Nationality, British. Profession, Cashier. Profession of Mother, Milliner. Profession of Father, Printer.

Question one. (Have films ever influenced you with regard to personal decisions or behaviour?)

In direct answer—Yes, but as far as I am concerned it was not the films themselves so much as the acting and personality of an actress, namely—Ann Sheridan.

For years I have been one of her greatest admirers, and have seen her in a great many films. I admire her 'Oomph', her wise-cracks, and her inimitable way of handling men—so that they invariably fall for her.

Although I haven't actually tried to emulate her, I have occaisonally (occasionally) found myself doing things as she would, and thinking the way that I imagine she does. I used to be rather timid, and quite selfconscious, especially when in strange company, but since becoming so interested in Ann, and to put it rather crudely—taking a few tips from her—I have acquired a great deal more confidance and feel that I am having much more enjoyment out of life. I am not any different however, as regards morals—and although I know that in private life Ann is divorced I still do not entirely agree with people being divorced, especially more times than one.

In many films, the most recent being: *Navy Blues*, *Juke Girl*, *Wings for the Eagle*, *The Man Who came to Dinner*, Ann Sheridan has played parts calling for plenty of glamour, and has played them very well. I can state with perfect truth that since seeing these films I have become more experienced in the art of feminine love-making, and attractiveness. Once I proved this to myself by having success at a party to be held in honour of a Pilot who had recently won his wings in America, from where he had just returned. Before going

I made preparations to look my very best, and managed to do my hair, make up, and dress quite well, the impressions which Ann had made on me helped me a lot in this. I went to the party and had a lovely time, and shortly afterwards I received a letter from a young London fellow who had also been at the party, and he invited me to spend a day in London with him. I went, met him again, and had a great time. After this I really felt that I owed my success to Ann, for giving me such a good idea of the technique of 'Glamour', and love-making.

Well, since then I have made myself 'Go Places', and have not felt self-conscious as I sometimes used to. Recently I met an American sailor who hails from the State of Texas, which incidentally is Ann Sheridan's native State. We are very good friends at present but of course I cannot say yet if a love affair will result, but I can say that without having seen the films of Anns' that I have, I would have probably have made a mess of things by being shy and uncertain.

In the film *Kings Row*, Ann had a very sympathetic part and I feel that I learnt something from seeing her acting in it, though of course not in the same way as the other films. Then in *Edge of Darkness* she played the rôle of a very brave, tough, Norwegian girl, this helped me to understand that there is more in life than just the superficial things. In *George Washington Slept Here*, Ann had a chance to show her sense of humour, and in *Shine On Harvest Moon* she again used her charm with great effect. These films have been an education to me, and I am serious about this, though I am afraid I haven't been able to explain very well what I mean. However I hope that you will be able to see exactly how I feel about it.

Question No. 2. (Have films ever appeared in your dreams?)

My answer to this question is No—I have never dreamt about films at any time.

I do hope that my experience concerning question one will help you with your investigation.

66. Miss . . .

Just a few lines in answer to your request:

First of all I will answer your questions regarding my age which is twenty, nationality British of course, profesion (profession) typist in the Wrens, Profession of parents Father office clerk Mother housewife, (a very clever one), for she picks all colour schemes from the Technicolour films we see so often now.

In answer to your questions, I can say that films have influenced me, mostly Technicolour musical films, such as, *Bathing Beauty*, they give you ideas of poise, self confidence and also dress sense which is the gateway to these two things, it enables you to pair off colours, which you would not dream of wearing unless you had seen how lovely they look.

Also from the films I have learned to love opera music, and taught myself to sing at the ships concerts, and have not yet had any eggs thrown, but will be always ready to catch them.

Films can also give you an idea of acting, when I see a part well acted I feel as if I would like to try the part myself, such as a good spy part, or the last part of *2,000 Women* in the concert hall, where they all sing, 'There'll always be an England.'

Films have never appeared in my dreams, and I have my own views on Love and Divorce, films would not influence me on those subjects.

I am not a very good letter writer, but hope I have been able to give you an idea of how films influence me.

67. Miss . . .

Please let me introduce myself first, I am nineteen years of age, female and British. For the past year since my Mother died, I have looked after the home, my Father and younger sister.

Before that, I was educated at High School, leaving at seventeen after passing my School-leaving Certificate. After which I worked in an office, learning shorthand and typing at night-school. Then I worked in a munitions factory for a while until called home, to look after the family.

My one and most interesting hobby has been films since I can remember, and I have kept an inventory of all the films I have ever seen, dating from about the age of four, which I can just remember, to the present day and the total number of films I have seen in my nineteen years up to date is: 1,350.

My Father, at present a ship's plumber in a 'dock-yard' has travelled to America and Canada, but has seen one film in the last fifteen years, and does not in the least share my enthusiasm for pictures.

Films have influenced me, on certain principals, one for instance behaviour, especially in concern with the opposite sex. In films men nearly always have good manners, even the 'bad' characters show a tendency for politeness here and there. Now most of the men I know, and boys especially my age, have no manners what-

CHARLES BOYER AND MARGARET SULLAVAN IN 'BACK STREET'

The fateful dilemma between family and business responsibilities and 'true love' (See Chapter IX, p. 178)

soever. The modern generation are lacking in that respect, I have heard it said that women in these times doing men's work are excuses for the man not to give up his seat in a bus or in general to treat her as an equivalent. Women whether doing a man's job or not get tired quicker and more easily than a man. But in some cases I must admit, a man is justified in remaining in his seat, as more often than not, he never even hears a 'thank-you' if he gives it up to a woman. All these tips should be noted by both sexes when seeing a picture, and perhaps someday, I may drop in a faint when some boys I know let me go in front of them or walk on the inside of the pavement, or show some manners.

I think too that some boys who must have too much imagination go so far as to copy boys on the films, such as the 'Dead End Kids' they see it on the films, stealing, lying and cheating, and in the film they get away with it, and think in real life they can do the same. Candidly I don't like such pictures.

Women's and men's fashions on the films generally appeal to me, like most women. But in some cases they are absolutely ridiculous, such as in *Lady in the Dark* Ginger Rogers wore some wonderful creations and I honestly preferred the simple modes, and got a great laugh at some of the others especially the ones the film actress Phyllis Brooks wore. I like the simple and plain fashions and try to make my own clothes resemble them. But I don't like the over dressed woman's clothes and many girls do try to copy these and especially in this country where the climate is so different and changeable the effect is ridiculous instead of stunning. But I do prefer men's fashions on the films, and they do influence me on what the well dressed man should wear. In regard to both sexes if there are too-broad a shoulder or not enough, or none too shapely a leg, they do know how to camoflage (camouflage) the defect from which tips and hints I do try to copy.

I expect I would not be truthful if I said that films do not influence me on the question of love, because like many other women they do, as I expect they do man about woman. Everyone has his or her favourite actor or actress about whom they build a secret ambition, to fall in love with someone just like them. *Love Story* intrigued me very much, the hero was what every girl dreams about, handsome, well dressed, thoughtful, kind and well mannered and in meeting one of the opposite sex, it is only natural to try and find those qualities in him. But also, there is the other type of hero that appeals to me, the character that is ruthless, brutal, and yet so calm and smooth tongued, such a part as Humphrey Bogart or

George Sanders play in *Casablanca* which I thought a wonderful picture and *The Moon and Sixpence*.

In real life though people are so different, the film stars themselves when they are themselves minus, script grease-paint and elaborate costume are the same the whole world over, as other people, tempers, emotions, thoughts so that when we admire them we are really admiring the part they are playing in the film, and this I always bear in mind, before I am led astray.

Love can be influenced by films, so in some cases divorce may be too, but I am afraid I can't write about that, as I am not married yet, to go further not even in love yet. But I don't think they would influence me on the point of divorce as you have to love someone very much to love their bad points as well as their good, and as I stated before films are only in a make-believe world, and love and divorce are reality, the same as stars are off the screen part of the human race.

Make up appeals to a woman and rather influences myself in regard to such problems. But of course in the Hollywood dream world make up is the most important essential of all. But when applied to yourself very powerful flood lighting has to be taken into consideration, and if, say, in everyday life we were to use make up to such an extent as the movie stars do, we would look ridiculous freaks. But the contours of the mouth where lipstick should and should not go is a useful hint to me, the same applies as to the application of powder and rouge. But of course considerably toned down.

Planning of houses has always interested and influenced me, I know for a fact that most houses in America are the latest in modern house planning, and when you see such wonderful appliances for labour saving, and wonderful electricity and cool storage planning on the films, well you feel that you just have to do something about it. Of course the kitchen mostly appeals to me, being a woman, but I daresay it will appeal to some men too in the way of comfortable living rooms, better lighting system, and where there is no help needed for such a house such as helping wife or mother to wash up, or carry coals as she is tired of doing it herself. Also it must be pleasing for a husband to come home from work, to a neat and pretty wife, owing to many labour saving devices, than a wife who is tired out and looks it too.

Films are educational, some more than others, and some hardly at all, but I like educational films and I think there should be more of them, sometimes they influence either one way or another. Such as in the film *The Adventures of Mark Twain*, it was, what I would call a very educational picture, being a writer 'Mark Twain' influenced me a lot, I have always wanted to write a book, and now I feel more determined than ever to write one, also I learnt a lot from that picture such about 'Mark Twain's' real name, his life, ambitions and humour, also a very slight bit about Haley's Comet. But every picture I see there is always some little bit of knowledge I learn that I didn't know before.

As to ever dreaming about any picture, I must confess I never have, although I don't know why, because my mind is so much full of them, that why I shouldn't dream of them remains a complete mystery to me. But of course I have had one or two real nasty nightmares through seeing a horror picture. But the nightmare has not actually been about the film itself. I must add that I enjoy horror or murder mystery films, and with a little modesty can generally detect the murderer and the clues and mistakes he makes before any of my other friends can, who happen to be with me at the time.

68. Miss . . .

I am not very clever at wording this kind of letter, but would like to help, if possible, the investigation.

1. I took a great liking to Deanna Durbin's hair style in *First Love*, copied it as near as possible and found it suited me better than any other style. I also took a great interest (which I never had before) in the more serious music, after seeing the films *Dangerous Moonlight* and *The Great Lie*.

2. I don't know whether this is correct for this question but I remember dreaming I went to a cinema to see George Sanders and Mary Maguire in *The Outsiders*, but what I dreamed was not a bit like the actual film.

Aged 21. Nationality, English. No profession—just ordinary factory worker.

3. A TENTATIVE INTERPRETATION

We have printed the above documents in the exact form in which we received them without any regard to grammatical or orthographical correctness. (Only in those very rare cases where the text was in danger of remaining unintelligible have we for example allowed ourselves to put a stop and to begin a new sentence.)

It might, of course, be objected that the documents are marked by a high degree of 'rationalisation' in so far as any answer to questions formulated by an investigator may reflect a gap between *immediate* experience and its formulation in words and sentences. There is no doubt that the questions have guided the authors in writing these documents, but I do not think they have marred in any way their sincerity. Indeed the sincerity with which the questions have been answered is perhaps the most striking general note of almost all the documents.

The writers felt, I believe, a profound urge to help in an investigation, the importance of which they fully realised. One must also be aware of the fact that the majority of the contributors can have felt only little attraction by the offered prizes, as the money involved was inconsiderable. What may have been much more attractive is the distinction of becoming a prize-winner. In addition one has to bear in mind that most of the contributors are what one considers as 'movie fans'. The more violent characteristics of a 'movie fan' are certainly not absent from the documents (*See* document 1). But, generally speaking, the contributors reveal themselves as ardent picturegoers—and nothing else. Moreover, the 'movie fan' phenomenon has not yet taken in this country such acute forms as in the U.S.A. Until now we have not made a film star into an honorary mayor of any British town. The fact that the British 'movie fan' remains unorganised indicates a profound difference between the still sound civic sense of the average Britisher and his American counterpart. It would be a fascinating task to undertake a sociological analysis of the fan-mail of British actors and actresses. It would probably also show that British film stars have, to an infinitely greater degree than their American *compères*, a private life of their own. Perhaps one day I shall implement the findings of this book by such an analysis.

Anyway, as far as our present authors are concerned, I am fairly convinced that their views on the moral and psychological impact of films on their lives may be regarded as *representative* of the great majority of the cinema-going public in Great Britain though, being 'fans' they may reflect film reactions with a somewhat greater intensity or perhaps it would be safer to say with a greater degree of 'rationalisation'. For an individual who is able to write about such intimate and delicate experiences may ultimately be freer from the magic of film than the person who goes twice or three times a week to his or her local cinema without ever attempting to bring film influence to his or her consciousness. I have tried to interview people under twenty, e.g. my local coal boy, and I was never able to get more out of him than the admission 'I liked this film', or 'this was a pretty film'. Their or his reaction is difficult to assess except by very careful case study. It may well be that such a study would make the material collected here colourless and insignificant. But before we reach such a stage in the social investigation of film our academic psychologists will have to give up a considerable amount of their prejudices.

Naturally I have tested the problem whether our documents have such a representative character. I have talked to and interviewed in the course of about five months very many people: workers, employees, clerks, members of the professional classes, members of the aristocracy, middle class people, housewives, etc. I have kept notes of these interviews and only because they taught me the documents printed can be regarded as representative—though with some important qualifications about which I shall say more presently—have I decided to publish them as they stand.

Perhaps I should insert here an example of one of my interviews. Here it is:

Mrs. B. on Films

I interviewed to-day Mrs. B. about films. She lives in our street which is a typical North Paddington street (workers, employees, and a few lower middle class people make up our street's social colour). Mrs. B. is twenty-three, her husband is in the army; at present he is in Austria. Mrs. B. is attractive, nicely dressed. She lives with her parents and another sister who is a few years older.

Mrs. B. is frank with me. She probably believes I am a good married man and father and, in spite of my being an 'intellectual' who has written books and has thousands of them on the walls of his home, finds that I am at ease with workers. I have also fulfilled, to the street's satisfaction, my duties as a member of our local Civil Defence.

Mrs. B. is a war worker in a factory. She admits that films are the main topic of her and her colleagues' conversation. Of newspapers she reads only 'an interesting headline' and the gossip column. Mrs. B. also admits that she copies dresses and hair-do's from films. She is frankly envious of some of film stars' clothes and becomes at times—for this reason—dissatisfied with her home life. Her screen idol is Bette Davis or Greer Garson. She imitates the latter's hair style.

When she has seen 'a good film' she and her sister come home and re-enact scenes and sequences to the delight of their family, not to mention their own enjoyment and thrill. She is very fond of acting. She 'thinks' also about films before she goes to sleep, for instance whether certain decisions and problems as seen on the screen were right or wrong.

Mrs. B. regards film as an educational instrument. Films also take her 'out' from her social surroundings. She very much liked *They Were Sisters,* this being a film which showed life as it might happen in her own family. She disliked *The Fifth Chair.* This type of American humour is 'too sophisticated'. She prefers British comedians.

Mrs. B. also admits—this on interrogation—that when faced with a decision, she might ask herself 'what would Bette Davis or Greer Garson do in such a situation?' Her male screen idol is Robert Taylor 'because he has such an expression in his eyes' (I wonder what her husband looks like).

It is obvious from these notes which I am writing down a few hours after our conversation that all the main trends of my *Picturegoer* documents recur. Whether you live in Wales, in Scotland, in Bath or Ipswich, your personality is shaped by film. Mrs. B. may think very rightly that she discovers her own personality by seeing a film. In reality her personality conforms to a type of film star; in this case Miss Davis and Miss Garson. This process must ultimately lead, and has already led, to a pauperisation of the human race which is terrifying.

It would be a fascinating task to make an attempt of a contemporary 'anthropology'. Take Robert Taylor, M. Boyer, Mr. Laurence Olivier, and take Miss Durbin, Miss Garson, and Miss Davis and a few more film actors and actresses, and you may be able to arrive at a complete anthropological typology of which no La Rochefoucauld, Pascal or Jung could ever dream.

Another question may perhaps be raised with regard to our documents. Why have you asked the question about dreams?

I am, of course, fully aware that accurate dream observation by laymen is exceedingly difficult to obtain. Yet I thought that I should risk some degree of inaccuracy, as the advantage of gaining some help on the more obvious psychological material might be considerable.

In addition, film reactions without an appreciation of the relevance of day-dream and *Einschlaftraum* and ultimately dream itself seemed to me to be utterly incomplete. So I offer this material to psychologists as very preliminary material for further study. It would be impertinent for me to attempt an appreciation of the dream material myself. I should like only to say that several of the dream descriptions (e.g., No. 40) appear to me as quite remarkable and important, while others (e.g., No. 33) are vague. In any case, they should enable us to form an idea of the extent to which the film experience leads to dreaming (in all forms), and also of how very important it would seem to make a thorough study of nightmares as resulting from films.

When I say the documents are representative I do not mean this in any way in a *numerical* sense. No attempt is made in this book to arrive at quantitative results. Not that I think that quantitative results are unobtainable. But I think, until we have studied the qualitative structure of film experience, any *quantitative* appreciation must remain vague.

Nor does this mean that we have overlooked certain numerical facts our documents may be able to tell us. Here for example, is a tabulated list of some points which are perhaps not unimportant:

Total Number of Protocols: 68.

Men	-	-	-	-	19	*c.* 28	per cent.
Women	-	-	-	49	*c.* 72	,, ,,

Age Groups

Under 20 years	-	-	-	29	42.6	,, ,,
20 to 25 years inclusive	-	-	15	22	,, ,,
26 ,, 30 ,, ,,	-	-	6	8.8	,, ,,
31 ,, 40 ,, ,,	-	-	3	4.4	,, ,,
Over 40 years	-	-	-	8	11.7	,, ,,
Unspecified	-	-	-	7	*c.* 10	,, ,,
Married	-	-	-	8	11.7	,, ,,
Single	-	-	-	-	52	*c.* 76	,, ,,
Unspecified	-	-	-	8	11.7	,, ,,

(Nearly all in this category are very probably single but do not actually state the fact).

It is certainly significant that 72 per cent of all the contributors are women and that 42.6 per cent are under twenty years of age. The film industry is, I believe, particularly conscious of the latter fact (the term conscious is not identical with the term conscientious!). It is also interesting to note that members of the employee class form the majority of those who have contributed.

Finally I give a list of the regional distribution of our contributors. Only 11 per cent come from the London area. In order to guard the anonymity of the writers I felt I was not justified in attaching the place names to the individual contributions.

Regional Distribution

Nottingham.
South Shields.
Wirral, Cheshire.
Dunstable, Beds.
Wallsend on Tyne.
Grimsby, Lincs.
London, S.E.6.
Coventry.
Tooting, S.W.17.
Walsall.
Slough.
Plymouth.
Brighton.
Hounslow.
Rhyl, N. Wales.
Dorking, Surrey.
Sussex village.
Edinburgh.
West Byfleet, Surrey.
Liverpool.
Weston-super-Mare.
Caithness.
Glasgow.
Ealing.
Stirling.
Aberdeen.
Loughborough.
Cardiff.
Rotherham.
London, S.E.5.
Golders Green.
Cradley Heath, Staffs.
Cardiff.

Wakefield.
Stockton-on-Tees.
Bury, Lancs.
Cardiff.
Northolt.
Boxmoor, Herts.
Gillingham, Kent.
Kent.
Llandudno.
Olton, B'ham.
Wishaw, Lanark.
Australia.
Nr. Pershore.
Finchley.
Leeds.
Chichester.
Wembley.
Plymouth.
Newport, Mon.
Islington.
London, S.E.23.
Southsea.
Bridgwater, Somerset.
Colchester.
Hove.
Harrow.
Farningham, Kent.
Bradford.
Tingley, Yorks.
Grays, Essex.
London, N.7.
Eire, village.

The regional distribution is perhaps the strongest indication of the representative character of the documents. Wherever we may be, the same films, for good or worse, follow us.[1]

Consequently, the typification of the reaction structure can hardly appear striking. I do not intend to discuss the impact on fashions, hair styles and mannerisms. In this respect the documents speak for themselves. Moreover, Professor Blumer and Mrs. Thorp have given us ample illustrations of this side of film influence. Count the Bette Davises, the Greer Garsons or David Nivens you may meet every day when you travel to your office!

There are other points which are equally well documented by our contributions: The influence of films on reading (*See* 21, 33, 54), on musical interest (33), the entirely unexplored field of film influence on speech and vocabulary (33, 40), or the importance of colour emotions (24, 40, 53, 66). With regard to the latter problem

[1] From my film diary, 7th August 1945.
Direct observations of audiences are extremely difficult.

I saw to-day for the second time the film *Under the Clock*, directed by Vincente Minelli. This time I saw this film in Norwich whereas the first time I saw it in a West End theatre in London.

There was one scene in particular where I wanted to compare the behaviour of a London with a Norfolk audience. A soldier on embarkation leave for two days meets an office girl in New York and they decide to marry (it is a fine, genuinely sentimental picture which has the great merit that two people take at least twenty-four hours before they decide to marry. Something quite unusual on the contemporary screen). Now after they have spent their first night together, we see them having breakfast. For almost five minutes they do not say a word. (She pours out coffee, he looks at her.) Now, this silence struck me very much when I saw the film in London (actually in my memory there was no music either; but there is, unfortunately, 'soft' music on the sound-track as I ascertained to-day).

The London audience listened in silence to this 'silent' scene whereas in my Norfolk audience there was a considerable amount of laughing.

What does this different behaviour mean in terms of audience reactions? Does the more 'sophisticated' London audience feel the subtle touch of the scene: when two lovers remain silent because they have so much to say to each other? Is the Norfolk audience—I saw the film in the *early* afternoon—of a cruder type? Or at least those who did laugh? It is possible. Perhaps one must live in a big city to understand the melody of loneliness and silence between people who love each other. Perhaps what is here deep for the city dweller is natural and obvious for the spectator in Norfolk. He laughs because the *profondeur* of the city dweller must remain unintelligible to him. His—the country dweller's—*profondeur* is altogether different.

I continue these notes. Any such conclusions about audiences are naturally what Lord Keynes would call 'rash generalisations'. Yet they are perhaps not quite beside the point, for they may help me to lay the foundations for more specified investigations.

What I said above about loneliness you may find—perhaps for the first time in Western thought?—in the famous discussion by Pascal of 'divertissement' in his *Pensées* (No. 139: Brunschvicg edition). I quote only the relevant first sentence:

only the Russians, under the spiritual leadership of Eisenstein,[1] have to my knowledge made serious sociological-psychological investigations. And yet it would seem imperative to study the psychological and sociological aspects of colour emotions, particularly in view of the fact that most people visit the cinema from the 'cradle to the grave' and if I am not mistaken it is particularly the child's mind which is so extremely susceptible to the effect of colour. Our psychologists have studied colour emotions in industrial psychology. The entire field of the 'technicolour picture' has so far been neglected, though of course, not being a psychologist

'Quand je me suis mis quelquefois à considérer les diverses agitations des hommes et les périls et les peines où ils s'exposent, dans la cour, dans la guerre, d'où naissent tant de querelles, de passions, d'entreprises hardies et souvent mauvaises, etc., j'ai découvert que tout le malheur des hommes vient d'une seule chose, qui est de ne pas savoir demeurer en repos, dans une chambre.'

Here Pascal expresses admirably the despair of the city dweller.

To test the justification of my thesis whether there is a fundamental difference of film behaviour between a London and a Norwich audience, I saw another film yesterday which I had previously seen in a North Paddington cinema. There the mainly proletarian audience expressed by hissing its violent disagreement with the main male character's vileness. The audience sided distinctly with the party who stood for moral justice.

I insert a note on this film from the *Eastern Evening News* (August 7th, 1945):

'Haymarket.—James Mason gives another excellent character study in *They Were Sisters*, in which he appears as a gay and heartless young man. The story traces the lives of three sisters, whose successes, tragedies and quiet happiness could easily be the lot of any average family. The sister whose character is the strength on which the others draw is played by Phyllis Calvert. Anne Crawford takes the part of the glamorous one and Dulcie Gray appears as the unfortunate. The story is taken from the novel by Dorothy Whipple, and Arthur Crabtree has directed.'

Was there any contrast in the behaviour of a Norfolk audience? I believe there was. People remained completely *silent* (when later on there was a Walt Disney Donald Duck picture shown they laughed merrily). Perhaps the different behaviour of the two audiences may be *tentatively* explained in this way: The London proletarian audience expresses openly its sense of moral indignation. Here social standards exercise no restraint. Such an audience may be classified by its affinity to a child audience who hisses the 'bad man'. Note the phenomenon of *participation mystique*.

The Norfolk audience may be (it was market day) an audience of village dwellers. There is *participation mystique* too, but 'the badness' as shown in the film is made so explicit that, I believe, the Norfolk audience is silently shocked because country people are not so consciously wicked as the behaviour shown on the screen. They were flabbergasted, awed. They may remain silent because they see something fancifully strange to them. There is wickedness amongst them too, but of a cruder, more natural type. The 'sophisticated' wickedness of the town dweller has not yet taken possession of them. The London proletarian audience 'knows all about it', but just because they know they condemn 'the bad man'. So I do think the results of both film visits in Norwich are in conformity with each other.

[1] Cf. Eisenstein, *The Film Sense*. London 1943. *See* here the fascinating chapter on *Colour and Meaning*.

266

I may be unaware of investigations either already made or in progress.

The vistas of a sociology of film are indeed immense. I deliberately ask only questions which I feel incompetent to answer. In these fields an expert knowledge is required which definitely goes beyond the mental compass of one single individual. Never have I felt so clearly the urgent need of more intimate co-operation in the social sciences as now, since my 'naiveté' and curiosity led me to undertake these film investigations. I can only wish that this book may be taken as the most urgent and sincere plea for an energetic co-operative research into some of the problems raised here.

As I have tried to explain in the Foreword of this book, I came to be interested in film reactions from sociological studies on the organisational structure of political parties, studies which I intend to continue, once I have brought these volumes on film reactions to a preliminary conclusion. The example of pre-Nazi Germany made me inclined to believe that even so-called non-political films can become an instrument for shaping political opinions. Consequently I am less interested in the intricate psychological mechanisms which seem to underlie film reactions than in those structural features which may help us to explain the sociological implications of films.

In this connection it is interesting to note that various of our contributors speak of films as vehicles to their becoming aware of their own personalities (No. 7 is in this respect of particular importance, but see also Nos. 26, 28, 30, 40, 49, 65). What strikes me is the fact that the plot-consciousness is hardly developed at all. Plots are introduced only to explain an attitude or a character, perhaps rather a type. This, of course, presupposes a fairly low educational level. To the careful reader of our Secondary Schoolgirls' essays, it will be obvious that, as compared with the latter, the present documents are nearer to our children's essays of North Paddington. The average filmgoer with the educational equipment of most of our contributors identifies himself either with certain actors or actresses, or with certain sequences of the plot (more rarely with a film as a whole). If this interpretation is correct, it would explain the relatively stereotyped or rather typified character of our documents. What may appear to the contributors as self-realisation is in fact a process of conforming to a type: Greer Garson, Bette Davis, Robert Taylor, Laurence Olivier, etc. It is, therefore, not surprising that films tend to become the most effective weapon of levelling down individual differences of human beings.

267

This process of identification would deserve the most careful study. '*Identification* is distinguished',[1] writes Jung, 'from *imitation* by the fact that identification is an *unconscious* imitation, whereas imitation is a conscious copying. . . . Identification is not always related to persons but also to things (for instance a spiritual movement . . .) and to psychological functions.' Though I cannot bring myself to accept Jung's definition of the 'unconscious', the process of identification appears to be adequately described. 'Identification' is clearly related to *participation mystique*! 'This term', writes Jung[2] again, 'connotes a peculiar kind of psychological connection with the object wherein the subject is unable to differentiate himself clearly from the object to which he is bound by an immediate relation that can only be described as partial identity. . . . It does not apply to the whole subject-object relation, but only to certain cases in which the phenomenon of this peculiar relatedness appears. It is a phenomenon that is best observed among the primitives; but it occurs not at all infrequently among civilised men, although not with the same range of intensity . . .' I have shortened Jung's enlightening definition somewhat. Whether or not Jung would be prepared to allow its application to the film experience, I am unable to say. Naturally the process of *participation mystique* does not explain the whole complexity of the film experience. You usually do not sit through a whole film in complete obliviousness. Let me give an example which I take from my own psychological attitudes as I noted them in my 'film diary'. I have recently seen a film *To Have and Have Not*, with Humphrey Bogart and Miss Lauren Bacall (the latter is an 'offspring' of the Marlene Dietrich tradition). Though I saw this film with the explicit purpose of the social scientist, I have to admit that there were fairly long sequences where I was completely absorbed by what was going on on the screen. The conversations between Mr. Bogart and Miss Bacall, in short the very obvious sexual side of this film, made me only smile, but the 'shooting scenes' drowned the sociological interest completely. For a while anyway. I also would not dream of imitating Mr. Bogart's behaviour towards women, nor is Miss Bacall 'my type'. But this is perhaps beside the point. What alone *is* interesting is the fact that certain *instincts* in us are brought to such a state of response that our rational faculties diminish or even disappear for a while. (I know that most people react to some films in this way, including our superior intellectuals. The difference

[1] Cf. Jung, *Psychological Types*, pp. 551 sq.
[2] Cf. *Ibid.* p. 572 sq.

268

lies in the instincts which respond, and in the intensity of their responses. Whereas I respond to the shooting scenes, my neighbour may respond to Miss Bacall's 'sex appeal'.)

So far, psychologists have left us completely in the dark with regard to these experiences. We have neither adequate descriptions of the processes involved, nor a satisfactory and *accepted* instinct psychology which could be applied. There appear to exist only psychologies, but not yet *one* psychology as a branch of an integrated social science.

Against the background of these very tentative remarks we can now turn to those accounts in our documents which tell us of the direct moral influence of films (see Nos. 7, 10, 11, 13, 16, 31, 32, 38, 39, 40, 46, 48, 52, 56, 58, 59, 60, 61, 63). An analysis of these parts of our material clearly indicates the immense constructive possibilities of film. They can build up and strengthen individual, group, and state morale, but they can also undermine and destroy them completely.

I believe our contributors generally tend to prove the positive and constructive effect of films and I see no reason to contradict them. Films like *The Song of Bernadette*, *A Tree Grows in Brooklyn*, *The Gentle Sex*, *The Way Ahead*, *The Lamp Still Burns*, *Tawny Pipit*, *The Way to the Stars*, and many others may have helped many millions to a greater awareness of their individual and civic responsibilities, without interfering with their natural desire for 'entertainment' and 'escape'. Yet the films just mentioned form in no way the majority of British and American film production. One need only glance through the *Monthly Film Bulletin of the British Film Institute* in order to see what type of film still prevails and must prevail as long as the State leaves it to 'private enterprise' alone to decide what films ought to be made and distributed. For it is not the production of films which is the crux of the matter. One need only mention films like *Message from Canterbury* or the many first-rate Russian and French films which are shown only in special theatres like the 'Academy' or 'Tatler' in London to illustrate this point. 'The Public' does not get the films it wants; the managers of the big exhibitor circuits ultimately form the public taste.

Clearly the box-office returns are only a very crude method of measuring public taste. A film, for example, like *Going My Way* was never expected to be such a roaring box-office success as it turned out to be. Undoubtedly the buyers and previewers of the circuit which acquired the film were unable to gauge the deep-seated need of the British war-time public for a simple and sincere religious message, even when it wore a Catholic garment as in this film. Nor would it be fair to say that you can show a good film everywhere. A charming, but somewhat sophisticated society comedy like *On Approval* will not be appreciated in a cinema with a prevailing proletarian audience. Nor will a cinema audience of war-time Bristol which enjoys thrillers and slap-stick comedy readily accept the tender and delicate atmosphere of a film like *Tawny Pipit*. All these differences in group or regional standards are ironed out by the rigid method of film distribution.

Our material would, I think, not justify any conclusions about different standards and norms of *group* appreciations. I have collected a considerable amount of material on this problem which naturally interests the film industry most, but in view of the *introductory* nature of this book and also of my limited strength and facilities to carry this investigation through, I decided to withhold this material for the time being.

Finally there is the thorniest question as to whether film reactions have a class structure. Naturally all social phenomena have a class structure, but to analyse the class structure of film experiences is a by no means easy undertaking.

In this respect certain conclusions may be drawn from our documents. We have noted for instance that the majority of our contributors are members of the 'employee' class. The ambitions and attitudes of this class are certainly different from the social behaviour of the manual worker.[1] Whilst the former tend to be more 'showy' and more interested in the *status quo* of their section of society, the latter are perhaps less interested in fashions than in a revolutionary or evolutionary change. I should also not hesitate to suggest that from a certain age upwards (perhaps 30), manual workers go less to the cinema than their 'black-coated' colleagues. On the other hand, I am inclined to believe that in recent years films may have helped to create a common outlook, anyway in the younger age-groups, for both classes. Furthermore this common outlook is (intentionally or not) decisively coloured in favour of the 'employee' mentality, for instance, in films like *You Can't Take It With You*, *The Shop Around the Corner*, and *This Happy Breed*. These three films apparently mean to interpret the daily lives of the employee. The second film admits the *insecurity* of the employee's job and life, but glosses over this insecurity by showing how the shop-assistant may eventually climb to the position of a

[1] Cf. my essay on *The New Middle Classes*, which I allowed myself to reprint as Appendix IV to this book.

manager. *This Happy Breed* does not raise the problem of unemployment at all. We are made familiar with the happy and unhappy moments of a 'typical employee family'—so that we may see our image in their lives. (Remember what we said above about self-identification and *participation mystique*.) Happiness and contentment—on the whole—are meant to prevail in this film. 'Revolution' or radical social change is in a kindly and persuasive spirit rejected. Political and social adjustments come by themselves. It is this kind of drug which we mean when we indicate the general tendency of contemporary British and American films to create the employee mentality. Even in a film like *A Tree Grows in Brooklyn* the *laissez-faire* society which to-day exists only in Professor Hayek's book *The Road to Serfdom* is suggested as the only legitimate method of correcting social adjustment.

I am, of course, not unaware of the fact that films like *Of Mice and Men* or *Grapes of Wrath* do exist, but their existence is outweighed by those films which glorify the *status quo* of the Western type of society.

This tendency to make films with, as it were, an ideology in bottles is strengthened by the scarcity with which—for the time being—Russian and French films are shown. If foreign films come to be included in the circuit systems, a real international ideology or rather common world outlook could easily be created. Such an outlook might provide the necessary cement for treaties which, after all, are only written on paper. I would suggest that a *State corporation* for film distribution might fulfil a most vital function. What such a corporation might lose on films, if there were any loss, the State might win by one battleship less to build.

The middle and professional classes and the upper strata of our society are naturally less open to film influence. Here the factor of better education is telling. I do not think I need say much on this point. To any reader who compares the secondary schoolgirl essays with the essays I have given as counter-examples by proletarian children, the importance and urgency of a sensible sociological film appreciation is evident. It is perhaps not yet too late to introduce film appreciation in the regular curriculum of primary and secondary schools (see Chapter 1 of this book).

The sociological meaning of films and their interpretation can naturally not be separated from the influence of films on our instincts and emotions. In this respect our document No. 6 is of particular relevance. (The authoress, a member of the medical profession, was kind enough to grant me a lengthy interview in which we discussed all points raised in her contribution with complete frankness.) It is this influence on our emotional life which makes a social study of film so imperative.

Our present material must be regarded only as a beginning. The documents which I shall publish in the third volume of this series are already nearer to the emotional sphere of the film experience. Ultimately, only by prolonged case studies for which Weizsäcker in his *Studien zur Pathogenese* has given an example, will it be possible to establish a firm inter-relation of a psychological and a sociological study of film.

Perhaps I may be allowed to indicate where, in my opinion, contemporary psychologists have failed us—so far. If I examine the present documents, I am astonished at the poverty of values of which account is given (see Nos. 35, 37, 43, 44, 52, 60). This is naturally not the fault of the contributors; it is the films which are to blame. I give an example: take a film like *To Have and Have Not*. What are the values which this film carries?

Excitement, lust, passion, beauty, love, bravery, self-sacrifice, heroism, friendship, family, patriotism.

I hope I have omitted nothing of 'importance'. Moreover, I have mentioned only the positive values because the negative ones never triumph in films. These are the very same values, though with some modifications and additions, which you find in our documents or in other films with a similar theme. Now I would contend that our real life is—still—very much richer. Furthermore, the values in our real lives are less listable.

In other words, social attitudes are varied, subtle, full of meaning, transitional and enigmatic. The great literature of all languages demonstrates my point: take Hamlet's character; take Goethe's Princess in his *Tasso*. Whole libraries have been written about their attitudes, because they are *ineffabile*. In contrast the very essence of film appears to be static; speed cannot replace the profoundness of the human soul. Film directors are, admittedly, struggling with this problem. There are many sequences in Charlie Chaplin's films or in René Clair's films, not to mention Eisenstein's films which come near to the immortal images of great art. Yet, generally speaking, this function of art, to make us aware of the infinity of the human world, is not helped by film. On the contrary we are made into types, until we may be unable to appreciate what life is really all about.

Naturally film is not the cause of this process though it has undoubtedly become a means of speeding up its tempo. Film is

LE DERNIER MILLIARDAIRE

Banco (Max Dearly), self-declared dictator of Casinario, whose mind was touched at the commencement of his rule by a blow on the head, forces the ministers to wear shorts and bark good-night to him

FROM 'LA KERMESSE HÉROÏQUE'

only a by-product of our industrial civilisation. But the problem needs, so it seems to me, careful consideration and study.

In this respect I speak of the failure of modern psychology. I firmly believe that one can learn more about the *ordre du coeur* from La Rochefoucauld and Pascal (who was the author of this term) than from the most up-to-date text-book on psychology or ethics. In fact what we need is a content-psychology. It was Dilthey who devoted fifty years of his life to the formulation of such a new psychology. The classical philosophies of Aristotle and Thomas Aquinas had formulated the value patterns for their ages. Pascal lived and taught in their tradition. Such content patterns of a psychological and ethico-sociological theory cannot consist in formalised and consequently empty 'relationships'. They must, to a much higher degree, become individualised without losing thereby their scientific accuracy. To give an illustration. Take, for example, the chapter headings of Chapter VI of McDougall's widely read *Introduction to Social Psychology*: 'Sentiments of three primitive types: love, hate and respect—the genesis of Hate—Parental love as a type of highly complex sentiment—Active Sympathy and its rôle in the genesis of the sentiment of affection between persons', and compare this classification with one sentence from La Rochefoucauld's *Maximes*: 'Quand nous sommes las d'aimer, nous sommes bien aises qu'on nous devienne infidèle pour nous dégager de notre fidélité.'

The difference between these two types of psychology is significant. It is La Rochefoucauld who, in my opinion, is nearer the truth, in spite of the fact that he wrote his *Maximes* two hundred and fifty years before McDougall published his *Introduction*. It is easier to understand the moral phenomena by taking into account the French court society of the seventeenth century than by applying the generalising scientificism of Professor McDougall to our own historic situation.

This is a very heretical point of view and I put it forward with all diffidence.

Thus it seems to me that only if we re-discover the unity of psychology and ethics, sociology and philosophy, which was self-evident in the Europe of Athens, Thomas Aquinas and Pascal, we may be able to formulate anew our contemporary value patterns and thus perhaps give guidance to those who, like ourselves, are lost in the present emptiness.

It is with these ideas in mind that I suggest our documents ought to be considered.

CHAPTER 10

Conclusions and Postulates

The preceding studies have approached a sociological interpretation of film from the consumer's end. We attempted to describe the significance and meaning of the film phenomenon in our contemporary society through the medium of film audiences. No attempt has been made to enter into a *full* sociological analysis of the audience phenomena. This obvious and theoretically regrettable neglect may perhaps be justified if we submit that cinema audiences are generally not crowds in the sense in which crowd-sociology uses this term.

We think here particularly of Gustave Le Bon's famous book on *Psychologie des Foules*. Apart from the fact that Le Bon's abstract conception of sociology fails to appreciate the important national differences in crowd structures, the cinema audiences become crowds perhaps only in cases of panic. Otherwise the audiences consist either of individuals or mainly pairs, or bands (friends, relatives, groups of friends) who seek what the film industry calls 'entertainment'. I am under the impression that in our large cities the atomised type of cinema-goer and the autark pair form the majority. (With regard to child audiences it may be that group cinema-visitors form the majority.) Nor did we pay attention to the inter-communication which exists among the cinema millions. It is well known, for example, that in factories, shops, and offices—during work and leisure hours—talk about films is probably the most frequent type of conversation.

The playhouses have been roofed since the second half of the seventeenth century,[1] a fact of very far-reaching consequences for any historico-sociological interpretation of audiences. The film, too, is seen in the dark. (It is even darker in the cinema than in the theatre, also a fact not without its sociological implications!) Yet

[1] Cf. L. Hotson, *The Commonwealth and Restoration Theatre*, Cambridge (U.S.A.) 1928, pp. 81 sqq.

doubt whether this darkness produces 'the comfortable community feeling' of which some writers who have written about the cinema, have told us. You may add the warmth in winter, but his, too, does not bring you nearer to your fellow cinema-goer. All these and related phenomena deserve a close study.

Apart from these problems, it must be emphasised that an entirely different methodological approach might be possible. One could choose one's starting-point from the film itself. The sociologist would then have to take specific films, for example, American, British, French, Russian films and analyse their meaning. Take, for instance, recent films like *A Tree Grows in Brooklyn* or *Under the Clock* as examples of American films, *Blithe Spirit* or *Waterloo Road* as British ones, *Quai des Brumes* as an exemplary type of a French film, *Lermontov* or the *Gorki* films as Russian examples. One would probably soon discover that the language, or better perhaps the categories', of the films mentioned reveal *structurally* different interpretations of different national societies. The emotional tempi, he behaviour patterns, the moral norms which films *visualise* show distinct and profound differences in spite of Hollywood's universalism. In a British or American film you may see a love-scene of an unmarried couple as shadows through a closed window; in a French film you see the same pair free and natural as lovers feel when they have satisfied their longing for each other. One would have to write a sociologically conceived history of the British, American, and French nations to elucidate the full implications of such and other differences. The national meanings of films are as different as La Rochefoucauld's *Sentences et Maximes* from William Penn's *Fruits of Solitude*.

It is to be hoped that such analytical and sociological film interpretations will be undertaken in the near future. They would of course have to be implemented with material which it is difficult if not impossible to obtain now. We should need access to sincere accounts of film directors. What was their *original* intention when they undertook to direct a specific film?[1] To what extent was their original intention modified, if not destroyed, by the producer

---

[1] I do not, of course, mean publications of the type of *The Making of Henry V* by C. Clayton Hutton, a book which is obviously only meant as uncritical propaganda for those who made this film. Such a book is utterly worthless from our point of view. It would be interesting to have an account, for instance, of Duvivier's making of *The Tales of Manhattan* or similar films. In the meantime the sociologist must be content with such information as he may find in film novels like *I Lost My Girlish Laughter*, London 1938, or *Leben ohne Geheimnis* by Vicki Baum, Berlin 1932.

interest? What part did the anticipation of the censorship complex play?—a question which is of particular relevance with regard to American and British films. (In Russia the political structure of the censorial system must play a considerable rôle as those who are familiar with the studio history of the film *Peter the Great* will have to admit.) French films have perhaps such an *intensive* personal note, because there is practically no moral censorship of French films, whereas the Puritan tradition in England and U.S.A. is still powerfully alive. Jeremy Collier has not written in vain.

Film director and script writer live in a concrete society. Their works must consequently reflect or interpret the social life of which they are a part. To analyse where life meets art is perhaps one of the subtlest problems the sociologist has to face. Perhaps I may illustrate this point. Last year—the Allies had just landed in France—I saw in a repertoire cinema in Cambridge Fritz Lang's film, *The Testament of Doctor Mabuse*, a film which I had previously seen in Berlin in 1932. It struck me now to what a surprising extent this film reflects the state of German society in those years when the Nazi advent was imminent. The film is well-known. I need not say anything about its morbid and destructive character. It may clearly stand as a symbol of Nazism. One actor in particular fascinated me. He was by no means a leading figure. Just an ordinary sub-gangster. When hunted down by the police, he refused to surrender. Crazily he went down shooting . . .

> *Wenn die Germanen untergehn,*
> *Dann muss die Welt in Flammen stehn.*

His hooligan face and attitude were unforgettable. (In 1932 I was not struck by the sociological significance of this figure, or of the film, though I remembered one or two frightening sequences in it.) I have never come across a more intimately illustrated relationship between a film and the historic phase of a concrete society.

When I discussed my observation with one of our most sensitive film directors, he was able to solve my problem. He related how Lang had seen this hooligan in Berlin's West End and did not rest until he had him before the camera. When I asked the same friend: do you ever think of the public when you work with the camera?, he quietly said: *never*.

As sociology of literature is still in its infancy, it will be evident that a sociology of film choosing, its starting point from such an objective' point of view will have to meet considerable difficulties. But these difficulties can be solved and they must be solved, provided we intend to use the most powerful 'educational' instrument of our time constructively.

As history of literature studies, or should study, the development of forms (e.g., of plays, and novels), the emergence of *subjects* and their relation to the social problems of epoch and generation, so the sociological history of film might study, for instance, the stress on the intimacy and holiness of family life in recent American and British films (*Until We Meet Again, Under the Clock, This Happy Breed, Perfect Strangers*) as a definite stage in the historic development of the cinema. Wars tend to uproot family lives. Here the film assumes the function of visualising (and unfortunately of romanticising) values which are adrift. So much about a different approach towards a sociology of film.

Clearly it is not for the author to summarise his book which has painfully become part of his life. Yet two main conclusions appear to stand out in my mind:

(1) Many of my contributors attribute to film that it helps them to discover their 'personalities'. In fact, just the opposite is true. When you adapt your behaviour according to the vision you have of Miss Greer Garson, you do not become a Greer Garson (or a Laurence Olivier), you only identify yourself with a type, for you don't know anything about Miss Greer Garson's personality, you only see a film type. So all over the country, from North to South, from East to West, we meet the same pitiful Greer Garsons or Laurence Oliviers, but the individualities in our time are on the verge of disappearing altogether.

It is important to contrast here the theatre and the cinema. Sir Max Beerbohm, in a recent broadcast, has given an admirable illustration of their difference. He is speaking of the Edwardian theatre.[1]

'Actors and actresses were certainly regarded with far greater interest than they are nowadays. The outstanding ones inspired something deeper than interest. It was with excitement, with wonder and with reverence, with something akin even to hysteria, that they were gazed upon. Some of the younger of you listeners would, no doubt, if they could, interrupt me at this point by asking, "But surely you don't mean, do you, that our parents and grandparents were affected by them as we are by cinema stars?" I would assure you that those idols were even more ardently worshipped

[1] Cf. 'The Listener', *Playgoing*, by Sir Max Beerbohm, Oct. 11th, 1945.

than are yours. Yours, after all, are but images of idols, mere shadows of glory. Those others were their own selves, creatures of flesh and blood, there, before our eyes. They were performing in our presence. And of our presence they were aware. Even we, in all our humility, acted as stimulants to them. The magnetism diffused by them across the footlights was in some degree our own doing. You, on the other hand, have nothing to do with the performances of which you witness the result. These performances—or rather those innumerable rehearsals—took place in some far away gaunt studio in Hollywood or elsewhere, months ago. Those moving shadows will be making identically the same movement at the next performance, or rather at the next record; and in the inflexions of those voices enlarged and preserved for you there by machinery not one cadence will be altered. Thus the theatre has certain advantages over the cinema, and in virtue of them will continue to survive.'

Shadow and a living relationship between actor and audience is indeed the formula which defines the structural difference between cinema and theatre. Yet theatrical art—all art—is *no* life. It is rather an interpretation of life. The greater art is, the more intense and deep is its interpretation of life. Art is more than life. It is a symbolic expression of life. And only symbolic art is real art.[1] While, in principle, the cinema may become art—and there are undoubtedly examples of film classics—and thus interpret or condense life, yet most films are, to use Sir Max's brilliant formula again—shadows.

I hope this book comes into the hands of many of those who so generously and trustingly helped me with collecting its material. To them (and to my other readers) I should like to say: In my mind, though I may have seen as many pictures as you have (good and bad ones), *not one* film star is present in the sense in which Hamlet, or Goethe's Princess (*Torquato Tasso*) or Rilke's Malte Laurids Brigge *live* in me. This permanent spiritual ever-presence film cannot give, because our *eye* is weaker than our mind. It does not *hold* sight impressions as our imagination does. You get shape, form, but very rarely *profondeur*, depth. If you get depth from film, you must use your mind to hold it.

(2) The second conclusion at which I have arrived, a conclusion which has increasingly hardened in me, is that the majority of films

---

[1] Cf. Cassirer, *An Essay on Man: An Introduction to a Philosophy of Human Culture*, New Haven (Yale University Press 1945), where the reader will find an exposition of the significance and implication of the term 'symbol'.

we see are pernicious to our nervous system. They are a mere drug which undermines our health, physical and spiritual. 'No man', wrote Francis Gentleman in the eighteenth century, 'can be hardy enough to deny, that a well-regulated drama is worthy support in the most polished, learned, or moral state.' Yet, as the drama of his time appeared to him conducive to vice, his intention was 'to strip off the serpent's shining coat, and to show the poison which lurks within'.[1] The same applies to the cinema to-day.

You may go to-day or to-morrow and see in any London suburb or in any town in England *The Woman in the Window* or *The Strange Affair of Uncle Harry*. In both films you see a murder case which is not supposed to have happened in reality, but about which the would-be murderer dreams. Naturally, with all the tricks of a make-believe reality. Have you ever dreamt of murdering somebody? If not, go and see these films, they will give you—pleasant dreams. Our social life is—without such films—full of problems of the most serious and urgent nature, social, and personal; why is it necessary that we create artificially nightmares and cruel psychological refinements? Where does this constant drugging lead us? It must naturally make us unfit to master our lives as they are.

This leads us to certain postulates which may be implicit in the preceding pages of this book, but which now perhaps need some further elucidation. Here, too, my views have considerably hardened since these studies were begun.

There is first the entire complex of films for children, with all its related problems. It would appear that in the light of the evidence submitted in this book the cinema clubs of the commercial film organisations will have to be terminated. Children's cinema clubs ought to be supervised by educational authorities and run under the authority of communal bodies.

Municipal authorities, e.g., those of Birmingham, Manchester, London, could easily build children's cinemas of their own and thus link the cinema of our young with other leisure activities. I am fully aware that such a suggestion may entail the danger of increasing bureaucratisation, but it seems to me that this danger may be more readily accepted than the present commercial practices to which the children are exposed.

Regional and communal children's cinemas would have the additional advantage of making the children familiar with local

[1] Cf. A. C. Ward, *Specimens of English Dramatic Criticism XVII-XX Centuries*, Oxford 1945, from which the above quotation is taken.

traditions and tastes. It would also be possible then to enlist th
help of regional universities for a serious study of those psychologica
and educational problems which this book has rather put that
solved.

In addition, considering the infancy of the children's film, I de
not hesitate to suggest that the central State authorities (Ministr
of Education and Ministry of Information) should go into featur
film production for children. Such a production unit could easil
be linked up with a State film-distributing corporation, the
necessity for which I shall discuss presently. So far we have only
discussed suggestions with regard to children's films, or cinema:
for child audiences.

Any suggestion of this kind must raise the problem of film
censorship. I have given examples of some of the recent activitie:
of the British Board of Film Censors in several passages in this book.
The problem is fairly simple. Only a trained child-psychologist can
say what kind of film may be shown to a young picture-goer, but
I do not think that such an expert has ever been asked to sit
regularly on a censorial committee of the British Board of Film
Censors. But, apart from the problem of what is and what is not
suitable for children, the censorship for adult films, too, needs
thorough revision. We no longer live in the age before the first
Reform Bill.[1]

Read, for instance, the following instructions 'Re "U" and "A"
films', being an extract from Annual Report 1928. (This extract
represented an up-to-date instruction in July, 1945.)

'It is hardly possible to give a list of the numerous grounds for
discrimination between the "U" and "A" films, but the broad
principle which has always regulated the Board's decision is that
nothing shall be shewn under the first category which is calculated
to impair, in the juvenile mind, respect for morality and good
conduct. Therefore, no film is passed as a "U" subject which deals
with irregular sex problems, or exaggerated love-making, or incidents shewing unhappy family jars and dissensions, or unhappy
marital relations, or "crime", especially such as is capable of
imitation, or any incident in which the recognised Authorities of
the Law are held up either to odium or ridicule. Extreme violence
and horrors, calculated to frighten children, are also debarred

---

[1] Miss Dorothy Knowles' book *The Censor, the Drama and the Film*, 1900-1934,
is still the best account of the censorship problem in Great Britain. Yet Miss
Knowles does not believe in state censorship, whereas I think it is the only
method of getting rid of the present anomalous system.

from this class, and obviously anything which brings religion into contempt or ridicule.'

These sentences allow us a glance at the mind of our film censors. Our moral conceptions have, we presume, not changed since Jane Austen wrote her novels. There is no doubt that the rigidity and stubbornness with which these norms are upheld (and this applies also to some extent to the Hays' Codes) influence film production to a considerable extent and produce the sterility and emptiness of emotional situations which make many adult films so boring and so uninspiring.

I am inclined to believe that only a State censorship of films would ensure a high standard of quality—social and artistic.[1] By virtue of a State censorship of film we would remove the present anomaly that local government authorities are not bound by the voluntary character of the censorial central body. Moreover the House of Commons, which takes so little interest in film matters now, would, once a State censorship is established, have ultimate control over the minister under whose guidance the censorship would have to function. In this way a public control of the censorial activities would be guaranteed.

There is another point which must be stressed in this context. It is common knowledge that neither film exhibitors, nor the audiences, nor the police take much notice of the legal provision that children under sixteen are not allowed to see 'A' films if unaccompanied by adults. The London area seems to be leading in this respect. I could easily give dozens of examples. The other day I saw *The Strange Affair of Uncle Harry* ('A') in a Kilburn theatre with perhaps a hundred children under the age of sixteen, not accompanied by adults. From the evidence I have collected I am inclined to believe that there is hardly one grown-up person under forty-five in this country who has not had an experience of shock, fright, terror or nightmare caused by a film in his early youth. (I shall publish further evidence of these facts in the second volume of my *Sociology of Film*.) I would therefore suggest enforcing existing legal provisions, while I am quite prepared to admit children from fourteen years upwards to see 'A' films, once a sensible censorial system has been instituted.

We have now come to the last point of these concluding con-

---

[1] The *Lichtspielgesetz* as resolved by the *Nationalversammlung* in Weimar (R.G.Bl. Nr. 107, S.953) worked—on the whole—rather well. It offered, perhaps, more 'freedom' than was compatible with the political health of the Weimar Republic.

siderations. Should the film industry continue in its present owner-ship structure? I very much doubt it, though I do realise the dangers, particularly to the independent producer, arising from its nationalisation. In the long run I am almost certain that national-isation is unavoidable. The film companies are commercial under-takings. They must, therefore, primarily think in terms of profit. Yet the service they provide is of an essentially different nature from food or clothing. If food is bad, the State machinery has ample means to deal with the merchant who sells it. In the case of the amusement industry the 'bad food' is sold—to the detriment of the audiences. Their moral health is undermined, if not ulti-mately destroyed. To sell 'soul' needs an expert knowledge which the present structure of the film industry cannot provide. The most pious and noble motives must fail when the system as such is objectively wrong, because you cannot sell 'soul', even if disguised under the cloak of 'entertainment'.

Yet the sociologist should not propagate Utopias. For the next five years Parliament has its hands full. So we should, perhaps, confine ourselves to suggestions which are practicable here and now.

I think it is feasible to form a State Distributing Corporation which might import (and export) those films which the dictatorial heads of the big distributing agencies either do not like or which they think not profitable. Such a State Distributing Agency would certainly create new and powerful bonds of understanding, for example, with Soviet Russia and France. Moreover, it would enter into important and effective competition with the existing circuit monopolies. Last but not least, the profits of such an organisation might be invested in making intelligent feature films, for which those directors who still have their own ideas and refuse to be bought up by the monopolistic and purely commercial film interests might be won.

I envisage also that communal authorities might build their own cinemas and administer them (I believe this is the case in Norway). From such communal cinemas beneficial and construc-tive ideas would permeate the State which, otherwise, as we have seen, is bound to decay in an age of increasing centralisation.

APPENDIX I

Some Observations on the Drama
among Democratic Nations[1]

When the revolution which subverts the social and political state of an aristocratic people begins to penetrate into literature, it generally first manifests itself in the drama, and it always remains conspicuous there.

The spectator of a dramatic piece is, to a certain extent, taken by surprise by the impression it conveys. He has no time to refer to his memory or to consult those more able to judge than himself. It does not occur to him to resist the new literary tendencies which begin to be felt by him; he yields to them before he knows what they are.

Authors are very prompt in discovering which way the taste of the public is thus secretly inclined. They shape their productions accordingly; and the literature of the stage, after having served to indicate the approaching literary revolution, speedily completes its accomplishment. If you would judge beforehand of the literature of a people which is lapsing into democracy, study its dramatic productions.

The literature of the stage, moreover, even among aristocratic nations, constitutes the most democratic part of their literature. No kind of literary gratification is so much within the reach of the multitude as that which is derived from theatrical representations. Neither preparation nor study is required to enjoy them: they lay hold on you in the midst of your prejudices and your ignorance. When the yet untutored love of the pleasures of the mind begins to affect a class of the community, it instantly draws them to the stage. The theatres of aristocratic nations have always been filled with spectators not belonging to the aristocracy. At the theatres alone the higher ranks mix with the middle and lower classes;

---

[1] Alexis de Tocqueville: *Democracy in America*. New York, 1845. Vol. II, first book, Ch. xix.

there alone do the former consent to listen to the opinion of the latter, or at least to allow them to give an opinion at all. At the theatre, men of cultivation and of literary attainments have always had more difficulty than elsewhere in making their taste prevail over that of the people, and in preventing themselves from being carried away by the latter. The pit has frequently made laws for the boxes.

If it be difficult for an aristocracy to prevent the people from getting the upper hand in the theatre, it will readily be understood that the people will be supreme there when democratic principles have crept into the laws and manners—when ranks are intermixed—when minds, as well as fortunes, are brought more nearly together—and when the upper class has lost, with its hereditary wealth, its power, its precedents, and its leisure. The tastes and propensities natural to democratic nations, in respect to literature, will therefore first be discernible in the drama, and it may be foreseen that they will break out there with vehemence. In written productions, the literary canons of aristocracy will be gently, gradually, and, so to speak, logically modified; at the theatre they will be riotously overthrown.

The drama brings out most of the good qualities, and almost all the defects, inherent in democratic literature. Democratic peoples hold erudition very cheap, and care but little for what occurred at Rome and Athens; they want to hear something which concerns themselves, and the delineation of the present age is what they demand.

When the heroes and the manners of antiquity are frequently brought upon the stage, and dramatic authors observe the rules of antiquated precedent, that is enough to warrant a conclusion that the democratic classes have not yet got the upper hand in the theatres.

Racine makes a very humble apology in the preface of the *Britannicus* for having disposed of Junia among the Vestals, who, according to Aulus Gallius, he says, 'admitted no one below six years of age nor above ten.' We may be sure that he would neither have accused himself of the offence, nor defended himself from censure, if he had written for our contemporaries.

A fact of this kind not only illustrates the state of literature at the time when it occurred, but also that of society itself. A democratic stage does not prove that the nation is in a state of democracy, for, as we have just seen, even in aristocracies it may happen that democratic tastes affect the drama; but when the spirit of aristocracy reigns exclusively on the stage, the fact irrefragably demonstrates that the whole of society is aristocratic; and it may be boldly inferred that the same lettered and learned class, which sways the dramatic writers, commands the people and governs the country.

The refined tastes and the arrogant bearing of an aristocracy will rarely fail to lead it, when it manages the stage, to make a kind of selection in human nature. Some of the conditions of society claim its chief interest; and the scenes which delineate their manners are preferred upon the stage. Certain virtues and even certain vices are thought more particularly to deserve to figure there; and they are applauded while all others are excluded. Upon the stage, as well as elsewhere, an aristocratic audience will meet only personages of quality, and share the emotions of kings. The same thing applies to style: an aristocracy is apt to impose upon dramatic authors certain modes of expression which give the key in which everything is to be delivered. By these means the stage frequently comes to delineate only one side of man, or sometimes even to represent what is not to be met with in human nature at all—to rise above nature and to go beyond it.

In democratic communities the spectators have no such partialities, and they rarely display any such antipathies: they like to see upon the stage that medley of conditions, of feelings, and of opinions, which occurs before their eyes. The drama becomes more striking, more common, and more true. Sometimes, however, those who write for the stage in democracies also transgress the bounds of human nature—but it is on a different side from their predecessors. By seeking to represent in minute detail the little singularities of the moment and the peculiar characteristics of certain personages, they forget to portray the general features of the race.

When the democratic classes rule the stage, they introduce as much licence in the manner of treating subjects as in the choice of them. As the love of the drama is, of all literary tastes, that which is most natural to democratic nations, the number of authors and of spectators, as well as of theatrical representations, is constantly increasing among these communities. A multitude of composed elements so different and scattered in so many different places, cannot acknowledge the same rules or submit to the same laws. No concurrence is possible among judges so numerous, who know not when they may meet again; and therefore each pronounces his own sentence on the piece. If the effect of democracy is generally to question the authority of all literary rules and conventions, on the stage it abolishes them altogether, and puts in their place nothing but the whim of each author and of each public.

The drama also displays in an especial manner the truth of what I have said before in speaking more generally of style and art in democratic literature. In reading the criticisms which were occasioned by the dramatic productions of the age of Louis XIV, one is surprised to remark the great stress which the public laid on the probability of the plot, and the importance which was attached to the perfect consistency of the characters, and to their doing nothing which could not be easily explained and understood. The value which was set upon the forms of language at that period, and the paltry strife about words with which dramatic authors were assailed, are no less surprising. It would seem that the men of the age of Louis XIV attached very exaggerated importance to those details, which may be perceived in the study but which escape attention on the stage. For, after all, the principal object of a dramatic piece is to be performed, and its chief merit is to affect the audience. But the audience and the readers in that age were the same: on quitting the theatre they called up the author for judgment to their own firesides.

In democracies, dramatic pieces are listened to, but not read. Most of those who frequent the amusements of the stage do not go there to seek the pleasures of the mind but the keen emotions of the heart. They do not expect to hear a fine literary work but to see a play; and, provided the author writes the language of his country correctly enough to be understood, and that his characters excite curiosity and awaken sympathy, the audience is satisfied. They ask no more of fiction and immediately return to real life. Accuracy of style is therefore less required, because the attentive observance of its rules is less perceptible on the stage.

As for the probability of the plot, it is incompatible with perpetual novelty, surprise, and rapidity of invention. It is therefore neglected and the public excuses the neglect. You may be sure that if you succeed in bringing your audience into the presence of something that affects them, they will not care by what road you brought them there; and they will never reproach you for having excited their emotions in spite of dramatic rules.

The Americans very broadly display all the different propensities which I have here described when they go to the theatre; but it must be acknowledged that as yet a very small number of them go to theatres at all. Although playgoers and plays have prodigiously increased in the United States in the last forty years, the population indulges in this kind of amusement with the greatest reserve. This is attributable to peculiar causes which the reader is already acquainted with, and of which a few words will suffice to remind him.

The Puritans who founded the American Republics were not only enemies to amusements, but they professed an especial abhorrence for the stage. They considered it as an abominable pastime; and, as long as their principles prevailed with undivided sway, scenic performances were wholly unknown among them. These opinions of the first fathers of the colony have left very deep marks on the minds of their descendants.

The extreme regularity of habits and the great strictness of manners which are observable in the United States have as yet opposed additional obstacles to the growth of dramatic art. There are no dramatic subjects in a country which has witnessed no great political catastrophes and in which love invariably leads by a straight and easy road to matrimony. People who spend every day in the week in making money, and the Sunday in going to church, have nothing to invite the Muse of Comedy.

A single fact proves that the stage is not very popular in the United States. The Americans, whose laws allow of the utmost freedom and even licence of language in all other respects, have nevertheless subjected their dramatic authors to a sort of censorship. Theatrical performances can only take place by permission of the municipal authorities. This may serve to show how much communities are like individuals; they surrender themselves unscrupulously to their ruling passions, and afterward take the greatest care not to yield too much to the vehemence of tastes which they do not possess.

No portion of literature is connected by closer or more numerous ties with the present condition of society than the drama. The drama of one period can never be suited to the following age, if in the interval an important revolution has changed the manners and the laws of the nation.

The great authors of a preceding age may be read; but pieces written for a different public will not attract an audience. The dramatic authors of the past live only in books. The traditional taste of certain individuals, vanity, fashion, or the genius of an actor, may sustain or resuscitate for a time the aristocratic drama among a democracy; but it will speedily fall away of itself—not overthrown, but abandoned.

APPENDIX 2

Children's Cinemas and Films in the Soviet Union[1]

In the Soviet Union there are cinemas in which the box-office windows are fixed not far above the floor. Also, above the box-offices hangs a placard bearing the significant inscription: 'No admission for adults without children.' At the entrance to the foyer, in the corridors, the happy, many-voiced buzzing of children's voices can be heard. These children's cinemas constitute a complicated organism. There are things not usually to be found in the ordinary cinemas, for the children's cinemas serve the interests and satisfactions of the young audience's needs.

For instance, there is a room full of toys, in which the little visitors can spend their time without boredom until the commencement of the performance.

In another room, eager chess-players of school age fight their battles on the chequered boards. A group of children, eager for knowledge, surrounds a large cupboard of books; here they find literature in which much can be learnt concerning the heroes of the film being shown; for all who have a closer interest in cinematography, an exhibition of decorational sketches, models of architectural structures for films, cameras and projection apparatus and albums with photographs of popular actors in well-known rôles, are provided.

In a cosily furnished corner of the foyer a discussion on a recently seen film is in progress. The little patrons of the cinema argue heatedly and passionately; here, also, some important director or actor is waiting for a chance to speak. He has the chance of taking part in the conversations of the little ones, and of answering their questions.

Now all are pouring towards the stage in the foyer. A short concert, especially arranged for the children, begins.

[1] Translated from *Der Sowjetfilm* by L. Tschernjowski, Moscow, 1941. I am most grateful to the representative of *Mezhdunarodnaja Kniga*, Moscow, in the United Kingdom for allowing us to publish this chapter.

288

The children's cinemas are real 'Republics of the art of the film' for youth. One of the main characteristics of these cinemas is the great pedagogical work undertaken in connection with the performances. Another is the earnest and responsible attitude of those working in the making of films towards the living, knowledge-seeking child audience.

The leading principle on which the whole organisation of children's films in the U.S.S.R. is based, is: real art for the small citizens! A serious attitude towards this work for the children, without the typical 'condescension'.

Films for children are not produced as a by-product, but constitute a particularly important sphere in Soviet film production. The large studio 'Sojusdetfilm' (Studio for child and youth films) is concerned exclusively with the production of films for children and young people. Important directors, authors, and actors work there. Schools, the organisation of the Communist Youth League, and higher educational institutions are closely connected with children's films. The basis for this is the particular attention paid by the State to the education of the growing generation.

The repertoire of the 1940-41 season gives an indication of the variety of themes and types of children's films.

We find, for instance, the film version of the legend *Wassilissa the Beautiful* (a film which takes up a whole evening); also films from literary works, mainly classics (*Mirgerod* after a tale by Gogol, *Tom Kenty*, Mark Twain's novel, *The Prince and the Beggarmaid*, etc.).

Great attention is also paid to adventure films, which satisfy the child's interests in travels, in the study of nature, etc. Recently, for instance, the following films were shown: *Gaitschi*, a description of the life of the peoples in the extreme North of Russia; *Siberia*, a romantic story of children in the far-away Siberian Taiga, whose dream it is to find a pipe which was supposed to have been left in that region by Stalin, while he was exiled there during the Czarist régime; *Timur and His Gang*, a film about the stirring adventures of young pioneers during the summer holidays.

It is interesting to analyse the content of this film a little. The young pioneer, Timur, with childish enthusiasm, organises a gang of boys of the same age for romantic adventures, during the summer holidays. The 'gang' is equipped with a whole arsenal of telephones, signals and so on, all constructed by the boys. The grown-ups regard Timur's gang most suspiciously and take them for nothing but a mischief-making group of boys. The attraction of a romantic mystery does not allow Timur to tell the grown-ups the truth about his gang. But soon this truth becomes evident to the audience. Timur and his comrades have charged themselves with helping all the families from which some member has been called up into the Red Army. Secretly the boys saw some wood in the evening for the father of a Red Army man; they fill the water reservoir in the yard belonging to the house of a Red Commander's mother; unseen, they bring a small girl, whose father fell at the front, flowers and toys.

Delicately and lyrically this film shows the transformation, which the new Soviet reality has brought about in the thoughts of children. The usual content of children's play—the enthusiasm for the legendary figures of robbers, knights, magicians, etc.—finds its completion in the fulfilment of social duties, in the service of the fatherland which one aids with personal work.

The problems of the schools are treated extensively in children's films. For the pupils in more advanced forms there are biographical films, for instance one about the great Russian poet, Lermontow, another about the Russian Polar explorer, Georgi Sedow. The studio 'Sojusdetfilm' has produced during the last two or three years an artistic film trilogy from the autobiographical works, *My Childhood, Amongst Strangers, My Universities* by Maxim Gorki. This great work has been done by one of the best directors of children's films, Mark Donskoi.

'Sojusdetfilm' produces yearly ten feature-length and ten to fifteen short films for children and young people. Besides this, no less than ten trick films for younger children are turned out by another studio, 'Multfilm'. It has also become a tradition in all other studios of the U.S.S.R. to produce at least one children's film per year.

Just as the film is the youngest branch of the Soviet arts, so the children's film is the youngest branch in the art of the film. Much of the work is still in the stage of experimentation: for instance, some main problems of children's films such as interpretation on the part of the director, and the working out of the actor's style.

Those working in this branch of film art are often at variance: is a modernisation of the folk- or fairy-tale legitimate, or should it be transmitted in the original form of folklore? How should such a delicate and complicated problem as 'calf love' be treated? What educational effects are produced by adventure films? How can one interpret for children social problems which are agitating the whole country? Of especial importance are moral problems, which obviously interest young people, and which must find expression in the film. Educationists, parents, and delegates of social organisations take part in discussions on these problems.

However, the broadest 'parliament of opinions' for all these practical problems the children's film finds amongst its vital, lively and sensitive audience, amongst the children themselves. As a rule, every completed film is discussed critically by children in schools, in 'Young Pioneer' clubs, and at children's conferences which the studio 'Sojusdetfilm' calls in. Thus, in Moscow alone, such consultations, for instance about the fairy-tale *By Command of the Pike*, took place in the 'Palace of the Young Pioneers'; at a children's meeting a thousand strong, in the First Children's Cinema, and in the central office of the journalists, as well as in several schools. In other cities, too, such consultations with children about the same film took place.

In the speeches of the young critics an astounding earnestness and great sense of responsibility can be felt. Apart from the individual judgment—'I like it'—'I don't like it', we often notice rather touching efforts, on the part of the children, to express themselves on certain general principles.

Here are a few extracts from the minutes of the discussion on the film, *By Command of the Pike*, held at the 'Palace of the Young Pioneers'.

A schoolboy, Oranowski, finds the film interesting. He has only a few remarks to make about the somewhat unsatisfactory sound performance. But he also takes into consideration some other points such as: is the director's conception of the hero of the film, the peasant's son, Temelja, correct?

'Perhaps I am wrong, but Temelja did not emerge as I know him in the fairy-tale. Temelja appears in many fairy-tales—I have read them all—and he is always a simple, lazy peasant boy. But with you he is such a cultured person, just like a scholar. He immediately knows who the Czar is and what the Czar intends to do. Possibly it is more correct to regard Temelja like that, but then it isn't the same as in the fairy-tale. It isn't like that in the fairy-tale.'

Werschinin, an older schoolboy, disagrees with Oranowski:

'I don't agree at all with the way in which Oranowski judges Temelja. Hasn't he noticed that in Temelja simplicity is coupled with cunning, when he blinks his eyes and whispers his magic word, 'By command of the Pike', in the presence of the Czar? What is so odd about Temelja being clever enough to use the magic power which has been given to him? Temelja is a peasant, and the peasant

291

is a practical sort of person. I liked Temelja better in the film than in the book; he is more interesting and more correct.'

The discussion becomes more and more heated. In the end, the script writer and director have to explain in popular terms their conception of the character of the popular hero in the fairy-tale before the attentive and serious audience. But as pupils of more advanced classes are also present, they have to refer to works on folklore and literary authorities.

Next to this central problem, which stimulated the passionate discussion, dozens of smaller questions emerged. The attentive eyes of the children do not overlook a single detail; they are used to realistic, truthfully artistic form, even if it is a question of fairy-tales. Why is one landscape decoration painted badly? What is the reason for the hero's delay with his answer? Why is the magic horse seen so indistinctly in some particular scene?

Also, all actors playing in this film take part in the discussion. Without a trace of embarrassment, members of the meeting criticise the good and bad points of each actor's performance, and show in this respect an exact knowledge of cinematographic terminology. The actors listen attentively to these criticisms and answer them in their speech at the end.

An extensive correspondence between the film studios and the youthful members of the audience completes this lively discussion. One department of the studio is exclusively concerned with carrying on this correspondence and analysing the numerous opinions, inquiries, demands, and suggestions of the children; it also organises circular questionnaires among the children.

Many letters are also received from adults. For instance, the matron of a kindergarten describes in her letter how the children, after a performance of the film *By Command of the Pike*, make use of the themes of this film in their play.

A good many letters contain sound suggestions from young cinema-goers for making films about particular themes. All sorts of suggestions are made, from the filming of *Don Quixote* or the production of a film on Newton to such 'problematical' themes as truthfulness, social conscience, patriotism, individualism, and collectivism, etc.

In one of these letters the writer says: 'I am told that you are making a film about a boy who is always thinking only of himself, and who is reformed under the influence of his school-friends. In my opinion such a theme is not really likely to have a great interest for either older or younger school-children. I should like to see in the cinema a good, truthful film about friendship. And not only one, but several. Friendship is an important matter for all of us, beginning in the seventh and eighth forms. Approximately at this age children start to think seriously about what they are doing, and a lot of questions appear then. Comrades of the "Detfilm", it is your direct duty not to shirk this great problem, and to make a film about it . . .'

Many correspondents want a film made about the Young Pioneer, Pawlik Morosow, one of the children's favourite heroes, who was murdered in his native village by an enemy of the Revolution, whom he had denounced. In numerous letters, films about the childhood of eminent men are demanded.

There are also correspondents who seriously offer their own services or help.

Bussja Petscherskaja, a schoolgirl in the fourth form, writes that she has seen the film, *Wassilissa the Beautiful*, and thinks it is essential that a second part to this film should appear in which the story of the hero is brought to an end, and where 'we see what happens to everyone'. 'When I came out of the cinema I said to daddy that I should like to write a second series, of course not so that you should make the film from it, but just because it may be useful sometime. But daddy told me that I had better not do that before I have left school. I should like to ask you whether daddy has advised me correctly. Of course, I write gratuitously.'

A great feature is made of songs and, in general, of music in the children's films; some young cinema-goers sometimes find them a little monotonous, not interesting enough, or too difficult for them to sing.

'The songs for children's films are written by grown-ups. But it would be better if children wrote their own songs and that only then the grown-ups made the music for them . . . I can write poems about everything: about travels, about the sea, about Stalin, about the heroes and others. I write poems quickly. For instance if you need something about a train, I write it on the same day as I receive your letter. Don't be afraid to ask me when you need something.'

The author of this letter is eight years old.

This living, organic connection of the film world with its young patrons is one of the most interesting aspects of this new but very promising field of work.

The specific world of the children's film, which has much in common with education, also shows itself in the work of directors with the young actors. It happens frequently in children's films that children are called in as actors, sometimes even in leading rôles, although scripts are usually written for adult actors.

The creative task demands tense and thorough educational work with each child on the part of the director. Decisive is the rejection, on principle, of every 'child prodigy' stunt, so that both the child and the parents are prevented from acquiring harmful ideas as to the 'great talent' of the little actor. Children and adolescents who take part at the shooting must feel as unconstrained and natural in the film studio as at school or at home. They must therefore be guarded from all possible influences of unhealthy 'artistic' exaggeration, and from the psychologically ill effects often connected with this.

In the Soviet children's film, a 'professionalisation' of youthful actors is hardly possible. New little actors, who, by their external or other characteristics, are suitable for a particular part, are chosen for each film from schools, cultural and educational institutions.

The film, *The Foundling*, made in 1940 by the children's film director, Tatjana Lukaschewitsch, is an example of the specifically educational work of the directors. For the casting of the main part a six-year-old girl was 'engaged'. She had to portray a very complicated and even partly dramatic part in the film: a child runs away from home through the carelessness of the parents, comes to strangers, lives through various adventures, but retains, in spite of all, her childish seriousness and her sincerity towards the adults. And precisely out of this arise the charming comical situations of this interesting film. The audiences were stunned by the natural acting of the heroine. It appeared to be a clever trick or the result of an extraordinary ability on the part of the child to imagine herself in the part.

The situation, however, was quite different. The normal life, the habits of the child, remained completely undisturbed throughout the period of shooting. An atmosphere was quite simply created for the child, in which she felt that she was 'on a visit to Aunt Tanja' (the director).

In her notes on this film, the directress tells of the enormous difficulties which she had to overcome in order to obtain the complete trust of the child, so that she would 'play her usual games in such a manner as to be in accordance with the composition and action of the film'. Of course, practically not one scene in this film was acted consciously by the child. Movements, intonations, moods, putting in of speech, all these were achieved by the director with the help of simple child games, which were invented before the camera, with the indispensable dolls taking part, by the little 'actress's' grandmother, the workers of the film studio and the director herself.

In order to take a few words, to be spoken in tears, four days were necessary. The work was undertaken with so much tact, delicacy, and precaution, that the conscience of the child reflected the dramatic as well as the comical elements in the dialogue merely as 'games', invented by 'Aunt Tanja'. This 'playing' has left no ill effects of any kind on the health and well-being of the child. When the 'heroine' saw the completed film for the first time, she recalled excitedly every detail of her entertaining 'game', which, for her, had become merely a pleasant memory having not the slightest connection with the film world.

A Modern Psychologist on Films[1]

The main difference between the traditional academic psychology and the modern type is the closer relatedness of the latter to everyday life and its varieties and complexities. The psychoanalysis of Freud, and still more the individual-psychology[2] of Adler, also mark a change in this respect. But an up-to-date social psychology cannot live up to its task and ideal unless it takes the objects of its research from the kaleidoscopic stage of actual social life. Science, essentially, investigates given phenomena; and only after conclusions have been drawn from this part of research does the possibility present itself, and therefore the task, of applying some of the new knowledge for planned and constructive activity.

The present writer thinks, for instance, that the discussion of films, however briefly, should on no account be ommitted from this small volume on social research and social reform. I know of hardly any other device or cultural institution of the present day that plays so important a part in the mental processes governing the masses as the cinema. People go there not simply to spend their leisure; they obviously go there because they receive something that supplements their life of concrete reality. They go there to SATISFY THEIR FANTASY—A SATISFACTION WHICH IS AN ESSENTIAL PART OF THE LIFE OF THE INDIVIDUAL.

It is in the main sexual problems and the large field of the struggle for bread, money, and position, that attract people's interest; to a lesser degree they derive satisfaction from a just and happy end of a plot, vindicating the supreme validity of the educational principle: 'Be good and you will be blessed'. The lifelike presentation in the 'movies' appears better fitted to satisfy the

---

[1] From *Man and His Fellowmen*, by Samuel Lowy, London 1944. I am much indebted to Messrs. Kegan, Paul, Trench, Trubner & Co., Ltd., for kindly allowing me to reprint this passage from Mr. Lowy's book.

[2] The expression, as used by Adler, refers to the UNITY of the personality in aiming, behaving and producing neurotic character-traits.

imagination of the people than books and lectures presenting in mere words the triumph of virtue and of justice.

I am perhaps not greatly mistaken in saying that the vicarious satisfaction of sexual and aggressive tendencies, providing compensation for what concrete life has not given to the individual—love, happiness, appreciation, success, position, supremacy—constitutes the main gift which the 'movies' are able to present, with such variation and regular frequency, with such appeal to individuals of all types, on a scale which has apparently been approached by nothing else yet known in social history. The overwhelming majority of people feel more or less frustrated, feel more or less a tendency toward revenge and aggression under the influence of the particular conditions of their life. And there is no doubt about the satisfaction-value of the cinema-plays on this point. By the process of identification with the actors of the play the spectators gain a temporary satisfaction of their own ambitions and of their tendencies to revenge.

Still more obvious is the temporary satisfaction and compensation for subjective deficiencies in that other sphere of human life, love and sex. I have used the expressions compensation and satisfaction. For these are, in fact, two different thirsts than can be quenched through the enjoyment of the 'pictures'. The first type of fantasy-compensation is that for elementary, socially justified expectations which the average individual cherishes, but the fulfilment of which frequently falls short of his hopes.

A modest and warm-hearted girl marries a similarly modest boy, who, like her, wishes to find a loving and sincere companion for life. They both dream of deep and eternal happiness, and they promise it to each other. The first years of their marriage are, however, full of the struggle for existence, and for the bringing up of their child, born in the first year. There is still, undoubtedly, much left of the love of the first months, but the fatigue of the day, and the cares of the economic struggle, force the manifestation of this love more and more into the background of mere good intentions. Soon, however, the small business develops; the husband, previously tied up by the difficulties of narrow financial means, now becomes occupied with the troubles of a big business. His commercial interests require social intercourse with other, even bigger business men, in hotels, in clubs, and at sports meetings; whilst his wife, essentially still a modest wife, and mother now of two small children, stays mostly at home. There is no sign of infidelity on his side, or of conscious dissatisfaction; but there is little cultivation of love, still less any increase of love, only a friendly co-existence without either having time for the other. Regularly on week-ends both go out together to the 'pictures' and enjoy the love-happiness of elegantly dressed actors, enjoy the passionate meetings of the imaginary people—and they are compensated for what they themselves have not, for what they cannot have, owing to ignorance at the start of their marriage, and no less owing to the social conditions of our age, which absorb the weak individual entirely into the acquisitive process of business and production.

Now an illustration of the other kind of satisfaction. There is a decent girl, well educated and charming, whose only admitted plan for life is to marry an educated and kind-hearted professional man. In this she succeeds. The young man, in addition, is quite handsome, though far removed from the athletic actor, and certainly not a 'lady's man'. He is greatly in love with his charming wife; and she, too, seems to be happy. At times they go to the cinema, and more frequently to a 'show'; and, to the surprise of the serious and strictly monogamic husband, his charming wife never stops being enthusiastic about the 'sweetness' and the 'handsome figure' of this or that actor, about his 'beautiful smile', and similar things. The embarrassed husband cannot join in the praise, since he begins to have feelings of inferiority; above all, he is puzzled, because many of the men on the stage who are admired by his wife are, in his opinion, anything but strikingly handsome. I know this from his complaints during a training analysis: I also had the opportunity of knowing his wife more closely before she was married to him, and I am satisfied that she is a decent wife, and also that she would never have thought of marrying an actor or an opera singer, however handsome. Her conscious aims were always directed towards science, a monogamous, happy marriage, and a religious spirit in the home; and all this is hardly to be expected in the general run of actors.

The solution is clear: the charming wife does not even realise how polygamous she, in fact, is; how much within her psyche she is craving for the love or attention of famous and elegant actors, who, however, are at the same time the ideal of numerous other girls. Not that our woman would in reality exchange her husband for such a one. Had she the choice once again, and the opportunity of choosing between both types, undoubtedly she would decide again for that type which her husband represents. The other man is only the object of her fantasy-life; she, though unaware of this, wishes to enjoy him, but simply and solely during her occasional revelling in a 'picture' or a 'show'. The realm of fantasy—far from actuality —is the field of her longed-for satisfaction, desired by her 'polygamy' complex. This is consequently a satisfaction, but not a compensation for what is being wished in concrete actuality, consciously wished but not entirely attained.

People under psycho-analysis not infrequently dream about particular scenes they have seen in the 'pictures'. They naturally refuse at first to submit such a dream to analysis, stating that it is simply a reproduction. But, in fact, one can frequently find that the part of the film picked out by the dream-process has an intrinsic bearing on the deepest problems, mostly difficult conflicts, of the dreamer. A young man suffers much from jealousy because of his fiancée's behaviour, but because of his passionate attachment to her he cannot decide to break off the engagement. He sees the picture *Pittsburgh*, and in his dream of the following night he finds himself in a merry company at a dance. He recognises the origin of this dream-motive from the picture of the previous night, where there were two scenes of a dance. He realises, however, only with the help of the analyst, who happened to know the picture, what is being hinted at by this dream. One hero of the play is an energetic but not quite reliable man, who because of financial ambitions, marries the daughter of a steel magnate, but thinks that he can keep up his intimate friendship with a girl whom he loves; the latter, being of a good character, refuses to agree. There are two scenes of a dance at which the fiancée, and later wife, of the unscrupulous young man meets the other girl. No doubt the dream-fragment expresses the secret wish of the dreamer to be also unscrupulous enough to marry a 'decent woman of social position' and somehow to keep up simultaneously the passionate relationship with the girl he irrationally likes but intellectually despises.

But, as has been said, visiting the cinema means to most people on frequent occasions, at least a substantial satisfaction. And implicitly a poisonous factor. Because 'pictures' mostly present solutions that are far from being real possibilities. The acting figures of plays are mostly unmarried, or else without children or dependent relatives to care for. They can wish, and aim at, almost anything; and even if in the play they meet with handicaps, they do many things, and attain things, which are entirely out of reach for the average human being. 'Pictures', whilst satisfying the psyche for two hours, operating after the fashion of alcohol or a sedative drug, may drop into the mind the additional seed of the desire for the unattainable, instead of solving the difficulty.

I have pointed out how unsuccessful marriages—and unsuccessful careers in general—are mostly the result of neurotic inhibitions and subconscious tendencies. The 'pictures' dramatically describe the existing tragedies of life—but the only remedy they advise is: intrigue, aggression, and adultery; and all this in a way exceeding the real possibilities for average men and women. Surely the great success of films is indicative of the fact that they do give something substantial to the public. However, they could give more: true life and true solutions, or hints at prevention. I am not thinking of the usual propaganda films, in which the artificiality of the setting and the tendency is so obvious; nor of that type of lukewarm sentimentalism the remoteness of which from true life is manifest to everybody. I mean a more serious type of art produced with the help of the highest institutions of public education and science, supported by the State, and finally in fact appreciated by the wider public. People should learn to live; youth should be given illustrations of why and how to avoid situations that lead inevitably to insoluble difficulties.

Above all, the 'pictures' stimulate eroticism undesirably—a process IN MARKED CONFLICT WITH OUR ACTUAL SOCIAL NEED of self-restraint and sublimation; and they attack the ideal of monogamous love. Though to interfere with such a state of affairs is against the principle of freedom; yet to do so to a certain degree for the sake of the well-being of people, for the sake of their better mental harmony, is to serve at least as important a social need as that of unlimited freedom. After all, there is no total freedom for the consumption of alcohol—scandalous behaviour of the drunkard is opposed by the authorities—and nobody invokes in this respect the principle of freedom.

In creating and supporting a really intellectual type of film production,[1] and gaining more or less public approval for the more realistic type of 'picture' as suggested above, interference with the other type of film may even prove superfluous. THE SOCIAL PROCESS itself may turn the taste and the requirements of the masses into a more desirable direction; and the enjoyment of that other type of film may be limited to the psychopaths, or to exceptional moments in the life of 'normals'.

[1] This does not necessarily mean restricting films to the 'serious' type.

APPENDIX 4

The New Middle Classes

In the course of the last hundred years, no political doctrine has proved more fatal than Marx's prophecy, which he formulated in a simplified way in the *Communist Manifesto*:

'Of all the classes that stand face to face with the bourgeoisie to-day the proletariat alone is a really revolutionary class. The other classes decay and finally disappear in the face of modern industry: the proletariat is its special and essential product.

The lower middle class—the small manufacturer, the shop-keeper, the artisan, the peasant—all these fight against the bourgeoisie to save from extinction their existence as fractions of the middle class. They are therefore not revolutionary but conservative. Nay, more, they are reactionary, for they try to roll back the wheel of history. If they are revolutionary, *they are only so in view of their impending transfer into the proletariat* (our italics); they thus, defend not their present, but their future, interests; they desert their own standpoint to place themselves at that of the proletariat.'

Marx was clearly convinced that the final struggle over the political and social organisation of modern society would be between two classes only—the bourgeoisie and the proletariat. The non-proletarian group between these two classes would be absorbed into the great mass of the proletariat inevitably, as it were.

In this form the Marxist doctrine gained a hold over the European, or at least the continental proletariat[1] and, in an increasingly irreligious age, held them with almost the force of religion. If, however, we examine the actual course of social development, we see that the prophecy has been completely disproved. To take the

---

[1] For the sake of historical objectivity it should be made clear that Marx in some of his later writings openly revised his earlier teaching, for example by 1860 he had formed quite a different opinion from the one he held in 1850 as to the power of resistance of French peasants to their impending transfer into the proletariat. Cf. my edition of *Marx's Eighteenth Brumaire*, Berlin, 1932.

example of Germany, the proportion of workers to the whole of the occupied population actually declined.[1] In Great Britain, between 1851 and 1921 it remained comparatively unaltered at about 50 per cent to 55 per cent. There has, however, been a striking increase in the numbers of salaried employees of all grades, skilled technicians and officials—the new class, very difficult to define, which stands midway between the workers and the employers.

Marx, of course, when he was expounding the fundamentals of his social philosophy, was unable to observe this class and form an estimate of its position in society, because it was only in process of formation in the 1840's. Now it has become clear that the highly complex organisation of the modern economic system needs an ever-increasing supply of technical and administrative personnel. Their numbers are increasing at a far greater rate than those of the workers. In Germany, between 1907 and 1925, this group increased by 111 per cent, though the workers increased by only 12 per cent. In England, during the same period, the tendency is similar though the increase is not so great. The salaried employees increased by 56 per cent as compared with a 7 per cent increase for the workers. In America, in the ten years between 1909 and 1919, both social groups increased considerably, the workers by 38 per cent and the salaried employees by more than double that percentage—83 per cent. For every 100 industrial workers in Germany there are 15·4 employees, in U.S.A. 15·9, in Great Britain 10·8, in France 10·7. There is every sign that this tendency is being maintained.[2]

The existence and social significance of this new class has been more widely recognised and studied in Germany and America than it has been in Great Britain and other countries. In Germany it has been called the *Mittel-* or *Zwischen-Schichten*. It is a generally accepted fact now that this class, because of its frustration and social insecurity, played a large part in the rise to power of the Fascist party in Germany and Italy. It is another matter, however, whether its aspirations or any material improvement in its position and security have been realised under Fascist rule.

There is no English translation for *Mittel-Schichten*, nor has its political and social significance been realised by more than a handful of people. No books have so far been devoted to the study of this class, though many touch on it in passing. Census reports

---

[1] Germany: 1895, 56·8 per cent; 1907, 55·1 per cent; 1925, 45·1 per cent.

[2] Cf. E. Lederer. *Die Umschichtung des Proletariats*. Die Neue Rundschau. Aug. 1929, p. 145 sq.

do not recognise its existence, which makes the search for statistical data a somewhat laborious process. Broadly speaking, it is the class between the working class and the upper-middle class, though there is no very sharp division at either end of the scale. In England it cannot be called the middle class, since that implies the employer and rentier class, which has a fair degree of social security and a certain chance of realising its social aspirations. 'Salaried class' is not an adequate term either, as the higher-salary earners belong, in all respects, to the English middle class proper. Harold Lasswell, the American sociologist, called them 'middle income-skilled groups'; this hardly covers the case either, for, though many skilled technicians may properly be said to belong to it, the majority of skilled workers belong to the working class.

A description of the types of people who belong to it and of their social habits may give a clearer picture of this class than any comprehensive label, as it is not easy to integrate all these widely different types, with their great diversity of interests, into a single sociological concept. The class as such may be roughly divided into five major groups:

(1) *Skilled technicians.*

There is a large group of skilled technicians, particularly in the newer industries such as the motor-car, aircraft and electrical industries, who, by reason of their social background, education and method of training, cannot be placed in the working class proper. They are highly qualified people, often earning good salaries, but, because they have no property background, are entirely dependent on their ability to earn. They have therefore a high consumption power in relation to their social security.

(2) *Commercial and financial employees of all types.*

The second large group is made up of all the salaried employees, working in commerce, finance and insurance. It includes small independent shopkeepers, shop assistants, commercial travellers, insurance agents and canvassers, bank clerks and clerical workers. These again have no property background, but the nature of their work, and their own inclinations too, demand that they maintain a certain standard of life—housing, dress, etc., which is immediately endangered if once they lose employment. This standard must be maintained at least outwardly during a period of unemployment, as it materially affects the prospects of obtaining new employment.

(3) *Personal Service.*

This group includes domestic servants, waiters and waitresses, assistants in hairdressing and beauty culture establishments, cinema and theatre attendants, porters and lift attendants. Their employment, too, is dependent on the outward maintenance of a certain standard of life, which is not always easy on the salaries which they earn.

(4) *Public Administration and Public Utility Services.*

Lower-grade civil servants who are doing responsible work but who have little prospect of rising in the social scale come into this fourth group, together with officials and clerical workers in the local Government services. Officials in the transport services and post-office and telegraph workers may also be included.

(5) *The Lower Professions.*

It is more difficult to decide which of the professional groups can rightly be considered as part of the *Mittel-Schichten*. Members of the medical and both branches of the legal profession cannot be included. These professions are of very ancient standing, their members have an assured place in society, the training is a lengthy and expensive process, the technique required for the practice of the profession is of the highest order, and the possibilities of remuneration are very great. Of the next professional grade—dentists, architects, engineers, vets, surveyors, accountants, etc.—very many members of these professions may fall outside the *Mittel-Schichten* group, though the majority probably fall within it. The low professional groups—pharmacists, opticians, nurses, midwives, estate agents, auctioneers, etc.—can be grouped within the *Mittel-Schichten*. They are skilled, but less highly so than the higher professions; they are unlikely to have any property background and are therefore dependent on earning. The nature of their work demands the maintenance of a high standard of life, although their social position is not assured.

The underlying characteristic of the whole *Mittel-Schichten* class is its frustration, which is the result of social insecurity and lack of political power. Its members both need and wish to maintain a fairly high standard of life. Socially they seek to emulate the upper middle class, even if this results only in a cheap imitation. They wish to have good housing accommodation, detached or semi-detached and with a garden, though this involves the aid of a building society. They wish to have up-to-date furniture, radio sets and motor-cars, though these must be bought on the hire-purchase basis. They want to dress well, and in many cases this is essential to their work also. They wish to enjoy life as people in the films and in the illustrated papers seem to. While they are in employment, they have a chance of realising many of these things, but, because they have no property or alternative means of income, their life is always insecure and they have little prospect of rising in the social scale. The mass civilisation of the present-day bourgeoisie, though its standards and attitude to life are empty and meaningless, appears to the new middle class as a goal worth striving after. The shopgirl, to take only one sociological type, makes her face up, manicures her hands, and does her hair after the manner of the ladies she serves from behind the counter. She tries, in her private life as well as in her appearance, to create an illusion, which compensates her for a salary which is below the average working-class wage, and for the general lack of prospects of her class. We still know very little about the sociological structure of these new social strata, with their new standards and outlook, which are growing up in the existing system. Certainly Tarde's laws of imitation have a decisive bearing on this point. Only a social crisis—revolution or war, or sometimes both—reveals the substitute character of this class's imitation of the upper middle class. The airman, formerly a commercial traveller or bank clerk, who now pilots his Hurricane to victory, knows that after this war he cannot return to the same meaningless way of life. A new social order must be created and he must have a constructive part to play in it.

As a class, the *Mittel-Schichten* are not well integrated and have not much interest in combining, as the working class does, to improve their material conditions or to make themselves a more powerful political force in the community. They are represented by no political party and have few people in Parliament who will look after their interests there. Unlike the upper middle class, they cannot afford political candidatures, and owing to their inability and aversion to a combination they do not enjoy the opportunities which Trade Unionism gives to the working class. This fact—that they are politically a negative body—makes them a potential danger to the community, since, as happened in Germany and Italy, and recently in France, they will throw their lot in with anyone who seems to promise them the security and opportunities for the exercise of power which they lack. They cannot be appealed to by proletarian slogans, because they have no sympathy with the working class and their one fear is that they will sink down into its ranks. On the other hand, while they may affect to despise the social habits of the upper middle class, their main aspiration is to rise up and attain the social status of their employers. Anyone who holds out the possibility of this to them will receive their full support. This situation has already arisen in many countries in Europe, but in Great Britain there is still a possibility of avoiding it. This could be done by recognising the social needs of this class and giving it a constructive part, which it at present lacks, to play in the life of the community.[1]

Two points now emerge clearly: (1) that the new social groups, to which this article is devoted, for lack of other standards and because of their uncertainty as to the future organisation of society, adopt the standards of the bourgeoisie; (2) that these groups consider themselves fundamentally different from the proletariat, and wish to be considered so by others. Perhaps some further explanation of these points is needed.

Modern society is largely determined by bourgeoisie standards and outlook on life, and the bourgeoisie usually considers that the modern working-class movement is a threat to its rights of property. There exists, perhaps, no better description of these standards than de Tocqueville's. He, as early as 1848, experienced the decline of the bourgeoisie and the rising tide of the proletariat.

'L'esprit particulier de la classe moyenne devint l'esprit général du gouvernement; il domina la politique extérieure aussi bien que les affaires du dedans; esprit actif, industrieux, souvent déshonnête, généralement rangé, téméraire quelquefois par vanité et par égoisme, timide par tempérament, modéré en toute chose, excepté dans le goût du bien-être, et médiocre; esprit, qui, mêlé à celui du peuple ou de l'aristocratie, peut faire merveille, mais qui, seul, ne produira jamais qu'un gouvernement sans vertu et sans grandeur.'[2]

---

[1] Though this essay was published in Christopher Dawson's *Dublin Review* in January 1941, I had no hesitation in reprinting it here in the context of these studies on the sociology of film. I do not think that the outcome of the General Election in 1945 has made the argument of 1940 superfluous. On the contrary. What was then written under the immediate impression of the 'Battle for England' and the first blitz on London, must not be forgotten to-day.

For the time being, the British *Mittel-Schichten* have decided to throw their weight on the side of the Labour Party, but they have not *joined* the Labour Party—yet. They still *can* throw their weight in an opposite direction, if Labour should fail to pay attention to the subtle aspirations and demands of these new social groups. It seems, therefore, to me that my essay, though distinctly bearing the atmosphere of 1940, may serve as a timely reminder. The text of Chapter IX will have shown to what extent films have contributed to shaping the ideology of 'the new middle classes'.

[2] Cf. Alexis de Tocqueville's *Souvenirs*, Paris 1893, p. 6.

It is clear from this quotation that de Tocqueville conceived the future pattern of values in Western Society as a 'mixture' of bourgeois, proletarian and aristocratic virtues.

The breakdown of mediaeval society is only a negative expression for the origins of modern capitalism. The 'free' bourgeois opportunities which afford means of rising in the social scale became an alternative for a world previously conceived in terms of estates and religious order. But the victory of bourgeois society was only a Pyrrhic victory, and modern nationalism is, as its early connection with liberalism proves, only a property category, written in large letters, the crisis of which we are now witnessing in the second world war.

At the turn of the century the 'free' bourgeois world was becoming more and more the prisoner of its own achievements. Social opportunities were becoming visibly more restricted. The modern mass state demands an ever-increasing executive and administrative apparatus, and, moreover, the state itself is becoming a great industrial and commercial *entrepreneur*. With this development the bourgeoisie cannot compete, so, completely misunderstanding the historical situation, it comes to regard the working class as its greatest enemy, because it threatens its privileges. In Italy, Germany, and France too, the bourgeoisie tried, by every means in its power, to play off the new middle classes against the industrial working class. This factor goes a long way towards explaining the emergence of Fascist state systems in these countries. The history of the Fascist countries, however, which has yet to be written, shows that Fascism, when it has once gained power, is not able to solve the problem of the middle groups, but rather has to dominate them, the bourgeoisie and the working classes alike. The Fascist state is the incarnation of pure force, which sacrifices the solution of social problems to its inhuman desire for power.

England has so far escaped this Fascist danger, and there are several possible reasons why it will not be seriously exposed to it in the future. This is at once obvious, if one compares the English social system and state organisation with the French. French democracy since 1789 has always shown a more equalitarian tendency, while the English state is definitely based on a certain feeling of freedom in all classes. The equalitarian tendency in England—in marked contrast to France and the other short-lived democracies of the continental powers—has been conceived as an evolutionary process. 1832, 1867, 1911, 1918, are the milestones on this road to democracy, which has been attained gradually and by a series of successful compromises. While on the Continent the aristocracy ceased in 1789 to be the leading political force, and the political sphere was more or less put on the same level as the industrial system, the English ruling class allowed itself continually to be regenerated from below.

It is an aristocracy of achievement, and entry to this class is theoretically attainable by social effort. If we succeed—and this war affords us every opportunity of doing so—in overcoming the complex structure of aristocratic privilege—to name only one example, the public schools—then it will be possible to regenerate the existing aristocracy with new blood from the working class and the new middle classes which have hitherto been held down. When this takes place all classes in English society will gain responsibility for the government of their country. The process has already started, and will be accelerated by the war. After the war it will continue as a permanent evolutionary process.

There are other tendencies which also point to the strengthening of common rather than sectional interests—the exchange between town and country, which, as a result of aerial bombardment, has affected millions of people and the common destiny of English towns. These things have brought together all sections of the English people in a way which could not have occurred in any other circumstances.

The interpretation of these common responsibilities and experiences in new institutional forms, not only through the re-shaping of the English educational system, but also through the extension of the social services, measures for farmers, employees, and workers, communal feeding and later new town planning, etc., will guarantee that England will preserve a political *élite*, open to all social groups, which is controlled by a formally and democratically elected parliament.

Only where there is unity of political responsibility can the danger of tyranny by a Fascist minority be avoided. This holds good not only for the British Isles, but equally for the Empire, whose political spirit has been characterised by Burke in the following unforgettable words:

'Do not dream that your letters of office and your instructions, and your suspending clauses, are the things that hold together the great contexture of this mysterious whole. These things do not make your government. Dead instruments, passive tools as they are, it is the spirit of the English communion that gives all their life and efficacy to them. It is the spirit of the English constitution, which, infused through the mighty mass, feeds, unites, invigorates, vivifies, every part of the Empire, even down to the minutest member.'

Burke's idea of an organic state, which he strongly maintained against the French revolutionaries of 1789, is unquestionably the heritage of the British nation; though it may not be explicit in its inner consciousness, it is still sound political wisdom to-day. The Marxian prophecy, which was quoted above, has proved itself a false myth. English political thought is not only free from the bourgeois formalism of France, but has also withstood the influence of Marxism. We can therefore hope that England will succeed in establishing the new social integration of all classes, which the present world crisis demands and which, according to the mediae-val Christian Catholic analogy, assigns to each social group its positive function in society. In this way only can freedom of the individual be reconciled with the administrative and organisational needs of the modern mass state.

APPENDIX 5

Report to Film Research

Name of School .... Class ....
Boy or Girl .... Age ....
Nationality.......................... Religion ....
Occupation of Father or
    Mother .... Place of Birth ....

1. How many times during the week do you usually go to the
    pictures? ....
    How many times during the week would you like to go?

    ....
    How many times do you usually stay through a show?

    ....
    What cinema do you usually go to? ....
    How far is it from your home? ....

2. Must you ask your parents for permission before you can go
    to the pictures? ....
    Do you go because your parents or brothers and sisters make
    you go? ....
    Do you ever go, even though your parents don't want you to?

    ....
    Or would you rather not go at all? ....

3. Place the number, 1, before the kind of picture you like best,
    the number, 2, before the kind you like next best, the num-
    ber, 3, before the kind you like next, and so on.

    ....Cowboy Pictures   ....Ghost Pictures
    ....Comedies   ....War Pictures
    ....News Reels   ....Historical Pictures
    ....Love Pictures   ....Serials or follow-up
                                         Pictures.
    ....Musicals   ....Detective Pictures
    ....Gangster Pictures   ....Educational Pictures (on
                                         travels to foreign
                                         countries, etc.)

..........Cartoons (like Walt Disney's)

..........Documentaries (like *Western Approaches* or *The March of Time*)

4. I usually go to the pictures (use check mark to show which).

..........By myself

..........With my parents.

..........With brothers or sisters.

..........With other grown-up people.

..........With a bunch of boys.

..........With a boy friend.

..........With a bunch of girls.

..........With a girl friend.

5. After a film I usually (use check mark to show which).

..........Start to play at what I have seen in the film.

..........Talk to my friends about the picture.

..........Imagine myself acting as they did in the film.

..........Talk to my parents about the picture.

(If you usually do something else after you see a film, say what it is).

6. Who are your three favourite men film stars, and who are your three favourite women film stars?

Men Stars.	Women Stars.
1.	1. ....
2.	2. ....
3.	3. ....

7. Place the number, 1, before the kind of film scene you like best, the number, 2, before the kind of film scene you like next best, the number, 3, before the kind you like next, and so on.

..........Sad scenes

..........Love scenes

..........Religious scenes

..........Ghost scenes

..........Scenes which show loyalty or true friendship

..........Fighting scenes

..........Murder scenes

..........Funny scenes

..........Scenes of unselfish action

8. Do your parents ever tell you that some films are bad for boys and girls? ....

What kind do they say are bad? ....

Do you agree with them? ....

9. Which of the following kinds of life do the films usually show in an interesting way? (Show by a check mark.)

..........Home life.

..........Hard work.

..........Life of the criminal.

..........Fighting.

..........Wealthy or rich life.

..........Having a good time.

..........Honest work.

10. Do you always want the good man in the pictures to win?..........

Do you ever want the bad or tough man to win?..............................

11. Do you day dream about what you see in the films? ....

How much do you do this? ....

..........a lot. ....once in a while.

..........sometimes. ....never.

12. Do you or your companions play at what you see in the films?

....

..........a lot. ....once in a while.

..........sometimes. ....never.

13. Would you rather be one of the good people or one of the bad people in these games? ....

14. Do any kind of motion pictures make you want to get a lot of money easily?...

What kind of pictures, if any, do this? ....

15. When you see an exciting film do you want to (show by check mark)

..........Do something brave and daring?

..........Behave roughly or fight someone?

..........Go out and have a good time?

..........Talk to others about what you have just seen?

..........Start to play an exciting game?

..........Imagine yourself having a lot of adventure?

16. When you see a thrilling gangster picture, do you

..........Feel sorry for the gangster?

..........Feel that you want to be a gangster?

..........Imagine yourself being one, doing big and
              daring things, and fooling the police?

..........Want to be a policeman?

..........Feel that every gangster ought to be caught
              and punished?

..........Think nothing about what you have just seen?

17. Have films ever made you

..........Want to stay away from school?

..........Want to run away from home?

..........Want to go out and have a lot of fun?

..........Want to break into a house and take something?

..........Want to take things from other people?

18. Have the pictures ever led you to do anything wrong, or that you feel you shouldn't have done?

....

....

If so, what kind of picture did you see, and what did you do?

....

....

19. Have you seen any film which made you want to be really
    good? ....
    What was the name of the film and what was it about?

    ....

    For how long were you good? ....
20. Do you think that films make boys or girls do bad things? ....
    What, for instance? ....
    Do you think that films make boys or girls do good things?...........
    What, for instance? ....
    Do you think that films make no difference to how boys or
    girls behave? ....
21. Do you think that the punishment which the bad man gets in
    films stops boys from doing bad things? ....
22. What kind of pictures, if any, do you think are not true to life?

    ....

    Why? ....
23. What kind of film would you like to have made?

    ....

    ....

24. Place the number, 1, before the one you do most, the number,
    2, before the one you do next most, the number, 3, before
    the one you do next, and so on.
    ....Reading stories.
    ....Playing or talking about what you see in
             films.
    ....Playing other games, such as football,
             marbles, skipping rope, and so on.
    ....Day-dreaming.
    ....Working about the house for your family.
    ....Working for other people.
    ....Doing your home work.
    If you care, you may sign your name here:

    _____

    THANK YOU

BIBLIOGRAPHY

Only those books not referred to in footnotes or text are listed. I also wish to point out that my bibliography makes no attempt at giving a complete list of all studies which may be of relevance in these wide fields.

Furthermore, I only mention those works which I have found useful and which may help the reader towards further clarification of problems discussed in the present studies.

THEATRE—DRAMA—GENERAL—GREEK AND ROMAN THEATRE—OTHER EPOCHS

BAB, J., *Das Theater im Lichte der Soziologie*, Leipsic, 1931.

BENTLEY, G. E., *Shakespeare and Johnson: Their Reputations in the Seventeenth Century Compared*, 2 vols., Chicago, 1945.

BLAIR, H., *Lectures on Rhetoric and Belles Lettres*, 3 vols., London, 1790.

CRUTTWELL, C. T., *A History of Roman Literature*, London, 1898.

DISHER, M. W., *Fairs, Circuses and Music Halls*, London, 1942.

DONALDSON, J. W., *The Theatre of the Greeks*, London, 1849.

FÉNELON, *Lettre à l'Académie*, Paris, 1935.

GEFFCKEN, *Die griechische Tragoedie*, Leipsic, 1918.

GIDE, A., *L'évolution du théatre*, Manchester, 1939.

GREEN, F. C., *Diderot's Writings on the Theatre*, Cambridge, 1936.

GREGOR, J., *Weltgeschichte des Theaters*, Vienna, 1933.

HASTINGS, C., *The Theatre: its Development in France and England, and a History of its Greek and Latin Origins*, London, 1901.

HOTSON, *The Commonwealth and Restoration Stage*, Cambridge, Mass., 1928.

JOURDAIN, E. F., *The Drama in Europe in Theory and Practice*, London, 1924.

KLEIST, H. v., *Ueber das Marionettentheater*, in *Werke*, ed. Erich Schmidt, Leipsic, s.a.

KNIGHTS, L. C., *Drama and Society in the Age of Johnson*, London, 1937.

LESSING, G. E., *Hamburgische Dramaturgie*, in *Saemtliche Werke*, Stuttgart, s.a.

LOMÉNIE, L. DE, *Beaumarchais et son temps*, 2 vols., Paris, 1873.

NICOLL, A., *A History of Restoration Drama, 1660-1700*, Cambridge, 1940.

NICOLL, A., *A History of Late Eighteenth Century Drama, 1750-1800*, Cambridge, 1927.

NICOLL, A., *A History of Early Nineteenth Century Drama, 1800-1850*, 2 vols., Cambridge, 1930.

NICOLL, A., *The Development of the Theatre: a Study of Theatrical Art from the Beginnings to the Present Day*, London, 1937.

NICOLL, A., *British Drama: an Historical Survey from the Beginnings to the Present Time*, London, 1945.

REYNOLDS, E., *Early Victorian Drama*, Cambridge, 1936.

ROUSSEAU, J. J., *Lettre à d'Alembert sur les spectacles*, in *Petits Chefs-d'Oeuvres de J. J. Rousseau*, Paris, 1876.

SCHILLER, F., *Die Schaubuehne als moralische Anstalt betrachtet*, in *Werke*, Stuttgart, s.a.

SIMMEL, G., *Zur Philosophie des Schauspielers*, in *Fragmente und Aufsaetze*, Munich, 1923.

VERRALL, A. W., *Euripides: the Rationalist*, Cambridge, 1895.

WEIL, H., *Etudes sur le Drame Antique*, Paris, 1897.

WELLS, ST. B., *A Comparison between the Two Stages: a late Restoration Book of the Theatre*, Princeton, 1942.

WITKOWSKI, G., *Das deutsche Drama des 19. Jahrhunderts*, Berlin, 1923.

ELIZABETHAN THEATRE

HANKINS, J. E., *The Character of Hamlet and Other Essays*, The University of North Carolina Press, 1944.

LAWRENCE, W. J., *The Elizabethan Playhouse and Other Studies*, Stratford-upon-Avon, 1913.

SYMONDS, J. A., *Shakespeare's Predecessors in the English Drama*, London, 1884.

TILLYARD, E. M. W., *Shakespeare's History Plays*, London, 1944.

WARD, A. W. and WALLER, A. R. (Editors), *The Cambridge History of English Literature*, vols. V and VI, Cambridge, 1910 (with extensive bibliographies).

WILSON, J. D., *Life in Shakespeare's England*, Pelican edition, 1944.

HISTORY AND SOCIAL HISTORY

BAILEY, C. (Editor), *The Legacy of Rome*, Oxford, 1924.

BEARD, C. and M. R., *America in Midpassage*, London, 1939.

BIBLIOGRAPHY

BEARD, C. A. and M. R., *A Basic History of the United States*, New York, 1944.

BURCKHARDT, J., *Die Zeit Constantins des Grossen*, Leipsic, 1929.

BURCKHARDT, J., *Griechische Kulturgeschichte*, 3 vols., Leipsic, s.a.

BURCKHARDT, J., *Weltgeschichtliche Betrachtungen*, Leipsic, s.a.

BURY, J. B., *History of Greece*, London, 1902.

BURY, J. B., *A History of the Roman Empire*, London, 1930.

COCHRAN, TH. C. and MILLER, W., *The Age of Enterprise: a Social History of Industrial America*, New York, 1942.

FRIEDLAENDER, L., *Darstellungen aus der Sittengeschichte Roms*, 2 vols., Leipsic, 1901.

HAZARD, P., *La crise de la conscience Européenne, 1680-1715*, 3 vols., Paris, 1935.

JAEGER, W., *Paideia: the Ideals of Greek Culture*, 3 vols., Oxford, 1939, and later.

LAISTNER, M. L. W., *A Survey of Ancient History*, New York, 1929.

LIVINGSTONE, R. W. (Editor), *The Legacy of Greece*, Oxford, 1928.

MEYER, E., *Geschichte des Altertums*, Vierter Band, Stuttgart, 1912.

MOMMSEN, TH., *The History of Rome*, 5 vols., London, 1894.

MURRAY, G., *Five Stages of Greek Religion*, London, 1935.

ROSTOVTZEFF, M., *The Social and Economic History of the Roman Empire*, Oxford, 1926.

SALMON, E. T., *A History of the Roman World*, London, 1944.

TREVELYAN, G. M., *English Social History*, London, 1944.

WILAMOWITZ-MOELLENDORFF, U. V. and NIESE, B., *Staat und Gesellschaft der Griechen und Roemer*, Leipsic, 1910.

MYTH. PRIMITIVES

CASSIRER, E., *Die Begriffsform im mythischen Denken*, Leipsic, 1922.

LIPS, J. E., *The Savage Hits Back or the White Man through Native Eyes*, London, 1937.

MALINOWSKI, B., *Sex and Repression in Savage Society*, London, 1937.

MALINOWSKI, B., *Crime and Custom in Savage Society*, London, 1940.

MEAD, M., *Growing Up in New Guinea*, Pelican edition, 1942.

MEAD, M., *Coming of Age in Samoa*, Pelican edition, 1943.

VICO, G., *Scienza Nuova*, 1911.

WUNDT, W., *Elemente der Voelkerpsychologie*, Leipsic, 1913.

316

BIBLIOGRAPHY
ETHICS—VALUES—VALUATION

CARRITT, E. F., *The Theory of Morals: an Introduction to Ethical Philosophy*, Oxford, 1930.

HARTMANN, N., *Ethik*, Berlin and Leipsic, 1926.

HOBHOUSE, L. T., *Morals in Evolution: a Study in Comparative Ethics*, London, 1929.

LÉVY-BRUHL, L., *La Morale et la Science des Moeurs*, Paris, 1903.

MOORE, G. E., *Ethics*, Oxford, 1944.

ROSS, W. D., *Aristotle*, London, 1937.

SCHELER, M., *Der Formalismus in der Ethik und die materiale Wertethik*, Halle, 1927.

SCHELER, M., *Wesen und Formen der Sympathie*, Bonn, 1923.

SCHELER, M., *Das Ressentiment im Aufbau der Moralen*, in *Vom Umsturz der Werte*, Leipsic, 1923.

SIDWICK, H., *Outlines of the History of Ethics*, London, 1931.

WESTERMARCK, E., *Ethical Relativity*, London, 1932.

SOCIOLOGY—GENERAL—SPECIALISED STUDIES

GINSBERG, M., *Studies in Sociology*, London, 1932.

HEHN, V., *Goethe und das Publikum*, in *Gedanken ueber Goethe*, Berlin, 1909.

LEAVIS, Q. D., *Fiction and the Reading Public*, London, 1939.

MACIVER, R. M., *Society: a Textbook of Sociology*, New York, 1944 (with valuable bibliographies).

MANNHEIM, K., *Diagnosis of Our Time*, London, 1943.

SCHUECKING, L. L., *The Sociology of Literary Taste*, London, 1944.

VEBLEN, TH., *The Theory of the Leisure Class*, New York, 1928.

SOCIAL CLASSES—SOCIAL STRATIFICATION

BOUGLÉ, C., (Editor), *Inventaires III, Classes Moyennes*, Paris, 1939 (with important bibliographies).

CARR-SAUNDERS, A. M. and JONES, D. C., *A Survey of the Social Structure of England and Wales*, Oxford, 1937.

DREYFUSS, C., *Beruf und Ideologie der Angestellten*, Munich, 1933.

JONES, D. C., (Editor), *The Social Survey of Merseyside*, London, 1934.

KRACAUER, S., *Die Angestellten*, Frankfurt, 1930.

MANNHEIM, K., *Man and Society in an Age of Reconstruction: Studies in Modern Social Structure*, London, 1940.

317

BIBLIOGRAPHY

Mess, H. A., *Social Groups in Modern England*, London, 1944.

Ranulf, S., *Moral Indignation and Middle Class Psychology*, Copenhagen, 1938.

Typology

Gaus, J. M., *Great Britain: a Study of Civic Loyalty*, Chicago, 1929.

Madariaga, S. de, *Englishmen, Frenchmen, Spaniards*, Oxford, 1929.

Mead, M., *The American Character*, Pelican edition, 1944.

Spranger, E., *Lebensformen*, Halle, 1927.

Method

Bartlett, F. C., Ginsberg, M., and others, *The Study of Society*, London, 1939 (Indispensable; contains also important bibliographies).

Cantril, H., *Gauging Public Opinion*, Princeton, 1944.

Dilthey, W., *Der Aufbau der geschichtlichen Welt in den Geisteswissenschaften*, in *Gesammelte Schriften*, vol. VII, Leipsic, 1927.

Hodges, H. A., *Wilhelm Dilthey: an Introduction*, London, 1944.

Lundberg, G. A., *Social Research: a Study in Methods of Gathering Data*, London, 1942.

Lynd, R. S. and H. M., *Middletown: a Study in Contemporary American Culture*, New York, 1929.

Lynd, R. S. and H. M., *Middletown in Transition: a Study in Cultural Conflicts*, New York, 1937.

Film

Allen, J., *I Lost my Girlish Laughter*, London, 1941.

Altman, G., *Ça c'est du cinéma*, Paris, 1931.

Betts, E., (Editor), *The Private Life of Henry VIII*, London, 1934.

Box, S., *Film Publicity*, London, 1937.

Durant, H. W., *The Problem of Leisure*, London, 1938.

Eisenstein, S., *The Cinema*, in *U.S.S.R. Speaks for Itself*, vol. IV, *Culture and Leisure*, London, 1941.

Groll, G., *Film: die neuentdeckte Kunst*, Munich, 1937.

Iros, F., *Wesen und Dramaturgie des Films*, Zuerich, 1938.

London, R., *Film Music*, London, 1936.

Manvell, R., *Film*, Pelican edition, 1944 (with annotated bibliography).

318

BIBLIOGRAPHY

MARCHAUD, R. ET WEINSTEIN, P., *L'art dans la Russie nouvelle: le Cinéma*, Paris, 1927.

MARSHALL, H., *Soviet Cinema*, London, 1945.

MOUSSINAC, L., *Naissance du Cinéma*, Paris, 1925.

MOUSSINAC, L., *Le Cinéma soviétique*, Paris, 1928.

PETERS, C. C., *Motion Pictures and Standards of Morality*, New York, 1933.

REPORTS :

The Film in National Life, London, 1932.

The Film in National Life, being the proceedings of a conference held by the British Film Institute in Exeter, April, 1943.

ROBSON, E. W. and M. M., *The Film Answers Back: an Historical Appreciation of the Cinema*, London, 1939.

ROTHA, P., *Celluloid: the Film To-day*, London, 1931.

ROTHA, P., *Documentary Film*, London, 1936.

SELDES, G., *Movies for the Millions*, London, 1937.

SHAND, P. M., *Modern Theatres and Cinemas*, London, 1930.

SHUTTLEWORTH, F. K., and MAY, M. A., *The Social Conduct and Attitudes of Movie Fans*, New York, 1933.

SPOTTISWOODE, R., *A Grammar of Film*, London, 1935.

VARIOUS AUTHORS :

L'Art cinématographique, vol. I-VIII, Paris, 1926-1931.

WAPLES, D. (Editor), *Print, Radio and Film in a Democracy*, Chicago, 1942.

PSYCHOLOGY—GENERAL

BARTLETT, F. C., *The Problem of Noise*, Cambridge, 1934.

BECK, M., *Psychologie: Wesen und Wirklichkeit der Seele*, Leiden, 1938.

BERGSON, H., *Laughter: an Essay on the Meaning of the Comic*, London, 1911.

BERGSON, H., *L'Evolution créatrice*, Paris, 1924.

BINSWANGER, L., *Einfuehrung in die Probleme der allgemeinen Psychologie*, Berlin, 1922.

BLEULER, E., *Lehrbuch der Psychiatrie*, Berlin, 1920.

DEWEY, J., *Human Nature and Conduct*, New York, 1930.

DOLLARD, J. and others, *Frustration and Aggression*, London, 1944.

DREVER, J., *Instinct in Man*, Cambridge, 1921.

DUMAS, G., *Traité de Psychologie*, 2 vols., Paris, 1923.

BIBLIOGRAPHY

FLUGEL, J. C., *A Hundred Years of Psychology*, London, 1941.

FROMM, E., *The Fear of Freedom*, London, 1942.

HELMHOLTZ, H. v., *Die Lehre von den Tonempfindungen*, Brunsvig, 1913.

GINSBERG, M., *The Psychology of Society*, London, 1933.

JAMES, W., *Psychology: Briefer Course*, London, 1892.

KOEHLER, W., *Dynamics in Psychology*, London, 1942.

MACCURDY, J. T., *Problems in Dynamic Psychology*, Cambridge, 1923.

MACCURDY, J. T., *The Psychology of Emotions, Morbid and Normal*, London, 1925.

McDOUGALL, W., *An Outline of Psychology*, London, 1923.

MILLER, N. E. and DOLLARD, J., *Social Learning and Imitation*, London, 1945.

MURCHISON, C. (Editor), *A Handbook of Social Psychology*, Worcester, Mass., 1935.

MURPHY, G., *General Psychology*, New York, 1933.

MURPHY, G., *A Briefer General Psychology*, New York, 1935.

SEIDEL, A., *Bewusstsein als Verhaengnis*, Bonn, 1927.

THOULESS, R. H., *General and Social Psychology*, London, 1943 (with bibliographies).

WEIZSAECKER, V. v., *Aeztliche Fragen: Vorlesungen ueber allgemeine Therapie*, Leipsic, 1935.

WEST, R., *Conscience and Society*, London, 1942.

CHILD PSYCHOLOGY—CINEMA

BOVET, P., *Le sentiment religieux et la psychologie de l'enfant*, Paris, s.a.

BUEHLER, CH., *From Birth to Maturity*, London, 1943.

CLAPARÈDE, E., *Psychologie de l'enfant et Pédagogie expérimentale*, Geneva, 1920.

CONSITT, F., *The Value of Films in History Teaching*, London, 1931.

DALE, E., *Children's Attendance at Motion Pictures*, New York, 1935.

FLEMING, C. M., *The Social Psychology of Education*, London, 1944.

GEORGE, W. H., *The Cinema in School*, London, 1935.

HADFIELD, J. A., *Psychology and Morals*, London, 1939.

ISAACS, S., *The Nursery Years: the Mind of the Child from Birth to Six Years*, London, 1945.

ISAACS, S., *Intellectual Growth in Young Children*, London, 1944.

ISAACS, S., *Social Development in Young Children*, London, 1933.

JAENSCH, E. R., and HENTZE, R., *Grundgesetze der Jugendentwicklung*, Leipsic, 1939.

BIBLIOGRAPHY

JEPHCOTT, A. P., *Girls Growing Up*, London, 1942.

KATZ, D., and KATZ, R., *Conversations with Children*, London, 1936.

KOFFKA, K., *The Growth of the Mind: an Introduction to Child Psychology*, London, 1931.

MARKEY, J. F., *The Symbolic Process and its integration in Children*, London, 1928.

PETERSON, R. C., and THURSTONE, L. L., *Motion Pictures and the Social Attitudes of Children*, New York, 1933.

PIAGET, J., *Judgment and Reasoning of the Child*, London, 1928.

PIAGET, J., *The Child's Conception of the World*, London, 1929.

PIAGET, J., *The Moral Judgment of the Child*, London, 1932.

PIAGET, J., and INHELDER, B., *Le développement des quantités chez l'Enfant*, Paris, 1941.

PIAGET, J., and SZEMINSKA, A., *La genèse du nombre chez l'Enfant*, Paris, 1941.

Report of the Conference on Films for Children, Nov. 20th and 21st, 1936, British Film Institute.

The Recreational Cinema and the Young, League of Nations, Geneva, 1938.

The Purpose and Content of the Youth Service, Ministry of Education, His Majesty's Stationery Office, 1945.

RENSHAW, S., MILLER, V. L., MARQUIS, D. P., *Children's Sleep: a Series of Studies on the Influence of Motion Pictures*, New York, 1933.

SPRANGER, E., *Psychologie des Jugendalters*, Leipsic, 1928.

STERN, W., *Psychologie der fruehen Kindheit: bis zum sechsten Lebensjahre*, Leipsic, 1927.

DREAM INTERPRETATION

FREUD, S., *Die Traumdeutung*, Leipsic, 1919.

LEONHARD, K., *Die Gesetze des normalen Traeumens*, Leipsic, 1939.

RATCLIFF, A. J. J., *The Nature of Dreams*, London, 1943.

VARENDONCK, J., *The Psychology of Day Dreams*, London, 1921.

COLOUR

GOETHE, W., *Schriften zur Naturwissenschaft*, in *Saemtliche Werke*, ed. v. d. Hellen, Stuttgart, s.a.

HELMHOLTZ, H. v., *Vortraege und Reden*, 2 vols., Brunswick, 1903.

KATZ, D., *The World of Colour*, London, 1935.

BIBLIOGRAPHY
POLITICAL RELIGION

CATTELL, R. B., *Psychology and the Religious Quest*, London, 1938.

JAMES, W., *The Varieties of Religious Experience*, London, 1928.

LASSWELL, H. D., *World Politics and Personal Insecurity*, New York, 1935.

LASSWELL, H. D., *Politics: Who Gets What, When, How*, New York, 1936.

SIMMEL, G., *Die Religion*, Frankfurt, 1922.

TCHAKHOTINE, S., *Le viol des Foules par la Propagande politique*, Paris, 1939.

THOULESS, R. H., *An Introduction to the Psychology of Religion*, Cambridge, 1923.

VOEGELIN, E., *Die politischen Religionen*, Stockholm, 1939.

WALLAS, G., *Human Nature in Politics*, London, 1908.

CENSORSHIP

G.M.G. (Anonymous), *The Stage Censor: an Historical Sketch, 1544-1907*, London, 1908.

HARLEY, J. E., *World-wide Influences of the Cinema: a Study of Official Censorship and the International Cultural Aspects of Motion Pictures*, Los Angeles, 1940.

KNOWLES, D., *The Censor, the Drama and the Film, 1900-34*, London, 1934.

A POSTSCRIPT AFTER READING THE PROOFS

It may be doubted whether, as the basis of government becomes more and more democratic, the supervision of public entertainments will not become more rather than less exacting and severe.

T. H. S. Escott, *England: Its People, and Pursuits,* New and Revised Edition, London 1885, p. 550

More than five months have elapsed since the last chapter of this book was written. I have added only a page or two to Chapter VI so as not to delay publication, but I can assure those readers who have followed me so far that the companion volume to this work is nearing completion.

In making a sociological study of the film one must, unfortunately, see those films which, like the Roman circuses, attract the masses—and not merely confine one's interest to those films which Miss Lejeune or Richard Winnington recommends us to see. Amongst such recent mass attractions I should like to mention: *The Wicked Lady, Pink String and Sealing Wax, Scarlet Street, The Fallen Angel, The Spiral Staircase, Shock.* All these films have a common denominator: they are sordid, play (successfully one presumes) on the lowest instincts of our contemporary masses, and must without exception do immeasurable harm to the growing generation, for the *present* legislation in this country allows children, if they are accompanied by adults, to see films of this type. The film *Shock* is perhaps the leading recent film in this category. I regret to say that no British daily paper has written about it as courageously as the American paper P.M. (March 14th, 1946).

These remarks do not imply that I regard films of this type as desirable for adults; quite the contrary. An age which has the paramount task of laying the foundations of a Social Service State must formulate its spiritual priorities and values as clearly as it devises its legislative measures in the social and economic field. All political beliefs fall, in the author's view, into the same category as religious beliefs, in spite of secularised forms. The basic contention of this book is that films provide a technique for shaping

323

'political' beliefs. This spiritual power which films may possess is *at present* directed by the 'laws' of *laissez-faire*. If it is left uncontrolled, the achievements in the field of economic and social reconstruction may soon be undermined.

It should be stressed that the integration of the producer-distributor-exhibitor complex of the British film monopoly *necessitates* State control over the value patterns of films, quite apart from economic control. This same would also naturally apply to the 'independent' producer, distributor, and exhibitor. Such 'spiritual' controls will require *very careful* consideration, if interference with political and cultural freedom is to be avoided, but a workable control system could easily be centred in a newly-devised censorial system. At the same time the artistic and cultural standard of a cinema like *The Academy* in London must under all circumstances be maintained. Here 'control' would appear to be quite unnecessary or purely formal. Generally speaking, however, value controls are in our opinion unavoidable though it is not within the scope of this book to devise their mechanisms.

I wish to express my gratitude to the Editor of *The Times* for printing an abbreviated version of Chapter IV. This article provoked considerable discussion, which was ultimately wound up by an admirable leading article in the issue of 28th January, 1946. My *Times* article deliberately did not refer to the Advisory Council, under the Chairmanship of Lady Allen of Hurtwood, as this Council has no influence whatsoever over the *majority* of films actually shown to children. In addition I should like to add here that I, in company with Government officials, had the opportunity of observing an Odeon Children's Cinema Club in operation in London during May 1946. To my regret the observations made during my visits last year remain up-to-date and must stand. Only one addition to the 'Club Promise'—to be careful when crossing a road—appeared as a noteworthy innovation!

May 1st, 1946.

I add a further book-list which should be used in conjunction with the earlier bibliography.

SUPPLEMENTARY BOOK-LIST

ABRAMS, M., *The Condition of the British People* 1911-1945, London, 1945.

ALLPORT, G. W., *The Use of Personal Documents in Psychological Science*, New York, 1942 (with invaluable bibliographies).

POSTSCRIPT AFTER READING THE PROOFS

BAECHLIN, P., *Der Film als Ware*, Basel, 1945.

BERGSON, H., *The Two Sources of Morality and Religion*, London, 1935.

BLATZ, W. E., *Understanding the Young Child*, London, 1944.

DUPOUY, *Rome et les Lettres Latines*, Paris, 1924.

FOWLER, W. WARDE, *Social Life at Rome in the Age of Cicero*, London, 1922.

GAUPP, R., *Psychologie des Kindes*, Leipzig, 1912.

GOOCH, G. P., AND OTHERS, *The German Mind and Outlook*, London, 1945.

GRAEBNER, F., *Das Weltbild der Primitiven*, Munich, 1924.

HALL, V., JR., *Renaissance Literary Criticism*, New York, 1945.

HERFORD, C. H., *A Sketch of the History of the English Drama in its Social Aspects*, Cambridge, 1881.

JACOBS, L., *The Rise of the American Film*, New York, 1939.

JASPERS, K., *Psychologie der Weltanschauungen*, Berlin, 1925.

JONES, A. E., *Juvenile Delinquency and the Law*, Pelican Books, 1945.

KRANEFELDE, *Die Psychoanalyse Psychoanalytische Psychologie*, Berlin, 1930.

McDOUGALL, W., *An Outline of Abnormal Psychology*, London, 1926.

MILLAR, J., *An Historical View of the English Government*, 4 vols. London, 1812.

MOLEY, R., *Are We Movie-Made?* New York, 1938.

MONNEROT, J., *Les Faits sociaux ne sont pas des Choses*, Paris, 1946.

Parliamentary Debates, 16th November, 1945.

Parliamentary Debates, 18th March, 1946.

PEAR, T. H., *Psychological Implications of the Culture-Pattern Theory*, Bulletin of the John Rylands Library, Manchester. July, 1945.

SCHOLZ, W. VON, *Kleists, Grillparzers, Immermanns und Grabbes Dramaturgie*, Muenich, 1912.

SYDOW, E. VON, *Form und Symbol*, Potsdam, 1929.

Tribune, November 16th, 1945.

WHEELER, O. A., *The Adventure of Youth*, London, 1946.

YOUNG, K., *A Handbook of Social Psychology*, London, 1946.

INDEX